CREATIVE
HOMEOWNER®

Two-Story
House Plans
Bible

CREATIVE HOMEOWNER®, Upper Saddle River, New Jersey

COPYRIGHT © 2007

CRE🏠TIVE
HOMEOWNER®

A Division of Federal Marketing Corp.
Upper Saddle River, NJ

VP/Editorial Director: Timothy O. Bakke
Production Manager: Kimberly H. Vivas

Home Plans Editor: Kenneth D. Stuts
Home Plans Designer Liaison: Timothy Mulligan

Design and Layout: Arrowhead Direct (David Kroha, Cindy DiPierdomenico, Judith Kroha); Maureen Mulligan

Cover Design: 3R1 Group

Current Printing (last digit)
10 9 8 7 6 5 4 3 2 1

Two-Story House Plans Bible
Library of Congress Control Number: 2006934226
ISBN-10: 1-58011-338-9
ISBN-13: 978-1-58011-338-0

CREATIVE HOMEOWNER®
A Division of Federal Marketing Corp.
24 Park Way
Upper Saddle River, NJ 07458
www.creativehomeowner.com

Note: The homes as shown in the photographs and renderings in this book may differ from the actual blueprints. When studying the house of your choice, please check the floor plans carefully.

Photo Credits
All landscape illustrations by Steve Buchanan

Front cover: *main plan* 121127, page 194; *top to bottom plan* 211076, page 310; *plan* 561002, page 223; *plan* 211076, page 310 **page 1:** *plan* 161036, page 27 **page 3:** *top to bottom plan* 161022, page 23; *plan* 161044, page 305; *plan* 321054, page 188 **page 4:** *plan* 141035, page 174 **page 5:** *top to bottom plan* 481035, page 276 **page 6:** *top to bottom plan* 161105, page 366; *plan* 161104, page 368 **page 7:** *plan* 481021, page 269 **page 74:** www.davidduncanlivingston.com **pages 75–76:** *all* Mark Lohman **page 77:** *top* Jessie Walker; *bottom* Brian Vanden Brink **page 78:** Tria Giovan **page 81:** *top both* Mark Lohman; *bottom* www.davidduncanlivingston.com **page 152:** courtesy of Central Fireplaces **pages 153–155:** courtesy of Aladdin Steel Products **page 157:** George Ross/CH **page 158:** Randall Perry **page 159:** courtesy of Heatilator **pages 206–213:** illustrations by Warren Cutler **pages 256–257:** *both* courtesy of Kraftmaid Cabinetry **page 258:** *both* courtesy of Wellborn Cabinets **page 259:** courtesy of Kraftmaid Cabinetry **page 260:** courtesy of Wellborn Cabinets **page 261:** *top left* courtesy of Merillat; *top right* courtesy of Wellborn Cabinets; *bottom left* courtesy of Merillat Industries **pages 350–353:** *all* John Parsekian/CH **page 354:** *left* H. Armstrong Roberts; *right* Jessie Walker **page 355:** *both* Charles Mann **page 356:** Tim Street-Porter/Beateworks, architect: Paul Williams **page 373:** *plan* 121114, page 199 **page 377:** *top to bottom plan* 131031, page 340; *plan* 121066, page 95; *plan* 121150, page 166 **page 384:** *plan* 391067, page 110; *plan* 131067, page 63; *plan* 151232, page 274 **back cover:** *main plan* 211076, page 310; *top plan* 561002, page 222

Contents

Getting Started

Maybe you can't wait to bang the first nail. Or you may be just as happy leaving town until the windows are cleaned. The extent of your involvement with the construction phase is up to you. Your time, interests, and abilities can help you decide how to get the project from lines on paper to reality. But building a house requires more than putting pieces together. Whoever is in charge of the process must competently manage people as well as supplies, materials, and construction. He or she will have to

- Make a project schedule to plan the orderly progress of the work. This can be a bar chart that shows the time period of activity by each trade.
- Establish a budget for each category of work, such as foundation, framing, and finish carpentry.
- Arrange for a source of construction financing.
- Get a building permit and post it conspicuously at the construction site.
- Line up supply sources and order materials.
- Find subcontractors and negotiate their contracts.
- Coordinate the work so that it progresses smoothly with the fewest conflicts.
- Notify inspectors at the appropriate milestones.
- Make payments to suppliers and subcontractors.

You as the Builder

You'll have to take care of every logistical detail yourself if you decide to act as your own builder or general contractor. But along with the responsibilities of managing the project, you gain the flexibility to do as much of your own work as you want and subcontract out the rest. Before taking this path, however, be sure you have the time and capabilities. Do you also have the

time and ability to schedule the work, hire and coordinate subs, order materials, and keep ahead of the accounting required to manage the project successfully? If you do, you stand to save the amount that a general contractor would charge to take on these responsibilities, normally 15 to 30 percent of the construction cost. If you take this responsibility on but mismanage the project, the potential savings will erode and may even cost you more than if you had hired a builder in the first place. A subcontractor might charge extra for hav-

Acting as the builder, above, requires the ability to hire and manage subcontractors.

Building a home, opposite, includes the need to schedule building inspections at the appropriate milestones.

ing to return to the site to complete work that was originally scheduled for an earlier date. Or perhaps because you didn't order the windows at the beginning, you now have to pay for a recent cost increase. (If you had hired a builder in the first place he or she would absorb the increase.)

Hiring a Builder to Handle Construction

A builder or general contractor will manage every aspect of the construction process. Your role after signing the construction contract will be to make regular progress payments and ensure that the work for which you are paying has been completed. You will also consult with the builder and agree to any changes that may have to be made along the way.

Leads for finding builders might come from friends or neighbors who have had contractors build, remodel, or add to their homes. Real-estate agents and bankers may have some names handy but are more likely familiar with the builder's ability to complete projects on time and budget than the quality of the work itself.

The next step is to narrow your list of candidates to three or four who you think can do a quality job and work harmoniously with you. Phone each builder to see whether he or she is interested in being considered for your project. If so, invite the builder to an interview at your home. The meeting will serve two purposes. You'll be able to ask the candidate about his or her experience, and you'll be able to see whether or not your personalities are compatible. Go over the plans with the builder to make certain that he or she understands the scope of the project. Ask if they have constructed similar houses. Get references, and check the builder's standing with the Better Business Bureau. Develop a short list of builders, say three, and ask them to submit bids for the project.

Contracts

Lump-Sum Contracts

A lump-sum, or fixed-fee, contract lets you know from the beginning just what the project will cost, barring any changes made because of your requests or unforeseen conditions. This form works well for projects that promise few surprises and are well defined from the outset by a complete set of contract documents. You can enter into a fixed-price contract by negotiating with a single builder on your short list or by obtaining bids from three or four builders. If you go the latter route, give each bidder a set of documents and allow at least two weeks for them to submit their bids. When you get the bids, decide who you want and call the others to thank them for their efforts. You don't have to accept the lowest bid, but it probably makes sense to do so since you have already honed the list to builders you trust. Inform this builder of your intentions to finalize a contract.

Cost-Plus-Fee Contracts

Under a cost-plus-fee contract, you agree to pay the builder for the costs of labor and materials, as verified by receipts, plus a fee that represents the builder's overhead and profit. This arrangement is sometimes referred to as "time and materials." The fee can range between 15 and 30 percent of the incurred costs. Because you ultimately pick up the tab—whatever the costs—the contractor is never at risk, as he is with a lump-sum contract. You won't know the final total cost of a cost-plus-fee contract until the project is built and paid for. If you can live with that uncertainty, there are offsetting advantages. First, this form allows you to accommodate unknown conditions much more easily than does a lump-sum contract. And rather than being tied down by the project documents, you will be free to make changes at any point along the way. This can be a trap, though. Watching the project take shape will spark the desire to add something or do something differently. Each change costs more, and the accumulation can easily exceed your budget. Because of the uncertainty of the final tab and the built-in advantage to the contractor, you should think twice before entering into this form of contract.

Contract Content

The conditions of your agreement should be spelled out thoroughly in writing and signed by both parties, whatever contractual arrangement you make with your builder. Your contract should include provisions for the following:

- The names and addresses of the owner and builder.
- A description of the work to be included ("As described in the plans and specifications dated . . .").
- The date that the work will be completed if time is of the essence.
- The contract price for lump-sum contracts and the builder's allowed profit and overhead costs for changes.
- The builder's fee for cost-plus-fee contracts and the method of accounting and requesting payment.
- The criteria for progress payments (monthly, by project milestones) and the conditions of final payment.
- A list of each drawing and specification section that is to be included as part of the contract.
- Requirements for guarantees. (One year is the standard period for which contractors guarantee the entire project, but you may require specific guarantees on

When submitting bids, all of the builders should base their estimates on the same specifications. Once the work begins, communicate with your builder to keep the work proceeding smoothly.

Inspect your newly built home, if possible, before the builder closes it up and finishes it.

certain parts of the project, such as a 20-year guarantee on the roofing.)
- Provisions for insurance.
- A description of how changes in the work orders will be handled.

The builder may have a standard contract that you can tailor to the specifics of your project. These contain complete specific conditions with blanks that you can fill in to fit your project and a set of "general conditions" that cover a host of issues from insurance to termination provisions. It's always a good idea to have an attorney review the draft of your completed contract before signing it.

Working with Your Builder

The construction phase officially begins when you have a signed copy of the contract and copies of any insurance required from the builder. It's not unheard of for a builder to request an initial payment of 10 to 20 percent of the total cost to cover mobilization costs, those costs associated with obtaining permits and getting set up to begin the actual construction. If you agree to this, keep a careful eye on the progress of the work to ensure that the total paid out at any one time doesn't get too far out of sync with the actual work completed.

What about changes? From here on, it's up to you and your builder to proceed in good faith and to keep the channels of communication open. Even so, changes of one sort or another beset every project, and they usually add to its cost.

Light at the End of the Tunnel.

The builder's request for a final inspection marks the end of the construction phase—almost. At the final inspection meeting, you and the builder will inspect the work, noting any defects or incomplete items on a "punch list." When the builder tidies up the punch list items, you should reinspect. Sometimes, builders go on to another job and take forever to clean up the last few details, so only after all items on the list have been completed satisfactorily should you release the final payment, which often accounts for the builder's profit.

Some Final Words

Having a positive attitude is important when undertaking a project as large as building a home. A positive attitude can help you ride out the rigors and stress of the construction process.

Stay Flexible. Expect problems, because they certainly will occur. Weather can upset the schedule you have established for subcontractors. A supplier may get behind on deliveries, which also affects the schedule. An unexpected pipe may surprise you during excavation. Just as certain, every problem that comes along has a solution if you are open to it.

Be Patient. The extra days it may take to resolve a construction problem will be forgotten once the project is completed.

Express Yourself. If what you see isn't exactly what you thought you were getting, don't be afraid to look into changing it. Or you may spot an unforeseen opportunity for an improvement. Changes usually cost more money, though, so don't make frivolous decisions.

Finally, watching your home go up is exciting, so stay upbeat. Get away from your project from time to time. Dine out. Take time to relax. A positive attitude will make for smoother relations with your builder. An optimistic outlook will yield better-quality work if you are doing your own construction. And though the project might seem endless while it is under way, keep in mind that all the planning and construction will fade to a faint memory at some time in the future, and you will be getting a lifetime of pleasure from a home that is just right for you.

Plan #181224

Dimensions: 36' W x 39'8" D

Levels: 2

Square Footage: 1,727

Main Level Sq. Ft.: 837

Upper Level Sq. Ft.: 890

Bedrooms: 3

Bathrooms: 2

Foundation: Basement

Material List Available: Yes

Price Category: C

Images provided by designer/architect.

This elegant home occupies a small footprint.

Features:

- Living Room: This two-story gathering place features a cozy fireplace and tall windows, which flood the room with natural light.

- Kitchen: This island kitchen has plenty of cabinet and counter space. It is open to the breakfast room.

- Upper Level: On this level you will find a balcony that overlooks the living room. Also, there are three bedrooms and a large bathroom.

- Garage: This one-car garage has room for a car plus some storage area.

Main Level Floor Plan

Copyright by designer/architect.

Upper Level Floor Plan

Front View

Kitchen

Master Bath

Dining Room/Living Room

Master Bath

Plan #161024

Dimensions: 54'4" W x 26'8" D
Levels: 2
Square Footage: 1,698
Main Level Sq. Ft.: 868
Upper Level Sq. Ft.: 830
Bonus Space Sq. Ft.: 269
Bedrooms: 3
Bathrooms: 2½
Foundation: Basement
Materials List Available: No
Price Category: C

The covered porch, dormers, and center gable that grace the exterior let you know how comfortable your family will be in this home.

Features:

- Great Room: Walk from windows overlooking the front porch to a door into the rear yard in this spacious room, which runs the width of the house.

- Dining Room: Adjacent to the great room, the dining area gives your family space to spread out and makes it easy to entertain a large group.

- Kitchen: Designed for efficiency, the kitchen area includes a large pantry.

- Master Suite: Tucked away on the second floor, the master suite features a walk-in closet in the bedroom and a luxurious attached bathroom.

- Bonus Room: Finish the 269-sq.-ft. area over the 2-bay garage as a guest room, study, or getaway for the kids.

This home, as shown in the photograph, may differ from the actual blueprints. For more detailed information, please check the floor plans carefully. *Images provided by designer/architect.*

Main Level Floor Plan

Copyright by designer/architect.

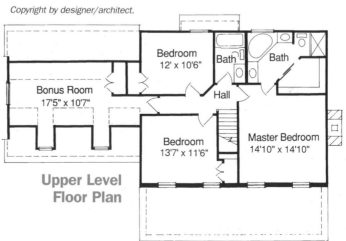

Upper Level Floor Plan

Plan #121031

Dimensions: 52' W x 51'4" D

Levels: 2

Square Footage: 1,772

Main Level Sq. Ft.: 1,314

Upper Level Sq. Ft.: 458

Bedrooms: 3

Bathrooms: 2½

Foundation: Basement

Materials List Available: Yes

Price Category: C

Images provided by designer/architect.

This home features architectural details reminiscence of earlier fine homes.

Features:

• Ceiling Height: 8 ft. unless otherwise noted.

• Foyer: This grand entry soars two-stories high. The U-shaped staircase with window leads to a second-story balcony.

• Great Room: You'll be drawn to the impressive views through the triple-arch windows at the front and rear of this room.

• Kitchen: Designed for maximum efficiency, this kitchen is a pleasure to be in. It features a center island, a full pantry, and a desk for added convenience.

• Breakfast Area: This area adjoins the kitchen. Both rooms are flooded with sunlight streaming from a shared bay window.

• Master Suite: The stylish bedroom includes a walk-in closet. Luxuriate in the whirlpool tub at the end of a long day .

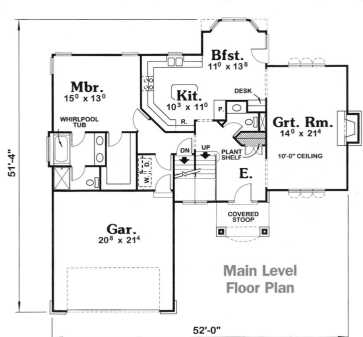

Main Level Floor Plan

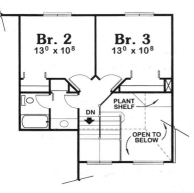

Copyright by designer/architect.

Upper Level Floor Plan

Plan #101014

Dimensions: 52' W x 28' D

Levels: 2

Square Footage: 1,598

Main Level Sq. Ft.: 812

Upper Level Sq. Ft.: 786

Bedrooms: 3

Bathrooms: 2½

Foundation: Slab, crawl space

Materials List Available: No

Price Category: C

Images provided by designer/architect.

This lovely Victorian home has a perfect balance of ornamental features and modern amenities.

Features:

• Ceiling Height: 8 ft. unless otherwise noted.

• Foyer: An impressive beveled glass-front door invites you into this roomy foyer.

• Kitchen: This bright and open kitchen offers an abundance of counter space to make cooking a pleasure.

• Breakfast Room: You'll enjoy plenty of informal family meals in this sunny and open spot next to the kitchen.

• Family Room: The whole family will be attracted to this handsome room. A full-width bay window adds to the Victorian charm.

• Master Suite: This dramatic suite features a multi-faceted vaulted ceiling and his and her closets and vanities. A separate shower and 6-ft. garden tub complete the lavish appointments.

Main Level Floor Plan

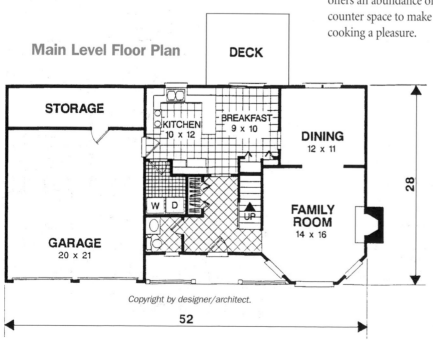

Copyright by designer/architect.

Upper Level Floor Plan

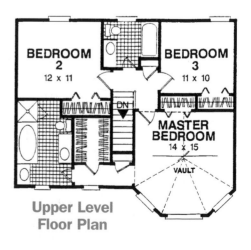

Plan #141025

Dimensions: 52' W x 36' D
Levels: 2
Square Footage: 1,721
Main Level Sq. Ft.: 902
Upper Level Sq. Ft.: 819
Bedrooms: 4
Bathrooms: 2½
Foundation: Basement
Materials List Available: Yes
Price Category: C

Images provided by designer/architect.

This traditional two-story home, with its typical roof and multi-directional ridge lines, presents a grand appearance. While modest in size, this lovely home incorporates many amenities found in much larger offerings.

Features:

- Living Room: This formal living room, certain to become a gathering place for friends and family, is accessible through an open foyer, with U-shaped stairs leading to the second floor.

- Dining Room: This formal dining room is particularly well-suited for those special entertainment occasions.

- Kitchen: This kitchen, which is designed for convenience and easy work patterns, makes food preparation a pleasure.

- Bedrooms: In addition to the master bedroom, this delightful home offers two secondary bedrooms. Also, you can convert the bonus room above the garage into a fourth bedroom.

Family Room

Main Level Floor Plan

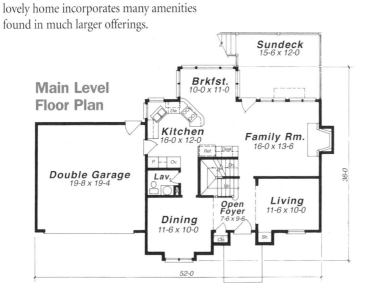

Sundeck 15-6 x 12-0
Brkfst. 10-0 x 11-0
Kitchen 16-0 x 12-0
Family Rm. 16-0 x 13-6
Double Garage 19-8 x 19-4
Lav.
Dining 11-6 x 10-0
Open Foyer 7-6 x 9-6
Living 11-6 x 10-0
52-0
36-0

Upper Level Floor Plan

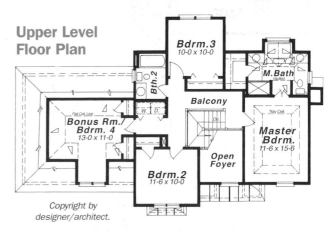

Bdrm.3 10-0 x 10-0
M.Bath
Bth.2
Balcony
Bonus Rm./ Bdrm. 4 13-0 x 11-0
Master Bdrm. 11-6 x 15-6
Open Foyer
Bdrm.2 11-6 x 10-0

Copyright by designer/architect.

Plan #181128

Dimensions: 36' W x 36' D
Levels: 2
Square Footage: 1,634
Main Level Sq. Ft.: 1,087
Second Level Sq. Ft.: 547
Bedrooms: 3
Bathrooms: 2
Foundation: Basement
Materials List Available: Yes
Price Category: C

This stone-accented rustic vacation home offers the perfect antidote to busy daily life.

CAD FILE AVAILABLE

Images provided by designer/architect.

Features:

- Ceiling Height: 8 ft. unless otherwise noted.

- Family Room: Family and friends will be unable to resist relaxing in this airy two-story family room, with its own handsome fireplace. French doors lead to the front deck.

- Kitchen: This eat-in kitchen features double sinks, ample counter space, and a pantry. It offers plenty of space for the family to gather for informal vacation meals.

- Master Suite: This first-floor master retreat occupies almost the entire length of the home. It includes a walk-in closet and a lavish bath.

- Secondary Bedrooms: On the second floor, two family bedrooms share a full bath.

- Mezzanine: This lovely balcony overlooks the family room.

- Basement: This full unfinished basement offers plenty of space for expansion.

Main Level Floor Plan

Upper Level Floor Plan

Copyright by designer/architect.

Plan #281002

Dimensions: 54' W x 33' D
Levels: 2
Square Footage: 1,859
Main Level Sq. Ft.: 959
Second Level Sq. Ft.: 900
Bedrooms: 3
Bathrooms: 2½
Foundation: Basement
Materials List Available: Yes
Price Category: D

This lovely three-bedroom home has the layout and amenities you need for comfortable living.

Features:

- Ceiling Height: 8 ft. unless otherwise noted.
- Foyer: Guests will walk through the lovely and practical front porch into this attractive foyer, with its vaulted ceiling.

- Living/Dining Room: Family and friends will be drawn to the warmth of the cozy, convenient gas fireplace in this combination living/dining room.

- Master Suite: You'll enjoy retiring at the end of the day to this luxurious master suite. It has a private sitting area with built-in storage for your books and television. Relax in the bath under its skylight.

- Kitchen: At the center of the main floor you will find this kitchen, with its eating nook that takes full advantage of the view and is just the right size for family meals.

- Deck: This large deck is accessible from the master suite, eating nook, and living/dining room.

Images provided by designer/architect.

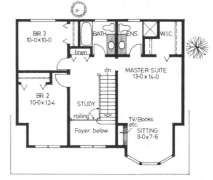

**Upper Level
Floor Plan**

**Main Level
Floor Plan**

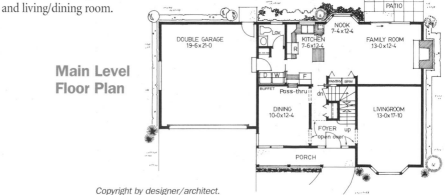

Copyright by designer/architect.

Images provided by designer/architect.

Plan #321060

Dimensions: 36' W x 46'8" D
Levels: 2
Square Footage: 1,575
Main Level Sq. Ft.: 802
Upper Level Sq. Ft.: 773
Bedrooms: 3
Bathrooms: 2½
Foundation: Basement
Materials List Available: Yes
Price Category: C

This stylish home is designed for a narrow lot but can complement any setting.

Features:

• Living Room: A masonry fireplace and large window area are the focal points in this spacious room.

• Dining Room: Open to the living room, the dining room has a large bay window that lets you enjoy the scenery as you dine.

• Breakfast Room: A bay window here lets morning sunlight help you greet the day.

• Kitchen: The center island gives extra work space as well as a snack bar. The adjacent laundry room and built-in pantry add to the convenience you'll find here.

• Master Suite: A vaulted ceiling and large walk-in closet make this room a treat, and the bath features a double vanity, tub, and separate shower.

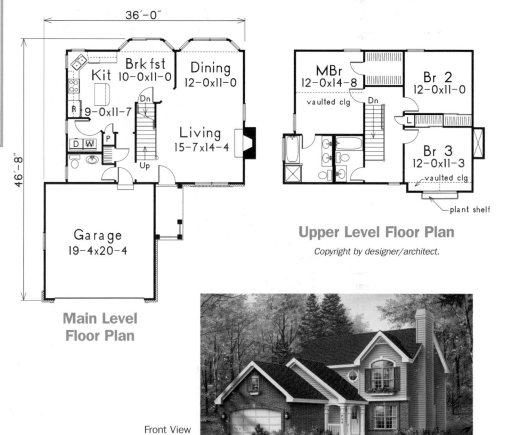

Main Level Floor Plan

36'-0"

46'-8"

Brk fst 10-0x11-0
Kit
Dining 12-0x11-0
9-0x11-7
Living 15-7x14-4
D W
Dn
Up
Garage 19-4x20-4

Upper Level Floor Plan

Copyright by designer/architect.

MBr 12-0x14-8
vaulted clg
Br 2 12-0x11-0
Dn
L
Br 3 12-0x11-3
vaulted clg
plant shelf

Front View

Plan #271010

Dimensions: 46'8" W x 43' D
Levels: 2
Square Footage: 1,724
Main Level Sq. Ft.: 922
Upper Level Sq. Ft.: 802
Bedrooms: 3
Bathrooms: 2½
Foundation: Basement
Materials List Available: Yes
Price Category: C

This traditional home features a wide assortment of windows that flood the interior with light and accentuate the open, airy atmosphere.

Features:

- Entry: A beautiful Palladian window enlivens this two-story-high space.

- Great Room: A second Palladian window brightens this primary gathering area, which is topped by a vaulted ceiling.

- Dining Room: Sliding glass doors connect this formal area to a large backyard deck.

- Kitchen: Centrally located, this kitchen includes a boxed-out window over the sink, providing a nice area for plants.

- Family/Breakfast Area: Smartly joined, this open space hosts a snack bar and a wet bar, in addition to a warming fireplace.

- Master Suite: Located on the upper floor, the master bedroom boasts corner windows, a large walk-in closet, and a split bath with a dual-sink vanity.

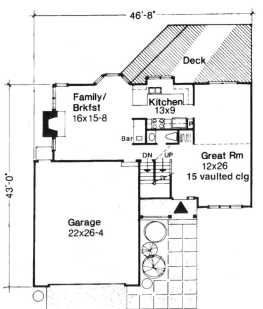

Main Level Floor Plan

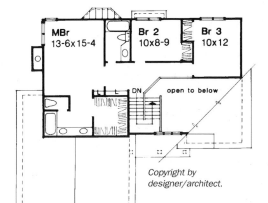

Upper Level Floor Plan

Copyright by designer/architect.

Plan #181126

Dimensions: 35' W x 30' D
Levels: 2
Square Footage: 1,468
Main Level Sq. Ft.: 958
Upper Level Sq. Ft.: 510
Bedrooms: 3
Bathrooms: 2
Foundation: Basement
Materials List Available: Yes
Price Category: B

A multiple-gabled roof and a covered entry give this home a charming appearance.

CAD FILE AVAILABLE

This home, as shown in the photograph, may differ from the actual blueprints. For more detailed information, please check the floor plans carefully.

Images provided by designer/architect.

Features:

- **Entry:** You'll keep heating and cooling costs down with this air-lock entry. There is also a large closet here.

- **Kitchen:** This efficient L-shaped eat-in kitchen has access to the rear deck.

- **Great Room:** This two-story space has a cozy fireplace and is open to the kitchen.

- **Master Bedroom:** Located on the main level, this area has access to the main bathroom, which has an oversized tub and a compartmentalized lavatory.

- **Bedrooms:** The two secondary bedrooms are located on the upper level and share a common bathroom.

Rear View

Main Level Floor Plan

Upper Level Floor Plan

Copyright by designer/architect.

Plan #161015

Dimensions: 55'4" W x 40'4" D

Levels: 2

Square Footage: 1,768

Main Level Sq. Ft.: 960

Upper Level Sq. Ft.: 808

Bedrooms: 3

Bathrooms: 2½

Foundation: Basement

Materials List Available: Yes

Price Category: C

One look at this dramatic exterior—a 12-ft. high entry with a transom and sidelights, multiple gables, and an impressive box window—you'll fall in love with this home.

Features:

- Foyer: This 2-story area announces the grace of this home to everyone who enters it.

- Great Room: A natural gathering spot, this room is sunken to set it off from the rest of the house. The 12-ft. ceiling adds a spacious feeling, and the access to the rear porch makes it ideal for friends and family.

- Kitchen: The kids will enjoy the snack bar and you'll love the adjoining breakfast room with its access to the rear porch.

- Master Suite: A whirlpool in the master bath and walk-in closets in the bedroom spell luxury.

- Laundry Area: Two large closets are so handy that you'll wonder how you ever did without them.

Images provided by designer/architect.

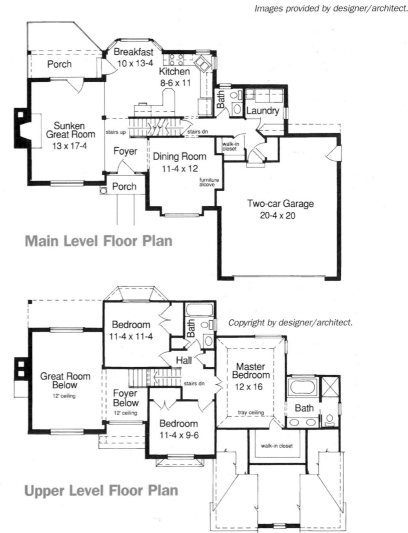

Main Level Floor Plan

Copyright by designer/architect.

Upper Level Floor Plan

Images provided by designer/architect.

Plan #181120

Dimensions: 32' W x 40' D
Levels: 2
Square Footage: 1,480
Main Level Sq. Ft.: 1,024
Second Level Sq. Ft.: 456
Bedrooms: 2
Bathrooms: 2
Foundation: Basement
Materials List Available: Yes
Price Category: B

Escape to this charming all-season vacation home with lots of view-capturing windows.

Features:

- Ceiling Height: 8 ft. unless otherwise noted.
- Living/Dining Area: The covered back porch opens into this large, inviting combined area. Its high ceiling adds to the sense of spaciousness.
- Family Room: After relaxing in front of the fireplace that warms this family room, family and guests can move outside onto the porch to watch the sun set.

- Kitchen: Light streams through a triple window in this well-designed kitchen. It's conveniently located next to the dining area and features a center island with a breakfast bar and double sinks.
- Master Suite: This first floor suite is located in the front of the house and is enhanced by its large walk-through closet and the adjoining private bath.

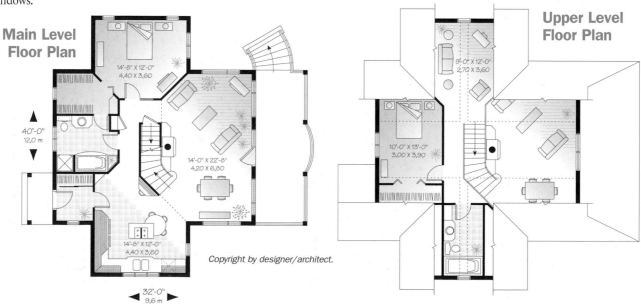

Main Level Floor Plan

14'-8" X 12'-0"
4,40 X 3,60

40'-0"
12,0 m

14'-0" X 22'-8"
4,20 X 6,80

14'-8" X 12'-0"
4,40 X 3,60

32'-0"
9,6 m

Upper Level Floor Plan

9'-0" X 12'-0"
2,70 X 3,60

10'-0" X 13'-0"
3,00 X 3,90

Copyright by designer/architect.

Plan #151016

Dimensions: 60'2" W x 39'10" D
Levels: 2
Square Footage: 1,783;
   2,107 with bonus
Main Level Sq. Ft.: 1,124
Upper Level Sq. Ft.: 659
Bonus Room Sq. Ft.: 324
Bedrooms: 3
Bathrooms: 2½
Foundation: Crawl space, slab,
   or basement
CompleteCost List Available: Yes
Price Category: C

An open design characterizes this spacious home built for family life and entertaining.

Images provided by designer/architect.

Features:

- Great Room: Enjoy the fireplace in this spacious, versatile room.
- Dining Room: Entertaining is easy, thanks to the open design with the kitchen.
- Master Suite: Luxury surrounds you in this suite, with its large walk-in closet, double vanities, and a bathroom with a whirlpool tub and separate shower.

- Upper Bedrooms: Window seats make wonderful spots for reading or relaxing, and a nook between the windows of these rooms is a ready-made play area.
- Bonus Area: Located over the garage, this space could be converted to a home office, a studio, or a game room for the kids.
- Attic: There's plenty of storage space here.

Bonus Room Above Garage

Copyright by designer/architect.

Main Level Floor Plan

Upper Level Floor Plan

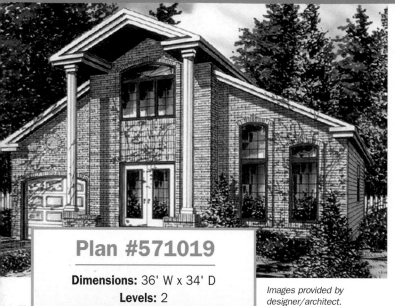

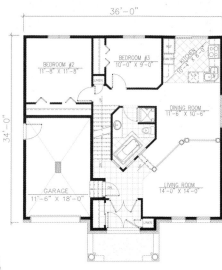

Main Level Floor Plan

Plan #571019

Dimensions: 36' W x 34' D

Levels: 2

Square Footage: 1,662

Main Level Sq. Ft.: 1,230

Upper Level Sq. Ft.: 432

Bedrooms: 4

Bathrooms: 2

Foundation: Basement

Material List Available: Yes

Price Category: C

Images provided by designer/architect.

Upper Level Floor Plan

Copyright by designer/architect.

Plan #121112

Dimensions: 44' W x 40' D

Levels: 2

Square Footage: 1,650

Main Level Sq. Ft.: 891

Upper Level Sq. Ft.: 759

Bedrooms: 3

Bathrooms: 2½

Foundation: Basement; crawl space for fee

Material List Available: Yes

Price Category: C

Images provided by designer/architect.

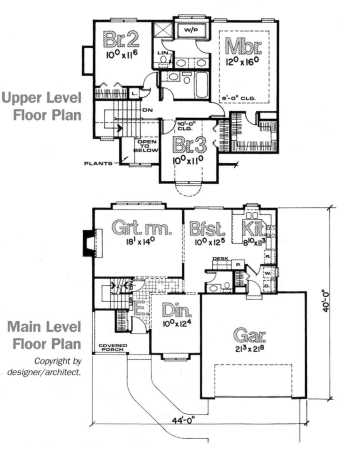

Upper Level Floor Plan

Main Level Floor Plan

Copyright by designer/architect.

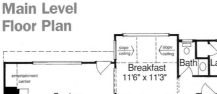

Plan #161022

Dimensions: 52'10" W x 38'2" D
Levels: 2
Square Footage: 1,898
Main Level Sq. Ft.: 1,065
Upper Level Sq. Ft.: 833
Bedrooms: 3
Bathrooms: 2½
Foundation: Basement
Materials List Available: No
Price Category: D

A covered porch and boxed window add to the charm of the stone exterior of this home.

CAD FILE AVAILABLE

Features:

- **Great Room:** This sunken room can be warmed by a fireplace on winter days and chilly evenings, and lit by natural light flowing through the bank of windows on the rear wall.

- **Kitchen:** You'll love the companionship that the snack bar in the kitchen naturally encourages. A large pantry in this area gives you ample storage space and helps to keep you organized.

- **Breakfast Room:** Quiet elegance marks this room with its sloped ceiling and arched windows that look out into the rear yard.

- **Master Suite:** Enjoy the vaulted ceiling and bath with a whirlpool tub.

- **Extra Spaces:** A loft on the second floor and a bonus room allow endless possibilities in this comfortable home.

Rear Elevation

Main Level Floor Plan

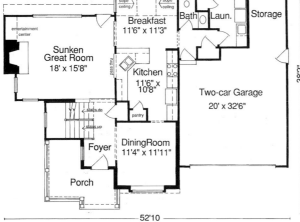

Upper Level Floor Plan

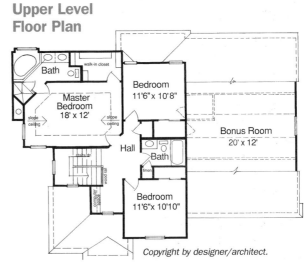

Copyright by designer/architect.

Plan #181133

Dimensions: 38' W x 40' D
Levels: 2
Square Footage: 1,832
Main Level Sq. Ft.: 1,212
Second Level Sq. Ft. 620
Bedrooms: 3
Bathrooms: 2
Foundation: Walkout; crawl space, slab, or basement for fee
Materials List Available: Yes
Price Category: D

Images provided by designer/architect.

Features:

- Ceiling Height: 8 ft.

- Family Room: Family and friends will be drawn to this large sunny room. Curl up with a good book before the beautiful see-through fireplace.

- Screened Porch: This porch shares the see-through fireplace with the family room so you can enjoy an outside fire on cool summer nights.

- Master Suite: This romantic first-floor master suite offers a large walk-in closet and a luxurious private bathroom enhanced by dual vanities.

- Secondary Bedrooms: Upstairs you'll find two generous bedrooms with ample closet space. These bedrooms share a full bathroom.

- Basement: This large walkout basement with large glass door is perfectly suited for future expansion.

You'll enjoy sunshine indoors and out with a wraparound deck and windows all around.

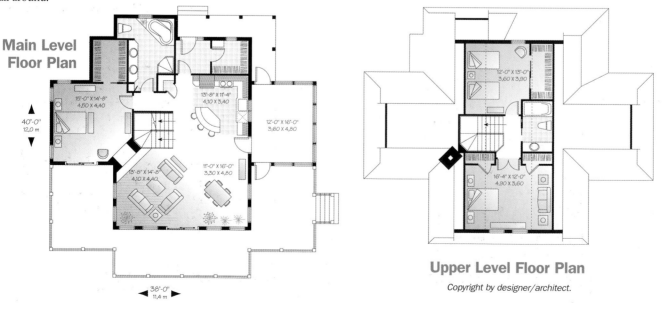

Main Level Floor Plan

15'-0" X 14'-8"
4,50 X 4,40

13'-8" X 11'-4"
4,10 X 3,40

12'-0" X 16'-0"
3,60 X 4,80

13'-8" X 14'-8"
4,10 X 4,40

11'-0" X 16'-0"
3,30 X 4,80

40'-0"
12,0 m

38'-0"
11,4 m

Upper Level Floor Plan

12'-0" X 13'-0"
3,60 X 3,90

16'-4" X 12'-0"
4,90 X 3,60

Copyright by designer/architect.

Plan #271012

Dimensions: 48' W x 29'10" D

Levels: 2

Square Footage: 1,359

Main Level Sq. Ft.: 668

Upper Level Sq. Ft.: 691

Bedrooms: 3

Bathrooms: 2½

Foundation: Basement

Materials List Available: Yes

Price Category: B

This home, as shown in the photograph, may differ from the actual blueprints. For more detailed information, please check the floor plans carefully.

Images provided by designer/architect.

This traditional home blends an updated exterior with a thoroughly modern interior.

Features:

- **Living Room:** This sunny, vaulted gathering room offers a handsome fireplace and open access to the adjoining dining room.
- **Dining Room:** Equally suited to intimate family gatherings and larger dinner parties, this space includes access to a spacious backyard deck.
- **Kitchen/Breakfast Nook:** Smartly joined, these two rooms are just perfect for speedy weekday mornings and lazy weekend breakfasts.
- **Master Suite:** A skylighted staircase leads to this upper-floor masterpiece, which includes a private bath, a walk-in closet, and bright, boxed-out window arrangement.
- **Secondary Bedrooms:** One of these is actually a loft/bedroom conversion, which makes it suitable for expansion space as your family grows.

Main Level Floor Plan

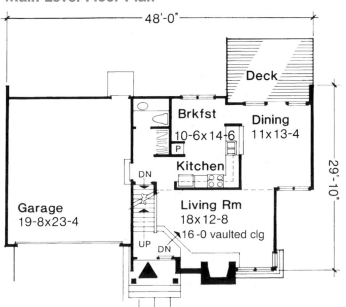

Upper Level Floor Plan

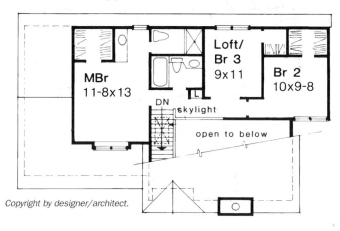

Copyright by designer/architect.

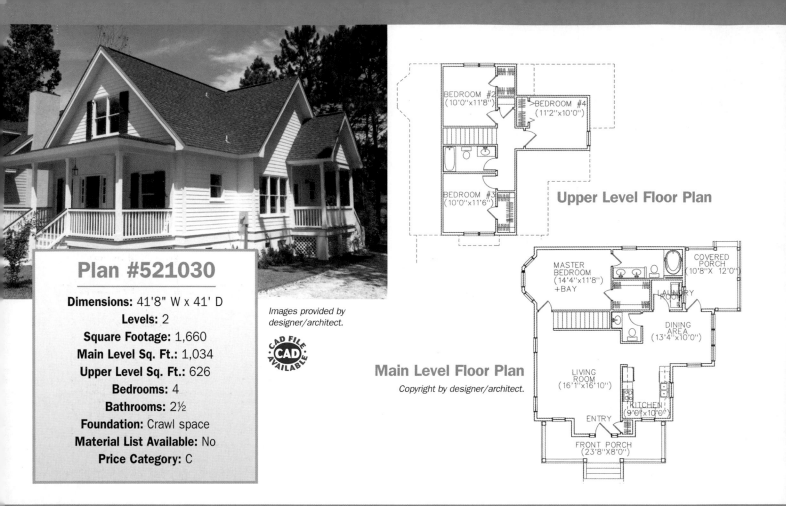

Plan #521030

Dimensions: 41'8" W x 41' D
Levels: 2
Square Footage: 1,660
Main Level Sq. Ft.: 1,034
Upper Level Sq. Ft.: 626
Bedrooms: 4
Bathrooms: 2½
Foundation: Crawl space
Material List Available: No
Price Category: C

Images provided by designer/architect.

Upper Level Floor Plan

Main Level Floor Plan
Copyright by designer/architect.

BEDROOM #2 (10'0"x11'8")
BEDROOM #4 (11'2"x10'0")
BEDROOM #3 (10'0"x11'6")

MASTER BEDROOM (14'4"x11'8") +BAY
COVERED PORCH (10'8"X 12'0")
LAUNDRY ROOM
DINING AREA (13'4"x10'0")
LIVING ROOM (16'1"x16'10")
KITCHEN (9'0"x10'0")
ENTRY
FRONT PORCH (23'8"X8'0")

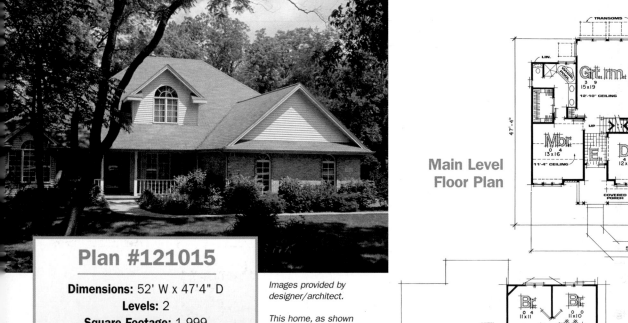

Plan #121015

Dimensions: 52' W x 47'4" D
Levels: 2
Square Footage: 1,999
Main Level Sq. Ft.: 1,421
Upper Level Sq. Ft.: 578
Bedrooms: 4
Bathrooms: 2½
Foundation: Basement
Materials List Available: Yes
Price Category: D

Images provided by designer/architect.

This home, as shown in the photograph, may differ from the actual blueprints. For more detailed information, please check the floor plans carefully.

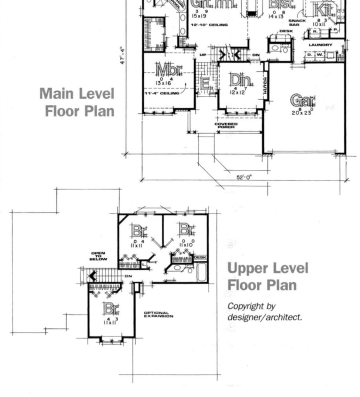

Main Level Floor Plan

Upper Level Floor Plan
Copyright by designer/architect.

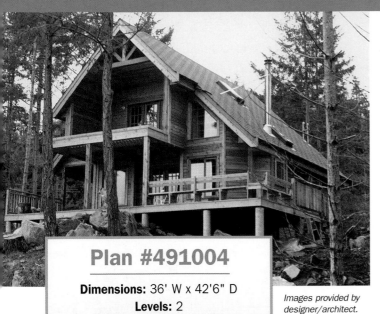

Main Level Floor Plan

Copyright by designer/architect.

36'-0"

42'-6"

WINDOW SEAT
13' VAULTED CLG.

LIV./DIN.
23' x 9'4" & 14'6"

WOOD STOVE

8'10" x 8'

GUEST
10'8" x 9'

Images provided by designer/architect.

Front View

Upper Level Floor Plan

STUDIO
15'4" x 11'8"
13' VAULTED CLG.

OPEN

BED RM.
15' x 9'
10' VAULTED CLG.

Plan #491004

Dimensions: 36' W x 42'6" D
Levels: 2
Square Footage: 1,154
Main Level Sq. Ft.: 672
Upper Level Sq. Ft.: 482
Bedrooms: 2
Bathrooms: 2
Foundation: Crawl space
Material List Available: Yes
Price Category: B

Main Level Floor Plan

34'-0"   4'-0"

34'-0"

BREAKFAST

KITCHEN

LIVING ROOM
16'-10" x 13'-0"

DINING ROOM
12'-6" x 12'-0"

GARAGE
12'-6" x 19'-0"

GARAGE (OPTION)
16'-6" x 19'-0"

Images provided by designer/architect.

BEDROOM #3
10'-6" x 13'-10"

BEDROOM #4
12'-8" x 9'-8"

BEDROOM #2
12'-6" x 12'-8"

MASTER BEDROOM
12'-6" x 16'-0"

Upper Level Floor Plan

Copyright by designer/architect.

Plan #571015

Dimensions: 38' W x 34' D
Levels: 2
Square Footage: 1,916
Main Level Sq. Ft.: 839
Upper Level Sq. Ft.: 1,077
Bedrooms: 4
Bathrooms: 1½
Foundation: Basement
Material List Available: Yes
Price Category: D

Plan #121094

Dimensions: 40'8" W x 46' D
Levels: 2
Square Footage: 1,768
Main Level Sq. Ft.: 905
Upper Level Sq. Ft.: 863
Bedrooms: 3
Bathrooms: 2½
Foundation: Basement
Materials List Available: Yes
Price Category: C

You'll love this design if you're looking for a home to complement a site with a lovely rear view.

Features:

- **Great Room:** A trio of lovely windows looks out to the front entry of this home. The French doors in this room open to the breakfast area for everyone's convenience.

- **Kitchen:** Designed to suit a gourmet cook, this kitchen includes a roomy pantry and an island with a snack bar.

- **Breakfast Area:** The boxed window here is perfect for houseplants or a collection of culinary herbs. A door leads to the rear porch, where you'll love to dine in good weather.

- **Master Suite:** On the upper level, the bedroom features a cathedral ceiling, two walk-in closets, and a window seat. The bath also has a cathedral ceiling and includes dual lavatories, a large dressing area, and a sunlit whirlpool tub.

Main Level Floor Plan

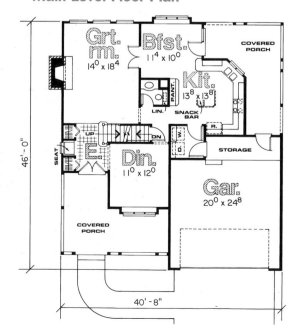

Upper Level Floor Plan

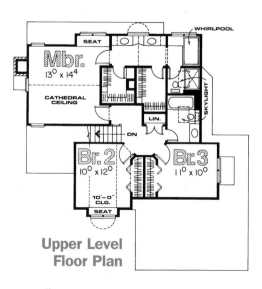

Copyright by designer/architect.

Plan #121084

Dimensions: 40' W x 42' D
Levels: 2
Square Footage: 1,728
Main Level Sq. Ft.: 845
Upper Level Sq. Ft.: 883
Bedrooms: 4
Bathrooms: 2½
Foundation: Basement
Materials List Available: Yes
Price Category: C

Images provided by designer/architect.

If you're looking for a home where the whole family will be comfortable, you'll love this design.

Features:

- **Great Room:** The heart of the home, this great room has a fireplace with a raised hearth, a sloped ceiling, and transom-topped windows.

- **Dining Room:** A cased opening lets you flow from the great room into this formal dining room. A built-in display hutch is the highlight here.

- **Kitchen:** What could be nicer than this wraparound kitchen with peninsula snack bar? The sunny, attached breakfast area has a pantry and built-in desk.

- **Master Suite:** A double vanity, whirlpool tub, shower, and walk-in closet exude luxury in this upper-floor master suite.

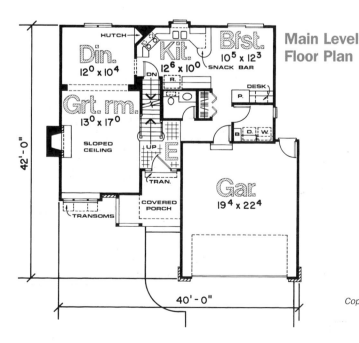

Main Level Floor Plan

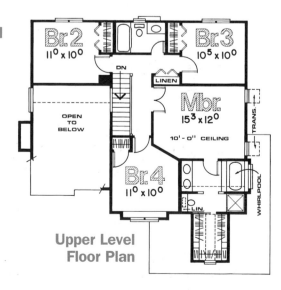

Upper Level Floor Plan

Copyright by designer/architect.

Plan #381174

Dimensions: 44' W x 63' D

Levels: 2

Square Footage: 1,685

Main Level Sq. Ft.: 1,250

Upper Level Sq. Ft.: 435

Bedrooms: 2

Bathrooms: 1

Foundation: Basement

Material List Available: Yes

Price Category: C

Main Level Floor Plan

Images provided by designer/architect.

Upper Level Floor Plan

Copyright by designer/architect.

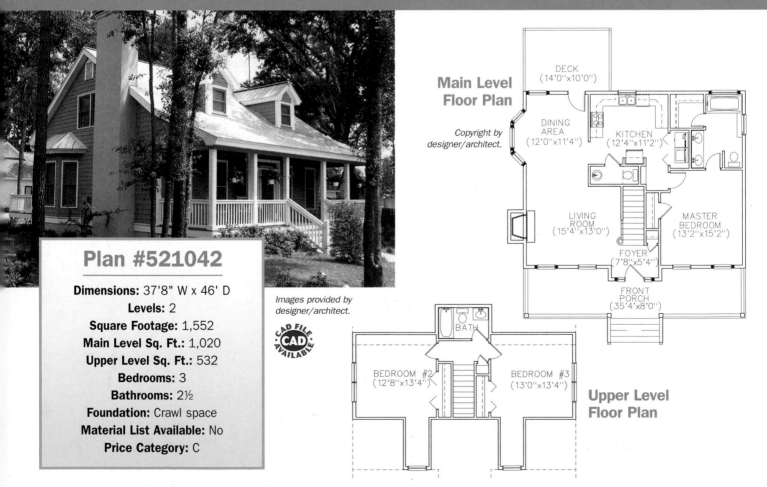

Plan #521042

Dimensions: 37'8" W x 46' D

Levels: 2

Square Footage: 1,552

Main Level Sq. Ft.: 1,020

Upper Level Sq. Ft.: 532

Bedrooms: 3

Bathrooms: 2½

Foundation: Crawl space

Material List Available: No

Price Category: C

Images provided by designer/architect.

CAD FILE AVAILABLE

Main Level Floor Plan

Copyright by designer/architect.

Upper Level Floor Plan

Plan #341283

Dimensions: 32' W x 38'9" D
Levels: 1.5
Square Footage: 1,786
Main Level Sq. Ft.: 1,197
Upper Level Sq. Ft.: 589
Bedrooms: 3
Bathrooms: 2½
Foundation: Crawl space, slab, basement or walkout
Material List Available: Yes
Price Category: C

Images provided by designer/architect.

CAD FILE AVAILABLE

Main Level Floor Plan

Upper Level Floor Plan

Copyright by designer/architect.

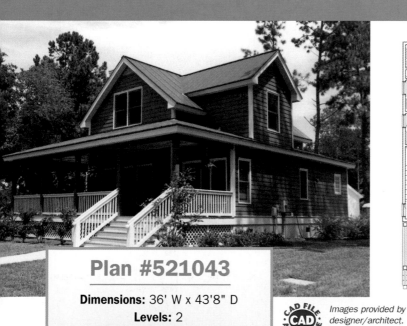

Plan #521043

Dimensions: 36' W x 43'8" D
Levels: 2
Square Footage: 1,536
Main Level Sq. Ft.: 1,038
Upper Level Sq. Ft.: 498
Bedrooms: 3
Bathrooms: 2½
Foundation: Crawl space
Material List Available: No
Price Category: C

CAD FILE AVAILABLE

Images provided by designer/architect.

Main Level Floor Plan

Copyright by designer/architect.

Side View

Upper Level Floor Plan

Plan #121086

Dimensions: 55'4" W x 37'8" D

Levels: 2

Square Footage: 1,998

Main Level Sq. Ft.: 1,093

Upper Level Sq. Ft.: 905

Bedrooms: 3

Bathrooms: 2½

Foundation: Basement

Materials List Available: Yes

Price Category: D

Images provided by designer/architect.

You'll love the open design of this comfortable home if sunny, bright rooms make you happy.

Features:

• Entry: Walk into this two-story entry, and you're sure to admire the open staircase and balcony from the upper level.

• Dining Room: To the left of the entry, you'll see this dining room, with its special ceiling detail and built-in display cabinet.

• Living Room: Located immediately to the right, this living room features a charming bay window.

• Family Room: French doors from the living room open into this sunny space, where a handsome fireplace takes center stage.

• Kitchen: Combined with the breakfast area, this kitchen features an island cooktop, a large pantry, and a built-in desk.

Main Level Floor Plan

Upper Level Floor Plan

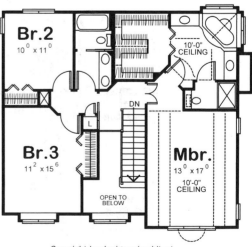

Copyright by designer/architect.

Plan #271011

Dimensions: 36' W x 40'8" D
Levels: 2
Square Footage: 1,296
Main Level Sq. Ft.: 891
Upper Level Sq. Ft.: 405
Bedrooms: 3
Bathrooms: 2
Foundation: Basement
Materials List Available: Yes
Price Category: B

Perfectly sized for a narrow lot, this charming modern cottage boasts space efficiency and affordability.

Features:

- **Living Room:** The inviting raised foyer steps down into this vaulted living room, with its bright windows and eye-catching fireplace.

- **Dining Room:** This vaulted formal eating space includes sliding-glass-door access to a backyard deck.

- **Kitchen:** Everything is here: U-shaped efficiency, handy pantry—even bright windows.

- **Master Suite:** Main-floor location ensures accessibility in later years, plus there's a walk-in closet and full bathroom.

- **Secondary Bedrooms:** On the upper floor, a bedroom and a loft reside near a full bath. The loft can be converted easily to a third bedroom, or use it as a study or play space.

CAD FILE AVAILABLE

Main Level Floor Plan

Upper Level Floor Plan

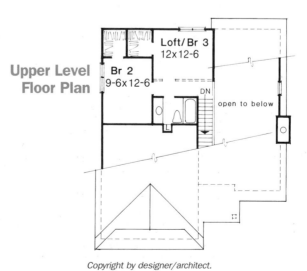

Main Level Floor Plan

16' VAULTED CLG.

GREAT ROOM
23' x 10'2" x& 16'6"

WOOD STOVE

KIT.
8'6" x 6'

GUEST
10'8" x 11'

W D

6'-0" 24'-0" 6'-0"

8'-0"

32'-0"

4'-6"

Images provided by designer/architect.

STUDIO
15'4" x13'4"
13' VAULTED CLG.

RAILING

OPEN

DN

BED RM.
15' x 11'
10' VAULTED CLG.

Upper Level Floor Plan

Copyright by designer/architect.

Rear View

Plan #491005

Dimensions: 36' W x 44'6" D
Levels: 2
Square Footage: 1,333
Main Level Sq. Ft.: 768
Upper Level Sq. Ft.: 565
Bedrooms: 2
Bathrooms: 2
Foundation: Crawl space
Material List Available: Yes
Price Category: B

CAD FILE AVAILABLE

Plan #181074

Dimensions: 42' W x 40' D
Levels: 2
Square Footage: 1,760
Main Level Sq. Ft.: 880
Upper Level Sq. Ft.: 880
Bedrooms: 3
Full Baths: 2½
Foundation: Full basement
Materials List Available: Yes
Price Category: C

Images provided by designer/architect.

20'-8" X 11'-4"
6,20 X 3,40

16'-8" X 11'-0"
5,00 X 3,30

15'-4" X 22'-8"
4,60 X 6,80

12'-8" X 15'-8"
3,80 X 4,70

Main Level Floor Plan

13'-4" X 9'-0"
4,00 X 2,70

11'-0" X 11'-0"
3,30 X 3,30

15'-4" X 15'-4"
4,60 X 4,60

12'-8" X 15'-8"
3,80 X 4,70

Upper Level Floor Plan
Copyright by designer/architect.

Plan #321057

Dimensions: 38' W x 39'4" D
Levels: 2
Square Footage: 1,524
Main Level Sq. Ft.: 951
Upper Level Sq. Ft.: 573
Bedrooms: 3
Bathrooms: 2½
Foundation: Basement
Materials List Available: Yes
Price Category: C

Images provided by designer/architect.

Main Level Floor Plan

Upper Level Floor Plan

Copyright by designer/architect.

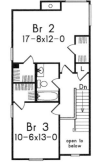

Plan #101015

Dimensions: 26' W x 46' D
Levels: 2
Square Footage: 1,647
Main Level Sq. Ft.: 1,288
Upper Level Sq. Ft.: 359
Bedrooms: 2
Bathrooms: 1
Foundation: Slab
Materials List Available: No
Price Category: C

Images provided by designer/architect.

CAD FILE AVAILABLE

Main Level Floor Plan

Upper Level Floor Plan

Copyright by designer/architect.

Plan #121064

Dimensions: 44' W x 40' D

Levels: 2

Square Footage: 1,846

Main Level Sq. Ft.: 919

Upper Level Sq. Ft.: 927

Bedrooms: 4

Bathrooms: 2½

Foundation: Basement

Materials List Available: Yes

Price Category: D

Images provided by designer/architect.

You'll love the features and design in this compact but amenity-filled home.

Features:

• Entry: A balcony overlooks this two-story entry, where a plant shelf tops the coat closet.

• Great Room: A trio of tall windows points up the large dimensions of this room, which is sure to be the hub of your home. Arrange the

furniture to create a cozy space around the fireplace, or leave it open to the room.

• Kitchen: You'll love to work in this well-designed kitchen area.

• Master Suite: On the second floor, this master suite features a tiered ceiling and two walk-in closets. In the bath, you'll find a double vanity, whirlpool tub, and separate shower.

Main Level Floor Plan

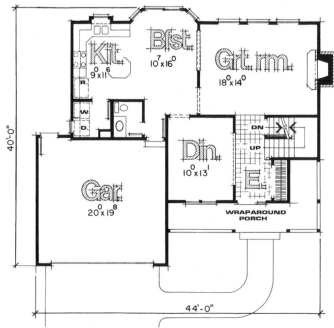

Upper Level Floor Plan

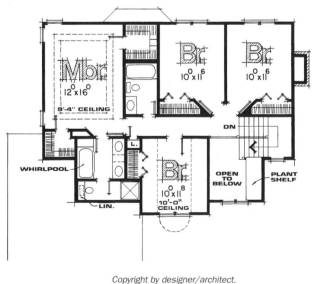

Copyright by designer/architect.

Plan #151213

Dimensions: 51' W x 46' D

Levels: 1

Square Footage: 1,231

Bedrooms: 3

Bathrooms: 2

Foundation: Crawl space or slab

CompleteCost List Available: Yes

Price Category: B

Images provided by designer/architect.

This cute brick ranch home is a great place to live.

Features:

• Foyer: This area welcomes you home with a handy coat closet.

• Great Room: A cozy fireplace and entry to the grilling porch make this gathering area special.

• Kitchen: This fully equipped kitchen is open into the breakfast room with a bay window looking out to the backyard.

• Master Bedroom: This master bedroom has a large walk-in closet and a private bathroom.

• Garage: In addition to two cars, there is room for storage.

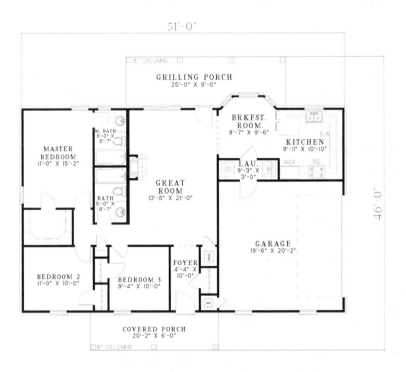

Copyright by designer/architect.

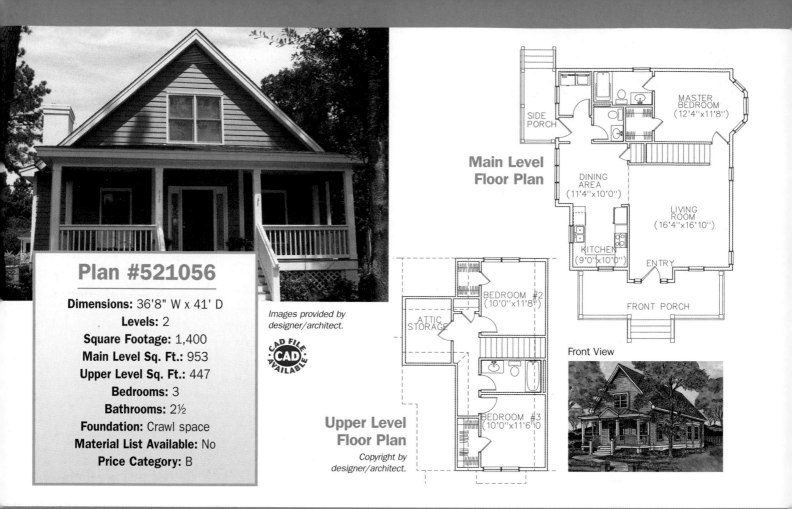

Plan #521056

Dimensions: 36'8" W x 41' D

Levels: 2

Square Footage: 1,400

Main Level Sq. Ft.: 953

Upper Level Sq. Ft.: 447

Bedrooms: 3

Bathrooms: 2½

Foundation: Crawl space

Material List Available: No

Price Category: B

Main Level Floor Plan

SIDE PORCH

MASTER BEDROOM (12'4"x11'8")

DINING AREA (11'4"x10'0")

LIVING ROOM (16'4"x16'10")

KITCHEN (9'0"x10'0")

ENTRY

FRONT PORCH

Images provided by designer/architect.

CAD FILE AVAILABLE

ATTIC STORAGE

BEDROOM #2 (10'0"x11'8")

BEDROOM #3 (10'0"x11'6")

Upper Level Floor Plan

Copyright by designer/architect.

Front View

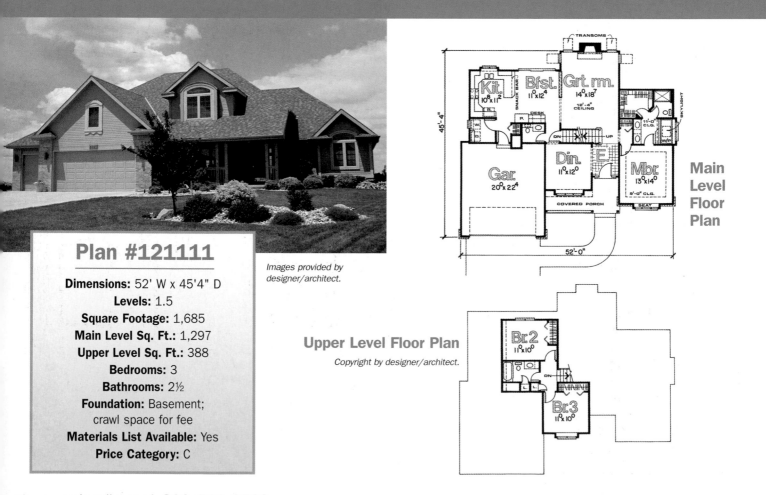

Plan #121111

Dimensions: 52' W x 45'4" D

Levels: 1.5

Square Footage: 1,685

Main Level Sq. Ft.: 1,297

Upper Level Sq. Ft.: 388

Bedrooms: 3

Bathrooms: 2½

Foundation: Basement; crawl space for fee

Materials List Available: Yes

Price Category: C

Images provided by designer/architect.

TRANSOMS

Kit. 10'x11'2

Bfst. 11'x12'4

Grt. rm. 14'x18'7
19'-4" CEILING

SNACK BAR

DESK

Gar. 20'x22'4

Din. 11'x12'0

Mbr. 13'x14'0
9'-0" CLG.

SKYLIGHT

COVERED PORCH

SEAT

45'-4"

52'-0"

Main Level Floor Plan

Upper Level Floor Plan

Copyright by designer/architect.

Br.2 11'x10'0

Br.3 11'x10'0

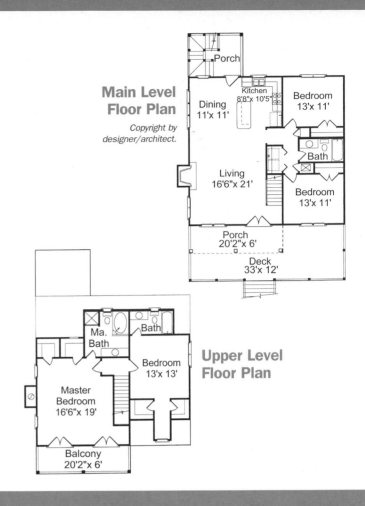

**Main Level
Floor Plan**

*Copyright by
designer/architect.*

Porch

Dining
11'x 11'

Kitchen
8'8"x 10'5"

Bedroom
13'x 11'

Bath

Living
16'6"x 21'

Bedroom
13'x 11'

Porch
20'2"x 6'

Deck
33'x 12'

Ma.
Bath

Bath

Bedroom
13'x 13'

**Upper Level
Floor Plan**

Master
Bedroom
16'6"x 19'

Balcony
20'2"x 6'

Plan #111047

Dimensions: 36' W x 54' D
Levels: 2
Square Footage: 1,863
Main Level Sq. Ft.: 1,056
Upper Level Sq. Ft.: 807
Bedrooms: 4
Bathrooms: 3
Foundation: Pier
Materials List Available: No
Price Category: D

*Images provided by
designer/architect.*

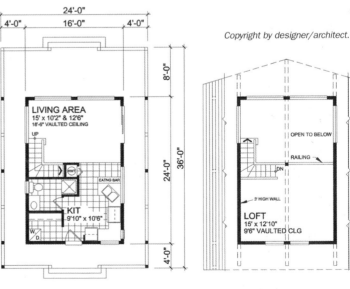

24'-0"

4'-0" 16'-0" 4'-0"

Copyright by designer/architect.

8'-0"

LIVING AREA
15' x 10'2" & 12'6"
18'-6" VAULTED CEILING

UP

24'-0"

36'-0"

OPEN TO BELOW

RAILING

KIT
9'10" x 10'6"

W.
D.

4'-0"

LOFT
15' x 12'10"
9'6" VAULTED CLG

3' HIGH WALL

DN

Plan #491001

Dimensions: 24' W x 36' D
Levels: 2
Square Footage: 582
Main Level Sq. Ft.: 384
Lower Level Sq. Ft.: 198
Bedrooms: 1
Bathrooms: 1
Foundation: Crawl space
Materials List Available: Yes
Price Category: A

**Main Level
Floor Plan**

**Upper Level
Floor Plan**

Plan #121044

Dimensions: 40' W x 55'8" D

Levels: 2

Square Footage: 1,923

Main Level Sq. Ft.: 1,351

Upper Level Sq. Ft.: 572

Bedrooms: 3

Bathrooms: 3

Foundation: Basement

Materials List Available: Yes

Price Category: D

Images provided by designer/architect.

The layout of this gracious home is designed with the contemporary family in mind.

Features:

• Ceiling Height: 8 ft. unless otherwise noted.

• Foyer: This elegant entry is graced with an open stairway that enhances the sense of spaciousness.

• Kitchen: Located just beyond the entry, this convenient kitchen features a center island that doubles as a snack bar.

• Breakfast Area: A sloped ceiling unites this area with the family room. Here you will find a planning desk for compiling menus and shopping lists.

• Master Bedroom: This bedroom has a distinctively contemporary appeal, with its cathedral ceiling and triple window.

• Computer Loft: Designed to house a computer, this loft overlooks the family room.

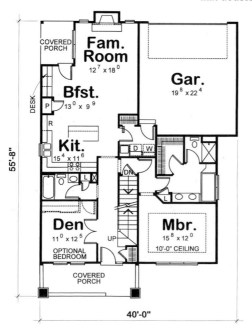

Main Level Floor Plan

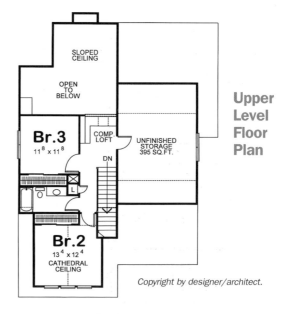

Upper Level Floor Plan

Copyright by designer/architect.

Plan #121045

Dimensions: 40' W x 48' D

Levels: 2

Square Footage: 1,575

Main Level Sq. Ft.: 787

Upper Level Sq. Ft.: 788

Bedrooms: 3

Bathrooms: 2½

Foundation: Basement

Materials List Available: Yes

Price Category: C

This home, as shown in the photograph, may differ from the actual blueprints. For more detailed information, please check the floor plans carefully.   *Images provided by designer/architect.*

This home is carefully laid out to provide the convenience demanded by busy family life.

Features:

- Ceiling Height: 8 ft.

- Family Room: This charming family room, with its fireplace and built-in cabinetry, will become the central gathering place for family and friends.

- Kitchen: This kitchen offers a central island that makes food preparation more convenient and doubles as a snack bar for a quick bite on the run. The breakfast area features a pantry and planning desk.

- Computer Loft: The second-floor landing includes this loft designed to accommodate the family computer.

- Room to Grow: Also on the second-floor landing you will find a large unfinished area waiting to accommodate the growing family.

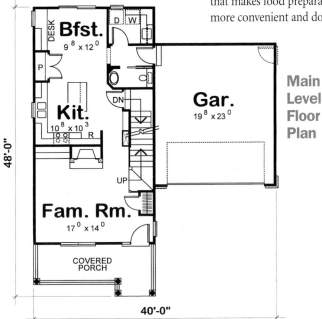

Main Level Floor Plan

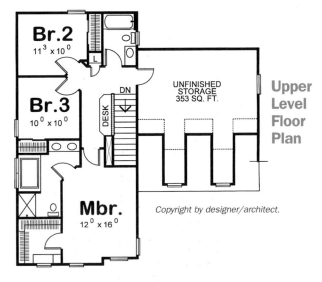

Upper Level Floor Plan

Copyright by designer/architect.

Plan #151026

Dimensions: 34' W x 66'8" D
Levels: 2
Square Footage: 1,574
Main Level Sq. Ft.: 1,131
Upper Level Sq. Ft.: 443
Bedrooms: 3
Bathrooms: 2½
Foundation: Crawl space, slab; optional full basement plan available for extra fee
CompleteCost List Available: Yes
Price Category: C

This French Country home gives space for entertaining and offers privacy.

Features:

- Great Room: Move through the gracious foyer framed by wooden columns into the great room with its lofty 10-ft. ceilings and gas fireplace.

- Dining Room: Set off by 8-in. columns, the dining room opens to the kitchen, both with 9-foot ceilings.

- Master Suite: Enjoy relaxing in the bedroom with its 10-ft. boxed ceiling and well-placed windows. Atrium doors open to the backyard, where you can make a secluded garden. A glass-bricked corner whirlpool tub, corner shower, and double vanity make the master bath luxurious.

- Bedrooms: Upstairs, two large bedrooms with a walk-through bath provide plenty of room as well as privacy for kids or guests.

Images provided by designer/architect.

Main Level Floor Plan

Upper Level Floor Plan

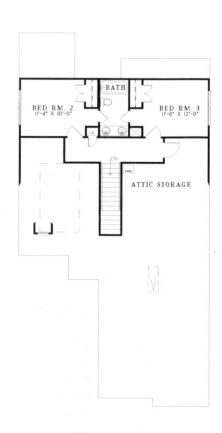

Copyright by designer/architect.

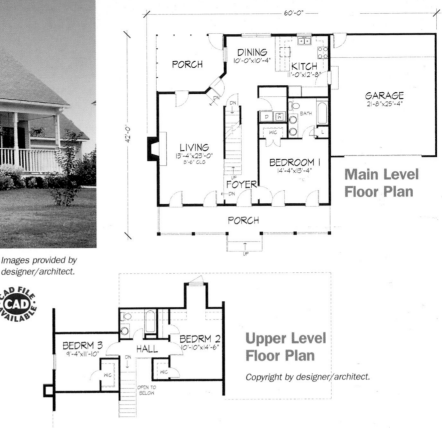

Main Level Floor Plan

Images provided by designer/architect.

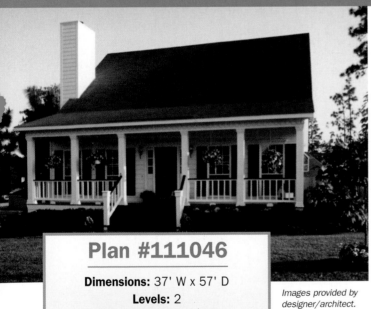

Plan #271097

Dimensions: 60' W x 42' D

Levels: 2

Square Footage: 1,645

Main Level Sq. Ft.: 1,136

Upper Level Sq. Ft.: 509

Bedrooms: 3

Bathrooms: 2

Foundation: Basement

Materials List Available: No

Price Category: C

Upper Level Floor Plan

Copyright by designer/architect.

CAD FILE AVAILABLE

Plan #111046

Dimensions: 37' W x 57' D

Levels: 2

Square Footage: 1,768

Main Level Sq. Ft.: 1,247

Upper Level Sq. Ft.: 521

Bedrooms: 3

Bathrooms: 2½

Foundation: Crawl space

Materials List Available: No

Price Category: C

Images provided by designer/architect.

Main Level Floor Plan

Upper Level Floor Plan

Copyright by designer/architect.

Plan #121085

Dimensions: 42' W x 54' D

Levels: 2

Square Footage: 1,948

Main Level Sq. Ft.: 1,517

Upper Level Sq. Ft.: 431

Bedrooms: 4

Bathrooms: 3

Foundation: Basement

Materials List Available: Yes

Price Category: D

You'll love the spacious feeling in this home, with its generous rooms and excellent design.

Features:

- Great Room: This room is lofty and open, thanks in part to the transom-topped windows that flank the fireplace. However, you can furnish to create a cozy nook for reading or a private spot to watch TV or enjoy some quiet music.

- Kitchen: Wrapping counters add an unusual touch to this kitchen, and a pantry gives extra storage area. A snack bar links the kitchen with a separate breakfast area.

- Master Suite: A tiered ceiling adds elegance to this area, and a walk-in closet adds practicality. The private bath features a sunlit whirlpool tub, separate shower, and double vanity.

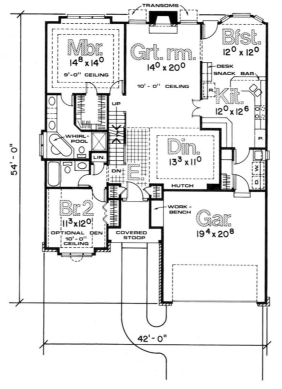

Main Level Floor Plan

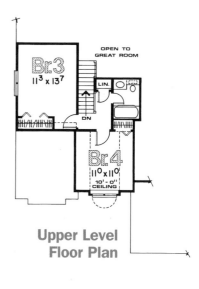

Upper Level Floor Plan

- Upper-Level Bedrooms: The upper-level placement is just right for these bedrooms, which share an amenity-filled full bathroom.

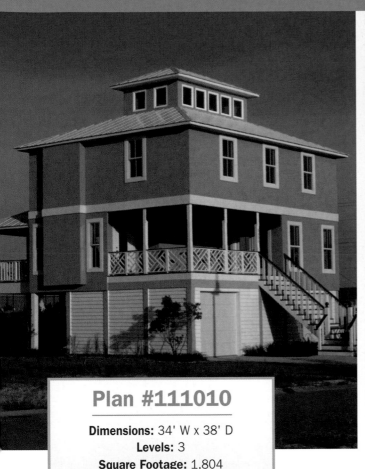

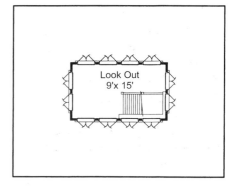

Plan #111010

Dimensions: 34' W x 38' D
Levels: 3
Square Footage: 1,804
Main Level Sq. Ft.: 731
Upper Level Sq. Ft.: 935
Third Level Sq.Ft.: 138
Bedrooms: 3
Bathrooms: 3
Foundation: Piers
Materials List Available: No
Price Category: D

This vacation home is designed for practicality and convenience.

Features:

- Porch: This cozy porch opens to the dining room and the living room. Relax on the porch, and invite a passing neighbor to join you for a cup of coffee.

- Living Room: French doors connect this brightly lit room to the porch. The corner fireplace adds warmth and elegance to the area.

- Kitchen: This island kitchen, with a snack bar, is open to the dining room and living room. A full bathroom and the laundry area are just a few steps away.

- Master Suite: This private retreat is located on the upper level close to the secondary bedrooms. Pass his and her closets that lead into the private bath, complete with an oversized tub.

Main Level Floor Plan

Copyright by designer/architect.

Deck
14'x 10'

Kitchen
10'6"x 13'9"

Dining
9'x 13'8"

Living
14'x 19'

Screen
Porch
19'6"x 10'

Upper Level Floor Plan

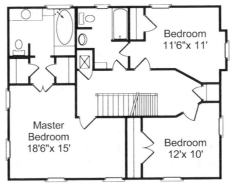

Master
Bedroom
18'6"x 15'

Bedroom
11'6"x 11'

Bedroom
12'x 10'

Third Level Floor Plan

Look Out
9'x 15'

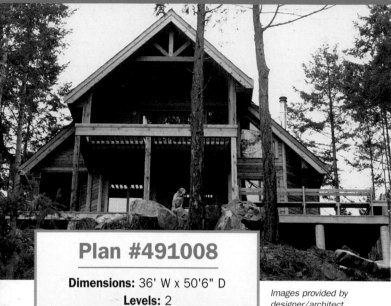

Main Level Floor Plan

Copyright by designer/architect.

DECK

GREAT ROOM
23'x19'6" & 16'8"

(VAULTED CLG.)

FLOOR LINE ABOVE

BREAKFAST BAR

WOOD STOVE

KITCHEN
10'x9'

BEDRM 2
11'x11'

LAV

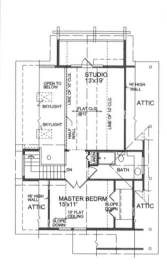

Plan #491008

Dimensions: 36' W x 50'6" D
Levels: 2
Square Footage: 1,644
Main Level Sq. Ft.: 955
Upper Level Sq. Ft.: 689
Bedrooms: 2
Bathrooms: 2
Foundation: Crawl space
Materials List Available: Yes
Price Category: C

Images provided by designer/architect.

STUDIO
13'x19'

OPEN TO BELOW

SKYLIGHT

SKYLIGHT

FLAT CLG @12

HALF WALL

ATTIC

LINEN

BATH

48" HIGH WALL
ATTIC

MASTER BEDRM
15'x11'

10' FLAT CEILING

SLOPE DOWN

ATTIC

SLOPE DOWN

Upper Level Floor Plan

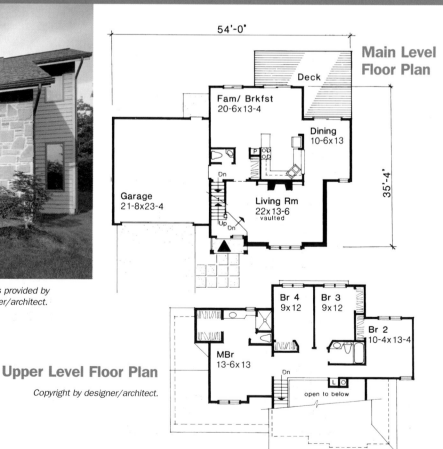

Main Level Floor Plan

54'-0"

35'-4"

Deck

Fam/ Brkfst
20-6x13-4

Dining
10-6x13

Garage
21-8x23-4

Living Rm
22x13-6
vaulted

Dn

Up Dn

Plan #271009

Dimensions: 54' W x 35'4" D
Levels: 2
Square Footage: 1,909
Main Level Sq. Ft.: 994
Upper Level Sq. Ft.: 915
Bedrooms: 4
Bathrooms: 2½
Foundation: Basement
Materials List Available: Yes
Price Category: D

Images provided by designer/architect.

Br 4
9x12

Br 3
9x12

Br 2
10-4x13-4

MBr
13-6x13

Dn

open to below

Upper Level Floor Plan

Copyright by designer/architect.

Plan #111041

Dimensions: 34' W x 32' D
Levels: 2
Square Footage: 1,743
Main Level Sq. Ft.: 912
Upper Level Sq. Ft.: 831
Bedrooms: 3
Bathrooms: 3
Foundation: Pier
Materials List Available: No
Price Category: C

You'll love the way this vacation home can accommodate a crowd or make a small family feel cozy and comfortable.

Features:

- Living Area: This easy-care living area is perfect for those times when you want to get away from it all—including extra housework.

- Kitchen: This kitchen is large enough for friends and family to chat with the cook or help with the dishes after a meal. You'll use the breakfast bar all day long for setting out drinks and snacks.

- Master Suite: Relax on the balcony off this master suit, and luxuriate in the bath with double vanities, a whirlpool tub, and a walk-in closet.

- Study: Adjacent to the master suite, this room lets you catch up on reading in a quiet spot.

- Porch: Let guests spill onto this convenient porch when you're hosting a party, or use it as outdoor space where the children can play.

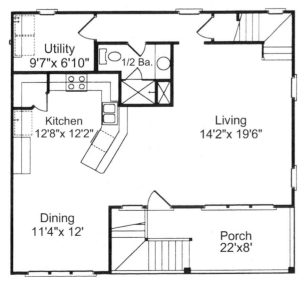

Main Level Floor Plan

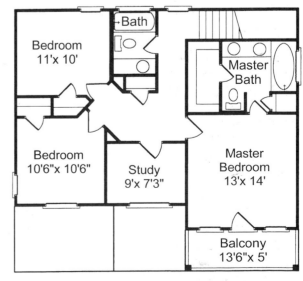

Upper Level Floor Plan

Plan #121027

Dimensions: 46' W x 48' D
Levels: 2
Square Footage: 1,660
Main Level Sq. Ft.: 1,265
Upper Level Sq. Ft.: 395
Bedrooms: 3
Bathrooms: 2½
Foundation: Basement
Materials List Available: Yes
Price Category: C

Images provided by designer/architect.

This elegant home is designed for architectural interest and gracious living.

Features:

- Ceiling Height: 8 ft. unless otherwise noted.

- Great Room: Family and guests will be drawn to this inviting, sun-filled room with its 13-ft. ceiling and raised-hearth fireplace.

- Formal Dining Room: An angled ceiling lends architectural interest to this elegant room. Alternately, this room can be used as a parlor.

- Master Bedroom: Corner windows are designed to ease window placement.

- Master Bath: The master bedroom is served by a private bath. The sunlit whirlpool bath invites you to take time to luxuriate and rejuvenate. There's a double vanity, separate shower, and a walk-in closet.

- Garage: This two bay garage offers plenty of space for storage in addition to parking.

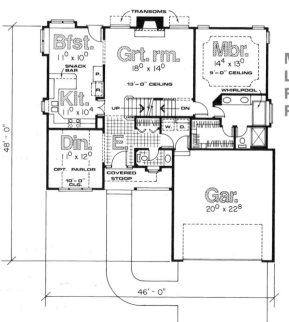

Main Level Floor Plan

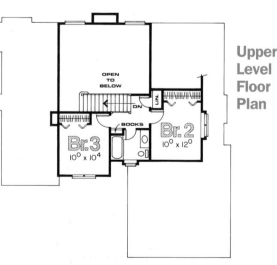

Upper Level Floor Plan

Copyright by designer/architect.

Plan #121033

Dimensions: 50'4" W x 47'4" D
Levels: 2
Square Footage: 1,987
Main Level Sq. Ft.: 929
Upper Level Sq. Ft.: 1,058
Bedrooms: 4
Bathrooms: 2½
Foundation: Basement
Materials List Available: Yes
Price Category: D

Images provided by designer/architect.

This spacious and practical home is designed with the growing family in mind.

Features:

- Ceiling Height: 8 ft.

- Great Room: This inviting room features a see-through fireplace that is sure to make it the central gathering place of the home.

- Flex Room: French doors flanking the see-through fireplace lead from the great room into this room that can be used as a dining room, music room or study.

- Eating Area: Open to the kitchen, this eating area is the perfect spot for informal meals.

- Garage: In addition to parking for two cars, this garage offers plenty of storage space. At the garage entrance, you'll find a powder room and a recycling area.

- Room to Grow: In addition to four bedrooms and a laundry room, the second level has 163 ft. of unfinished space for future expansion.

Main Level Floor Plan

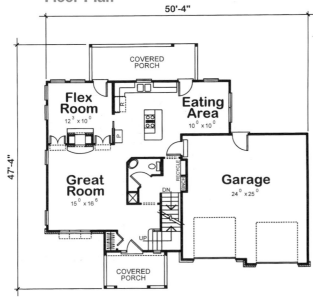

Upper Level Floor Plan

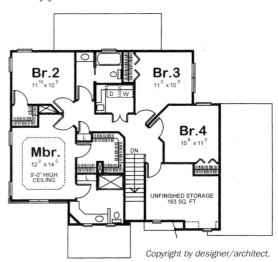

Copyright by designer/architect.

Plan #211070

Dimensions: 46' W x 68' D
Levels: 2
Square Footage: 1,700
Main Level Sq. Ft.: 1,160
Upper Level Sq. Ft.: 540
Bedrooms: 3
Bathrooms: 2½
Foundation: Crawl space or slab; basement option for fee
Materials List Available: Yes
Price Category: C

Images provided by designer/architect.

Upper Level Floor Plan

Main Level Floor Plan

Copyright by designer/architect.

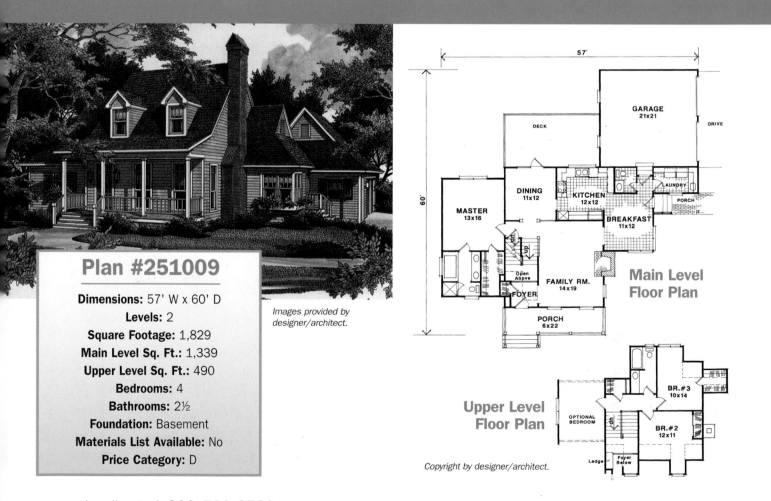

Plan #251009

Dimensions: 57' W x 60' D
Levels: 2
Square Footage: 1,829
Main Level Sq. Ft.: 1,339
Upper Level Sq. Ft.: 490
Bedrooms: 4
Bathrooms: 2½
Foundation: Basement
Materials List Available: No
Price Category: D

Images provided by designer/architect.

Main Level Floor Plan

Upper Level Floor Plan

Copyright by designer/architect.

Plan #111044

Dimensions: 43' W x 47' D
Levels: 2
Square Footage: 1,819
Main Level Sq. Ft.: 1,242
Upper Level Sq. Ft.: 577
Bedrooms: 3
Bathrooms: 2½
Foundation: Pier
Materials List Available: No
Price Category: D

Images provided by designer/architect.

Front View

Main Level Floor Plan

Deck

Breakfast 10'10"x 16'

Dining 13'x 12'

Kitchen 14'6"x 10'2"

Utility

Bath

WIC

1/2 Bath

Living 13'x 20'

Bedroom 12'x 15'

Porch

Copyright by designer/architect.

Upper Level Floor Plan

WIC

Bath

WIC

Bedroom 13'x 11'

Bedroom 12'x 11'

Open to Below

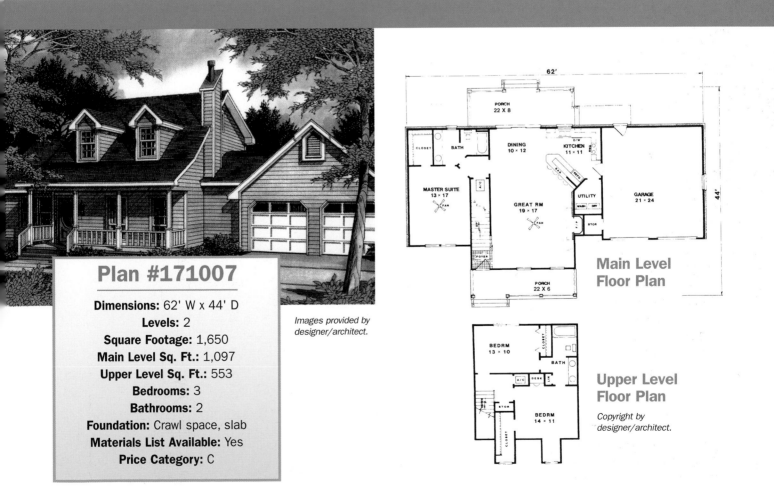

Plan #171007

Dimensions: 62' W x 44' D
Levels: 2
Square Footage: 1,650
Main Level Sq. Ft.: 1,097
Upper Level Sq. Ft.: 553
Bedrooms: 3
Bathrooms: 2
Foundation: Crawl space, slab
Materials List Available: Yes
Price Category: C

Images provided by designer/architect.

Main Level Floor Plan

62'

PORCH 22 X 8

CLOSET

BATH

DINING 10 × 12

KITCHEN 11 × 11

D/W

REFG

MASTER SUITE 13 × 17

A/C

GREAT RM 19 × 17

UTILITY
WASH DRY

GARAGE 21 × 24

STOR

44'

FOYER

PORCH 22 X 6

Upper Level Floor Plan

BEDRM 13 × 10

CLOSET

BATH

A/C

STOR

BEDRM 14 × 11

CLOSET

Copyright by designer/architect.

Plan #131024

Dimensions: 36' W by 54'4" D
Levels: 2
Square Footage: 1,635
Main Level Sq. Ft.: 880
Upper Level Sq. Ft.: 755
Bedrooms: 3
Bathrooms: 2½
Foundation: Crawl space, slab, or basement
Materials List Available: Yes
Price Category: D

Images provided by designer/architect.

You'll love the combination of early-American detailing on the outside and the contemporary, open layout of the interior.

Features:

• Ceiling Height: 8 ft.

• Front Porch: Use this wraparound front porch as an extra room when the weather's fine.

• Living Room: Separated only by columns, the open arrangement of the living and dining rooms enhances the spacious feeling in this home.

• Family Room/Kitchen: This combination family room/country kitchen includes a large work island and snack bar for convenience.

• Master Suite: A tray ceiling creates a contemporary look in the spacious master bedroom, and three closets make it practical. A compartmented full bath completes the suite.

• Bedrooms: Two additional bedrooms share a second full bath.

• Attic: Finish the attic space that's over the garage for even more living space.

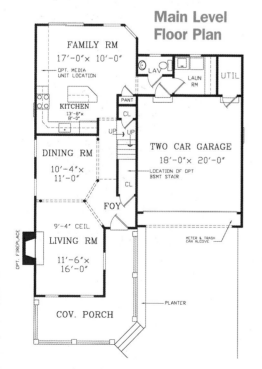

Main Level Floor Plan

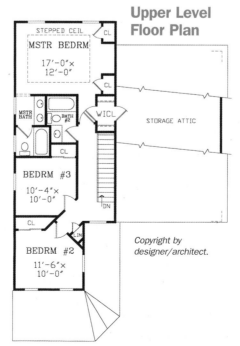

Upper Level Floor Plan

Copyright by designer/architect.

Rear Elevation

Plan #121035

Dimensions: 45'4" W x 38' D
Levels: 2
Square Footage: 1,471
Main Level Sq. Ft.: 716
Upper Level Sq. Ft.: 755
Bedrooms: 3
Bathrooms: 2½
Foundation: Basement
Materials List Available: Yes
Price Category: B

Images provided by designer/architect.

This convenient and elegant home is designed to expand as the family does.

Features:

- Ceiling Height: 8 ft. unless otherwise noted.
- Family Room: An open staircase to the second level visually expands this room where a built-in entertainment center maximizes the floor space. The whole family will be drawn to the warmth from the handsome fireplace.
- Kitchen: Cooking will be a pleasure in this

bright and efficient kitchen that features an island and a corner pantry. A snack bar offers a convenient spot for informal family meals.

- Dining Area: This lovely bayed area adjoins the kitchen.
- Room to Expand: Upstairs is 258 sq. ft. of unfinished area offering plenty of space for expansion as the family grows.
- Garage: This two-bay garage offers plenty of storage space in addition to parking for cars.

CAD FILE AVAILABLE

Main Level Floor Plan

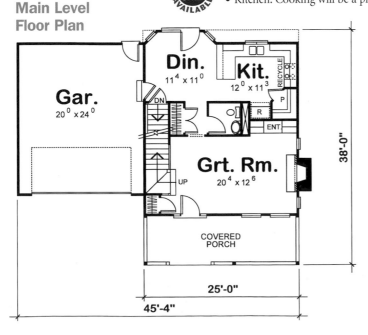

Upper Level Floor Plan

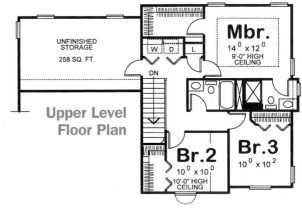

Copyright by designer/architect.

Main Level Floor Plan

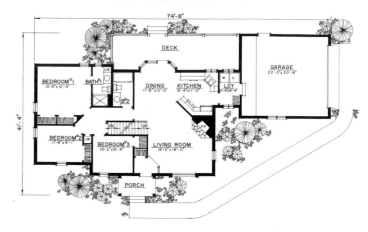

Images provided by designer/architect.

Plan #291009

Dimensions: 74'8" W x 41'4" D

Levels: 2

Square Footage: 1,655

Main Level Sq. Ft.: 1,277

Upper Level Sq. Ft.: 378

Bedrooms: 3

Bathrooms: 3

Foundation: Basement

Materials List Available: No

Price Category: C

Copyright by designer/architect.

Upper Level Floor Plan

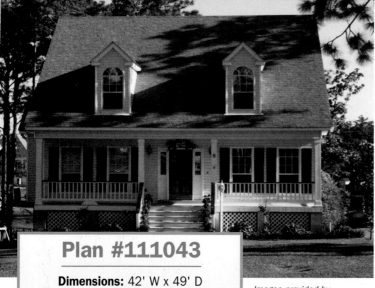

Main Level Floor Plan

Images provided by designer/architect.

Plan #111043

Dimensions: 42' W x 49' D

Levels: 2

Square Footage: 1,737

Main Level Sq. Ft.: 1,238

Upper Level Sq. Ft.: 499

Bedrooms: 3

Bathrooms: 2½

Foundation: Crawl space

Materials List Available: No

Price Category: C

Upper Level Floor Plan

Copyright by designer/architect.

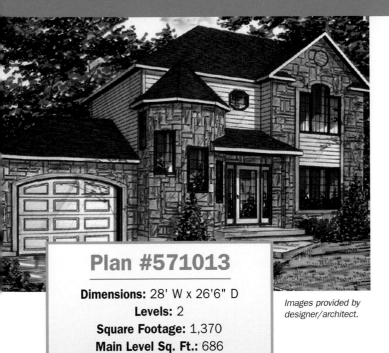

Plan #571013

Dimensions: 28' W x 26'6" D
Levels: 2
Square Footage: 1,370
Main Level Sq. Ft.: 686
Upper Level Sq. Ft.: 684
Bedrooms: 3
Bathrooms: 1½
Foundation: Basement
Material List Available: Yes
Price Category: B

Images provided by designer/architect.

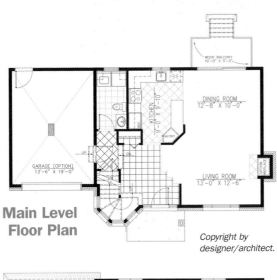

Main Level Floor Plan

Copyright by designer/architect.

Upper Level Floor Plan

Plan #281015

Dimensions: 32' W x 48' D
Levels: 2
Square Footage: 1,660
Main Level Sq. Ft.: 964
Upper Level Sq. Ft.: 696
Bedrooms: 4
Bathrooms: 2½
Foundation: Basement
Materials List Available: Yes
Price Category: C

Images provided by designer/architect.

Main Level Floor Plan

Copyright by designer/architect.

Upper Level Floor Plan

Plan #121036

Dimensions: 42' W x 43' D
Levels: 2
Square Footage: 1,297
Main Level Sq. Ft.: 603
Upper Level Sq. Ft.: 694
Bedrooms: 3
Bathrooms: 2½
Foundation: Basement
Materials List Available: Yes
Price Category: B

This bright and cheery home offers the growing family plenty of room to expand.

Features:

- Ceiling Height: 8 ft. unless otherwise noted.

- Living Room: Family and friends will be drawn to this delightful living room. A double window at the front and windows framing the fireplace bring lots of sunlight that adds to the appeal.

- Dining Room: From the living room, you'll usher guests into this large and inviting dining room.

- Kitchen: A center island is the highlight of this attractive and well-designed kitchen.

- Three-Season Porch: This appealing enclosed porch is accessible from the dining room.

- Master Bedroom: A dramatic angled ceiling highlights a picturesque window in this bedroom.

- Bonus Area: With 354 sq. ft. of unfinished area, you'll never run out of space to expand.

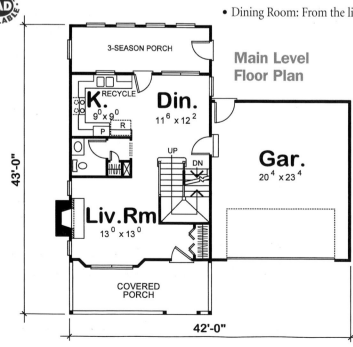

Main Level Floor Plan

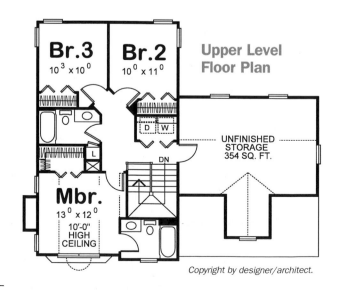

Upper Level Floor Plan

Plan #141012

Dimensions: 44'4" W x 38' D

Levels: 2

Square Footage: 1,870

Main Level Sq. Ft.: 1,159

Upper Level Sq. Ft.: 711

Bedrooms: 3

Bathrooms: 2½

Foundation: Basement

Materials List Available: Yes

Price Category: D

Images provided by designer/architect.

Country charm comes to mind with this classic two story design.

Features:

• Ceiling Height: 8 ft.

• Porch: This full shed porch with dormers creates a look few can resist.

• Living/Dining: This open living/dining area invites you to come in and sit a spell.

• Kitchen: This kitchen allows the host to see their guests from the sink through the opening in the angled walls.

• Breakfast Area: The cathedral ceiling in this breakfast area creates a sunroom effect at the rear of the house.

• Master Suite: This spacious master suite has all the amenities, including a double bowl vanity, corner tub, walk in closet, and 5-ft. shower.

• Bedrooms: Two large bedrooms upstairs share a hall bath.

• Balcony: This upstairs balcony is lit by the center dormer, creating a cozy study alcove.

Copyright by designer/architect.

Main Level Floor Plan

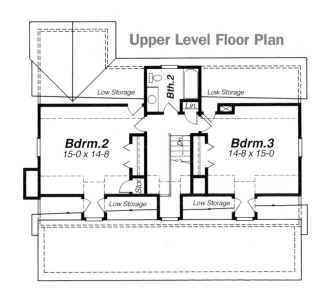

Upper Level Floor Plan

Plan #391072

Dimensions: 42' W x 35'10" D
Levels: 2
Square Footage: 1,787
Main Level Sq. Ft.: 877
Upper Level Sq. Ft.: 910
Bedrooms: 3
Bathrooms: 2½
Foundation: Basement
Material List Available: Yes
Price Category: C

Images provided by designer/architect.

A double-gable garage and covered front entrance add architectural interest to the exterior of the home.

Features:

• **Living Room:** The large bay window gives this gathering area an open and bright feeling. The fireplace adds a focal point to the room.

• **Kitchen:** This L-shaped kitchen opens to a breakfast nook that contains a bay window. The built-in pantry is conveniently located for storage of kitchen supplies.

• **Master Suite:** This private suite features a large sleeping area and a view of the back-yard. The master bath has a skylight, separate shower, tub, and walk-in closet.

• **Secondary Bedrooms:** Located in close proximity to the master suite, these two bedrooms feature walk-in closets and share a full bathroom with dual sinks.

Upper Level Floor Plan

Copyright by designer/architect.

BEDROOM 2 11'-8" X 10'-0"
MAST. BEDROOM 14'-4" X 13'-6"
BEDROOM 3 12'-0" X 13'-6"

Main Level Floor Plan

DECK
KITCHEN 12'-0" X 8'-0"
BRKFST. 8'-0" X 9'-6"
DINING 11'-6" X 12'-0"
LIVING ROOM 12'-0" X 17'-0"
SECOND FLOOR ABOVE
GARAGE 21'-8" X 21'-4"
ENTRY
WALK
DRIVEWAY

Plan #121040

Dimensions: 50' W x 48' D
Levels: 2
Square Footage: 1,818
Main Level Sq. Ft.: 1,302
Upper Level Sq. Ft.: 516
Bedrooms: 3
Bathrooms: 2½
Foundation: Basement
Materials List Available: Yes
Price Category: D

Offering plenty of architectural style, this home is designed with the busy modern lifestyle in mind.

Features:

- Ceiling Height: 8 ft. unless otherwise noted.

- Great Room: This is sure to be the central gathering place of the home with its volume ceiling, abundance of windows, and its handsome fireplace.

- Kitchen: This convenient and attractive kitchen offers a center island. It includes a snack bar that will get lots of use for impromptu family meals.

- Breakfast Area: Joined to the kitchen by the snack bar, this breakfast area will invite you to linger over morning coffee. It includes a pantry and access to the backyard.

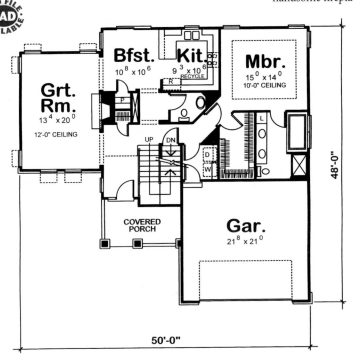

Main Level Floor Plan

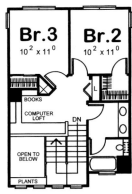

Upper Level Floor Plan

- Master Bedroom: This private retreat offers the convenience of a walk-in closet and the luxury of its own whirlpool bath and shower.

- Computer Loft: Designed with the family computer in mind, this loft overlooks a two-story entry.

Plan #141037

Dimensions: 40'4" W x 44' D

Levels: 2

Square Footage: 1,735

Main Level Sq. Ft.: 1,045

Upper Level Sq. Ft.: 690

Bedrooms: 3

Bathrooms: 2½

Foundation: Basement with drive under garage

Materials List Available: No

Price Category: C

Images provided by designer/architect.

Main Level Floor Plan

Sundeck 16-0 x 12-0
Brkfst. 9-0 x 7-8
Kit. 9-0 x 9-6
Dining 10-0 x 11-4
Lav.
M.Bath
Living Area 18-0 x 13-6
Master Bdrm. 15-6 x 13-6
Entry
Porch
44-0
40-4

Upper Level Floor Plan

Copyright by designer/architect.

Bth.2
Bdrm.2 12-2 x 14-8
Bdrm.3 13-2 x 14-4
Low Storage
Sitting

Plan #121110

Dimensions: 52' W x 45'4" D

Levels: 1.5

Square Footage: 1,855

Main Level Sq. Ft.: 1,297

Upper Level Sq. Ft.: 558

Bedrooms: 4

Bathrooms: 2½

Foundation: Full basement; crawl space for fee

Materials List Available: Yes

Price Category: D

Images provided by designer/architect.

Main Level Floor Plan

Copyright by designer/architect.

TRANSOMS
Kit. 10⁸ x 11²
Bfst. 11⁰ x 12⁴
Grt. rm. 14⁰ x 18⁷
13' - 8" CEILING
SNACK BAR
DESK
PANT.
WHIRLPOOL SKYLIGHT
Gar. 20⁰ x 22⁴
Din. 11⁰ x 12³
Mbr. 13⁰ x 14⁰
9' - 0" CLG.
COVERED PORCH
45'-4"
52'-0"

Front View

Upper Level Floor Plan

Br.2 11³ x 10³
Br.3 10⁰ x 11⁷
OPTIONAL UNFINISHED STORAGE 13⁰ x 13⁴
Br.4 11⁰ x 10⁰
10' - 0" CEILING

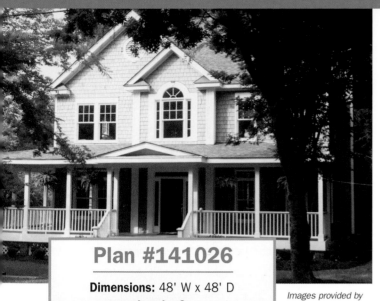

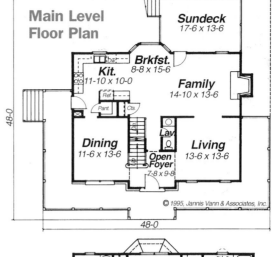

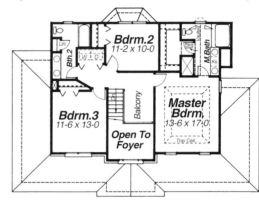

Plan #141026

Dimensions: 48' W x 48' D

Levels: 2

Square Footage: 1,993

Main Level Sq. Ft.: 1,038

Upper Level Sq. Ft.: 955

Bedrooms: 3

Bathrooms: 2½

Foundation: Basement

Materials List Available: Yes

Price Category: D

Images provided by designer/architect.

Main Level Floor Plan

Sundeck 17-6 x 13-6
Brkfst. 8-8 x 15-6
Kit. 11-10 x 10-0
Family 14-10 x 13-6
Dining 11-6 x 13-6
Living 13-6 x 13-6
Lav
Open Foyer 7-8 x 9-8
Ref
Pant. Cts
48-0
48-0

© 1995, Jannis Vann & Associates, Inc.

Upper Level Floor Plan

Bdrm.2 11-2 x 10-0
M.Bath
Bth.2
Lin
W
D
Bdrm.3 11-6 x 13-0
Balcony
Master Bdrm. 13-6 x 17-0
Open To Foyer
Tray Ceil

Copyright by designer/architect.

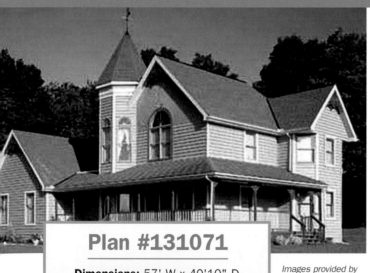

Plan #131071

Dimensions: 57' W x 40'10" D

Levels: 2

Square Footage: 1,992

Main Level Sq. Ft.: 1,146

Upper Level Sq. Ft.: 846

Bedrooms: 3

Bathrooms: 2½

Foundation: Crawl space, slab or basement

Material List Available: Yes

Price Category: E

Images provided by designer/architect.

Upper Level Floor Plan

ROOF
BED RM 11'-0" x 10'-0"
BED RM 13'-4" x 11'-0"
BATH
skylights
BATH
H
DECK
W.I.C.
MASTER SUITE 15'-4" x 12'-8"
high ceiling
railing
TOWER
ROOF
ROOF

Main Level Floor Plan

Copyright by designer/architect.

PORCH
BAY
2x6 studs for added insulation
railing
entertainment center
FAMILY RM 16'-0" x 13'-4"
skylights
DINING RM 13'-4" x 12'-0"
KITCH 13'-4" x 9'-0"
pantry
laundry
LAV.
LIVING RM 18'-0" x 15'-4"
W.I.C.
FOYER
brick fireplace
PORCH
TWO CAR GARAGE 21'-0" x 20'-0"
pull down stair to attic stor.
up
PORCH
railing
40'-10"
57'-0"

Plan #141044

Dimensions: 54'4" W x 30' D
Levels: 2
Square Footage: 1,855
Main Level Sq. Ft.: 874
Upper Level Sq. Ft.: 981
Bedrooms: 3
Bathrooms: 2½
Foundation: Basement
Material List Available: No
Price Category: D

This colonial-inspired home, with its compact footprint, features all the most-popular amenities.

Features:

- Family Room: Friends and family will feel right at home in this large gathering area. On nice days, step through the French doors and onto the rear patio for a relaxing drink.

- Dining Room: This dining room has plenty of space for your formal meals. Its location makes serving simple.

- Kitchen: This island kitchen will inspire the family chef to create a culinary treat at every meal. The double windows in the adjoining breakfast nook flood the whole area with natural light.

- Laundry Area: Conveniently located on the upper level near the bedrooms, this laundry area will save you many steps.

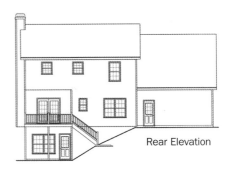

Rear Elevation

Main Level Floor Plan

Upper Level Floor Plan

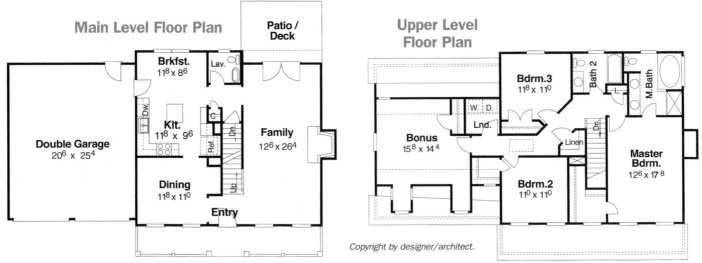

Copyright by designer/architect.

Plan #131067

Dimensions: 60'8" W x 29'4" D
Levels: 2
Square Footage: 1,909
Main Level Sq. Ft.: 1,159
Upper Level Sq. Ft.: 750
Bedrooms: 3
Bathrooms: 2½
Foundation: Crawl space, slab, or basement
Material List Available: Yes
Price Category: E

Images provided by designer/architect.

This dramatic contemporary home features large dormers and windows.

Features:

• Foyer: This cathedral-ceiling entry welcomes you into this home. The open and airy feeling of the space makes you feel comfortable.

• Family Room: This sunken room is the comfortable space in which you and your family can relax after a busy day. The sliding glass doors lead out to the rear patio.

• Kitchen: This U-shaped kitchen is open to the adjacent breakfast area and only a few steps to the washer and dryer.

• Master Suite: Located on the upper level with two secondary bedrooms, this retreat offers two large closets. The master bath is an added plus.

Main Level Floor Plan

Upper Level Floor Plan

Copyright by designer/architect.

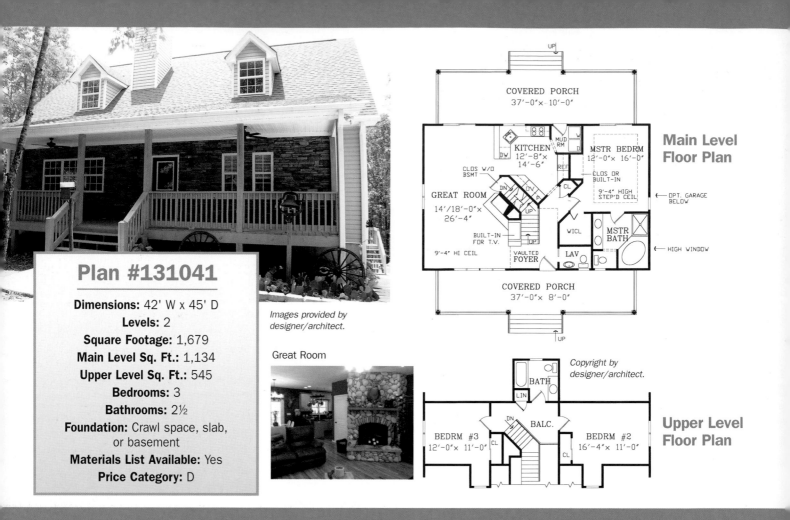

Plan #131041

Dimensions: 42' W x 45' D

Levels: 2

Square Footage: 1,679

Main Level Sq. Ft.: 1,134

Upper Level Sq. Ft.: 545

Bedrooms: 3

Bathrooms: 2½

Foundation: Crawl space, slab, or basement

Materials List Available: Yes

Price Category: D

Images provided by designer/architect.

Great Room

Copyright by designer/architect.

Main Level Floor Plan

Upper Level Floor Plan

Plan #111040

Dimensions: 37' W x 52' D

Levels: 2

Square Footage: 1,650

Main Level Sq. Ft.: 1,122

Upper Level Sq. Ft.: 528

Bedrooms: 4

Bathrooms: 2

Foundation: Pier

Materials List Available: No

Price Category: C

Images provided by designer/architect.

Main Level Floor Plan

Upper Level Floor Plan

Copyright by designer/architect.

Main Level Floor Plan

SUNDECK

DINING
14' x 12'
16'11" VAULTED CLG.

BR.
11' x 12'4"
10' VAULTED CLG.

LIVING
16' x 15'
16'11" VAULTED CLG.

FOYER

SEAT

SITTING

UP

COVERED PORCH

LDR

10'-0"

29'-6"

53'-0"

4'-0"

Plan #491006

Dimensions: 53' W x 29'6" D
Levels: 2
Square Footage: 1,470
Main Level Sq. Ft.: 1,130
Upper Level Sq. Ft.: 340
Bedrooms: 2
Bathrooms: 2
Foundation: Crawl space
Material List Available: Yes
Price Category: B

Images provided by designer/architect.

Front View

BALCONY

BR.
12'2" x 10'
10' VAULTED CLG.

LOFT
VAULTED

OPEN TO BELOW

RAILING

PLANT LEDGE

OPEN

DN

Upper Level Floor Plan

Copyright by designer/architect.

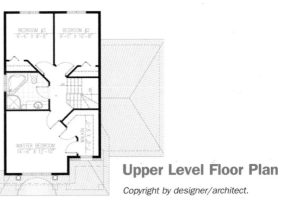

Main Level Floor Plan

BEDROOM #3
9'-6" x 9'-6"

BEDROOM #2
9'-0" x 10'-8"

MASTER BEDROOM
14'-6" x 12'-10"

Plan #571007

Dimensions: 20' W x 34' D
Levels: 2
Square Footage: 1,308
Main Level Sq. Ft.: 648
Upper Level Sq. Ft.: 660
Bedrooms: 3
Bathrooms: 1½
Foundation: Basement
Material List Available: Yes
Price Category: B

Images provided by designer/architect.

Upper Level Floor Plan

Copyright by designer/architect.

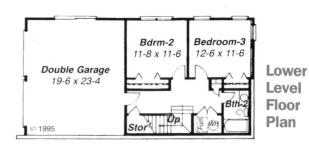

Double Garage
19-6 x 23-4

Bdrm-2
11-8 x 11-6

Bedroom-3
12-6 x 11-6

Bth-2

Stor. | Up | Furn. | WH

© 1995

**Lower
Level
Floor
Plan**

Copyright by designer/architect.

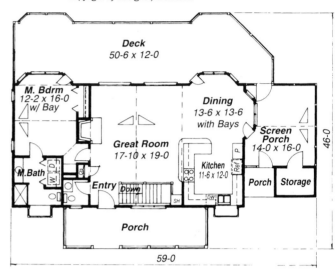

Deck
50-6 x 12-0

M. Bdrm
12-2 x 16-0
w/ Bay

Dining
13-6 x 13-6
with Bays

Screen
Porch
14-0 x 16-0

Great Room
17-10 x 19-0

Kitchen
11-6 x 12-0

Ref | P

M. Bath | W/D

Entry | Down

Porch | Storage

Porch

46-0

59-0

**Main Level
Floor Plan**

*Images provided by
designer/architect.*

Plan #141024

Dimensions: 59' W x 46' D
Levels: 2
Square Footage: 1,732
Main Level Sq. Ft.: 1,128
Lower Level Sq. Ft.: 604
Bedrooms: 3
Bathrooms: 2½
Foundation: Basement
Materials List Available: Yes
Price Category: C

Plan #121172

Dimensions: 48' W x 48' D
Levels: 1.5
Square Footage: 1,897
Main Level Sq. Ft.: 1,448
Upper Level Sq. Ft.: 449
Bedrooms: 3
Bathrooms: 2½
Foundation: Slab; basement for fee
Material List Available: Yes
Price Category: D

*Images provided by
designer/architect.*

*This home, as shown
in the photograph, may
differ from the actual
blueprints. For more
detailed information,
please check the floor
plans carefully.*

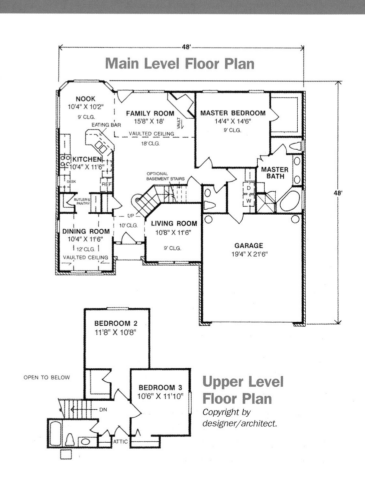

48'

Main Level Floor Plan

NOOK
10'4" X 10'2"
9' CLG.

FAMILY ROOM
15'8" X 18'
VAULTED CEILING
18' CLG.

MASTER BEDROOM
14'4" X 14'6"
9' CLG.

EATING BAR

KITCHEN
10'4" X 11'6"

MASTER
BATH

REF

OPTIONAL
BASEMENT STAIRS

DESK

BUTLER'S
PANTRY

UP

10' CLG.

D | W

DINING ROOM
10'4" X 11'6"
12' CLG.

LIVING ROOM
10'8" X 11'6"
9' CLG.

GARAGE
19'4" X 21'6"

VAULTED CEILING

48'

BEDROOM 2
11'8" X 10'8"

BEDROOM 3
10'6" X 11'10"

OPEN TO BELOW

DN

ATTIC

**Upper Level
Floor Plan**

*Copyright by
designer/architect.*

Plan #131056

Dimensions: 40' W x 54' D
Levels: 1.5
Square Footage: 1,396
Main Level Sq. Ft.: 964
Upper Level Sq. Ft.: 432
Bedrooms: 3
Bathrooms: 2
Foundation: Slab or basement
Materials List Available: Yes
Price Category: C

This ruggedly handsome home is a true A-frame. The elegance of the roof virtually meeting the ground and the use of rugged stone veneer and log-cabin siding make it stand out.

Features:

• Living Room: This area is the interior high-light of the home. The large, exciting space features a soaring ceiling, a massive fireplace, and a magnificent window wall to capture a view.

• Side Porch: The secondary entry from this side porch leads to a center hall that provides direct access to the first floor's two bedrooms, bathroom, kitchen, and living room.

• Kitchen: This kitchen is extremely efficient and includes a snack bar and access to the screened porch.

• Loft Area: A spiral stairway leads from the living room to this second-floor loft, which overlooks the living room. The area can also double as an extra sleeping room.

Images provided by designer/architect.

Main Level Floor Plan

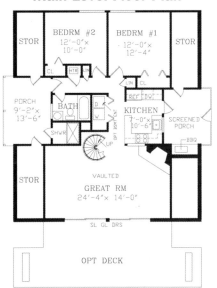

Upper Level Floor Plan

Copyright by designer/architect

Rear View

Great Room

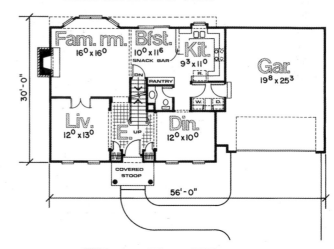

Main Level Floor Plan

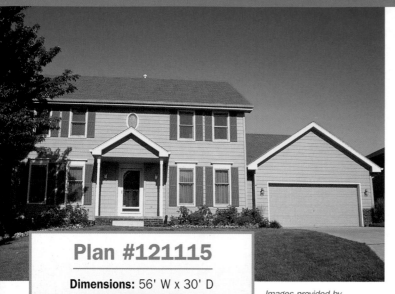

Plan #121115

Dimensions: 56' W x 30' D

Levels: 2

Square Footage: 1,993

Main Level Sq. Ft.: 1,000

Upper Level Sq. Ft.: 993

Bedrooms: 4

Bathrooms: 2½

Foundation: Basement; crawl space for fee

Material List Available: Yes

Price Category: D

Images provided by designer/architect.

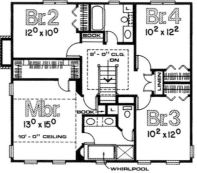

Upper Level Floor Plan

Copyright by designer/architect.

Plan #111042

Dimensions: 34' W x 30' D

Levels: 2

Square Footage: 1,779

Main Level Sq. Ft.: 907

Upper Level Sq. Ft.: 872

Bedrooms: 3

Bathrooms: 2½

Foundation: Pier

Materials List Available: No

Price Category: C

Images provided by designer/architect.

Main Level Floor Plan

Upper Level Floor Plan

Copyright by designer/architect.

Plan #121153

Dimensions: 62' W x 42'6" D
Levels: 1.5
Square Footage: 1,984
Main Level Sq. Ft.: 1,487
Upper Level Sq. Ft.: 497
Bedrooms: 3
Bathrooms: 2½
Foundation: Slab; basement for fee
Material List Available: Yes
Price Category: D

Images provided by designer/architect.

Features:

- **Living Room:** This two-story gathering area is available for family and friends. The fireplace adds a focal point to the room.

- **Kitchen:** This peninsula kitchen features a raised bar open to the breakfast area. The breakfast area boasts French doors that lead to the future rear deck.

- **Master Suite:** Residing on the main level is this beautiful retreat, which boasts a tray ceiling. The master bath features dual vanities, whirlpool tub, and a separate toilet area.

- **Upper Level:** Two secondary bedrooms are found on this level. A large full bathroom is centrally located for easy access.

A stone and stucco exterior give this home an elegant look.

Main Level Floor Plan

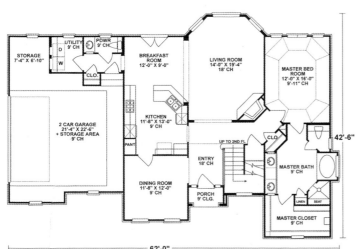

Upper Level Floor Plan

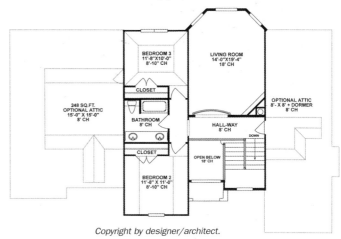

Copyright by designer/architect.

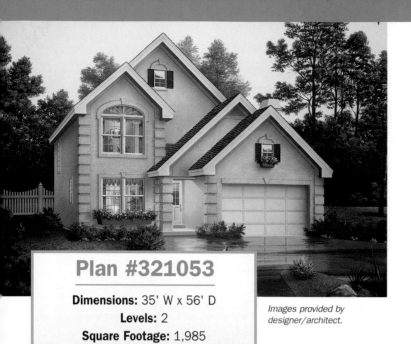

Plan #321053

Dimensions: 35' W x 56' D

Levels: 2

Square Footage: 1,985

Main Level Sq. Ft.: 1,114

Upper Level Sq. Ft.: 871

Bedrooms: 4

Bathrooms: 3½

Foundation: Basement

Materials List Available: Yes

Price Category: D

Images provided by designer/architect.

Main Level Floor Plan

Copyright by designer/architect.

MBr 17-0x13-10
Deck
Kitchen 11-4x12-0
Great Rm 13-7x18-8 Sunken vaulted
Dining 11-4x12-0
Garage 18-4x21-4
35'-0"
56'-0"

Br 3 12-4x12-5
Br 2 11-0x12-5
open to below
Br 4 11-4x13-3

Upper Level Floor Plan

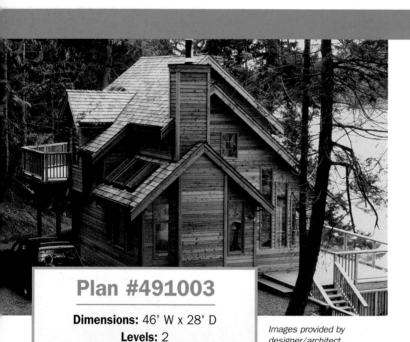

Plan #491003

Dimensions: 46' W x 28' D

Levels: 2

Square Footage: 1,235

Main Level Sq. Ft.: 893

Upper Level Sq. Ft.: 342

Bedrooms: 3

Bathrooms: 2

Foundation: Crawl space

Material List Available: Yes

Price Category: B

Images provided by designer/architect.

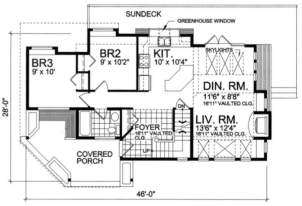

Main Level Floor Plan

SUNDECK
GREENHOUSE WINDOW
BR3 9' x 10'
BR2 9' x 10'2"
KIT. 10' x 10'4"
SKYLIGHTS
DIN. RM. 11'6" x 8'8" 16'11" VAULTED CLG.
FOYER 16'11" VAULTED CLG.
LIV. RM. 13'6" x 12'4" 16'11" VAULTED CLG.
COVERED PORCH
28'-0"
46'-0"

Upper Level Floor Plan

Copyright by designer/architect.

SUNDECK
SKYLIGHTS
MBR 13'6" x11'8" 11' VAULTED CLG. PLANT LEDGE OVER
DN
OPEN TO BELOW
OPEN TO BELOW

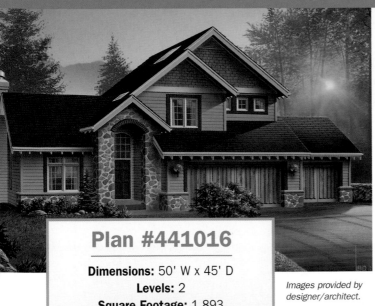

Plan #441016

Dimensions: 50' W x 45' D
Levels: 2
Square Footage: 1,893
Main Level Sq. Ft.: 1,087
Upper Level Sq. Ft.: 806
Bedrooms: 3
Bathrooms: 2½
Foundation: Crawl space; slab or basement for fee
Materials List Available: No
Price Category: D

Images provided by designer/architect.

CAD FILE AVAILABLE CAD

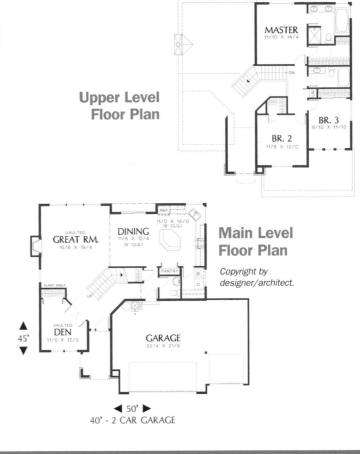

Upper Level Floor Plan

Main Level Floor Plan

Copyright by designer/architect.

MASTER 11/10 X 14/4

BR. 3 9/10 X 11/10

BR. 2 11/8 X 12/0

REF 11/0 X 14/0 (9' CLG)

VAULTED GREAT RM. 16/6 X 19/4

DINING 11/6 X 12/4 (9' CLG)

PANTRY

PLANT SHELF

UP

VAULTED DEN 11/0 X 12/0

GARAGE 32/4 X 21/6

45'

50'

40' · 2 CAR GARAGE

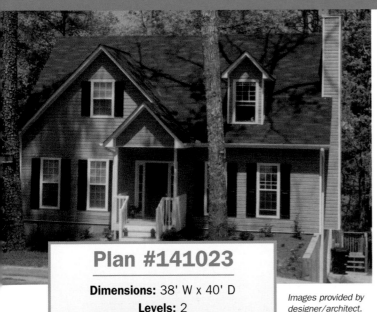

Plan #141023

Dimensions: 38' W x 40' D
Levels: 2
Square Footage: 1,715
Main Level Sq. Ft.: 1,046
Upper Level Sq. Ft.: 669
Bedrooms: 3
Bathrooms: 2½
Foundation: Basement
Materials List Available: Yes
Price Category: C

Images provided by designer/architect.

Main Level Floor Plan

Upper Level Floor Plan

Copyright by designer/architect.

38-0

Deck 16-0 x 12-0

Skylights

Breakfast

Kitchen 9-0 x 9-6

Dining Area 9-10 x 11-4

Bath

M. Bath

Living Area 18-0 x 13-6

Master Bedroom 15-6 x 13-6

Porch

© 1989

32-0

8-0

Bath

Bedroom 2 15-8 x 13-4

Down

Bedroom 3 15-6 x 11-0

Plan #121089

Dimensions: 54' W x 51'8" D
Levels: 2
Square Footage: 1,976
Main Level Sq. Ft.: 1,413
Upper Level Sq. Ft.: 563
Bedrooms: 4
Bathrooms: 2½
Foundation: Basement
Materials List Available: Yes
Price Category: D

Images provided by designer/architect.

Enjoy the natural light that streams into every room through a variety of window types.

Features:

• Entry: This two-story entryway is distinguished by its many windows, which flood the area with light.

• Great Room: Tall windows frame the large fireplace in this room. A high, sloped ceiling accentuates its spacious dimensions, and its convenient position makes it a natural

gathering place for friends and family.

• Kitchen: An island provides an extra measure of convenience in this well-designed kitchen. The sunny breakfast area with its many windows is defined by the snack bar that it shares with the kitchen area.

• Master Suite: Placed in the opposite side of the home for privacy, this master suite features unusual detailing on the ceiling. The bath includes a corner whirlpool tub and double vanity.

Main Level Floor Plan

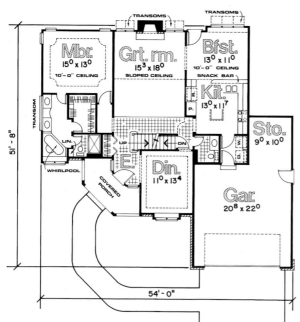

Upper Level Floor Plan

Copyright by designer/architect.

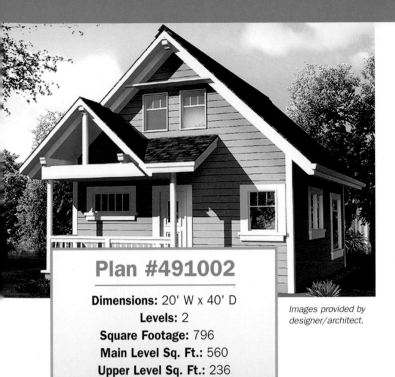

Plan #491002

Dimensions: 20' W x 40' D
Levels: 2
Square Footage: 796
Main Level Sq. Ft.: 560
Upper Level Sq. Ft.: 236
Bedrooms: 1
Bathrooms: 1
Foundation: Crawl space
Material List Available: Yes
Price Category: A

Images provided by designer/architect.

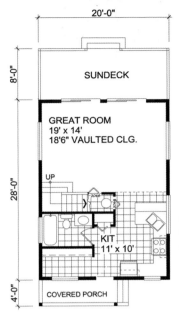

Main Level Floor Plan

SUNDECK

GREAT ROOM
19' x 14'
18'6" VAULTED CLG.

UP

KIT
11' x 10'

COVERED PORCH

20'-0"
8'-0"
28'-0"
4'-0"

Upper Level Floor Plan

OPEN TO BELOW

RAILING

DN

RAILING

SLEEPING LOFT
19' x 10'
9'6" VAULTED CLG.

Copyright by designer/architect.

Plan #121014

Dimensions: 52' W x 47'4" D
Levels: 2
Square Footage: 1,869
Main Level Sq. Ft.: 1,421
Upper Level Sq. Ft.: 448
Bedrooms: 3
Bathrooms: 2½
Foundation: Basement
Materials List Available: Yes
Price Category: D

Images provided by designer/architect.

CAD FILE AVAILABLE

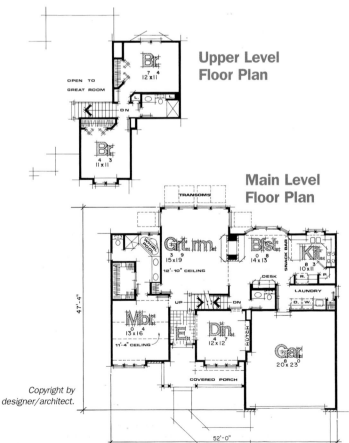

Upper Level Floor Plan

OPEN TO GREAT ROOM

Br
12 x 11

DN

Br
11 x 11

Main Level Floor Plan

TRANSOMS

Grt. rm.
15 x 19
12'-10" CEILING

Bfst.
14 x 13

Kit.
10 x 11

SNACK BAR

DESK

LAUNDRY

Mbr.
13 x 16
11'-4" CEILING

UP   DN

Din.
12 x 12

HUTCH

Gar.
20 x 23

COVERED PORCH

47'-4"

52'-0"

Copyright by designer/architect.

Choosing Curtains and Draperies

Long ago, but not so far in the past, curtains were just a way to keep out the cold or extreme light. Today, these fabric-based coverings can still be used to control the amount of natural light in a room and limit heat gain in the summer and heat loss during the winter. But technology and the modern insulating qualities of glass allow curtains and draperies to be more, or even less, than practical. With limitless combinations of fabric, color, and trim, these window treatments can be simply decorative.

Throughout this article, the terms "draperies" and "curtains" are used interchangeably. But to some people, they have slightly different meanings. Draperies are usually pleated, lined, and floor length, with a tailored, formal style. They are attached via hooks to a traverse rod; a cord mechanism is used to close them. Curtains are normally suspended from rods by rings, tabs, ties, or a rod-pocket casing; they look less formal.

When choosing curtains or draperies for your windows, make note of how far you will be able to retract the panels. Stack-back refers to how compactly curtains or draperies can be drawn back on a rod. When there is minimal wall space around a window or when you want to maximize a view, the depth of the stack-back is a concern.

Curtain Basics

Curtains encompass three basic styles: panels, cafés, and tiers. Heading variations, including pocket casings, tabs, loops, ties, grommets, and pleats, can change the personality of each style. In addition, curtains can be lined, unlined, or—for extra body and insulation—interlined. All of these elements work together to influence the ultimate appearance of your window treatment.

Types of Curtains

The basic panel is the most versatile and straightforward type of window dressing. It can be any length and have any type of heading. It can be hung straight, without any adornment, or tied back in one of the various positions. It looks wonderful with all sorts of hardware, including traverse rods, decorative poles with finials, curtain rings, café clips, tiebacks, and holdbacks. This multipurpose treatment can be made in a variety of fabrics with trimmings—from fringe to gimp—to reflect any decor.

A café curtain covers the lower half of a window. A longer version goes approximately three-quarters up the window, leaving a small section at the top of the window exposed. Café curtains are usually hung from a pole by rings, clips, tabs, ties, or a rod-pocket heading. This type of casual treatment suits cottage-style interiors. Similar to café curtains, tiered curtains are a team of two half curtains covering the upper and lower sections of a window. They, too, have a homey, comfortable ambiance and are hung on curtain rods.

Curtain Lengths

The curtain length influences the style of the treatment. A sill-length curtain has a casual air; drapery that falls to the floor connotes elegance. Curtain lengths also affect activity in the area near a window. Are the windows close to a breakfast table? If so, shorter curtains are less intrusive and leave clearance around the table. Is there a heat source underneath the window? Curtains should never touch or block a radiator, heat vent, or heating unit. Is the treatment hung on or around a glazed door? Make sure that it doesn't block the opening and that you can open and close the door—and the curtain, if desired—easily.

Curtain lengths can camouflage problems, too. Is the window awkwardly shaped? Or is there an architectural flaw that you would like to conceal? A floor-length treatment, hung above the window frame, can help disguise the problem. In some rooms, windows may be different widths and lengths. If this is the case, plan the largest window treatment first. Dress the remaining windows in a scaled-down version of this treatment. For visual unity, install all the upper hardware at the same height.

In general, a window treatment looks best when it falls in line with the sill or floor. The most common lengths for drapery are sill, below sill, floor, and puddled. As the description implies, a sill-length curtain skims the windowsill. Favored for horizontal windows, it can start from the top of the window to the sill or, when café style, from the middle of the window to the sill. A curtain at this length is typically easy to operate, so it is a good

Below: These floor-length curtain panels feature a pleated heading. Small curtain, or drapery, hooks are used to attach the panels to the rings that run across the rod.

choice for a window that will be opened and closed often.

The *below-sill length* falls at least 4 inches beneath the window frame so that it covers the apron, the horizontal board that runs under the sill. If the curtain is too far below the sill, however, it looks awkward and unfinished. A sill-length panel, too, can be used for café or three-quarter curtains, and it can cover up an unattractive window frame. It generally looks best on picture windows and above window seats.

A *floor-length* curtain makes a strong visual statement. Make sure that the curtain is only ½ inch above the floor because, like a hem that's too high on pants, floor-length treatments that fall short can suffer the "floods." (In humid areas, however, the curtain can be an inch off the floor to allow for the rise and fall of the fabric.) If you install layered drapery, the inner curtain can be ¼ to ½ inch shorter than the outer curtain.

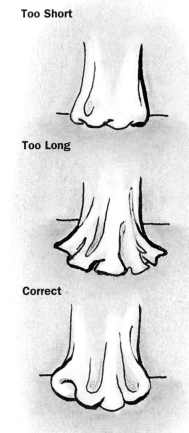

Too Short

Too Long

Correct

Above: In an older home, windows may be out of plumb, which could make long panels appear to be different lengths. To camouflage this, puddle the hemlines on the floor.

Below: The hems of these kitchen curtains sit slightly above the sills of the two windows. When same-size windows are adjacent, the curtains should be exactly the same length.

Above: When puddling curtains, increase the length of the fabric by at least 6 to 8 inches for the best results.

To avoid seeing the back of the heading from the outside, add 4 inches to the curtain's length so that it hangs above the window frame. This length works well with double-hung windows, bay windows, sliding glass doors, and tall, narrow openings, such as French doors.

Puddling is the term used for a floor-length curtain with an extra allowance of fabric that is arranged into a soft pouf (the puddle) on the floor. This is a dramatic length that falls 6 to 8 inches onto the floor. (For the correct length, see the illustrations on the opposite page.) Particularly appropriate for floor-to-ceiling windows, puddling has some drawbacks. A puddled curtain often needs adjustment, as it can be easily disarranged. Also, it isn't the right choice for high-traffic aisles or doorways, because the extra fabric can block the function of a door or cause someone to trip.

Tieback Positions

How a curtain frames an opening is an important part of a window dressing's overall design. You can leave a curtain hanging unadorned, but by using a tieback, you can create a sculpted silhouette of fabric against a window. You can also

Above: Ventilation is important in a bathroom, and so curtains should not interfere with the operation of a window. These sill-length panels are unobtrusive.

control the amount of light that comes into the room and create a dramatic frame that enhances a view or covers an unsightly one.

Where you position the tieback affects the way a curtain hangs. The curtain can be caught back in a dramatic swoop of fabric, or it can be gently held open, revealing a colorful contrasting lining. The traditional tieback positions—high, midway, and low—are some of the most effective placements. Looping a tieback around or just below a pole, angled *high*, creates a short curve of fabric; don't use this arrangement where the curtain is moved often. A tieback positioned *midway* shouldn't fall exactly in the center; the best placement is slightly above or below the middle of the curtain. Two-thirds of the way down the curtain is the proper place for a *low* tieback. When using this position, check that a tasseled tieback doesn't brush the floor, however.

A *center tie*—when one or two curtains are gathered at the middle so that they curve on both sides—can look impressive if it's on a bay or bow window. Use a rope tieback or, if the material is light-

SMARTtip

Curtain Weights

A breeze can stir up a floor-length curtain, leaving it in disarray. A curtain weight can minimize the problem, plus it helps drapery to hang more smoothly. You will find two types of curtain weights: disk weights and fabric-covered weights. A disk weight is a small, round piece of lead that is inserted into the hem at each corner and each seam. To prevent it from rubbing and wearing out the fabric, insert it into a pocket made of lining fabric or muslin. A fabric-covered weight consists of links of metal encased in a fabric tube. This type, which comes in different sizes to correspond to the weight of the fabric, is attached along the hem.

High Tie   **Midway Ties**   **Center Tie**

weight, literally knot the fabric. A crisscross arrangement requires two curtain rods and looks best with lightweight or sheer fabrics. When each panel is caught midway, the top halves overlap.

To create a *bishop's sleeve*, arrange two center ties at different points on a curtain (one high, one midway). Pull out the fabric above each tie to create a double tier of soft poufs. Try an *angled double tie* with a sheer undertreatment because the sinuous outline stands out against a gauzy backdrop. Slightly different from the bishop's sleeve, the two ties are arranged at the high and midway points on the panel so that the curtain swoops into graceful curves on only one side of the window.

What's Your Style?

Whether you are choosing curtains for an entire house or just one room, the process is the same. You need to make three basic decisions about your treatment. Will it be formal or informal? Lined or unlined? What type of heading? Once these decisions are made, you can finalize a design.

Formal Verses Informal Style

A room's window treatments are influenced by a number of elements, including the function of the space, the architectural style of the house, and the decorating preferences of the homeowner. The result is that the same windows can be treated quite differently. For example, picture a dining room with a bay window. That type of window is often given a multilayered, floor-length window dressing—in other words, a formal window treatment. But if you

prefer a more casual style, you can choose the informal look of café curtains with sill-length, tied-back side panels.

A Full Formal Treatment. Formal treatments often involve two or three layers. One layer, called the casement curtain, is installed inside the window's trim area. Typically it's a sheer, solid, or lace panel that lays straight or is gathered at the top. Overdraperies, often referred to simply as draperies, make up the second layer. Generally, they cover the window and the trim and, space permitting, extend beyond to the sides or the area above the window. The third, and optional, layer of a full formal window treatment is a valance, sometimes called a pelmet, which runs horizontally across the top of the window and covers the drapery or curtain heading. A hard valance, also called a cornice or a lambrequin, is usually made of wood and covered with fabric or upholstery. To some eyes, the window treatment is unfinished without this last element, but this is strictly a matter of taste. Luxurious, heavyweight fabrics, such as damasks, brocades, silks, tapestries, and velvets, enhance the sophistication of formal treatments. However, remember that these fabrics require professional cleaning every couple of years.

An Informal Treatment. Informal treatments may consist of one or two layers or nothing at all. If location and privacy considerations permit, a beautiful window looks attractive without a dressing—especially when there's also something pleasant to see outside. Sometimes simple casement curtains look attractive in casual rooms. If only the lower half of the window needs covering, café curtains offer privacy without blocking light. Fabrics that lend

Low Ties

Angled Double Ties

Crisscrossed Ties

Unlined Curtains. An *unlined curtain* diffuses daylight, but it does not exclude it. It is the simplest form of window dressing, and it is effective on its own or as an undertreatment. Because an unlined treatment lacks the extra thickness of a lining, it stacks back tightly. Choose a fabric with no right or wrong side so that it looks equally attractive from both the outside and inside of the window. Voile, lace, muslin, and sheers made of cotton or silk organza are the classic fabric choices for unlined treatments. Textured fabrics with open weaves are also suitable.

An unlined curtain filters light beautifully and provides a hazy screen from prying eyes. However, because it offers little privacy in the evening when lamps are turned on, consider pairing sheers with shades or blinds to maintain privacy where necessary. Sunlight damage is another drawback to

themselves to an informal look include all cottons, such as chintz, ticking, toile de Jouy, linen, gingham, and muslin. Unlike the fabric that is typical of formal draperies, most of these are washable.

Lining

The style of curtains—formal or informal—often dictates whether the treatment will be lined. Other considerations include how much natural light you want in a room and how long you expect the arrangement to last.

unlined curtains. Without a protective lining, the fabric deteriorates quickly.

Lined Curtains. A *lined* curtain has body, improving its appearance by creating softer, deeper folds. A lining blocks sunlight, protecting the curtain fabric and other elements in the room from fading, particularly where there is western or southern exposure. Sunlight also adds a yellow tint to unlined fabric that may throw off your room's color scheme. A lining preserves the true color of the face fabric. Linings increase privacy, reduce outside noise, and block drafts and dust. Check for linings treated to resist rot and sun damage. Once a lining has deteriorated, the curtain can be relined or hung without the lining. To achieve the best protection possible, buy the best quality lining fabric that you can afford.

If you line one curtain in a room, do the same to the rest so that the color and drape of the curtains match. Typically, lining fabric comes in white or off-white. Although colored linings are available, be aware that light shining through a lining affects the hue of a lightweight curtain fabric. Get samples of your intended lining and curtain fabric, and then test them together at the window for color change.

Interlinings. If you are set on having a colored lining, consider adding an *interlining*, which is a soft, blanket-like layer of material that is sandwiched between the lining and the curtain fabric. Like a lining, it increases the insulation and light-blocking qualities of the drapery, as well as extending the life of the curtains. It also gives a professional finish to pleats by improving the drape of the fabric. A lining is usually sewn on, but it can also be attached with special double tape or pinned on with buttonholes that slip over drapery hooks. The latter allows the lining and face fabric to be cleaned separately. If you need a dark bedroom during the daytime because you work nights, try a *blackout lining*, which almost completely blocks sunlight. Other specialty linings include *insulating* and *reflective* types. These types of linings can be sewn on, but they can also be hung on a separate rod and drawn closed only when needed.

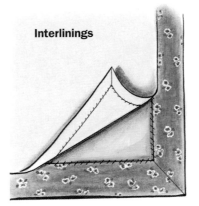

Interlinings

Top Left: Full formal draperies are installed just under the crown molding in this dining room. The symmetrical tails on the swag valance feature rosettes on the corners.

Top right: The floor-length curtains in this study have a black-out lining that completely blocks out the sun when the panels are drawn shut.

Below: Lots of unlined gathered cotton fabric keeps this bedroom light while providing a sense of soft enclosure.

Plan #481034

Dimensions: 84'8" W x 77'8" D
Levels: 2
Square Footage: 2,830
Main Level Sq. Ft.: 1,673
Upper Level Sq. Ft.: 1,157
Bedrooms: 3
Bathrooms: 2½
Foundation: Walkout
Materials List Available: No
Price Category: F

Images provided by designer/architect.

This European-influenced two-story home has stone accents and wide board siding.

Features:

- Great Room: The fireplace, flanked by built-in cabinets, is the focal point of this gathering area. Because the area is located just off the foyer, your guests can easily enter this area.

- Dining Room: This formal dining area features a built-in cabinet and a 9-ft,-high ceiling. The triple window has a view of the front yard.

- Kitchen: This large island kitchen is a bonus in any home. Open to the dinette and the great room, the area has a light and open feeling. The built-in pantry is ready to store all of your supplies.

- Master Suite: Occupying most of the upper level, this retreat boasts a vaulted ceiling in the sleeping area and a large walk-in closet. The master bath features his and her vanities and a large stall shower.

Rear View

Main Level
Floor Plan

Upper Level
Floor Plan

*Copyright by
designer/architect.*

Rear Elevation

Living Room

Kitchen

Plan #321051

Dimensions: 69'8" W x 46' D

Levels: 2

Square Footage: 2,624

Main Level Sq. Ft.: 1,774

Upper Level Sq. Ft.: 850

Bedrooms: 4

Bathrooms: 2½

Foundation: Basement

Materials List Available: Yes

Price Category: F

This home, as shown in the photograph, may differ from the actual blueprints. For more detailed information, please check the floor plans carefully.   *Images provided by designer/architect.*

The dramatic exterior design allows natural light to flow into the spacious living area of this home.

Features:

- **Entry:** This two-story area opens into the dining room through a classic colonnade.

- **Dining Room:** A large bay window, stately columns, and doorway to the kitchen make this room both beautiful and convenient.

- **Great Room:** Enjoy light from the fireplace or the three Palladian windows in the 18-ft. ceiling.

- **Kitchen:** The step-saving design features a walk-in pantry as well as good counter space.

- **Breakfast Room:** You'll love the light that flows through the windows flanking the back door.

- **Master Suite:** The vaulted ceiling and bayed areas in both the bed and bath add elegance. You'll love the two walk-in closets and bath with a sunken tub, two vanities, and separate shower.

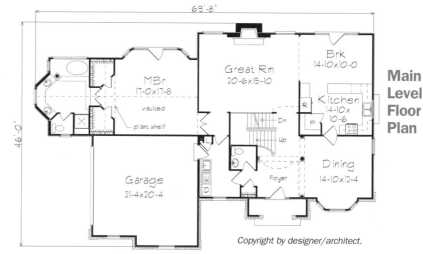

Main Level Floor Plan

Copyright by designer/architect.

Master Bath

Upper Level Floor Plan

Plan #311003

Dimensions: 70'10" W x 65'4" D

Levels: 2

Square Footage: 2,428

Main Level Sq. Ft.: 2,348

Upper Level Sq. Ft.: 80

Bedrooms: 3

Bathrooms: 2½

Foundation: Crawl space, slab

Materials List Available: Y

Price Category: E

If you admire the gracious colonnaded porch, curved brick steps, and stunning front windows, you'll fall in love with the interior of this home.

Features:

• Great Room: Enjoy the vaulted ceiling, balcony from the upper level, and fireplace with flanking windows that let you look out to the patio.

• Dining Room: Columns define this formal room, which is adjacent to the breakfast room.

• Kitchen: A bayed sink area and extensive curved bar provide visual interest in this well-designed kitchen, which every cook will love.

• Breakfast Room: Huge windows let the sun shine into this room, which is open to the kitchen.

• Master Suite: The sitting area is open to the rear porch for a special touch in this gorgeous suite. Two walk-in closets and a vaulted ceiling and double vanity in the bath will make you feel completely pampered.

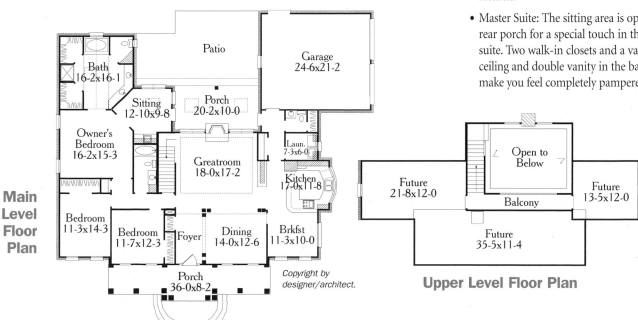

Main Level Floor Plan

Upper Level Floor Plan

Copyright by designer/architect.

Plan #121079

Dimensions: 50' W x 60' D
Levels: 2
Square Footage: 2,688
Main Level Sq. Ft.: 1,650
Upper Level Sq. Ft.: 1,038
Bedrooms: 4
Bathrooms: 3½
Foundation: Slab
Materials List Available: Yes
Price Category: F

You'll love this open design if you're looking for a home that gives a spacious feeling while also providing private areas.

Features:

- **Entry:** The cased openings and corner columns here give an attractive view into the dining room.

- **Living Room:** Another cased opening defines the entry to this living room but lets traffic flow into it.

- **Kitchen:** This well-designed kitchen is built around a center island that gives you extra work space. A snack bar makes an easy, open transition between the sunny dining nook and the kitchen.

- **Master Suite:** An 11-ft. ceiling sets the tone for this private space. With a walk-in closet and adjoining full bath, it will delight you.

Images provided by designer/architect.

This home, as shown in the photograph, may differ from the actual blueprints. For more detailed information, please check the floor plans carefully.

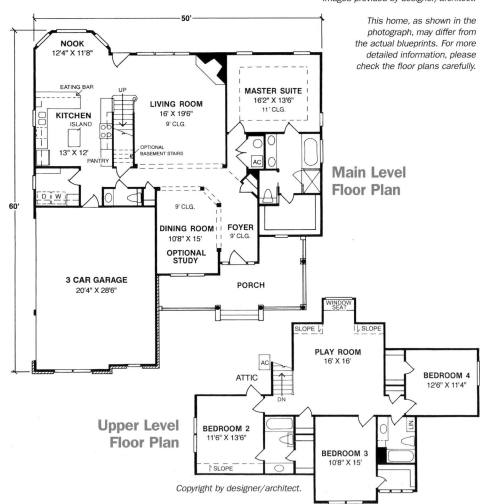

Main Level Floor Plan

Upper Level Floor Plan

Copyright by designer/architect.

Plan #141014

Dimensions: 72' W x 38' D

Levels: 2

Square Footage: 2,091

Main Level Sq. Ft.: 1,362

Upper Level Sq. Ft.: 729

Bedrooms: 3

Bathrooms: 2½

Foundation: Basement

Materials List Available: Yes

Price Category: D

Images provided by designer/architect.

The wraparound front porch and front dormers evoke an old-fashioned country home.

Features:

- Ceiling Height: 8 ft. unless otherwise noted.

- Living Room: This spacious area has an open flow to the dining room, so you can graciously usher guests when it is time to eat.

- Dining Room: This elegant dining room has a bay that opens to the sun deck.

- Kitchen: This warm and inviting kitchen looks out to the front porch. Its bayed breakfast area is perfect for informal family meals.

- Master Suite: The bedroom enjoys a view through the front porch and features a master bath with all the amenities.

- Flexible Room: A room above the two-bay garage offers plenty of space that can be used for anything from a home office to a teen suite.

- Study Room: The two second-floor bedrooms share a study that is perfect for homework.

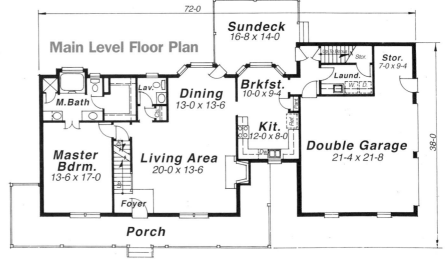

Main Level Floor Plan

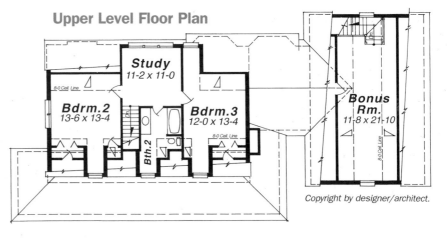

Upper Level Floor Plan

Copyright by designer/architect.

Plan #181034

Dimensions: 60' W x 44' D

Levels: 2

Square Footage: 2,687

Main Level Sq. Ft.: 1,297

Upper Level Sq. Ft.: 1,390

Bedrooms: 3

Bathrooms: 2½

Foundation: Full basement

Materials List Available: Yes

Price Category: F

Images provided by designer/architect.

Main Level Floor Plan

Upper Level Floor Plan

Copyright by designer/architect.

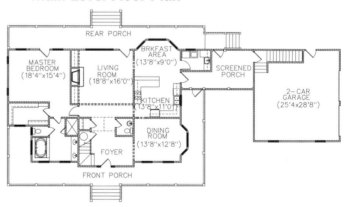

Plan #521006

Dimensions: 99'2" W x 47'5" D

Levels: 1.5

Square Footage: 2,818

Main Level Sq. Ft.: 1,787

Upper Level Sq. Ft.: 1,031

Bedrooms: 4

Bathrooms: 3½

Foundation: Crawl space

Material List Available: No

Price Category: F

Images provided by designer/architect.

Main Level Floor Plan

Upper Level Floor Plan

Copyright by designer/architect.

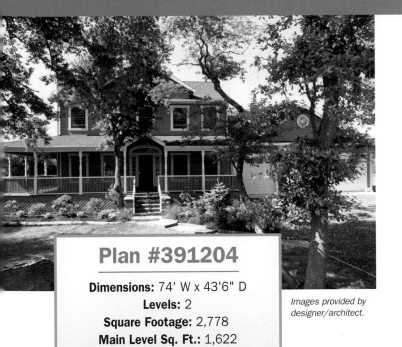

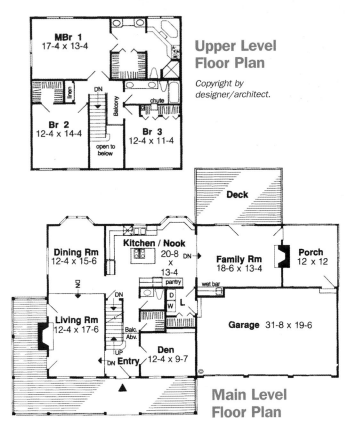

**Upper Level
Floor Plan**

*Copyright by
designer/architect.*

Plan #391204

Dimensions: 74' W x 43'6" D
Levels: 2
Square Footage: 2,778
Main Level Sq. Ft.: 1,622
Upper Level Sq. Ft.: 1,156
Bedrooms: 3
Bathrooms: 2½
Foundation: Basement
Material List Available: Yes
Price Category: F

*Images provided by
designer/architect.*

**Main Level
Floor Plan**

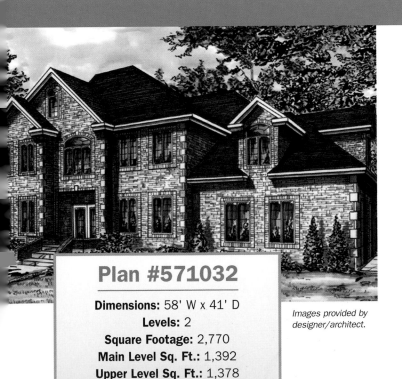

Plan #571032

Dimensions: 58' W x 41' D
Levels: 2
Square Footage: 2,770
Main Level Sq. Ft.: 1,392
Upper Level Sq. Ft.: 1,378
Bedrooms: 4
Bathrooms: 2½
Foundation: Basement
Material List Available: Yes
Price Category: F

*Images provided by
designer/architect.*

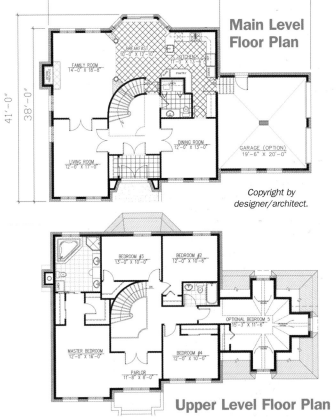

**Main Level
Floor Plan**

*Copyright by
designer/architect.*

Upper Level Floor Plan

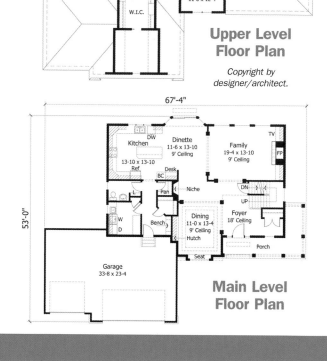

Upper Level Floor Plan

Copyright by designer/architect.

Images provided by designer/architect.

Main Level Floor Plan

Plan #481005

Dimensions: 67'4" W x 53' D

Levels: 2

Square Footage: 2,825

Main Level Sq. Ft.: 1,412

Upper Level Sq. Ft.: 1,413

Bedrooms: 4

Bathrooms: 2½

Foundation: Walkout basement

Material List Available: No

Price Category: F

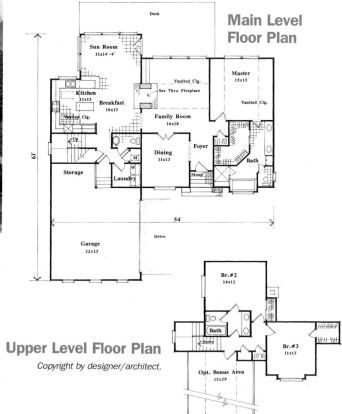

Main Level Floor Plan

Images provided by designer/architect.

Upper Level Floor Plan

Copyright by designer/architect.

Plan #251014

Dimensions: 54' W x 61' D

Levels: 2

Square Footage: 2,210

Main Level Sq. Ft.: 1,670

Upper Level Sq. Ft.: 540

Bedrooms: 3

Bathrooms: 2½

Foundation: Crawl space, basement

Materials List Available: Yes

Price Category: E

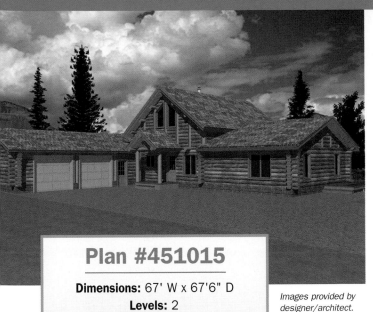

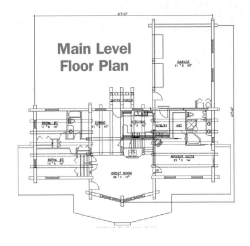

Main Level Floor Plan

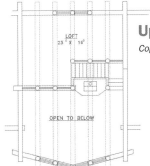

Upper Level Floor Plan

Copyright by designer/architect.

Rear View

Plan #451015

Dimensions: 67' W x 67'6" D

Levels: 2

Square Footage: 2,113

Main Level Sq. Ft.: 1,898

Upper Level Sq. Ft.: 215

Bedrooms: 3

Bathrooms: 2

Foundation: Crawl space

Material List Available: No

Price Category: D

Images provided by designer/architect.

CAD FILE AVAILABLE

Plan #381180

Dimensions: 85' W x 37' D

Levels: 2

Square Footage: 2,105

Main Level Sq. Ft.: 1,180

Upper Level Sq. Ft.: 925

Bedrooms: 4

Bathrooms: 3

Foundation: Basement

Material List Available: Yes

Price Category: D

Images provided by designer/architect.

Upper Level Floor Plan

Copyright by designer/architect.

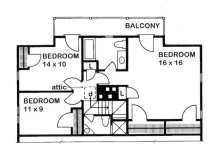

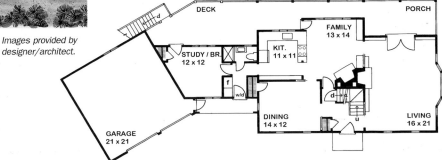

Main Level Floor Plan

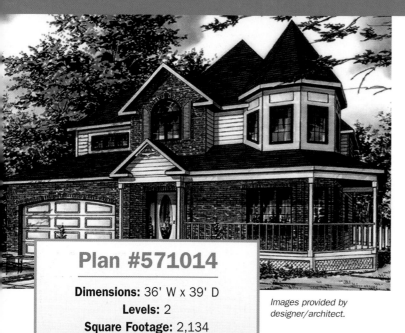

Upper Level Floor Plan

Main Level Floor Plan

Copyright by designer/architect.

Images provided by designer/architect.

Plan #571014

Dimensions: 36' W x 39' D

Levels: 2

Square Footage: 2,134

Main Level Sq. Ft.: 1,065

Upper Level Sq. Ft.: 1,069

Bedrooms: 3

Bathrooms: 2½

Foundation: Basement

Material List Available: Yes

Price Category: D

Main Level Floor Plan

Upper Level Floor Plan

Copyright by designer/architect.

Images provided by designer/architect.

Plan #391173

Dimensions: 61' W x 55' D

Levels: 2

Square Footage: 2,357

Main Level Sq. Ft.: 1,789

Upper Level Sq. Ft.: 568

Bedrooms: 3

Bathrooms: 2½

Foundation: Basement

Material List Available: Yes

Price Category: E

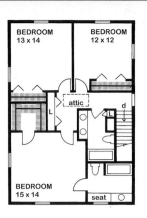

Upper Level Floor Plan

Copyright by designer/architect.

BEDROOM
13 x 14

BEDROOM
12 x 12

attic

BEDROOM
15 x 14

seat

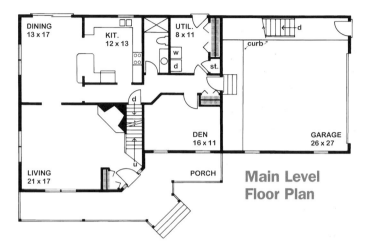

DINING
13 x 17

KIT.
12 x 13

UTIL.
8 x 11

curb

st.

DEN
16 x 11

GARAGE
26 x 27

LIVING
21 x 17

PORCH

Main Level Floor Plan

Images provided by designer/architect.

Plan #381178

Dimensions: 68' W x 42' D

Levels: 2

Square Footage: 2,360

Main Level Sq. Ft.: 1,370

Upper Level Sq. Ft.: 990

Bedrooms: 3

Bathrooms: 3

Foundation: Basement

Material List Available: Yes

Price Category: E

Upper Level Floor Plan

Bdrm 4
13-0 x 10-0

Bath 3

Bath 2

Bdrm-3
11-6 x 13-6

BAL
Open to Foyer

Bdrm 2
11-8 x 17-0

Copyright by designer/architect.

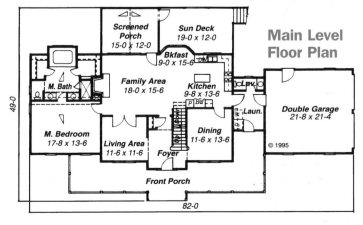

Screened Porch
15-0 x 12-0

Sun Deck
19-0 x 12-0

Bkfast
9-0 x 15-6

M. Bath

Family Area
18-0 x 15-6

Kitchen
9-8 x 13-6

Laun.

Double Garage
21-8 x 21-4

M. Bedroom
17-8 x 13-6

Living Area
11-6 x 11-6

Dining
11-6 x 13-6

Foyer

Front Porch

49-0

82-0

© 1995

Main Level Floor Plan

Images provided by designer/architect.

Plan #141017

Dimensions: 82' W x 49' D

Levels: 2

Square Footage: 2,480

Main Level Sq. Ft.: 1,581

Upper Level Sq. Ft.: 899

Bedrooms: 4

Bathrooms: 3½

Foundation: Crawl space, slab, or basement

Materials List Available: No

Price Category: E

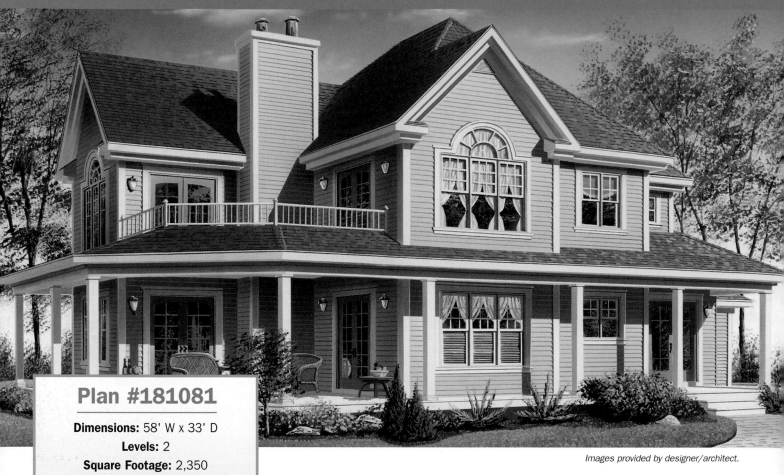

Plan #181081

Dimensions: 58' W x 33' D

Levels: 2

Square Footage: 2,350

Main Level Sq. Ft.: 1,107

Second Level Sq. Ft.: 1,243

Bedrooms: 3

Bathrooms: 2½

Foundation: Basement

Materials List Available: Yes

Price Category: E

Images provided by designer/architect.

This traditional country home features a wrap-around porch and a second-floor balcony.

Features:

- Ceiling Height: 8 ft. unless otherwise noted.

- Family Room: Double French doors and a fireplace in this inviting front room enhance the beauty and warmth of the home's open floor plan.

- Kitchen: You'll love working in this bright and convenient kitchen. The breakfast bar is the perfect place to gather for informal meals.

- Master Suite: You'll look forward to retiring to this elegant upstairs suite at the end of a busy day. The suite features a private bath with separate shower and tub, as well as dual vanities.

- Secondary Bedrooms: Two family bedrooms share a full bath with a third room that opens onto the balcony.

- Basement: An unfinished full basement provides plenty of storage and the potential to add additional finished living space.

Main Level Floor Plan

Copyright by designer/architect.

Upper Level Floor Plan

Plan #121066

Dimensions: 46' W x 41'5" D
Levels: 2
Square Footage: 2,078
Main Level Sq. Ft.: 1,113
Upper Level Sq. Ft.: 965
Bedrooms: 4
Bathrooms: 2½
Foundation: Basement
Materials List Available: Yes
Price Category: D

Images provided by designer/architect.

This lovely home has an unusual dignity, perhaps because its rooms are so well-proportioned and thoughtfully laid out.

Features:

- Family Room: This room is sunken, giving it an unusually cozy, comfortable feeling. Its abundance of windows let natural light stream in during the day, and the fireplace warms it when the weather's chilly.
- Dining Room: This dining room links to the parlor beyond through a cased opening.
- Parlor: A tall, angled ceiling highlights a large, arched window that's the focal point of this room.
- Breakfast Area: A wooden rail visually links this bayed breakfast area to the family room.
- Master Suite: A roomy walk-in closet adds a practical touch to this luxurious suite. The bath features a skylight, whirlpool tub, and separate shower.

Main Level Floor Plan

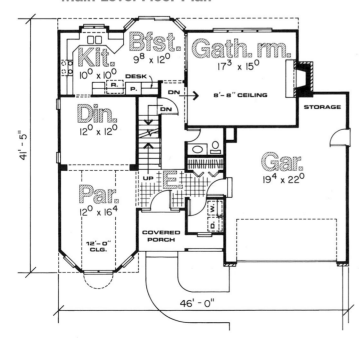

Upper Level Floor Plan

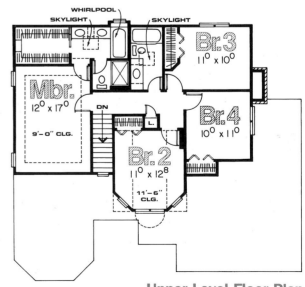

Copyright by designer/architect.

Plan #161045

Dimensions: 57' W x 49'8" D

Levels: 2

Square Footage: 2,077

Main Level Sq. Ft.: 1,532

Upper Level Sq. Ft.: 545

Bedrooms: 3

Bathrooms: 2½

Foundation: Basement

Materials List Available: Yes

Price Category: D

Images provided by designer/architect.

Multiple gables, arched windows, and the stone accents that adorn the exterior of this lovely two-story home create a dramatic first impression.

Features:

• Great Room: With multiple windows to light your way, grand openings, varied ceiling treatments, and angled walls let you flow from room to room. Enjoy the warmth of a gas fireplace in both this great room and the dining area.

• Master Suite: Experience the luxurious atmosphere of this master suite, with its coffered ceiling and deluxe bath.

• Additional Bedrooms: Angled stairs lead to a balcony with writing desk and to two additional bedrooms.

• Porch: Exit two sets of French doors to the rear yard and a covered porch, perfect for relaxing in comfortable weather.

Main Level Floor Plan

Copyright by designer/architect.

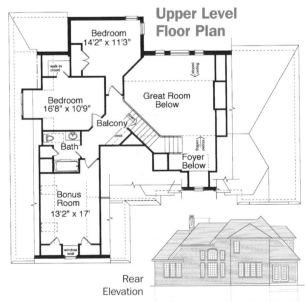

Upper Level Floor Plan

Rear Elevation

Plan #521005

Dimensions: 62' W x 104'2" D
Levels: 1.5
Square Footage: 2,932
Main Level Sq. Ft.: 2,026
Upper Level Sq. Ft.: 906
Bedrooms: 3
Bathrooms: 3½
Foundation: Slab
Material List Available: No
Price Category: F

This country home contains plenty of room for entertaining.

Features:

- Front Porch: This outdoor relaxing area attaches to the side screened porch. The breezeway attaches to the two-car garage.

- Foyer: This area welcomes you to the home. Pocket doors allow access to the computer room, which leads to the laundry room.

- Living Room: This large, centrally located gathering area features triple French doors, allowing the fun to spill out onto the rear covered deck. The fireplace adds a focal point to the room.

- Kitchen: An abundance of cabinets and counter space fill this island kitchen. A bay window creates a bright and warm space.

- Master Suite: This main-level oasis features a large walk-in closet. The master bath boasts a whirlpool tub and a separate shower.

CAD FILE AVAILABLE

LOWER DECK
(21'7"x8'4")

COVERED DECK
(20'0"x7'0")

SUNROOM
(14'4"x13'8")

MASTER BEDROOM
(14'4"x18'8")

DINING AREA
(12'8"x11'4")
+bay

LIVING ROOM
(16'10"x20'6")

KITCHEN
(12'8"x12'6")

FOYER
(10'8"x6'0")

SCREENED SIDE PORCH
(8'0"x11'4")

COMPUTER ROOM

LAUNDRY ROOM

FRONT PORCH
(57'0"x8'0")

Main Level Floor Plan

BREEZE WAY
(7'0"x11'6")

SERVICE YARD

2-CAR GARAGE
(21'4"x26'8")

GOLF CART AREA
(8'0"x15'4")

BONUS ROOM

Bonus Area Floor Plan

OPEN TO LIVING ROOM

BEDROOM #2
(14'4"x14'6")
+bay

BEDROOM #3
(12'8"x12'8")

Upper Level Floor Plan

Copyright by designer/architect.

RearView

Main Level Floor Plan

Upper Level Floor Plan

Images provided by designer/architect.

Copyright by designer/architect.

Plan #481016

Dimensions: 90'6" W x 63'10" D

Levels: 2

Square Footage: 2,845

Main Level Sq. Ft.: 1,587

Upper Level Sq. Ft.: 1,258

Bedrooms: 4

Bathrooms: 2½

Foundation: Basement

Material List Available: No

Price Category: F

Upper Level Floor Plan

Copyright by designer/architect.

Main Level Floor Plan

Plan #371127

Dimensions: 85'2" W x 42'4 1/2" D

Levels: 2

Square Footage: 2,427

Main Level Sq. Ft.: 1,788

Upper Level Sq. Ft.: 639

Bedrooms: 4

Bathrooms: 3

Foundation: Crawl space, slab, or basement

Material List Available: No

Price Category: E

Images provided by designer/architect.

Upper Level Floor Plan

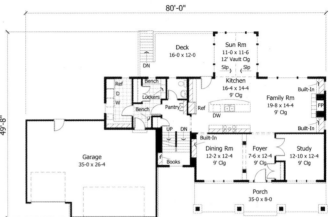

Plan #481017

Dimensions: 80' W x 49'8" D

Levels: 2

Square Footage: 2,982

Main Level Sq. Ft.: 1,563

Upper Level Sq. Ft.: 1,419

Bedrooms: 4

Bathrooms: 2½

Foundation: Basement

Material List Available: No

Price Category: F

Images provided by designer/architect.

Main Level Floor Plan

Copyright by designer/architect.

Plan #571030

Dimensions: 50' W x 40' D

Levels: 2

Square Footage: 2,155

Main Level Sq. Ft.: 1,210

Upper Level Sq. Ft.: 945

Bedrooms: 3

Bathrooms: 2½

Foundation: Basement

Material List Available: Yes

Price Category: D

Images provided by designer/architect.

Main Level Floor Plan

Upper Level Floor Plan

Copyright by designer/architect.

Plan #161017

Dimensions: 61' W x 37'6" D
Levels: 2
Square Footage: 2,653
Main Level Sq. Ft.: 1,365
Upper Level Sq. Ft.: 1,288
Bedrooms: 4
Bathrooms: 2½
Foundation: Basement
Materials List Available: Yes
Price Category: F

If a traditional look makes you feel comfortable, you'll love this spacious, family-friendly home.

Features:

- **Family Room:** Accessorize with cozy cushions to make the most of this sunken room. Windows flank the fireplace, adding warm, natural light. Doors leading to the rear deck make this room a family "headquarters."

- **Living and Dining Rooms:** These formal rooms open to each other, so you'll love hosting gatherings in this home.

- **Kitchen:** A handy pantry fits well with the traditional feeling of this home, and an island adds contemporary convenience.

- **Master Suite:** Relax in the whirlpool tub in your bath and enjoy the storage space in the two walk-in closets in the bedroom.

Images provided by designer/architect.

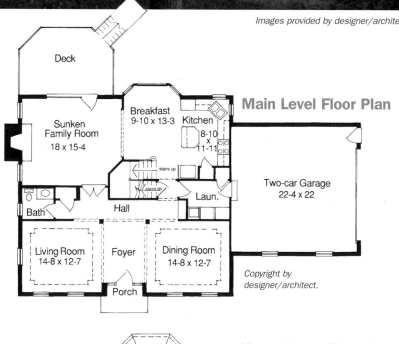

Main Level Floor Plan

Copyright by designer/architect.

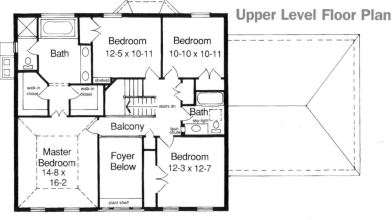

Upper Level Floor Plan

Plan #181085

Dimensions: 56'4" W x 44' D

Levels: 2

Square Footage: 2,183

Main Level Sq. Ft.: 1,232

Second Level Sq. Ft.: 951

Bedrooms: 3

Bathrooms: 2½

Foundation: Basement

Materials List Available: Yes

Price Category: D

Images provided by designer/architect.

This country home features an inviting front porch and a layout designed for modern living.

CAD FILE AVAILABLE

Features:

- Ceiling Height: 8 ft.

- Solarium: Sunlight streams through the windows of this solarium at the front of the house.

- Living Room: Walk through French doors, and you will enter this inviting living room. Family and friends will be drawn to the corner fireplace.

- Formal Dining Room: Usher your guests directly from the living room into this formal dining room. The kitchen is located on the

other side of the dining room for convenient service.

- Kitchen: This generously sized kitchen is a delight, it offers a center island, separate eat-in area, and access to the back deck.

- Bonus Room: This room just off the entry hall can become a family room, a bedroom, or an office.

- Master Suite: Curl up by the corner fireplace in this master retreat, with its walk-in closet and lavish bath with separate shower and tub.

Main Level Floor Plan

Upper Level Floor Plan

Copyright by designer/architect.

Plan #461092

Dimensions: 81' W x 54' D
Levels: 2
Square Footage: 2,844
Main Level Sq. Ft.: 2,128
Upper Level Sq. Ft.: 716
Bedrooms: 4
Bathrooms: 4
Foundation: Slab or basement; crawl space for fee
Material List Available: No
Price Category: F

Enjoy country living at its best in this well-designed home.

Images provided by designer/architect.

Features:

- Dining Room: Located at the entry, this formal dining room features a nook for your hutch. Pocket doors lead into the foyer, adding the ability for the space to work as a home office.

- Guest Suite: This main-level suite offers your guests privacy while staying connected to what is happening in other parts of the house. The accessible full bathroom is a bonus for the area.

- Master Suite: Located on the main level, this retreat boasts two large walk-in closets. The master bath features a whirlpool tub and a stall shower.

- Upper Level: This level is home to the two secondary bedrooms, each with a walk-in closet. Each bedroom has a private bathroom.

Rear View

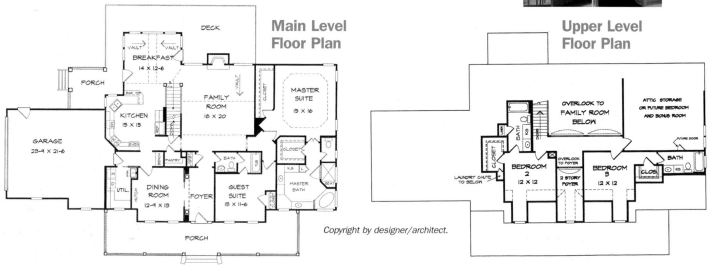

Main Level Floor Plan

Upper Level Floor Plan

Copyright by designer/architect.

Upper Level Floor Plan
Copyright by designer/architect.

Bedroom
13' x 10'2"

Bedroom
13' x 12'4"

Dn

Plan #361543

Dimensions: 50' W x 67' D

Levels: 2

Square Footage: 2,222

Main Level Sq. Ft.: 1,700

Upper Level Sq. Ft.: 522

Bedrooms: 3

Bathrooms: 2½

Foundation: Crawl space

Material List Available: No

Price Category: E

Images provided by designer/architect.

CAD FILE AVAILABLE

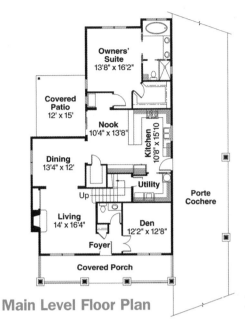

Owners' Suite
13'8" x 16'2"

Covered Patio
12' x 15'

Nook
10'4" x 13'8"

Kitchen
10'8" x 15'10"

Dining
13'4" x 12'

Utility

Up

Porte Cochere

Living
14' x 16'4"

Den
12'2" x 12'8"

Foyer

Covered Porch

Garage
20' x 24'

Main Level Floor Plan

Plan #491007

Dimensions: 36' W x 50'6" D

Levels: 2

Square Footage: 2,414

Main Level Sq. Ft.: 864

Upper Level Sq. Ft.: 686

Lower Level Sq. Ft.: 864

Bedrooms: 3

Bathrooms: 1½

Foundation: Basement

Material List Available: Yes

Price Category: E

Images provided by designer/architect.

CAD FILE AVAILABLE

Upper Level Floor Plan
Copyright by designer/architect.

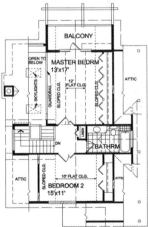

BALCONY

OPEN TO BELOW

MASTER BEDRM
13'x17'

ATTIC

SKYLIGHTS

GUARDRAIL

SLOPED CLG.

12' FLAT CLG.

SLOPED CLG.

DN

BATHRM

ATTIC

SLOPED CLG.

10' FLAT CLG.

BEDROOM 2
15'x11'

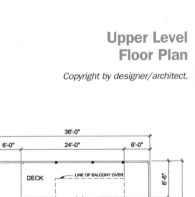

36'-0"

6'-0" 24'-0" 6'-0"

DECK

LINE OF BALCONY OVER

8'-6"

WOOD STORAGE

WINDOW SEAT

WINDOW SEAT

37'-6"

50'-6"

DN

VAULTED CLG.

GREAT ROOM
23'x16' & 15'8"

UP

DN

KIT
10'x10'

BEDRM 3
11'x11'

LAV

DECK

4'-6"

DN

Main Level Floor Plan

Front View

Plan #161037

Dimensions: 46' W x 59'4" D
Levels: 1
Square Footage: 2,469
Main Level Sq. Ft.: 1,462
Basement Level Sq. Ft.: 1,007
Bedrooms: 2
Bathrooms: 2½
Foundation: Walkout; basement for fee
Materials List Available: Yes
Price Category: E

Images provided by designer/architect.

A brick-and-stone facade welcomes you into this lovely home, which is designed to fit into a narrow lot.

Features:

- Foyer: This entrance, with vaulted ceiling, introduces the graciousness of this home.

- Great Room: A vaulted center ceiling creates the impression that this large great room and dining room are one space, making entertaining a natural in this area.

- Kitchen: Designed for efficiency with ample storage and counter space, this kitchen also allows casual dining at the counter.

- Master Suite: A tray ceiling sets this room off from the rest of the house, and the lavishly equipped bathroom lets you pamper yourself.

- Lower Level: Put extra bedrooms or a library in this finished area, and use the wet bar in a game room or recreation room.

Kitchen

Main Level Floor Plan

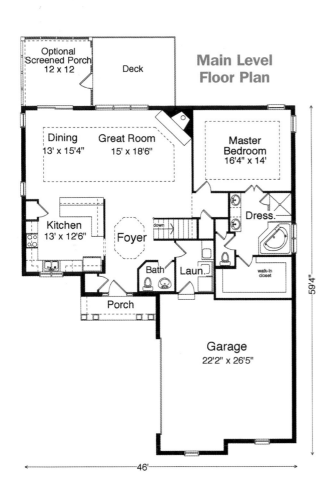

Optional Screened Porch 12 x 12

Deck

Dining 13' x 15'4"

Great Room 15' x 18'6"

Master Bedroom 16'4" x 14'

Kitchen 13' x 12'6"

Foyer

down

Dress.

Bath

Laun.

walk-in closet

Porch

Garage 22'2" x 26'5"

59'4"

46'

Basement Level Floor Plan

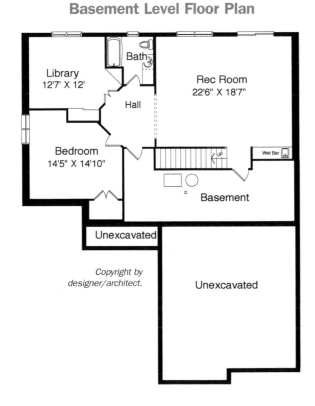

Library 12'7' X 12'

Bath

Hall

Rec Room 22'6" X 18'7"

Bedroom 14'5" X 14'10"

UP

Wet Bar

Basement

Unexcavated

Copyright by designer/architect.

Unexcavated

Rear Elevation

Great Room

Dining Room

Upper Level Floor Plan

Copyright by designer/architect.

Bedroom 11'10" x 10'4"

Bedroom 12' x 10'4"

Open to Great Room Below

Dn

Open to Entry Below

Vaulted Bedroom 12'6" x 10'4"

Covered Patio 12' x 10'

Kitchen 11' x 12'8"

Nook 11' x 13'

2 Story Great Room 15' x 18'

Utility

2 Story Entry

Living 12'6" x 12'8"

Owners' Suite 13' x 15'6"

Up

Garage 20' x 22'6"

Covered Porch

Main Level Floor Plan

Plan #361540

Dimensions: 54' W x 53' D
Levels: 2
Square Footage: 2,231
Main Level Sq. Ft.: 1,531
Upper Level Sq. Ft.: 700
Bedrooms: 4
Bathrooms: 2½
Foundation: Crawl space
Material List Available: No
Price Category: E

Images provided by designer/architect.

CAD FILE AVAILABLE

Upper Level Floor Plan

BEDROOM #2 14'-0" X 11'-0"

BEDROOM #3 14'-0" X 11'-0"

MASTER BEDROOM 12'-0" X 15'-0"

PARLOR 9'-4" X 7'-8"

BEDROOM #4 12'-6" X 12'-0"

BALCONY 10'-0" X 8'-6"

KITCHEN 9'-0" X 11'-0"

BREAKFAST 10'-0" X 11'-0"

FAMILY ROOM 16'-0" X 13'-2"

PANTRY

DINING ROOM 15'-6" X 10'-10"

GARAGE 13'-0" X 19'-0"

LIVING ROOM 12'-0" X 12'-6"

GARAGE (OPTION) 19'-0" X 19'-0"

Main Level Floor Plan

Copyright by designer/architect.

Plan #571006

Dimensions: 36' W x 40' D
Levels: 2
Square Footage: 2,409
Main Level Sq. Ft.: 1,142
Upper Level Sq. Ft.: 1,267
Bedrooms: 4
Bathrooms: 2½
Foundation: Basement
Material List Available: Yes
Price Category: E

Plan #131051

Dimensions: 64'4" W x 53'4" D

Levels: 2

Square Footage: 2,431

Main Level Sq. Ft.: 1,293

Upper Level Sq. Ft.: 1,138

Bedrooms: 4

Bathrooms: 2½

Foundation: Crawl space, slab, or basement

Materials List Available: Yes

Price Category: F

Gracious and charming with a wraparound front porch and a backyard terrace, this home also has a ready-to-finish third floor all-purpose room and a full bath.

Features:

- Main Level Ceiling Height: 8 ft.

- Family Room: A comfortable space for the entire family to gather, this delightful room can be warmed by a heat-circulating fireplace.

- Dining Room: A cozy dinette boasts a sliding glass door with access to a gorgeous backyard terrace with an optional calm reflecting pool.

- Kitchen: Adjoining the dining area, the kitchen offers plenty of storage and counter space. The laundry room and half-bath are nearby for convenience.

- Garage: The garage is tucked way back to keep it from intruding into the traditional facade.

Main Level Floor Plan

Images provided by designer/architect.

This home, as shown in the photograph, may differ from the actual blueprints. For more detailed information, please check the floor plans carefully.

Rear Elevation

Upper Level Floor Plan

Optional 3rd Level Floor Plan

Copyright by designer/architect.

Plan #391071

Dimensions: 73' W x 35'6" D
Levels: 2
Square Footage: 2,710
Main Level Sq. Ft.: 1,469
Upper Level Sq. Ft.: 1,241
Bedrooms: 4
Bathrooms: 2½
Foundation: Crawl space, slab, or basement
Material List Available: Yes
Price Category: F

Images provided by designer/architect.

This spacious family home is well suited for growing families.

Features:

- **Living Room:** This formal room flows into the dining room. The large group of front windows here will allow an abundance of natural light into the area.

- **Family Room:** This large family room opens to a screened porch as well as an optional side deck. Add the optional fireplace to increase the warmth and charm of the space.

- **Kitchen:** This efficient kitchen, complete with a bay window and cooktop island, opens to the cozy breakfast area, which boasts its own bay window for added space.

- **Upper Level:** Three generous secondary bedrooms gather around a full bathroom. The master suite takes advantage of a sprawling private bath and two walk-in closets.

Main Level Floor Plan

Copyright by designer/architect.

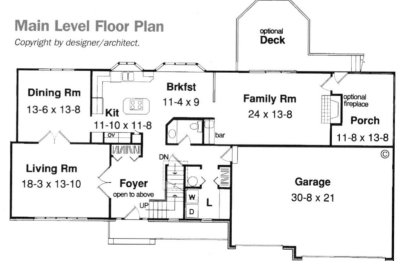

Upper Level Floor Plan

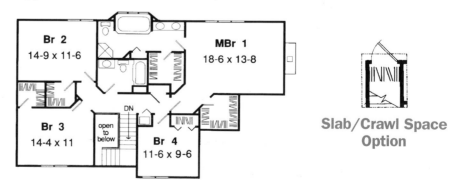

Slab/Crawl Space Option

108   order direct: 1-800-523-6789

Plan #401039

Dimensions: 69'8" W x 46' D

Levels: 2

Square Footage: 2,462

Main Level Sq. Ft.: 1,333

Upper Level Sq. Ft.: 1,129

Bedrooms: 4

Bathrooms: 2½

Foundation: Basement

Materials List Available: Yes

Price Category: E

A large wraparound porch graces the exterior of this home and gives it great outdoor livability.

Features:

• **Foyer:** This raised foyer spills into a hearth-warmed living room and the bay-windowed dining room beyond; French doors open from the breakfast and dining rooms to the spacious porch.

• **Family Room:** Built-ins surround a second hearth in this cozy gathering room.

• **Study:** Located in the front, this room is adorned by a beamed ceiling and, like the family room, features built-ins.

• **Bedrooms:** You'll find three family bedrooms on the second floor.

• **Master Suite:** This restful area, located on the second floor, features a walk-in closet and private bath.

• **Garage:** Don't miss the workshop area in this garage.

Upper Level Floor Plan

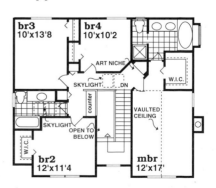

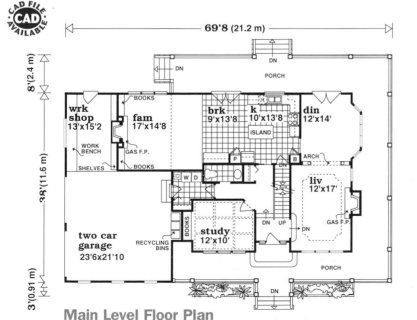

Main Level Floor Plan

Plan #391067

Dimensions: 69'8" W x 42' D
Levels: 2
Square Footage: 2,897
Main Level Sq. Ft.: 1,435
Upper Level Sq. Ft.: 1,462
Bedrooms: 4
Bathrooms: 2½
Foundation: Crawl space, slab, or basement
Material List Available: No
Price Category: F

Images provided by designer/architect.

This beautiful home has a stucco-and-stone facade that features detailing around the multipaned windows and a stone arch over the entrance.

Features:

- Foyer: This two-story foyer is the visitor's introduction to the spacious open layout of the home's first floor. An angled staircase cascading down to the foyer also enhances the first impression.

- Living Room: This formal living room is directly to the right of the foyer. A bump-out window provides a focal point and a view of the front yard.

- Kitchen: The gourmet of the family will find this kitchen efficient and convenient. An island work area, double sink with a garden window above, walk-in pantry, and ample counter and storage space have been included in the well-thought-out kitchen. The informal breakfast area is a bright, cheery place to start your day.

- Upper Level: The sleeping quarters are located on this upper level. A luxurious master suite awaits the owner with a pampering private bath and two walk-in closets. Three additional bedrooms share a full bathroom with a double vanity. Natural illumination streams into the common area from two skylights. A bonus room is provided for your family' future needs.

Copyright by designer/architect.

Main Level Floor Plan

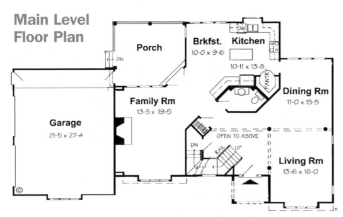

Upper Level Floor Plan

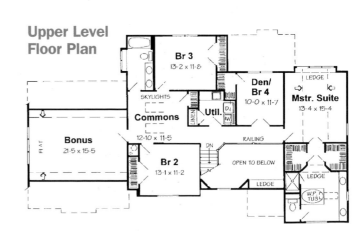

Plan #121098

Dimensions: 46' W x 47'10" D
Levels: 2
Square Footage: 2,292
Main Level Sq. Ft.: 1,158
Upper Level Sq. Ft.: 1,134
Bedrooms: 4
Bathrooms: 2½
Foundation: Basement
Materials List Available: Yes
Price Category: E

Images provided by designer/architect.

You'll love the graceful feeling of this lovely home, which is filled with style and wonderful amenities.

Features:

• **Great Room:** The hub of the home, this great room shares a see-through fireplace with the adjacent hearth room.

• **Kitchen:** A built-in desk and center island are highlights in this room which has been designed to make cooking a pleasure for both beginners and seasoned chefs.

• **Breakfast Area:** A bayed window lets sunlight stream into this lovely dining area.

• **Master Suite:** The luxury of a private bath with a shower, tub, and double vanity makes this area a welcome retreat.

• **Bedroom 4:** This room offers access to an unfinished area over the 2-bay garage below. You can use this room for extra storage or finish it as a game room or study for the children.

Main Level Floor Plan

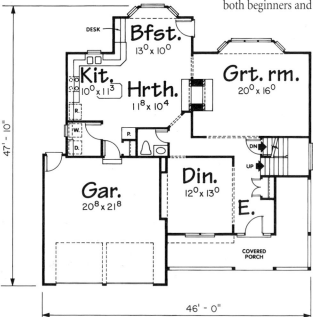

Upper Level Floor Plan

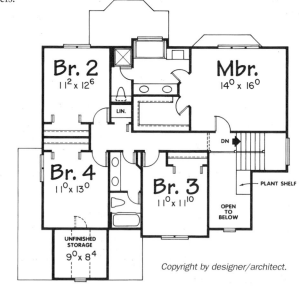

Copyright by designer/architect.

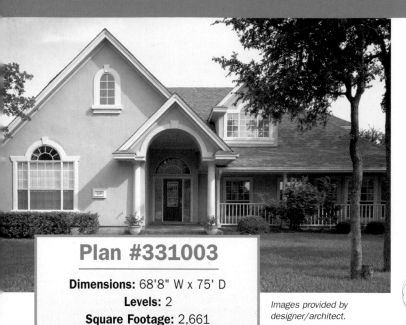

68'8"

75'0"

Main Level Floor Plan

Images provided by designer/architect.

Plan #331003

Dimensions: 68'8" W x 75' D

Levels: 2

Square Footage: 2,661

Main Level Sq. Ft.: 2,000

Upper Level Sq. Ft.: 660

Bedrooms: 4

Bathrooms: 3

Foundation: Crawl space, slab or basement

Materials List Available: No

Price Category: F

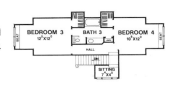

Upper Level Floor Plan

Copyright by designer/architect.

Plan #341295

Dimensions: 46' W x 58'8" D

Levels: 2

Square Footage: 2,188

Main Level Sq. Ft.: 1,569

Lower Level Sq. Ft: 619

Bedrooms: 3

Bathrooms: 2½

Foundation: Crawl space, slab, basement, or walkout

Materials List Available: Yes

Price Category: D

Images provided by designer/architect.

CAD FILE AVAILABLE

Upper Level Floor Plan

Main Level Floor Plan

Copyright by designer/architect.

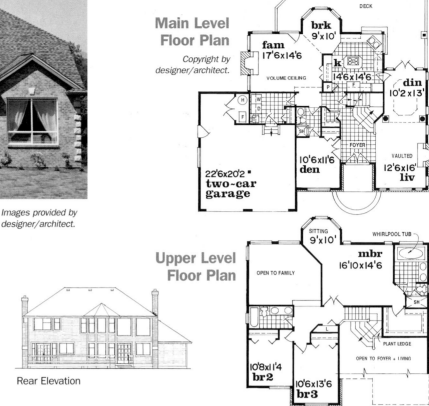

Main Level Floor Plan

Copyright by designer/architect.

DECK

brk 9'x10'

fam 17'6x14'6

k 14'6x14'6

din 10'2x13'

VOLUME CEILING

22'6x20'2 two~car garage

10'6x11'6 den

FOYER

VAULTED

12'6x16' liv

Plan #401015

Dimensions: 56' W x 50'4" D

Levels: 2

Square Footage: 2,618

Main Level Sq. Ft.: 1,464

Upper Level Sq. Ft.: 1,154

Bedrooms: 3

Bathrooms: 3

Foundation: Basement

Materials List Available: Yes

Price Category: F

Images provided by designer/architect.

Rear Elevation

Upper Level Floor Plan

SITTING 9'x10'

WHIRLPOOL TUB

mbr 16'10x14'6

OPEN TO FAMILY

SH

PLANT LEDGE

OPEN TO FOYER + LIVING

10'8x11'4 br2

10'6x13'6 br3

Plan #331002

Dimensions: 62'2" W x 66'8" D

Levels: 2

Square Footage: 2,299

Main Level Sq. Ft.: 1,517

Upper Level Sq. Ft.: 782

Bedrooms: 3

Bathrooms: 2½

Foundation: Crawl space, slab, or basement

Materials List Available: No

Price Category: E

Images provided by designer/architect.

62'2"

GARAGE 20'0x20'0

STO

SEAT

SPA

DECK

SEAT

66'8"

MUD RM

COVERED PORCH

BBQ

KITCHEN 12'8x10'0

UP

GREAT ROOM 16'8x17'4

M BATH

MORNING 13'0x10'0

DN

M BEDROOM 16'8x14'6

DINING 12'8x11'4

ENTRY 6'0x9'0

STUDY 12'4x11'4

COVERED PORCH

Main Level Floor Plan

STO

BEDRM 2 11'0x14'2

BATH 2

DN

STORAGE

AC

BEDRM 3 10'10x16'0

LINEN

STO

PLAYROOM 16'0x9'0

STO

Upper Level Floor Plan

Copyright by designer/architect.

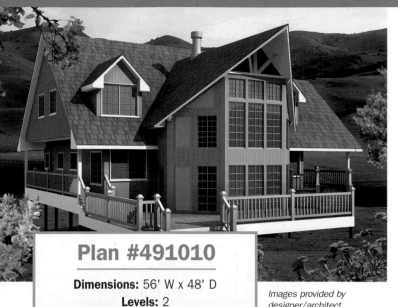

Plan #491010

Dimensions: 56' W x 48' D

Levels: 2

Square Footage: 2,682

Main Level Sq. Ft.: 1,559

Upper Level Sq. Ft.: 1,123

Bedrooms: 6

Bathrooms: 3

Foundation: Pier/Pole

Material List Available: Yes

Price Category: F

Images provided by designer/architect.

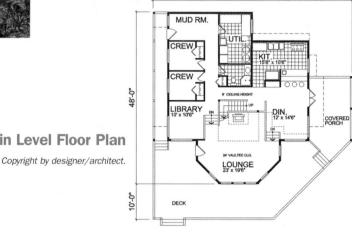

Upper Level Floor Plan

Main Level Floor Plan

Copyright by designer/architect.

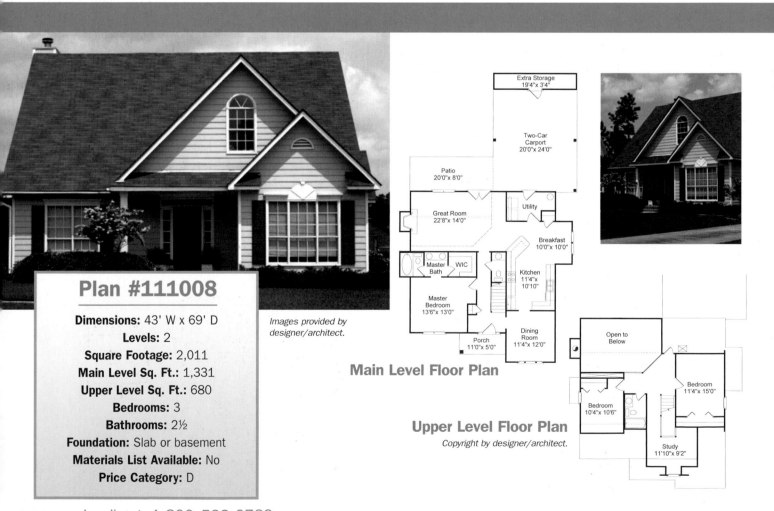

Plan #111008

Dimensions: 43' W x 69' D

Levels: 2

Square Footage: 2,011

Main Level Sq. Ft.: 1,331

Upper Level Sq. Ft.: 680

Bedrooms: 3

Bathrooms: 2½

Foundation: Slab or basement

Materials List Available: No

Price Category: D

Images provided by designer/architect.

Main Level Floor Plan

Upper Level Floor Plan

Copyright by designer/architect.

Plan #121029

Dimensions: 58'8" W x 54' D

Levels: 2

Square Footage: 2,576

Main Level Sq. Ft.: 1,735

Upper Level Sq. Ft.: 841

Bedrooms: 4

Bathrooms: 2½

Foundation: Basement

Materials List Available: Yes

Price Category: E

Images provided by designer/architect.

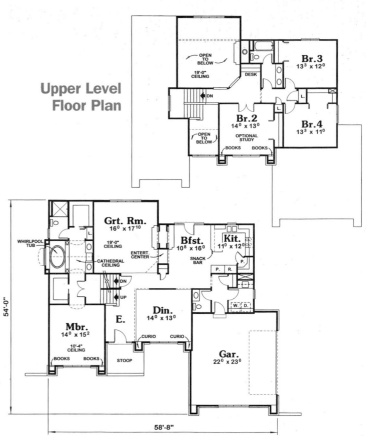

Upper Level Floor Plan

Main Level Floor Plan

Copyright by designer/architect.

Plan #121097

Dimensions: 58' W x 42'8" D

Levels: 2

Square Footage: 2,417

Main Level Sq. Ft.: 1,162

Upper Level Sq. Ft.: 1,255

Bedrooms: 4

Bathrooms: 2½

Foundation: Basement

Materials List Available: Yes

Price Category: E

Images provided by designer/architect.

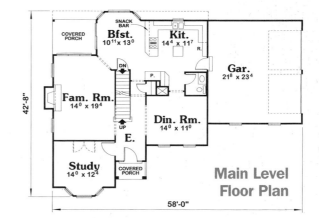

Main Level Floor Plan

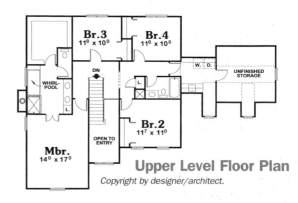

Upper Level Floor Plan

Copyright by designer/architect.

Main Level Floor Plan

Family 20-2x16-8
Brk 10-0x16-8
Kitchen 10-8x11-6
Living 11-0x14-8 Sunken
Dining 10-6x13-3
Garage 19-4x21-4
Porch 17-4x5-0
vaulted
Entry
42'-0"
49'-0"

Upper Level Floor Plan

Br 2 11-0x10-0
MBr 13-0x17-8 vaulted
Br 3 11-0x11-0
Br 4 10-6x11-0
open to below
vaulted

Images provided by designer/architect.

Copyright by designer/architect.

Plan #321050

Dimensions: 49' W x 42' D
Levels: 2
Square Footage: 2,336
Main Level Sq. Ft.: 1,291
Upper Level Sq. Ft.: 1,045
Bedrooms: 4
Bathrooms: 2½
Foundation: Basement
Materials List Available: Yes
Price Category: E

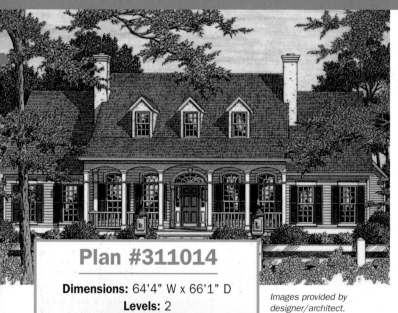

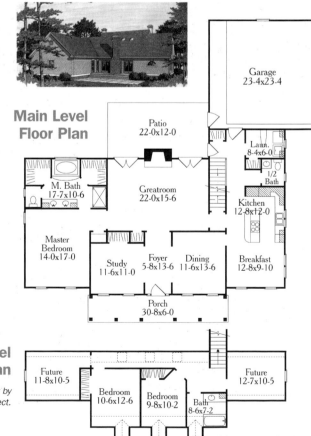

Main Level Floor Plan

Garage 23-4x23-4
Patio 22-0x12-0
Laun. 8-4x6-0
1/2 Bath
M. Bath 17-7x10-6
Greatroom 22-0x15-6
Kitchen 12-8x12-0
Master Bedroom 14-0x17-0
Study 11-6x11-0
Foyer 5-8x13-6
Dining 11-6x13-6
Breakfast 12-8x9-10
Porch 30-8x6-0

Upper Level Floor Plan

Future 11-8x10-5
Future 12-7x10-5
Bedroom 10-6x12-6
Bedroom 9-8x10-2
Bath 8-6x7-2

Images provided by designer/architect.

Copyright by designer/architect.

Plan #311014

Dimensions: 64'4" W x 66'1" D
Levels: 2
Square Footage: 2,344
Main Level Sq. Ft.: 1,791
Upper Level Sq. Ft.: 553
Bedrooms: 3
Bathrooms: 2½
Foundation: Crawl space, slab, or basement
Materials List Available: Yes
Price Category: E

Plan #131032

Dimensions: 69'2" W x 46' D
Levels: 2
Square Footage: 2,455
Main Level Sq. Ft.: 1,499
Upper Level Sq. Ft.: 956
Bedrooms: 4
Bathrooms: 3
Foundation: Crawl space, slab, or basement
Materials List Available: Yes
Price Category: F

Images provided by designer/architect.

If you love Victorian styling, you'll be charmed by the ornate, rounded front porch and the two-story bay that distinguish this home.

Features:

- Living Room: You'll love the 13-ft. ceiling in this room, as well as the panoramic view it gives of the front porch and yard.

- Kitchen: Sunlight streams into this room, where an angled island with a cooktop eases both prepping and cooking.

- Breakfast Room: This room shares an eating bar with the kitchen, making it easy for the family to congregate while the family chef is cooking.

- Guest Room: Use this lovely room on the first level as a home office or study if you wish.

- Master Suite: The dramatic bayed sitting area with a high ceiling has an octagonal shape that you'll adore, and the amenities in the private bath will soothe you at the end of a busy day.

Rear View

Main Level Floor Plan

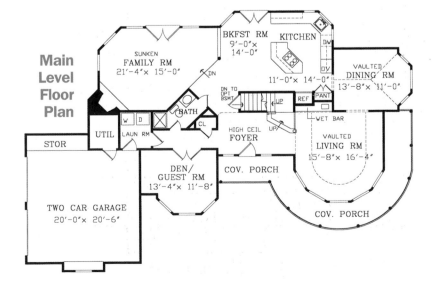

Upper Level Floor Plan

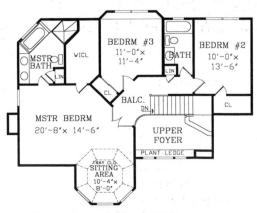

Copyright by designer/architect.

Plan #351087

Dimensions: 66'8" W x 70'8" D
Levels: 1.5
Square Footage: 2,250
Bedrooms: 4
Bathrooms: 3
Foundation: Crawl space or slab
Materials List Available: Yes
Price Category: E

Images provided by designer/architect.

CAD FILE AVAILABLE

The dashing contemporary-country style of brick and wood siding with attractive architectural details, like a string of dormers, makes this home's exterior as lovely as its interior.

Features:

- **Great Room:** Vaulted ceilings give this great room an enormous sense of freedom. The space also opens onto the rear covered porch for the overflow of relaxing warm-weather gatherings and features a fireplace and built-in storage for staying comfortable inside during the cold months.

- **Kitchen:** This efficiently designed kitchen features an L-shaped work area, a pantry, and an island with a raised eating bar. Because the space is open to the formal dining room, bay-windowed breakfast room, and large great room, you'll have plenty of mealtime possibilities.

- **Master Suite:** In a space of its own, the bedroom in this space speaks volumes of relaxation and privacy. One door leads onto the covered porch while the other leads to the expansive master bath, with its dual sinks, oversize jetted tub, stall shower, and his and her walk-in closets.

- **Secondary Bedrooms:** The other bedrooms have hallways of their own and are all just steps away from the other full bathrooms.

- **Flex Space:** A small room adjacent to the master bedroom is in perfect proximity for use as a home office, a nursery, or extra storage space. Above the garage is unfinished bonus space, which can be used however you like.

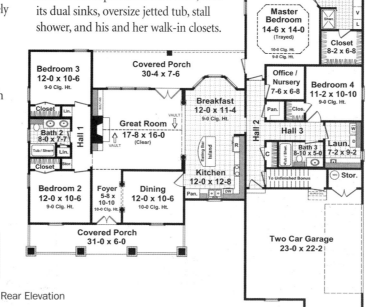

Rear Elevation

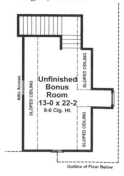

Bonus Area Floor Plan

Copyright by designer/architect.

Plan #401009

Dimensions: 70'8" W x 54' D
Levels: 2
Square Footage: 2,750
Main Level Sq. Ft.: 1,462
Upper Level Sq. Ft.: 1,288
Bedrooms: 4
Bathrooms: 2½
Foundation: Basement
Materials List Available: Yes
Price Category: F

A touch of Victoriana, including a turret roof over a wraparound porch with turned wood spindles, enhances the facade of this home.

CAD FILE AVAILABLE

Features:

- **Living Room:** This octagonal gathering area features a tray ceiling and a fireplace. An abundance of windows allows natural light to flood the room.

- **Kitchen:** The breakfast room is attached to this country kitchen, which features a built-in pantry. The fireplace located in the breakfast room adds warmth to the kitchen.

- **Master Suite:** This retreat features an octagonal sleeping area with a decorative ceiling. The master bath features a walk-in closet and a whirlpool tub.

- **Secondary Bedrooms:** Three additional bedrooms and a full bathroom share the upper level with the master suite.

Main Level Floor Plan

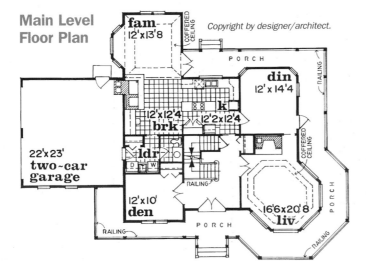

Copyright by designer/architect.

Upper Level Floor Plan

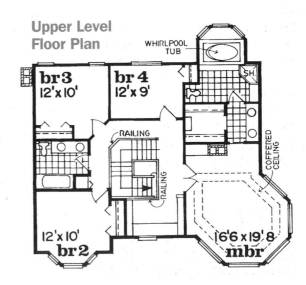

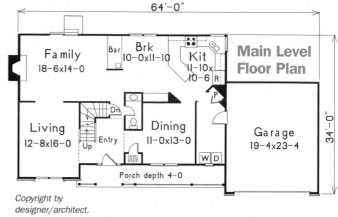

64'-0"

Family
18-6x14-0

Bar

Brk
10-0x11-10

Kit
11-10x
10-6

**Main Level
Floor Plan**

Living
12-8x16-0

Up   Entry   Dn

Dining
11-0x13-0

Garage
19-4x23-4

34'-0"

W D

Porch depth 4-0

*Copyright by
designer/architect.*

Plan #321041

Dimensions: 64' W x 34' D

Levels: 2

Square Footage: 2,286

Main Level Sq. Ft.: 1,283

Upper Level Sq. Ft.: 1,003

Bedrooms: 4

Bathrooms: 2½

Foundation: Crawl space, slab, or basement

Materials List Available: No

Price Category: E

*Images provided by
designer/architect.*

Upper Level Floor Plan

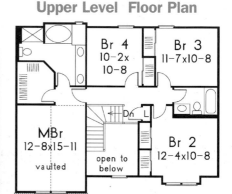

Br 4
10-2x
10-8

Br 3
11-7x10-8

MBr
12-8x15-11
vaulted

Dn L

open to
below

Br 2
12-4x10-8

Front View

Plan #301006

Dimensions: 60' W x 32' D

Levels: 2

Square Footage: 2,162

Main Level Sq. Ft.: 1,098

Upper Level Sq. Ft.: 1,064

Bedrooms: 3

Bathrooms: 2½

Foundation: Crawl space, slab, or basement

Materials List Available: Yes

Price Category: D

Copyright by designer/architect.

WOOD DECK

BREAKFAST
9-8 x 9-8

KITCHEN
12-0 x 13-6

LAUNDRY

GARAGE
22-0 x 22-0

DINING
13-6 x 13-6

GREAT ROOM
13-6 x 22-4

FOYER

PORCH

Main Level Floor Plan

*Images provided by
designer/architect.*

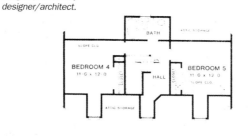

BATH

ATTIC STORAGE

BEDROOM 4
11-0 x 12-0

HALL

BEDROOM 5
11-0 x 12-0

Optional Third Level

BATH

WALK-IN
CLOSET

BEDROOM 2
13-6 x 12-0

WALK-IN
CLOSET

BATH

HALL

M. BEDROOM
13-6 x 16-0

TELEPHONE
NICHE

BEDROOM 3
13-6 x 12-0

Upper Level Floor Plan

Plan #131030

Dimensions: 51' W x 41'10" D
Levels: 2
Square Footage: 2,470
Main Level Sq. Ft.: 1,290
Upper Level Sq. Ft.: 1,180
Bedrooms: 4
Bathrooms: 2½
Foundation: Crawl space, slab, basement, or walkout
Materials List Available: Yes
Price Category: F

This home, as shown in the photograph, may differ from the actual blueprints. For more detailed information, please check the floor plans carefully.

Images provided by designer/architect.

If high ceilings and spacious rooms make you happy, you'll love this gorgeous home.

Features:

- **Family Room:** An 18-ft. vaulted ceiling that's open to the balcony above, a corner fireplace, and a wall of windows make this room feel special.
- **Dining Room:** This formal room, which flows into the living room, also opens to the front porch and optional backyard deck.
- **Kitchen:** A bright breakfast room joins with this kitchen and opens to the backyard deck.

- **Master Suite:** You'll smile when you see the 11-ft. vaulted ceiling, stunning arched window, and two walk-in closets in the bedroom. A skylight lets natural light into the private bath, with its spa tub, separate shower, and dual-sink vanity.
- **Bedrooms:** To reach these three charming bedrooms, you'll admire the view into the family room below as you walk along the balcony hall.

Main Level Floor Plan

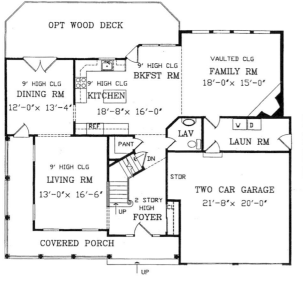

Upper Level Floor Plan

Copyright by designer/architect.

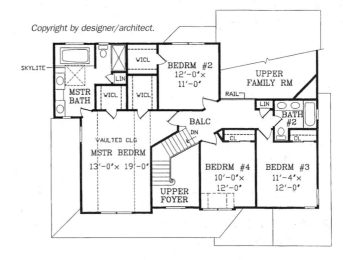

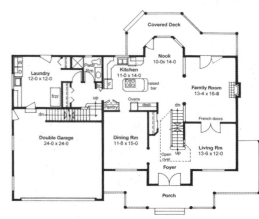

Main Level Floor Plan

Plan #281032

Dimensions: 66' W x 49' D

Levels: 2

Square Footage: 2,904

Main Level Sq. Ft.: 1,494

Upper Level Sq. Ft.: 1,410

Bedrooms: 4

Bathrooms: 2½

Foundation: Basement

Material List Available: Yes

Price Category: F

Images provided by designer/architect.

Rear Elevation

Upper Level Floor Plan

Copyright by designer/architect.

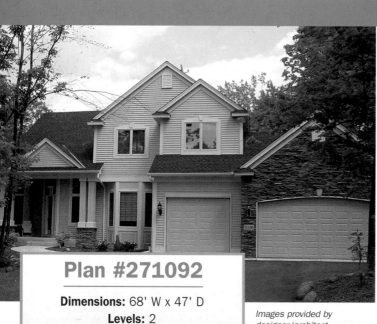

Plan #271092

Dimensions: 68' W x 47' D

Levels: 2

Square Footage: 2,636

Main Level Sq. Ft.: 1,596

Upper Level Sq. Ft.: 1,040

Bedrooms: 3

Bathrooms: 2½

Foundation: Daylight basement

Materials List Available: No

Price Category: F

Images provided by designer/architect.

CAD FILE AVAILABLE

Main Level Floor Plan

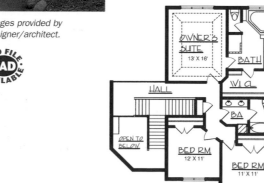

Upper Level Floor Plan

Copyright by designer/architect.

Main Level Floor Plan

Copyright by designer/architect.

Deck
Porch
Utility 14'9"x 5'9"
Master Bedroom 15'4"x 15'1"
Living 18'2"x 16'7"
Breakfast 14'9"x 9'
Ma. Bath
1/2 Ba.
Kitchen 12'9"x 14'5"
Foyer
Dining 15'4"x 12'7"
WIC
Porch
Porch

Plan #111009

Dimensions: 56' W x 49' D
Levels: 2
Square Footage: 2,514
Main Level Sq. Ft.: 1,630
Upper Level Sq. Ft.: 884
Bedrooms: 4
Bathrooms: 3½
Foundation: Basement
Materials List Available: No
Price Category: E

Images provided by designer/architect.

Upper Level Floor Plan

Basement Level Floor Plan

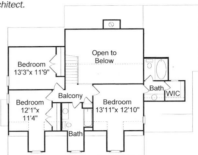

Bedroom 13'3"x 11'9"
Open to Below
Bedroom 12'1"x 11'4"
Balcony
Bedroom 13'11"x 12'10"
Bath
WIC
Bath

Future Gameroom 14'5"x 21'7"
Two-Car Garage

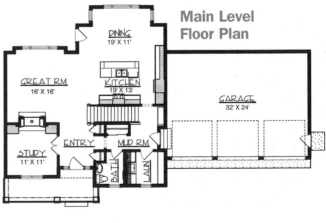

Main Level Floor Plan

DINING 19' X 11'
GREAT RM 16' X 16'
KITCHEN 19' X 13'
GARAGE 32' X 24'
STUDY 11' X 11'
ENTRY
MUD RM
BATH
LAUN

Plan #271091

Dimensions: 68' W x 43' D
Levels: 2
Square Footage: 2,854
Main Level Sq. Ft.: 1,219
Upper Level Sq. Ft.: 1,635
Bedrooms: 3
Bathrooms: 2½
Foundation: Daylight basement
Materials List Available: No
Price Category: F

Images provided by designer/architect.

CAD FILE AVAILABLE

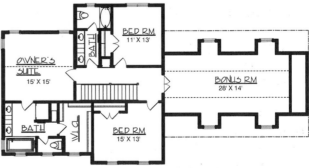

OWNER'S SUITE 15' X 15'
BATH
BED RM 11' X 13'
BONUS RM 28' X 14'
BATH
WIC
BED RM 15' X 13'

Upper Level Floor Plan

Copyright by designer/architect.

Main Level Floor Plan

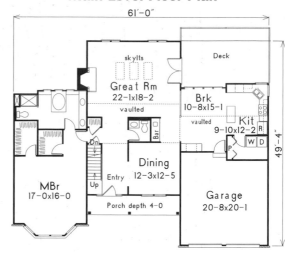

61'-0"

49'-4"

skylts

Great Rm
22-1x18-2
vaulted

Deck

Brk
10-8x15-1
vaulted

Kit
9-10x12-2

Bar

Dining
12-3x12-5

MBr
17-0x16-0

Entry

Porch depth 4-0

Garage
20-8x20-1

Dn

Up

W D

P

Images provided by designer/architect.

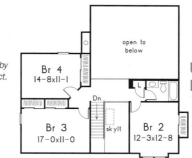

Upper Level Floor Plan

open to below

Br 4
14-8x11-1

Dn

Br 3
17-0x11-0

skylt

Br 2
12-3x12-8

Copyright by designer/architect.

Plan #321044

Dimensions: 61' W x 49'4" D
Levels: 2
Square Footage: 2,618
Main Level Sq. Ft.: 1,804
Upper Level Sq. Ft.: 814
Bedrooms: 4
Bathrooms: 2½
Foundation: Basement
Materials List Available: Yes
Price Category: F

SITTING
7' X 8'

DINETTE
11' X 10'

GREAT RM
22' X 14'

LAUN

KITCHEN
17' X 15'

MUD RM

STUDY
11' X 15'

ENTRY

DINING RM
11' X 13'

GARAGE
44' X 24'

Main Level Floor Plan

OWNER'S SUITE
19' X 13'

BED RM
13' X 10'

WLC

WLC

BATH

LOFT

WLC

BATH

BED RM
11' X 12'

Upper Level Floor Plan

Copyright by designer/architect.

Plan #271090

Dimensions: 78' W x 49' D
Levels: 2
Square Footage: 2,708
Main Level Sq. Ft.: 1,430
Upper Level Sq. Ft.: 1,278
Bedrooms: 3
Bathrooms: 2½
Foundation: Daylight basement
Materials List Available: No
Price Category: F

Images provided by designer/architect.

CAD FILE AVAILABLE

Plan #121025

Dimensions: 60' W x 59'4" D

Levels: 2

Square Footage: 2,562

Main Level Sq. Ft.: 1,875

Upper Level Square Footage: 687

Bedrooms: 4

Bathrooms: 2½

Foundation: Basement

Materials List Available: Yes

Price Category: E

Images provided by designer/architect.

Dramatic arches are the reoccurring architectural theme in this distinctive home.

Features:

- Ceiling Height: 8 ft. unless otherwise noted.
- Foyer: This is a grand two-story entrance. Plants will thrive on the plant shelf thanks to light streaming through the arched window.
- Great Room: The foyer flows into the great room through dramatic 15-ft.-high arched openings.
- Kitchen: An island is the centerpiece of this highly functional kitchen that includes a separate breakfast area.
- Office: French doors open into this versatile office that features a 10-ft. ceiling and transom-topped windows.
- Master Suite: The master suite features a volume ceiling, built-in dresser, and two closets. You'll unwind in the beautiful corner whirlpool bath with its elegant window treatment.

Main Level Floor Plan

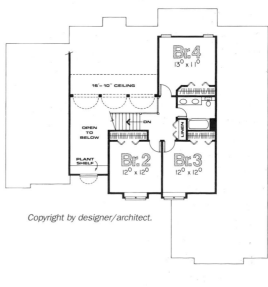

Upper Level Floor Plan

Copyright by designer/architect.

Plan #291015

Dimensions: 88'6" W x 58'3" D
Levels: 1.5
Square Footage: 2,901
Main Level Sq. Ft.: 2,078
Upper Level Sq. Ft.: 823
Bedrooms: 3
Bathrooms: 2½
Foundation: Basement
Materials List Available: No
Price Category: F

Images provided by designer/architect.

Upon entering this home, a cathedral-like timber-framed interior fills the eye.

Features:

- **Great Room:** This large gathering area's ceiling rises up two stories and is open to the kitchen. The beautiful fireplace is the focal point of this room.

- **Kitchen:** This island kitchen is open to the great room and the breakfast nook. Warm woods of all species enhance the great room and this space.

- **Master Suite:** This suite has a sloped ceiling and adjoins a luxurious master bath with twin walk-in closets that open to a sunroom with a private balcony.

- **Upper Level:** This upper level has an open lounge that leads to two bedrooms with vaulted ceilings and a generous second bath.

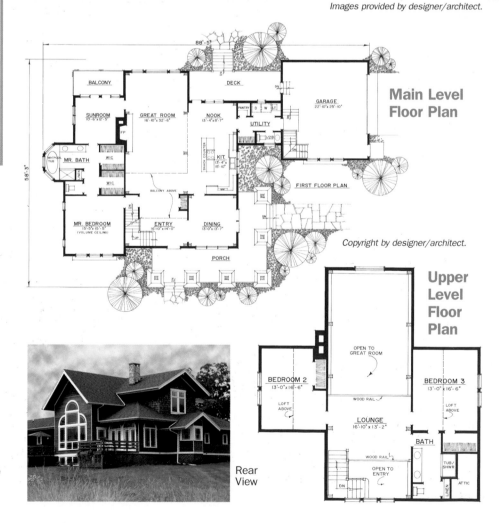

Main Level Floor Plan

Copyright by designer/architect.

Upper Level Floor Plan

Rear View

Master Bath

Dining Room

Kitchen

Rear Porch

Plan #121090

Dimensions: 60' W x 58' D
Levels: 2
Square Footage: 2,645
Main Level Sq. Ft.: 1,972
Upper Level Sq. Ft.: 673
Bedrooms: 4
Bathrooms: 2½
Foundation: Basement
Materials List Available: Yes
Price Category: F

Images provided by designer/architect.

You'll be amazed at the amenities that have been designed into this lovely home.

Features:

- Den: French doors just off the entry lead to this lovely room, with its bowed window and spider-beamed ceiling.

- Great Room: A trio of graceful arched windows highlights the volume ceiling in this room. You might want to curl up to read next to the see-through fireplace into the hearth room.

- Kitchen: Enjoy the good design in this room.

- Hearth Room: The shared fireplace with the great room makes this a cozy spot in cool weather.

- Master Suite: French doors lead to this well-lit area, with its roomy walk-in closet, sunlit whirlpool tub, separate shower, and two vanities.

Main Level Floor Plan

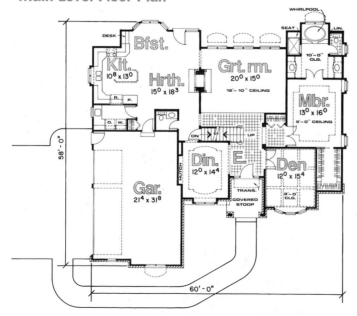

Upper Level Floor Plan

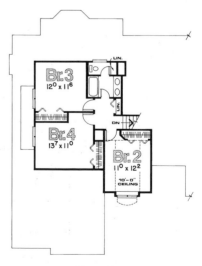

Copyright by designer/architect.

Plan #131029

Dimensions: 56'4" W x 46'6" D
Levels: 2
Square Footage: 2,936
Main Level Sq. Ft.: 1,680
Upper Level Sq. Ft.: 1,256
Bedrooms: 4
Bathrooms: 2½
Foundation: Crawl space, slab, or basement
Materials List Available: Yes
Price Category: G

Images provided by designer/architect.

This home is ideal if you love the look of a country-style farmhouse.

Features:

• **Foyer:** Walk across the large wraparound porch that defines this home to enter this two-story foyer.

• **Living Room:** French doors from the foyer lead into this living room.

• **Family Room:** The whole family will love this room, with its vaulted ceiling, fireplace, and sliding glass doors that open to the wooden rear deck.

• **Kitchen:** A beautiful sit-down center island opens to the family room. There's also a breakfast nook with a lovely bay window.

• **Master Suite:** Luxury abounds with vaulted ceilings, walk-in closets, private bath with whirlpool tub, separate shower, and dual sinks.

• **Loft:** A special place with vaulted ceiling and view into the family room below.

This home, as shown in the photograph, may differ from the actual blueprints. For more detailed information, please check the floor plans carefully.

Main Level Floor Plan

Copyright by designer/architect.

Upper Level Floor Plan

Rear Elevation

Main Level Floor Plan

WOOD DECK

FLOOR ABOVE

DINETTE
11-0 x 11-0

HALF WALL

FLOOR ABV.

LND

D W

PDR

KITCHEN
19-4 x 10-10

DW

REF.

FAMILY RM
13-8 x 18-0
GAS F.P.

DEN
12-0 x 12-0

ENTRY

STEP

BC

PANTRY

DESK

DN

LNDG

LIVING RM
13-8 x 13-0

GARAGE
22-0 x 24-0

DINING RM
STEPPED CEILING
12-0 x 14-0

FOYER

UP.

OPEN ABV.

PORCH

Upper Level Floor Plan

BEDRM 3
12-0 x 15-4

BATH 2

LINEN

TWL

HALL

BEDRM 4
10-8 x 15-0

SHWR

60"X60" W/POOL TUB

M BATH

TC

W.I.C.

DN

LNDG

M BEDRM
13-8 x 17-0

BEDRM 2
12-0 x 12-0

RAILING

BALCONY

SEAT

Copyright by designer/architect.

Plan #261012

Dimensions: 58' W x 47' D

Levels: 2

Square Footage: 2,648

Main Level Sq. Ft.: 1,452

Upper Level Sq. Ft.: 1,196

Bedrooms: 4

Bathrooms: 2½

Foundation: Basement

Materials List Available: No

Price Category: F

Images provided by designer/architect.

Rear Elevation

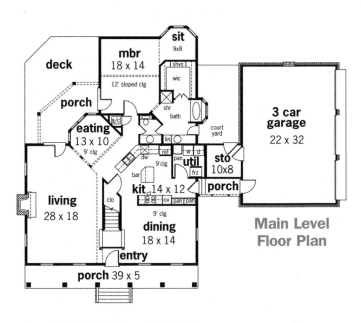

deck

sit
9x8

mbr
18 x 14

shvs

porch

12' sloped clg

wic

eating
13 x 10

9' clg

a/c

shr

bath

lin

court yard

3 car garage
22 x 32

living
28 x 18

clo

dw

ref

bar

w d

util

frz

sto
10x8

porch

kit 14 x 12

ov

pan pan

9' clg

dining
18 x 14

entry

porch 39 x 5

Main Level Floor Plan

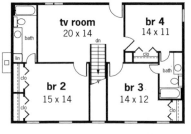

tv room
20 x 14

bath

dn

br 4
14 x 11

lin

clo

bath

Upper Level Floor Plan

Copyright by designer/architect.

br 2
15 x 14

clo

br 3
14 x 12

clo

clo

Plan #211071

Dimensions: 66' W x 66' D

Levels: 2

Square Footage: 2,954

Main Level Sq. Ft.: 1,984

Upper Level Sq. Ft.: 970

Bedrooms: 4

Bathrooms: 3½

Foundation: Slab; crawl space or basement for fee

Materials List Available: Yes

Price Category: F

Images provided by designer/architect.

Main Level Floor Plan

Plan #121120

Dimensions: 55'4" W x 37'8" D

Levels: 2

Square Footage: 2,131

Main Level Sq. Ft.: 1,093

Upper Level Sq. Ft.: 1,038

Bedrooms: 4

Bathrooms: 2½

Foundation: Basement; crawl space for fee

Materials List Available: Yes

Price Category: D

Images provided by designer/architect.

Upper Level Floor Plan

Copyright by designer/architect.

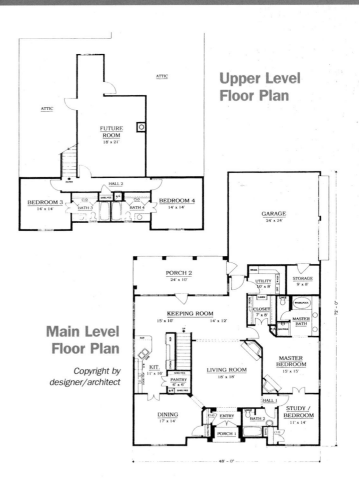

Upper Level Floor Plan

Plan #171018

Dimensions: 48' W x 72' D

Levels: 2

Square Footage: 2,599

Main Level Sq. Ft.: 1,967

Upper Level Sq. Ft.: 632

Bedrooms: 4

Bathrooms: 4

Foundation: Crawl space, slab

Materials List Available: Yes

Price Category: E

Images provided by designer/architect.

Main Level Floor Plan

Copyright by designer/architect

Plan #131026

Dimensions: 55'10" W x 41' D
Levels: 2
Square Footage: 2,796
Main Level Sq. Ft.: 1,481
Upper level Sq. Ft.: 1,315
Bedrooms: 4
Bathrooms: 2½
Foundation: Crawl space, slab, or basement
Materials List Available: Yes
Price Category: G

Images provided by designer/architect.

Handsome half rounds add to curb appeal.

Features:

• Ceiling Height: 8 ft.

• Library: This room features a 10-ft. ceiling with a bright bay window.

• Great Room: A 10-ft. ceiling adds to the spacious feeling of this room, while the corner fireplace gives it an intimate feeling. Sliding glass doors at the rear of the room open to the backyard.

• Dining Room: This formal room adjoins the great room, allowing guests and family to flow between the rooms, and it opens to the backyard through sliding glass doors.

• Breakfast Room: Turrets add a Victorian feeling to this room, which is just off the kitchen and overlooks the front porch.

• Master Suite: Privacy is assured in this suite, which is separated from the main part of the house. A compartmented bath and large walk-in closet add convenience to its beauty.

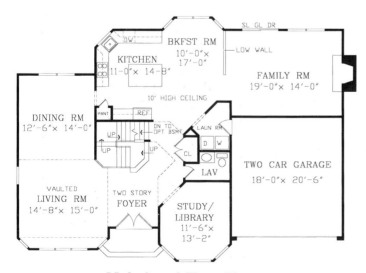

Main Level Floor Plan

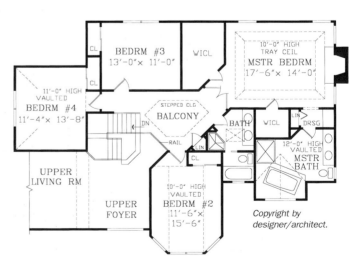

Upper Level Floor Plan

Plan #121093

Dimensions: 62' W x 60'8" D

Levels: 2

Square Footage: 2,603

Main Level Sq. Ft.: 1,800

Upper Level Sq. Ft.: 803

Bedrooms: 4

Bathrooms: 3½

Foundation: Basement

Materials List Available: Yes

Price Category: F

Images provided by designer/architect.

If you love family life but also treasure your privacy, you'll appreciate the layout of this home.

Features:

- Entry: This two-story, open area features plant shelves to display a group of lovely specimens.
- Dining Room: Open to the entry, this room features 12-ft. ceilings and corner hutches.
- Den: French doors lead to this quiet room, with its bowed window and spider-beamed ceiling.
- Gathering Room: A three-sided fireplace, shared with both the kitchen and the breakfast area, is the highlight of this room.
- Master Suite: Secluded for privacy, this suite also has a private covered deck where you can sit and recharge at any time of day. A walk-in closet is practical, and a whirlpool tub is pure comfort.

Main Level Floor Plan

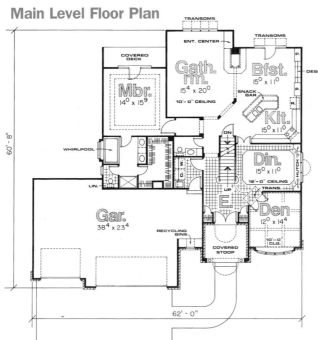

Upper Level Floor Plan

Copyright by designer/architect.

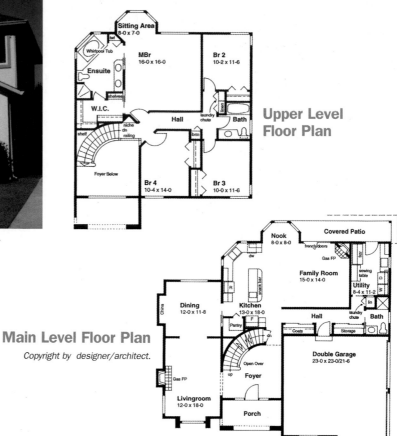

Upper Level Floor Plan

Main Level Floor Plan

Copyright by designer/architect.

Images provided by designer/architect.

Plan #281030

Dimensions: 50' W x 48'6" D

Levels: 2

Square Footage: 2,517

Main Level Sq. Ft.: 1,384

Upper Level Sq. Ft.: 1,133

Bedrooms: 4

Bathrooms: 3

Foundation: Basement

Materials List Available: Yes

Price Category: E

Main Level Floor Plan

Upper Level Floor Plan

Copyright by designer/architect.

Images provided by designer/architect.

Plan #171017

Dimensions: 84' W x 54' D

Levels: 2

Square Footage: 2,558

Main Level Sq. Ft.: 1,577

Upper Level Sq. Ft.: 981

Bedrooms: 4

Bathrooms: 2½

Foundation: Slab, crawl space

Materials List Available: Yes

Price Category: E

Main Level Floor Plan

Dressing
walk-in closet
Master Bedroom
14' x 14'1"
Sitting Area
11'2" x 9'4"
Porch
Foyer
Great Room
16' x 19'6"
Dining Room
12' x 13'10"
Breakfast
14' x 11'2"
Kitchen
Hearth Room
17' x 14'10"
Laun.
Two-car Garage
21' x 20'4"

63'4"
48'

Plan #161041

Dimensions: 63'4" W x 48' D

Levels: 2

Square Footage: 2,738

Main Level Sq. Ft.: 1,915

Upper Level Sq. Ft.: 823

Bedrooms: 4

Bathrooms: 3½

Foundation: Basement

Materials List Available: Yes

Price Category: F

Images provided by designer/architect.

Rear Elevation

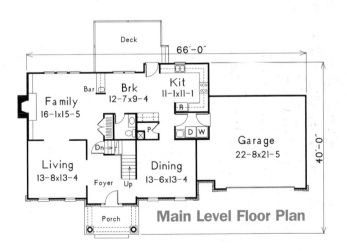

Great Room
Below
Balcony
Bedroom
17' x 12'6"
Bedroom
10' x 13'10"
Bath
Bedroom
12' x 10'6"
slope ceiling   slope ceiling

Upper Level Floor Plan

Copyright by designer/architect.

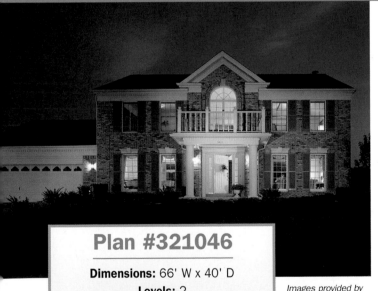

Plan #321046

Dimensions: 66' W x 40' D

Levels: 2

Square Footage: 2,411

Main Level Sq. Ft.: 1,293

Upper Level Sq. Ft.: 1,118

Bedrooms: 3

Bathrooms: 2½

Foundation: Basement

Materials List Available: Yes

Price Category: E

Images provided by designer/architect.

This home, as shown in the photograph, may differ from the actual blueprints. For more detailed information, please check the floor plans carefully.

Deck
66'-0"
Bar
Family
16-1x15-5
Brk
12-7x9-4
Kit
11-1x11-1
R
Living
13-8x13-4
Dn
Dining
13-6x13-4
P
D W
Garage
22-8x21-5
Foyer
Up
Porch
40'-0"

Main Level Floor Plan

Study
11-5x11-8
Br 3
11-11x10-0
MBr
13-8x15-4
Dn
open to
below
vaulted
Br 2
13-8x11-0

Upper Level Floor Plan

Copyright by designer/architect.

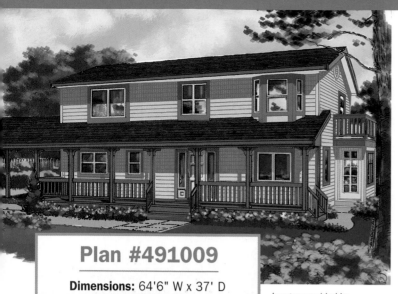

Main Level Floor Plan

LIV
15' x 17'

KIT
12' x 12'

DIN
14'2" x 12'

DOUBLE CARPORT
22'x22'

UTIL

DEN
10' x 12'2"

DN

UP

VERANDAH

2'-0"

28'-0"

7'-0"

22'-0"

42'-6"

Images provided by designer/architect.

Upper Level Floor Plan

Copyright by designer/architect.

BR 2
15' x 10'

MBR
17'6" x 14'4"

BALCONY

DN

OPEN

RAILING

BR 3
15' x 10'

LIN

SEAT

Plan #491009

Dimensions: 64'6" W x 37' D

Levels: 2

Square Footage: 2,215

Main Level Sq. Ft.: 1,149

Upper Level Sq. Ft.: 1,066

Bedrooms: 3

Bathrooms: 2½

Foundation: Basement

Material List Available: Yes

Price Category: E

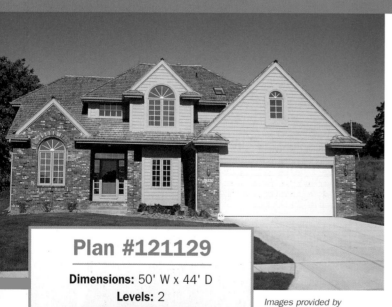

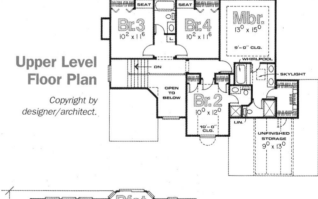

Upper Level Floor Plan

Copyright by designer/architect.

SEAT   SEAT

Br.3
10² x 11⁶

Br.4
10² x 11⁶

Mbr.
13⁰ x 15⁰

9'-0" CLG.

WHIRLPOOL

DN

SKYLIGHT

OPEN TO BELOW

Br.2
10⁰ x 12⁰

10'-0" CLG.

LIN.

UNFINISHED STORAGE
9⁰ x 13⁰

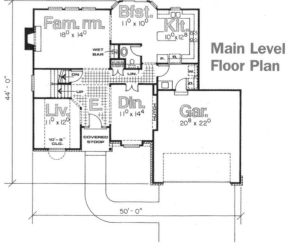

Main Level Floor Plan

44'-0"

Fam. rm.
18⁰ x 14⁰

Bfst.
11⁰ x 10⁰

Kit.
10⁰ x 12⁸

WET BAR

P.

DN

Liv.
11⁰ x 12⁰

E.

Din.
11⁰ x 14⁴

Gar.
20⁸ x 22⁰

UP

10'-8" CLG.

COVERED STOOP

50'-0"

Plan #121129

Dimensions: 50' W x 44' D

Levels: 2

Square Footage: 2,198

Main Level Sq. Ft.: 1,179

Upper Level Sq. Ft.: 1,019

Bedrooms: 4

Bathrooms: 3½

Foundation: Basement;
crawl space for fee

Material List Available: Yes

Price Category: D

Images provided by designer/architect.

CAD FILE AVAILABLE

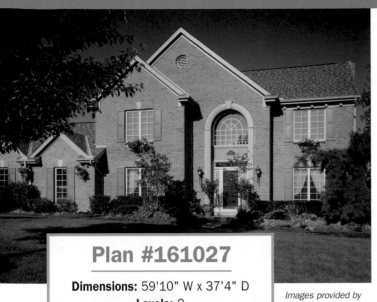

Plan #161027

Dimensions: 59'10" W x 37'4" D

Levels: 2

Square Footage: 2,388

Main Level Sq. Ft.: 1,207

Upper Level Sq. Ft.: 1,181

Bedrooms: 4

Bathrooms: 2½

Foundation: Basement

Materials List Available: No

Price Category: E

Images provided by designer/architect.

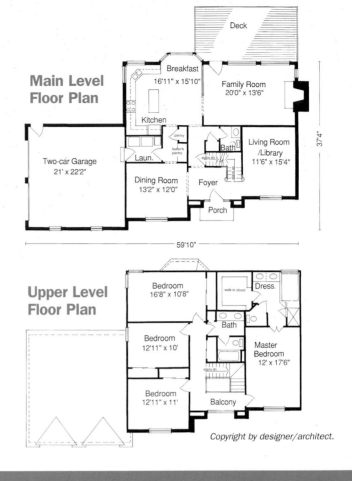

Main Level Floor Plan

Deck

Breakfast 16'11" x 15'10"

Family Room 20'0" x 13'6"

Kitchen

pantry

butler's pantry

Living Room /Library 11'6" x 15'4"

Bath

Laun.

stairs dn.

Dining Room 13'2" x 12'0"

Foyer

Two-car Garage 21' x 22'2"

Porch

37'4"

59'10"

Upper Level Floor Plan

Bedroom 16'8" x 10'8"

walk-in closet

Dress.

Bath

Bedroom 12'11" x 10'

Master Bedroom 12' x 17'6"

stairs dn.

Bedroom 12'11" x 11'

Balcony

Copyright by designer/architect.

Plan #161020

Dimensions: 60' W" x 50'4" D

Levels: 2

Square Footage: 2,082; 2,349 with bonus space

Main Level Sq. Ft.: 1,524

Upper Level Sq. Ft.: 558

Bedrooms: 3

Bathrooms: 2½

Foundation: Basement

Materials List Available: Yes

Price Category: D

Images provided by designer/architect.

Bedroom 11'1" x 13'3"

Bedroom 11'5" x 12'0"

Bath

bookshelves

computer desk

Balcony

wood rail

Foyer Below

Bonus Room 11'0" x 22'0"

wood rail

Upper Level Floor Plan

Master Bedroom 13'6" x 15'1"

Triple French Doors w/ arched window above

Great Room 17'4" x 21'2"

12' high ceiling

Dining Room 10'10" x 14'0"

Bath

Bath

hanging space

walk-in closet

Laun.

pass thru

Kitchen 12'4" x 11'6"

Foyer

pantry

Breakfast 11' x 9'4"

wood rail

Two-car Garage 22'9" x 22'0"

50'4"

Main Level Floor Plan

Copyright by designer/architect.

60'

Plan #131023

Dimensions: 78'8" W x 36'2" D
Levels: 2
Square Footage: 2,460
Main Level Sq. Ft.: 1,377
Upper Level Sq. Ft.: 1,083
Bedrooms: 4
Bathrooms: 3½
Foundation: Crawl space, slab, or basement
Materials List Available: Yes
Price Category: F

You'll love the modern floor plan inside this traditional two-story home, with its attractive facade.

Features:

• Ceiling Height: 8 ft.

• Living Room: The windows on three sides of this room make it bright and sunny. Choose the optional fireplace for cozy winter days and the wet bar for elegant entertaining.

• Family Room: Overlooking the rear deck, this spacious family room features a fireplace and a skylight.

• Dining Room: The convenient placement of this large room lets guests flow into it from the living room and allows easy to access from the kitchen.

• Kitchen: The island cooktop and built-in desk make this space both modern and practical.

Rear Elevation

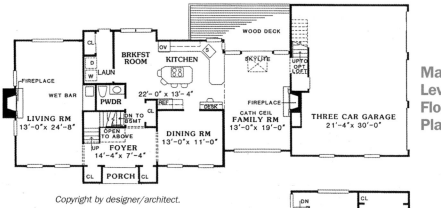

Main Level Floor Plan

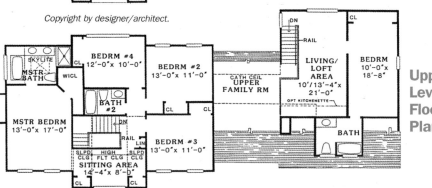

Upper Level Floor Plan

Plan #121021

Dimensions: 46' W x 48' D

Levels: 2

Square Footage: 2,270

Main Level Sq. Ft.: 1,150

Upper Level Sq. Ft.: 1,120

Bedrooms: 4

Bathrooms: 2½

Foundation: Basement

Materials List Available: Yes

Price Category: E

This home, as shown in the photograph, may differ from the actual blueprints. For more detailed information, please check the floor plans carefully.

Images provided by designer/architect.

With its wraparound porch, this home evokes the charm of a traditional home.

Features:

• Ceiling Height: 8 ft.

• Foyer: The dramatic two-story entry enjoys views of the formal dining room and great room. A second floor balcony overlooks the entry and a plant shelf.

• Formal Dining Room: This gracious room is perfect for family holiday gatherings and for more formal dinner parties.

• Great Room: All the family will want to gather in this comfortable, informal room which features bay windows, an entertainment center, and a see-through fireplace.

• Breakfast Area: Conveniently located just off the great room, the bayed breakfast area features a built-in desk for household bills and access to the backyard.

• Kitchen: An island is the centerpiece of this kitchen. Its intelligent design makes food preparation a pleasure.

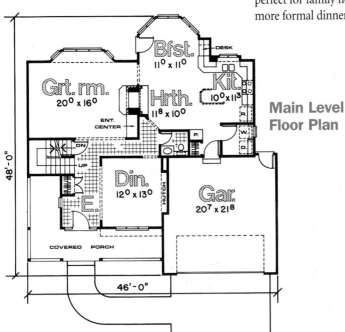

Main Level Floor Plan

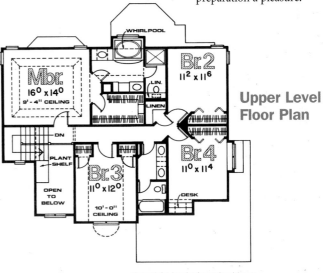

Upper Level Floor Plan

Copyright by designer/architect.

Main Level Floor Plan

- Dressing
- Breakfast 14' x 11'2"
- Great Room 16' x 19'6"
- Hearth Room 17' x 14'10"
- walk-in closet
- Kitchen
- Laun.
- Master Bedroom 14' x 14'1"
- Foyer
- Porch
- Dining Room 12' x 13'10"
- Two-car Garage 21' x 20'4"
- Sitting Area 11'2" x 9'4"

Main Level Floor Plan

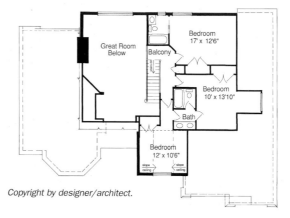

- Great Room Below
- Balcony
- Bedroom 17' x 12'6"
- Bedroom 10' x 13'10"
- Bath
- Bedroom 12' x 10'6"
- slope ceiling

Upper Level Floor Plan

Copyright by designer/architect.

Plan #161025

Dimensions: 63'4" W x 48' D

Levels: 2

Square Footage: 2,738

Main Level Sq. Ft.: 1,915

Upper Level Sq. Ft.: 823

Bedrooms: 4

Bathrooms: 3½

Foundation: Basement

Materials List Available: No

Price Category: F

Images provided by designer/architect.

This home, as shown in the photograph, may differ from the actual blueprints. For more detailed information, please check the floor plans carefully.

Plan #141028

Dimensions: 48' W x 36'4" D

Levels: 2

Square Footage: 2,215

Main Level Sq. Ft.: 1,075

Upper Level Sq. Ft.: 1,140

Bedrooms: 4

Bathrooms: 3

Foundation: Basement

Materials List Available: Yes

Price Category: E

Images provided by designer/architect.

This home, as shown in the photograph, may differ from the actual blueprints. For more detailed information, please check the floor plans carefully.

Main Level Floor Plan

- Patio / Sundeck
- Bdrm.4 11^0 x 12^0
- Two Story Living 16^4 x 14^6
- Brkfst. 10^0 x 13^4
- Kitchen 9^8 x 13^4
- Bath 3
- Open Foyer 7^2 x 11^{10}
- Dining 10^8 x 12^{10}
- Double Garage 19^4 x 21^8
- Pantry
- Ref.

Upper Level Floor Plan

- Bdrm.3 11^0 x 11^0
- Open To Living Area
- Laund.
- W.D.
- Master Bdrm. 13^6 x 17^6
- Bath 2
- Computer Station
- Opt. Plant Shelf Above
- Open To Foyer
- Bdrm.2 10^8 x 11^0
- M.Bath
- M.Clos.
- Low Storage

Copyright by designer/architect.

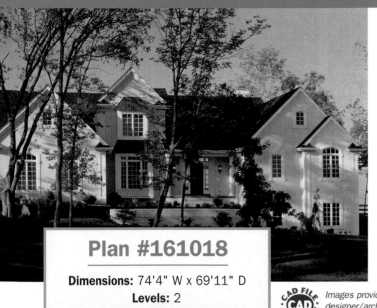

Upper Level Floor Plan

Copyright by designer/architect.

Bedroom 13' x 13'11"

Bath

Bonus Room 16'8" x 15

Balcony

Bedroom 13' x 13'4"

Great Room Below

949 Sq. Ft.

Main Level Floor Plan

Porch

Patio

Breakfast 13' x 10'5"

Laun.

Hall

Bath

Kitchen 17' x 13'2"

Garage 21'10" x 32'4"

Great Room 19'4" x 17'9"

Master Bedroom 13'8" x 17'9"

Dining Room 13' x 12'9"

Foyer

Hall

Bath

Porch

Bath

Dressing

69'-11"

74'-4"

2192 Sq. Ft.

CAD FILE AVAILABLE

Images provided by designer/architect.

Rear View

Plan #161018

Dimensions: 74'4" W x 69'11" D
Levels: 2
Square Footage: 2,816
+ 325 Sq. Ft. bonus room
Main Level Sq. Ft.: 2,231
Upper Level Sq. Ft.: 624
Bedrooms: 3
Bathrooms: 3 full, 2 half
Foundation: Basement
Materials List Available: No
Price Category: F

Plan #151534

Dimensions: 37'8" W x 71'6" D
Levels: 2
Square Footage: 2,237
Main Level Sq. Ft.: 1,708
Upper Level Sq. Ft.: 529
Bedrooms: 3
Bathrooms: 2½
Foundation: Crawl space or slab
CompleteCost List Available: Yes
Price Category: E

Images provided by designer/architect.

CAD FILE AVAILABLE

37'-8"

M. BATH

GARAGE 18'-4" X 19'-6"

MASTER SUITE 16'-8" X 14'-10"

LAU.

GRILLING PORCH

BREAKFAST ROOM 12'-4" X 12'-0"

GREAT RM. 16'-0" X 16'-8"

KITCHEN 13'-6" X 12'-0"

WET BAR

PANTRY

OFFICE / STUDY 13'-0" X 10'-0"

FOYER 7'-6" X 11'-0"

DINING 13'-2" X 12'-0"

COVERED PORCH 24'-4" X 8'-0"

71'-6"

Main Level Floor Plan

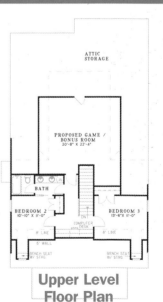

ATTIC STORAGE

PROPOSED GAME / BONUS ROOM 20'-8" X 22'-4"

BATH

BEDROOM 2 10'-10" X 11'-0"

BEDROOM 3 13'-6" X 11'-0"

COMPUTER DESK

Upper Level Floor Plan

Copyright by designer/architect.

Front View

Plan #131022

Dimensions: 54'8" W x 43' D

Levels: 2

Square Footage: 2,092

Main Level Sq. Ft.: 1,152

Upper Level Sq. Ft.: 940

Bedrooms: 4

Bathrooms: 2½

Foundation: Crawl space, slab, or basement

Materials List Available: Yes

Price Category: E

This home, as shown in the photograph, may differ from the actual blueprints. For more detailed information, please check the floor plans carefully.

Images provided by designer/architect.

You'll love the way this charming home reminds you of an old-fashioned farmhouse.

Features:

• Ceiling Height: 8 ft.

• Living Room: This large living room can be used as guest quarters when the need arises.

• Dining Room: This bayed, informal room is large enough for all your dining and entertaining needs. It could also double as an office or den.

• Garage: An expandable loft over the garage offers an ideal playroom or fourth bedroom.

Rear Elevation

Main Level Floor Plan

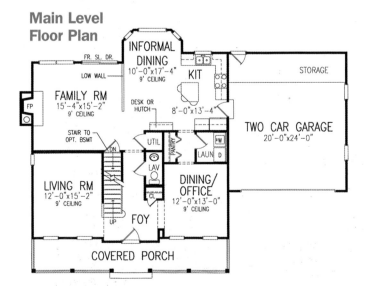

Upper Level Floor Plan

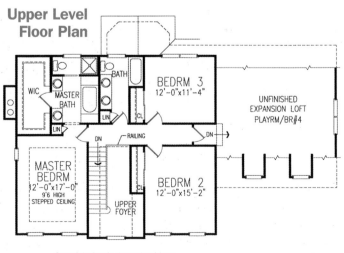

Copyright by designer/architect.

Plan #401012

Dimensions: 48' W x 52'6" D
Levels: 2
Square Footage: 2,301
Main Level Sq. Ft.: 1,180
Upper Level Sq. Ft.: 1,121
Bedrooms: 3-4
Bathrooms: 2½
Foundation: Basement
Materials List Available: Yes
Price Category: E

A turret roof, prominent bay window, and wraparound veranda designate this four bedroom design as classic Victorian. The plans include two second-level layouts – one with four bedrooms or one with three bedrooms and a vaulted ceiling over the family room.

Features:

- **Living Room:** This formal room has windows that overlook the veranda.

- **Family Room:** This gathering space includes a fireplace for atmosphere.

- **Kitchen:** This U-shaped kitchen has a sunny breakfast bay; you'll find a half-bath and a laundry room in the service area that leads to the two-car garage.

- **Master Suite:** This lavish area has an octagonal tray ceiling in the sitting room, a walk-in closet, and a private bath with a colonnaded whirlpool spa and separate shower.

Images provided by designer/architect.

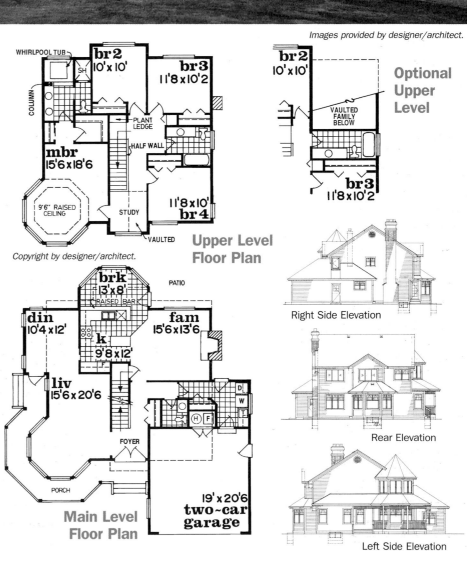

Copyright by designer/architect.

Upper Level Floor Plan

Optional Upper Level

Main Level Floor Plan

Right Side Elevation

Rear Elevation

Left Side Elevation

Plan #181063

Dimensions: 55' W x 41' D
Levels: 2
Square Footage: 2,037
Main Level Sq. Ft.: 1,347
Upper Level Sq. Ft.: 690
Bedrooms: 4
Bathrooms: 2
Foundation: Full basement
Materials List Available: Yes
Price Category: D

Quaint brick and stone, plus deeply pitched rooflines, create the storybook aura folks fall for when they see this home, but it's the serenely versatile interior layout that captures their hearts.

Features:

• Family Room: The floor plan is configured to bring a panoramic view to nearly every room, beginning with this room, with its fireplace and towering cathedral ceiling.

• Kitchen: This kitchen, with its crowd-pleasing island, has an eye on the outdoors. It also has all the counter and storage space a cook would want, plus a lunch counter with comfy seats and multiple windows to bring in the breeze.

• Bedrooms: Downstairs, you'll find the master bedroom, with its adjoining master bath. Upstairs, three uniquely shaped bedrooms, styled with clever nooks and windows to dream by, easily share a large bathroom.

• Mezzanine: This sweeping mezzanine overlooks the open living and dining rooms.

Images provided by designer/architect.

This home, as shown in the photograph, may differ from the actual blueprints. For more detailed information, please check the floor plans carefully.

Front View

Living Room

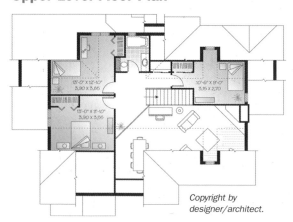

Main Level Floor Plan

Upper Level Floor Plan

Copyright by designer/architect.

Master Bath

Plan #401003

Dimensions: 64'6" W x 47' D
Levels: 2
Square Footage: 2,582
Main Level Sq. Ft.: 1,291
Upper Level Sq. Ft.: 1,291
Bedrooms: 4
Bathrooms: 3
Foundation: Basement
Materials List Available: Yes
Price Category: E

CAD FILE AVAILABLE

This home has a traditional feel, but it is filled with up-to-date amenities.

Features:

- Den: This is a versatile area; use it as a home office or a quiet room to get away from it all. Access to a full bathroom opens up the possibilities of the space as an extra bedroom.

- Kitchen: The light-filled breakfast nook is located just off this L-shaped kitchen, which features an island work center. Plenty of cabinets and counter space make the space very functional.

- Master Suite: This master suite is complete with a private sitting area and a walk-in closet. The master bath boasts a whirlpool tub and a bay window.

- Secondary Bedrooms: Three additional bedrooms located on the upper level round out this floor plan. Bedroom 4 features a walk-in closet.

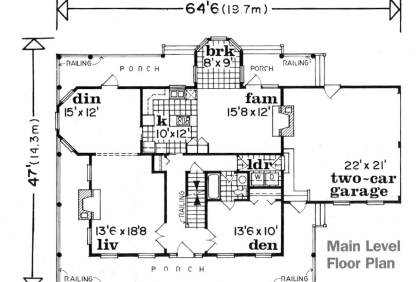

Main Level Floor Plan

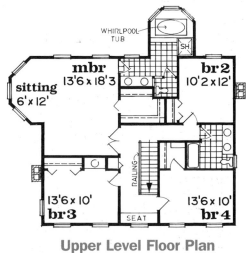

Upper Level Floor Plan

Copyright by designer/architect.

Main Level Floor Plan

Breakfast 11'4" x 10'4"

Family Room 17'5" x 15'4"

Bath

Laun. 11'8" x 8'8"

Kitchen 15'6" x 10'6"

Two-car Garage 19'8" x 23' 0"

Living Room 13'6" x 14'2"

Dining Room 11'6" x 13'6" to 15'6"

Foyer

Porch

arched ceiling

high ceiling

54'6"

41'10"

Copyright by designer/architect.

Upper Level Floor Plan

Bedroom 11'6" x 12'0"

Master Bedroom 15'0" x 14'5"

walk-in closet

Bedroom 11'8" x 11'0"

Bath

Balcony

Bath

stairs dn

Bedroom 11'4" x 13'6"

Foyer Below

plant shelf

slope ceiling

Plan #161019

Dimensions: 54'6" D x 41'10" W

Levels: 2

Square Footage: 2,428

Main Level Sq. Ft.: 1,309

Upper Level Sq. Ft.: 1,119

Bedrooms: 4

Bathrooms: 2½

Foundation: Basement

Materials List Available: No

Price Category: E

Images provided by designer/architect.

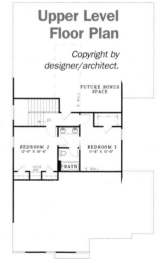

Upper Level Floor Plan

Copyright by designer/architect.

FUTURE BONUS SPACE

BEDROOM 2 12'-0" x 14'-4"

BEDROOM 3 11'-8" x 12'-0"

BATH

38'-10"

M. BATH

GARAGE 21'-0" x 20'-0"

W.I.C.

MASTER SUITE 16'-10" x 22'-2"

LAU.

BREAKFAST ROOM 11'-5" x 12'-0"

GRILLING PORCH 9'-0" x 20'-0"

COURT YARD PATIO

KITCHEN 12'-4" x 12'-0"

DINING 11'-8" x 14'-0"

FOYER 7'-4" x 16'-3"

GREAT ROOM 17'-6" x 18'-0"

COVERED PORCH 22'-0" x 8'-0"

70'-4"

Main Level Floor Plan

Plan #151530

Dimensions: 38'10" W x 70'4" D

Levels: 2

Square Footage: 2,146

Main Level Sq. Ft.: 1,654

Upper Level Sq. Ft.: 492

Bedrooms: 3

Bathrooms: 2½

Foundation: Crawl space or slab

CompleteCost List Available: Yes

Price Category: D

Images provided by designer/architect.

CAD FILE AVAILABLE

Front View

Main Level Floor Plan

Copyright by designer/architect.

Dining 13' x 15'
Breakfast 15'2" x 9'
Great Room 16' x 23'10"
Kitchen 16'6" x 9'
Dressing
walk-in closet
Laun.
Hall
Raised Foyer
Master Bedroom 13'2" x 16'
Two-car Garage 22' x 22'
Porch

Upper Level Floor Plan

Images provided by designer/architect.

Rear View

Bedroom 12'10" x 11'6"
Bedroom 11' x 11'6"
Bath
skylight
Great Room Below
Balcony
walk-in closet
Bonus Room 11' x 11'11"
skylight

Plan #161034

Dimensions: 56' W x 53' D
Levels: 2
Square Footage: 2,156
Main Level Sq. Ft.: 1,605
Upper Level Sq. Ft.: 551
Bedrooms: 3
Bathrooms: 2½
Foundation: Basement
Materials List Available: No
Price Category: D

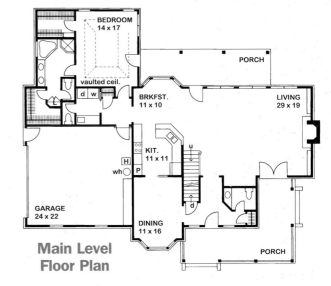

BEDROOM 14 x 17
vaulted ceil.
PORCH
BRKFST. 11 x 10
LIVING 29 x 19
KIT. 11 x 11
wh
P
GARAGE 24 x 22
DINING 11 x 16
PORCH

Main Level Floor Plan

Plan #381175

Dimensions: 66' W x 58' D
Levels: 2
Square Footage: 2,765
Main Level Sq. Ft.: 1,725
Upper Level Sq. Ft.: 1,040
Bedrooms: 4
Bathrooms: 3½
Foundation: Basement
Material List Available: Yes
Price Category: F

Images provided by designer/architect.

storage
BEDROOM 11 x 11
BEDROOM 11 x 11
stor.
UNFINISHED 405 sq. ft.
attic
BEDROOM 11 x 15
REC ROOM 12 x 19

Upper Level Floor Plan

Copyright by designer/architect.

Plan #181078

Dimensions: 58' W x 40' D
Levels: 2
Square Footage: 2,292
Main Level Sq. Ft.: 1,266
Upper Level Sq. Ft.: 1,026
Bedrooms: 4
Bathrooms: 2½
Foundation: Full basement
Materials List Available: Yes
Price Category: E

This two-story home will be a fine addition to any neighborhood.

Features:

• **Living Room:** This gathering area is open to the kitchen and will warm you with its cozy fireplace.

• **Kitchen:** This island kitchen has a raised bar that looks into the living room, and it provides access to the rear porch.

• **Master Suite:** This private area has a cozy fireplace in the sleeping area. The master bath features dual vanities, a walk-in closet, and a large tub.

• **Bedrooms:** The two additional bedrooms are located upstairs with the master suite and share the Jack-and-Jill bathroom.

Images provided by designer/architect.

This home, as shown in the photograph, may differ from the actual blueprints. For more detailed information, please check the floor plans carefully.

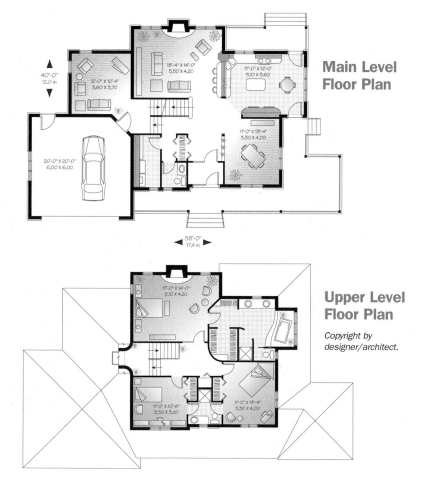

Main Level Floor Plan

Upper Level Floor Plan

Copyright by designer/architect.

Plan #401001

Dimensions: 56' W x 43'4" D
Levels: 2
Square Footage: 2,071
Main Level Sq. Ft.: 1,204
Upper Level Sq. Ft.: 867
Bedrooms: 3
Bathrooms: 2½
Foundation: Basement
Materials List Available: Yes
Price Category: D

This transitional design carries the best of both worlds—popular details of both traditional and contemporary architecture. The high rooflines allow for dramatic full-height windows and vaulted ceilings in the formal areas.

CAD FILE AVAILABLE

Features:

- **Open Plan:** The open casual areas include the hearth-warmed family room, bayed breakfast nook, and island kitchen.

- **Den:** Located just off the foyer, this room is a well-appreciated haven for quiet time. Note the half-bath just beyond the den.

- **Master Suite:** This area has two walk-in closets and a full bath with a separate shower and tub.

- **Bedrooms:** Three bedrooms occupy the second floor and include two family bedrooms—one with a vaulted ceiling.

- **Utility Areas:** A laundry alcove leads to the two-car garage with extra storage space.

Rear Elevation

Left Side Elevation

Right Side Elevation

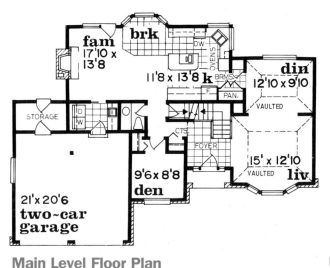

Main Level Floor Plan

Upper Level Floor Plan

Plan #441033

Dimensions: 67' W x 68' D
Levels: 2
Square Footage: 2,986
Main Level Sq. Ft.: 2,162
Upper Level Sq. Ft.: 824
Bedrooms: 3
Bathrooms: 2½
Foundation: Crawl space;
slab or basement for fee
Materials List Available: No
Price Category: F

Images provided by designer/architect.

This home, as shown in the photograph, may differ from the actual blueprints. For more detailed information, please check the floor plans carefully.

Dramatic design coupled with elegant architectural detailing brings this comfortable home a lovely facade.

Features:

- **Great Room:** This room is two stories tall; the fireplace is flanked by built-ins.

- **Dining Room:** The interior was specifically created for family lifestyles. This formal room, accented with columns, is also graced by the butler's pantry, which connects it to the kitchen for convenience.

- **Master Suite:** The left wing is dedicated to this suite. The extensive master bath, with spa tub, separate shower, and walk-in closet, complements the master salon, which features a tray ceiling and large window over looking the rear yard.

- **Upper Level:** The two family bedrooms are on the second floor; they share the full bathroom with double sinks. The games room opens through double doors just off the loft library.

Main Level Floor Plan

Upper Level Floor Plan

Copyright by designer/architect.

Rear Elevation

Front View

Plan #391062

Dimensions: 58'4" W x 53' D
Levels: 2
Square Footage: 2,525
Main Level Sq. Ft.: 1,409
Upper Level Sq. Ft.: 1,116
Bedrooms: 3
Bathrooms: 2½
Foundation: Crawl space, slab, or basement
Material List Available: Yes
Price Category: E

Images provided by designer/architect.

You'll never get bored with the rooms in this charming three-bedroom Victorian.

Features:

- **Foyer:** This foyer serves as the link between the living room and parlor, separating them and allowing each to have its own identity.

- **Dining Room:** In this room, with its hexagonal recessed ceiling, you can enjoy your after-dinner coffee while watching the kids playing on the deck. Because it is open to the living room, it is a great setting for parties.

- **Breakfast Room:** You can eat in this sunny breakfast room, which is just off the island kitchen. Step out onto the optional rear deck to enjoy the outdoors.

- **Master Suite:** You'll love this master suite's bump-out window and large walk-in closets. The master bath boasts dual sinks and a separate shower.

Rear View

Main Level Floor Plan

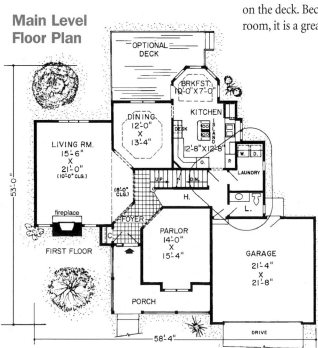

Crawl Space/Slab Option Floor Plan

Copyright by designer/architect.

Upper Level Floor Plan

Today's Fireplace Technology

Handsome and romantic, but drafty. Thirty years ago, you might have described a traditional fireplace in this way. But that was before technological advancements finally made fireplaces more efficient. Now, not only can you expect your fireplace to provide ambiance and warmth, you can relax knowing that your energy dollars aren't going up in smoke. Over the centuries, people had tried to improve the efficiency of the fireplace so that it would generate the maximum heat possible from the wood consumed. But real strides didn't come until the energy crisis of the early 1970s. That's when designers of fireplaces and stoves introduced some significant innovations. Today, fireplaces are not only more efficient, but cleaner and easier to use.

The traditional fireplace is an all-masonry construction, consisting of only bricks and mortar. However, new constructions and reconstructions of masonry fireplaces often include either a metal or a ceramic firebox. This type of firebox has double walls. The space between these walls is where cool air heats up after being drawn in through openings near the floor of the room. The warm air exits through openings near the top of the firebox. Although a metal firebox is more efficient than an all-masonry firebox, it doesn't radiate heat very effectively, and the heat from the fireplace is distributed by convection—that is, the circulation of warmed air. This im–provement in heating capacity comes from the warm air emitted by the upper openings. But that doesn't keep your feet toasty

on a cold winter's night—remember, warm air rises.

A more recent development is the ceramic firebox, which is engineered from modern materials such as the type used in kilns. Fires in ceramic fireboxes burn hotter, cleaner, and more efficiently than in all-masonry or metal fireboxes. The main reason is that the back and the walls of a ceramic firebox absorb, retain, and reflect heat effectively. This means that during the time the fire is blazing, more heat radiates into the room than with the other fireboxes. Heat radiation is boosted by the fact that most ceramic units are made with

The warm glow of a realistic-looking modern zero-clearance gas fire, below, can make the hearth the heart of any room in the house.

Zero-Clearance Fireplace

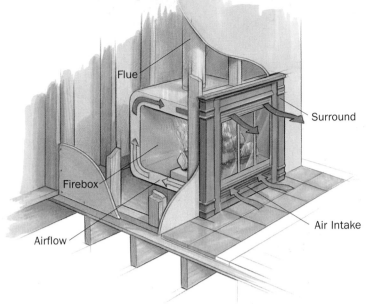

Flue

Surround

Firebox

Air Intake

Airflow

Traditional Masonry Fireplace

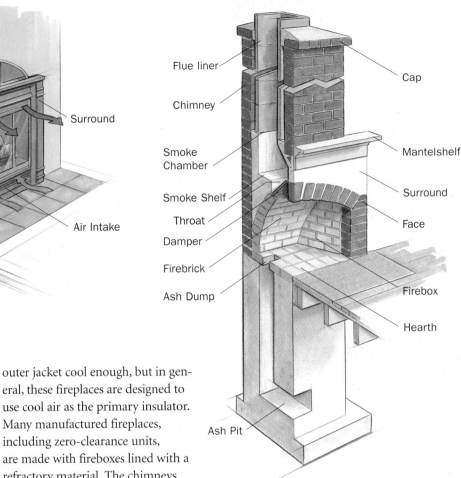

Flue liner

Chimney

Smoke Chamber

Smoke Shelf

Throat

Damper

Firebrick

Ash Dump

Ash Pit

Cap

Mantelshelf

Surround

Face

Firebox

Hearth

thick walls, and so the fire itself is not set as deeply into the hearth as it is with all-masonry or metal fireboxes. As a bonus, because heat is absorbed and retained by the material, the firebox actually radiates a significant amount of heat many hours after the fire has died down. By contrast, a metal firebox cools quickly once the heat source goes out.

In this type of efficient fireplace construction, a metal firebox is usually less expensive than a ceramic one, but the metal does break down over time, in a process professionals refer to as burnout. In addition, an air-circulating metal firebox can only be installed in masonry constructions that are built with ports for the intake of cool air and the discharge of warmed air, or in masonry fireplaces in which such ports can be added. On the other hand, ceramic fireboxes can be installed in any type of masonry fireplace and are not subject to burnout.

Manufactured Fireplaces

The metal fireplaces that are made today can be zero-clearance or freestanding. The zero-clearance units are so named because they can be installed safely against combustible surfaces such as wood. Any of a number of methods are used to keep the

outer jacket cool enough, but in general, these fireplaces are designed to use cool air as the primary insulator. Many manufactured fireplaces, including zero-clearance units, are made with fireboxes lined with a refractory material. The chimneys are also made of metal, and a variety of designs use noncombustible material or air as insulation to keep the outer surface at a safe temperature.

New-technology and traditional fireplaces are shown above. Woodstove-like inserts, below and opposite, make fireplaces more efficient.

The Advantages of a Manufactured Unit

There are some important pluses to choosing a zero-clearance manufactured fireplace. First is the price, which is relatively low, and second is the easy and quick installation. Also, these units are lightweight and can be installed over almost any type of flooring, including wood. This means they do not need elaborate foundations, which is another cost-saver. Manufactured fireplaces are also extremely efficient, and many are designed to provide both radiated heat from the firebox and convection heat from ducting.

Manufactured freestanding fireplaces are, in effect, stoves. They are available in an array of colors, finishes, shapes, and sizes. Like zero-clearance factory-built fireplaces, freestanding models are lightweight, offering the same advantages: no need for heavy masonry or additional reinforcement of flooring. And you have a choice of either a wood-burning or gas-powered unit. Heat efficiency is maximized because, in addition to the firebox, the chimney and all sides of the unit radiate heat into the room. Freestanding units may be the least expensive option because installation requires only a chimney hole and, depending on the type of flooring, a noncombustible pad. A major disadvantage is the space required for placement, because you cannot install most of these units near a combustible wall. Also, a freestanding fireplace is probably not the best choice for families with young children because so much heat is radiated from the exposed surfaces.

Hybrids

If you're looking for a way to get improved efficiency from a masonry fireplace, consider a gas insert (actually a prefabricated firebox equipped with gas logs). You can purchase either a venting insert or one that's nonventing. But be prepared to pay $1,500 to several thousand dollars for the unit in addition to the cost of installation. For a fraction of that amount you can simply replace real wood logs with ceramic logs powered by gas. Like inserts, these logs may or may not require venting. Consult an experienced plumber or heating contractor, and remember that once you convert to gas you cannot burn wood.

Improving a masonry fireplace on the inside by installing a metal firebox might also be an inspiration to think of the fireplace and mantel in a new design way. Pairing two or more finishing materials, such as metal and masonry, can make your fireplace a hybrid in more than one way. For example, combine a stone base with a metal hood and chimney to create a custom-designed fireplace that works as a room divider in a large space. The design options in terms of materials and technology are seemingly endless.

If you have plans for building an innovative custom design, carefully review them with an expert in fireplace construction and maintenance to make sure you're not doing something hazardous. Also, don't forget to check with your local building inspector so that you don't waste time and money on a project that may not comply with codes and regulations set forth where you live.

Enhancing the Basics

You can improve the efficiency of any manufactured fireplace, and of masonry and hybrid constructions as well, with a few extras. In a masonry fireplace, a device commonly referred to as a fresh-air intake accessory or an outside air kit may improve performance. A fresh-air accessory makes use of outside air instead of heated room air for combustion, thus improving the fireplace's efficiency. There is another way to make your fireplace more efficient that isn't high tech at all, however. Simply replace the traditional grate or firebasket with a superior design—one that provides greater air circulation and allows a better placement of logs. Another type, a heat-exchanger grate, works with a fan. The device draws in the room's air, reheats it quickly, and then forces it back into the room.

Capitalizing on Technology

Wood is the traditional fuel for a fireplace, and today's manufactured fireplaces offer designs that make the most of your cord of hardwood. However, wood is not the only fuel option. In fact, in some places, it's not an option at all. There are manufactured units that offer a choice of natural gas or propane as a fuel source, which heats ceramic logs designed to realistically simulate wood. The fire, complete with glowing embers, is often difficult to distinguish from one burning real wood.

In some areas of the country, fireplace emission regulations have become strict—in places such as much of Colorado and parts of Nevada and California so strict that new construction of wood-burning fireplaces has been outlawed. In these areas, manufactured units using alternative fuels allow homeowners all the benefits of a wood-burning fireplace without the adverse impact on air quality.

Most of the units available today also offer a variety of amenities, including built-in thermostatic control and remote-control devices for turning the fire on and off and regulating heat output.

The Importance of a Clean Sweep

Finally, one of the most important factors in the use of a fireplace or stove is the regular inspection and cleaning of the stovepipe, flue, and chimney. To understand why, remember that the burning of wood results in the combustion of solids as well as combustible gases. However, not everything that goes into the firebox is burned, no matter how efficient the appliance. One of the by-products of wood burning is the dark brown or black tar called creosote, a flammable substance that sticks to the linings of chimney flues.

Although the burning temperature of creosote is high, it can ignite and cause a chimney fire. It may be brief and without apparent damage, but a chimney fire may also be prolonged or intense and result in significant fire and smoke damage or, at worst, the loss of your home if the creosote buildup is great enough. Creosote causes other problems, too. It decreases the inside diameter of stovepipes and flues, causing slower burning. This makes burning less efficient and contributes to further deposits of creosote. In addition, because creosote is acidic, it corrodes mortar, metal, and eventually even stainless-steel and ceramic chimney liners.

To prevent costly and dangerous creosote buildup, have your chimney professionally cleaned by a qualified chimney sweep. How often depends on the amount of creosote deposited during the burning season, and this, in turn, depends largely on how and what kind of wood you burn. Professional sweeps usually recommend at least annual cleaning. Depending on where you live, you'll spend about $150, perhaps less, for a cleaning.

You'll enjoy a warm glow at the highest efficiency if you use a glass-front wood-burning or gas-fueled, right, fireplace insert.

Fireside Arrangements

Creating an attractive, comfortable setting around a fireplace should be easy. Who doesn't like the cozy ambiance of relaxing in front of a fire? But there are times when the presence of a fireplace in a room poses problems with the layout. A fireplace can take up considerable floor and wall space, and like any other permanent feature or built-in piece of furniture, its size or position can limit the design possibilities.

The Fireplace and the Space

What is the room's size and shape—large, small, square, long and narrow, L-shaped? Where is the fireplace located—in the center of a wall, to the side, or in a corner? What other permanent features, such as windows, doors, bookcases, or media units, will you have to work with in your arrangement? How much clearance can you allow around the furniture for easy passage? How close do you want to be to the fire? Think of these questions as you consider the design basics presented below.

Scale and Proportion. Remember the importance of spatial relationships. For example, a fireplace may seem large in a room with a low ceiling; conversely, it may appear small in a room with a vaulted ceiling. Size is relative. Applied to objects on the mantel or the wall above the fireplace, correct scale and proportion happen when the objects are the appropriate size for the wall or the fireplace.

Balance. Sometimes the architectural features of a mantel or surround are so strong, you'll have to match them with furnishings of equal visual weight. Or they may be so ornate or plain that you'll have to play them up or tone them down to make them work with the rest of the decor. That's balance. But balance also refers to arrangements: symmetrical, asymmetrical, and radial.

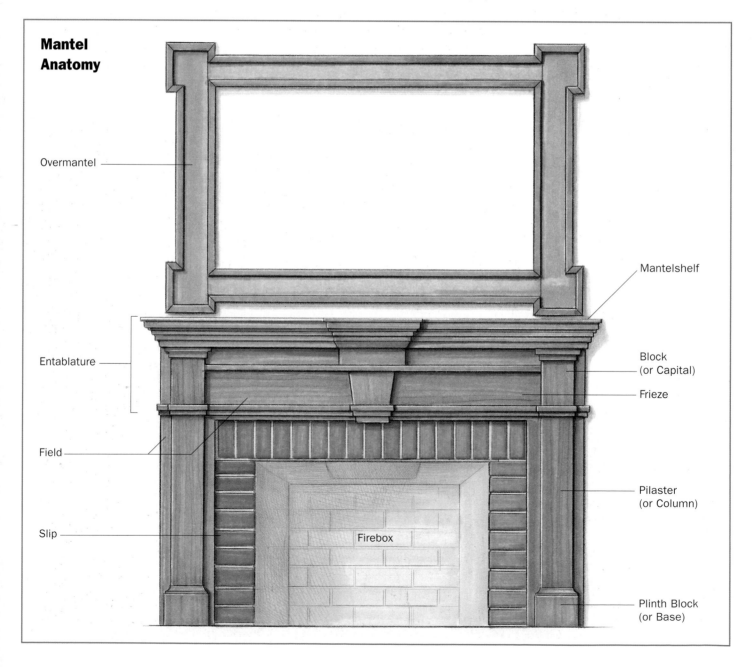

Mantel Anatomy

Overmantel

Mantelshelf

Entablature

Block (or Capital)

Frieze

Field

Pilaster (or Column)

Slip

Firebox

Plinth Block (or Base)

Line. Shape depends on line. Different types of lines suggest various qualities. Pay attention to the lines when you're creating arrangements and relationships among objects. Some lines are inherent in a room or an architectural feature, but you can modify them. For example: vertical lines are stately and dignified, which is just the look you want for your fireplace, but unfortunately, it's rather wide and squat instead. Solution? Create an arrangement above the fireplace that extends high on the wall, or hang a tall mirror or frame over than mantel.

What if the fireplace is too tall? Does it overwhelm the rest of the furniture? Add horizontal lines by moving seating pieces farther apart to the right and left of the hearth. Install wall art on the sides of the fireplace.

If the room is boxy, avoid grouping pieces at right angles to the fireplace and each other. Instead, de-emphasize the boxy shape by placing them on the diagonal to open the square. Use upholstered pieces with rounded arms or curvaceous cushions, legs, or frames. Create a radial arrangement. With the hearth as the central point, create a semicircular hub of furnishings that include seating and a small table or two.

Rhythm. Keep the eye moving at a measured pace by repeating motifs, colors, or shapes. For example, you might pick up the color from a tiled surround to use as an accent color in fabrics on upholstered pieces, curtains, pillows, throws, or other decorative accessories. Or repeat architectural features of the fireplace with other similar elements in the room, such as molding or other woodwork details.

Variety. Don't go overboard trying to match everything exactly. The most interesting rooms and arrangements mix objects of different sizes, shapes, lines, and sometimes even styles (as long as they are compatible).

Harmony. Create harmony among all of the parts of your design by connecting all of the elements either by color or motif. For example, in a display of family photos the frames may all be different shapes, styles, and heights, but because each one is made of brass, the overall appearance looks harmonious. Or you could assemble a wall vignette of frames over the fireplace, all different in finish but tied together by the subject matter of each one—all landscapes, for example, or all pink cabbage roses. Unifying diverse items in this way creates a finished-looking scheme.

How to Make a Hinged Fireboard

You'll need a hinged three-panel wooden fireplace screen, which you can buy or make. If you buy one, you'll have to sand and prime it thoroughly before applying the new finish over the existing one. Ideally, it's best to work on unfinished wood.

The screen used for this project features two 9 x 36-inch side panels and one 26 x 36-inch center panel that were cut from a ¾-inch-thick sheet of plywood. If you aren't handy with a circular saw or table saw, ask your local lumber supplier to cut the panels to your desired dimensions. Attach the side and center panels with two-way (piano) hinges, which are easy to install. Simply mark their location along the inside edges of the panel pieces, drill pilot holes, and then screw the hinges into place. To finish, prime the boards; then paint or stencil a design onto each panel. For Victorian authenticity, decoupage the panels with a motif cut out of a piece of fabric, wallpaper, old greeting cards, or postcards.

Symmetrical versus Asymmetrical Arrangements

If you like the symmetry of classic design, balance your arranged pieces accordingly. For example, position two sofas or love seats of the same size perpendicular to the fireplace and exactly opposite each other. Or place a single sofa parallel with the fireplace, with two chairs opposite one another and equidistant from both the sofa and the hearth. Try out a low coffee table or an oversize ottoman in the center of the arrangement. Leave the peripheral areas outside the main grouping for creating small impromptu conversation areas during parties and gatherings or to accommodate a modest dining area or home-office station.

If your design sense is less formal or contemporary, try an asymmetrical grouping in front of the fire. Turn seating pieces at a 45-degree angle from the hearth.

In a large open space, locate seating not directly in front of the hearth but slightly off to the side. Counterbalance the arrangement with a large table and chairs, a hutch, bookcases, or any element of relatively equal weight. This layout works especially well when the ceiling is vaulted (as most great rooms are) or when the hearth is massive. In many contemporary homes, especially where there is a zero-clearance unit, the fireplace is not on an outside wall, nor is it necessarily in a central location. This means you can put the fireplace almost anywhere.

Comfortable Arrangements

You may want an intimate environment in front of the fire, but the room is so large that it feels and looks impersonal. Large rooms afford lots of leeway for arranging, but people often make the mistake of pushing all of the furniture against the walls. If that's what you're doing, pull the major seating pieces closer together and near the fire, keeping a distance of only 4 to 10 feet between sofas and chairs. For the most comfortable result, create one or more small groupings that can accommodate up to four to six people in different areas of the room.

Modular Seating. Instead of a standard sofa and chairs, consider the convenience of modular seating, too, which comes in any number of armless and single-arm end pieces. The advantage of these separate upholstered units is that you can easily add, take away, or rearrange the modules to suit any of your layout or seating needs. Create an L or a U arrangement in front of the fire; subtract pieces, moving one or two outside of the area for an intimate

A raised hearth, above, reinforces the idea of a fireplace as a focal point, and it provides seating near the fire. Place other furniture to the sides of the hearth.

grouping. Use an area rug to further define the space. Or put the pieces together to make one large arrangement in any configuration. Versatile furnishings such as an ottoman with a hinged top or an antique trunk can double as seating, a low table, or storage.

A Quick Guide to Buying Firewood

How much wood you need to buy in a season depends on a number of factors, but there are three major variables: how often and how long you burn fires; the efficiency of your fireplace or stove; and the type of wood you burn. In general, hard, dense woods are ideal for fuel. As a rule of thumb, the wood from deciduous trees is best. (Deciduous trees are those that shed their leaves annually.) These include oak, maple, walnut, birch, beech, ash, and the wood from fruit trees such as cherry and apple.

Avoid burning wood from evergreens—those cone-bearing (coniferous) trees with needles instead of leaves. The wood of coniferous trees is soft and it will burn faster, so a greater volume of wood will be consumed per hour compared with hardwood. A greater problem with softwoods, however, is the resin content. Resin is the gummy substance that's used in the manufacture of some wood stains and shellacs, and when resin is burned it gives off a byproduct called creosote. Creosote, which is flammable, accumulates in flues and chimneys, and this buildup represents a potential fire hazard.

The wood you purchase should also be seasoned, which means that the tree should have been cut down at least six months or, preferably, a year prior to the burning of the wood. Ideally, the wood should be cut and split soon after the tree is felled, allowing for more effective drying. The moisture in unseasoned (or green) wood tends to have a cooling effect, preventing complete combustion and making it harder to keep a fire blazing. A low-burning fire also increases creosote. (It's okay to burn green wood occasionally, but make sure to use small logs or split sticks and add them to an already hot fire.)

Mantel Vignettes

A grouping of objects on your mantel can be as simple or complex as you like. To make your display lively, choose a variety of shapes and sizes. For dramatic impact, group related objects that you can link in theme or color.

Remember that a symmetrical arrangement has classical overtones and will reinforce the formality of traditional designs. Stick with similar objects: a pair of Chinese ginger jars or antique silver candlesticks arranged in mirror fashion on either side of the mantel equidistant from the center, for example. Or keep the look simple by placing a single but important object in the center; it could be a mantel clock, a floral arrangement, or some other objet d'art.

Asymmetry, on the other hand, brings a different dynamic to a mantel vignette with mismatched pieces. Try placing a large object to one side of the mantel, and then balance that piece by massing several small objects or a different type of object of similar scale on the opposite side. An example might be an arrangement of books of varying heights and sizes at one end of the mantel and a simple large vase at the other end. Or you might oppose tall thin candlesticks with one fat candle.

A simple brick wall, left, serves as a backdrop for a gleaming fireplace insert.

Plan #121078

Dimensions: 50' W x 48' D
Levels: 2
Square Footage: 2,248
Main Level Sq. Ft.: 1,568
Upper Level Sq. Ft.: 680
Bedrooms: 4
Bathrooms: 2½
Foundation: Slab
Materials List Available: Yes
Price Category: E

Images provided by designer/architect.

This home, as shown in the photograph, may differ from the actual blueprints. For more detailed information, please check the floor plans carefully.

Main Level Floor Plan

Upper Level Floor Plan

Copyright by designer/architect.

Plan #151484

Dimensions: 53'6" W x 76'10" D
Levels: 1.5
Square Footage: 2,211
Bedrooms: 3
Bathrooms: 2
Foundation: Crawl space or slab
CompleteCost List Available: Yes
Price Category: E

Images provided by designer/architect.

CAD FILE AVAILABLE

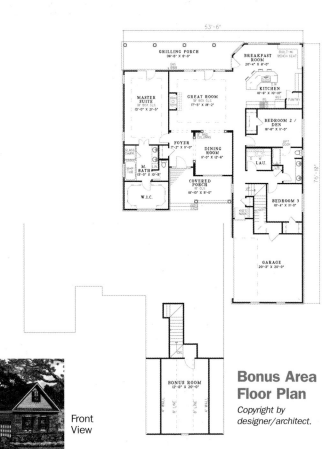

Front View

Bonus Area Floor Plan

Copyright by designer/architect.

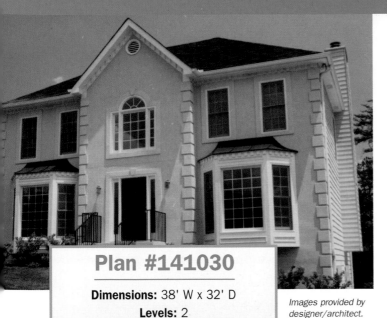

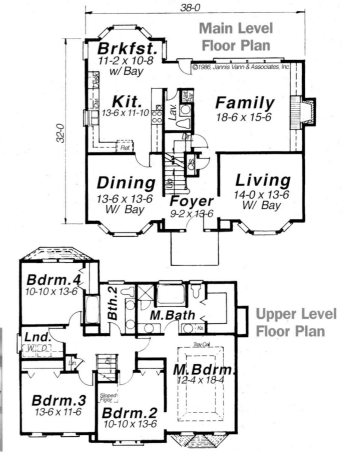

Main Level Floor Plan

Brkfst.
11-2 x 10-8
w/ Bay

©1986, Jannis Vann & Associates, Inc

Kit.
13-6 x 11-10

Family
18-6 x 15-6

Dining
13-6 x 13-6
W/ Bay

Living
14-0 x 13-6
W/ Bay

Foyer
9-2 x 13-6

38-0

32-0

Plan #141030

Dimensions: 38' W x 32' D

Levels: 2

Square Footage: 2,323

Main Level Sq. Ft.: 1,179

Upper Level Sq. Ft.: 1,144

Bedrooms: 4

Bathrooms: 2½

Foundation: Basement

Materials List Available: Yes

Price Category: E

Images provided by designer/architect.

Upper Level Floor Plan

Bdrm.4
10-10 x 13-6

Bth.2

M.Bath

Lnd.
W D

M.Bdrm.
12-4 x 18-4

Bdrm.3
13-6 x 11-6

Bdrm.2
10-10 x 13-6

Sloped Floor

Tray Ceil.

Plan #151015

Dimensions: 72'4" W x 48'4" D

Levels: 2

Square Footage: 2,789

Main Level Sq. Ft.: 1,977

Upper Level Sq. Ft.: 812

Bedrooms: 4

Bathrooms: 3

Foundation: Crawl space, slab, or basement

CompleteCost List Available: Yes

Price Category: F

Images provided by designer/architect.

CAD FILE AVAILABLE CAD

Main Level Floor Plan

72'-4"

48'-4"

MASTER BATH
17'-10" X 14'-2"

GREAT RM.
20'-6" X 17'-10"

BRKFAST RM.
12'-4" X 14'-4"

HEARTH RM.
9'-6" X 13'-4"

MEDIA CENTER

LAU.
6'-0" X 8'-6"

STRG

KITCHEN
12'-4" X 15'-8"

MASTER BEDROOM
17'-10" X 15'-2"

BATH

GARAGE
20'-0" X 20'-10"

STUDY / GUEST RM.
12'-4" X 17'-4"

DINING RM.
12'-4" X 12'-4"

FOYER

COVERED PORCH
33'-10" X 8'-0"

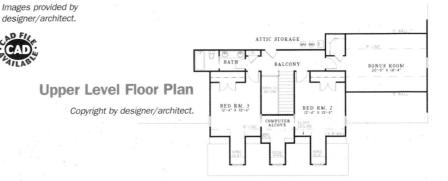

Upper Level Floor Plan

Copyright by designer/architect.

ATTIC STORAGE

BATH

BALCONY

BONUS ROOM
20'-0" X 14'-4"

BED RM. 3
12'-4" X 13'-4"

BED RM. 2
12'-4" X 13'-4"

COMPUTER ALCOVE

Plan #121160

Dimensions: 66'4½" W x 49'9½" D
Levels: 1.5
Square Footage: 2,188
Main Level Sq. Ft.: 1,531
Upper Level Sq. Ft.: 657
Bedrooms: 3
Bathrooms: 2½
Foundation: Slab; basement for fee
Materials List Available: Yes
Price Category: D

The standing-seam roof on the wraparound porch gives this home a charming country look.

CAD FILE AVAILABLE

Images provided by designer/architect.

Features:

• Family Room: The open design that leads to the adjoining breakfast area makes this space airy and welcoming. The room also features a tray ceiling. The fireplace adds to the comfortable feel of the space.

• Dining Room / Sunroom: Featuring three exterior walls with windows, this space can either be your formal dining room or your casual sunroom.

• Kitchen: This peninsula kitchen boasts a raised bar open to the breakfast room. The walk-in pantry is always a welcome feature.

• Master Suite: Located on the main level, this retreat features a bay window with a view of the backyard. The master bath features a large walk-in closet and dual vanities.

Front View

Main Level Floor Plan

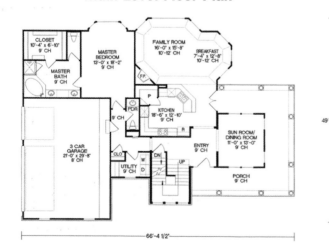

Upper Level Floor Plan

Copyright by designer/architect.

Plan #281001

Dimensions: 54' W x 47' D
Levels: 2
Square Footage: 2,423
Main Level Sq. Ft.: 1,388
Second Level Sq. Ft.: 1,035
Bedrooms: 3
Bathrooms: 2½
Foundation: Basement
Materials List Available: Yes
Price Category: E

This stately manor appears larger than it is and is filled with amenities for comfortable living.

Features:

• Ceiling Height: 8 ft. unless otherwise noted.

• Foyer: The grand entrance porch leads into this spacious two-story foyer, with an open staircase and architecturally interesting angles.

• Balcony: This second story has a balcony that overlooks the foyer.

• Living Room: This delightful living room seems even more spacious, thanks to its sloped vaulted ceiling.

• Dining Room: This elegant dining room shares the living room's sloped vaulted ceiling.

• Kitchen: This beautiful kitchen will be a real pleasure in which to cook. You'll love lingering over morning coffee in the breakfast nook, which is located on the sunny full-bayed wall.

• Family Room: Relax in this roomy family room, with its 9-ft. ceiling.

Images provided by designer/architect.

Main Level Floor Plan

Upper Level Floor Plan

Copyright by designer/architect.

Main Level Floor Plan

Plan #151018

Dimensions: 69' W x 69'10" D

Levels: 2

Square Footage: 2,755

Main Level Sq. Ft.: 2,406

Upper Level Sq. Ft.: 349

Bedrooms: 3

Bathrooms: 4½

Foundation: Crawl space, slab, or basement

CompleteCost List Available: Yes

Price Category: F

Images provided by designer/architect.

Upper Level Floor Plan

Copyright by designer/architect.

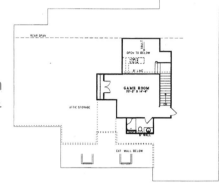

Main Level Floor Plan

Plan #141029

Dimensions: 55' W x 42' D

Levels: 2

Square Footage: 2,289

Main Level Sq. Ft.: 1,382

Upper Level Sq. Ft.: 907

Bedrooms: 4

Bathrooms: 2½

Foundation: Basement

Materials List Available: Yes

Price Category: E

Images provided by designer/architect.

Upper Level Floor Plan

Copyright by designer/architect.

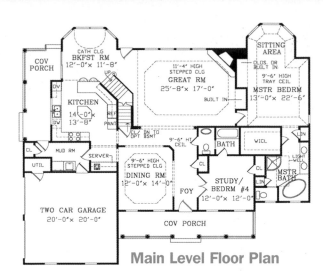

Main Level Floor Plan

Plan #131027

Dimensions: 62'4" W x 53'6" D
Levels: 2
Square Footage: 2,567
Main Level Sq. Ft.: 2,017
Upper Level Sq. Ft.: 550
Bedrooms: 4
Bathrooms: 3
Foundation: Crawl space, slab, or basement
Materials List Available: Yes
Price Category: F

Images provided by designer/architect.

This home, as shown in the photograph, may differ from the actual blueprints. For more detailed information, please check the floor plans carefully.

Upper Level Floor Plan

Copyright by designer/architect.

Plan #151384

Dimensions: 76'8" W x 77'7" D
Levels: 1.5
Square Footage: 2,742
Bedrooms: 3
Bathrooms: 2½
Foundation: Crawl space or slab
CompleteCost List Available: Yes
Price Category: F

Images provided by designer/architect.

CAD FILE AVAILABLE

Bonus Area Floor Plan

Copyright by designer/architect.

Front View

Plan #121150

Dimensions: 68'7" W x 57'4" D
Levels: 1.5
Square Footage: 2,639
Main Level Sq. Ft.: 2,087
Upper Level Sq. Ft.: 552
Bedrooms: 4
Bathrooms: 3½
Foundation: Slab; basement for fee
Material List Available: Yes
Price Category: F

Images provided by designer/architect.

Main Level Floor Plan

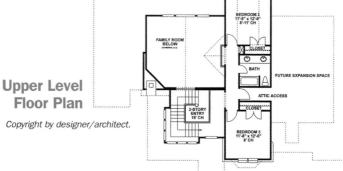

Upper Level Floor Plan

Copyright by designer/architect.

Plan #151019

Dimensions: 63'4" W x 53'10" D
Levels: 2
Square Footage: 2,947
Main Level Sq. Ft.: 1,407
Upper Level Sq. Ft.: 1,540
Bedrooms: 3
Bathrooms: 2½
Foundation: Crawl space, slab; optional full basement plan available for extra fee
CompleteCost List Available: Yes
Price Category: F

Images provided by designer/architect.

Main Level Floor Plan

Upper Level Floor Plan

Copyright by designer/architect.

Plan #151027

Dimensions: 37' W x 73' D

Levels: 2

Square Footage: 2,323

Main Level Sq. Ft.: 1,713

Upper Level Sq. Ft.: 619

Bedrooms: 3

Bathrooms: 3

Foundation: Crawl space, slab; optional basement plan available for extra fee

Materials List Available: No

Price Category: E

Images provided by designer/architect.

Copyright by designer/architect.

Plan #151028

Dimensions: 36' W X 69' D

Levels: 2

Square Footage: 2,252

Main Level Sq. Ft.: 1,694

Upper Level Sq. Ft.: 558

Bedrooms: 3

Bathrooms: 3

Foundation: Crawl space, slab; optional basement plan available for extra fee

CompleteCost List Available: Yes

Price Category: E

Images provided by designer/architect.

Copyright by designer/architect.

Plan #181228

Dimensions: 68' W x 36' D
Levels: 2
Square Footage: 2,393
Main Level Sq. Ft.: 1,279
Upper Level Sq. Ft.: 1,114
Bedrooms: 4
Bathrooms: 2
Foundation: Slab
Materials List Available: Yes
Price Category: E

Come home to this fine home, and relax on the front or rear porch.

Features:

- Living Room: This large, open entertaining area has a cozy fireplace and is flooded with natural light.

- Kitchen: This fully equipped kitchen has an abundance of cabinets and counter space. Access the rear porch is through a glass door.

- Laundry Room: Located on the main level, this laundry area also has space for storage.

- Upper Level: Climb the U-shaped staircase, and you'll find four large bedrooms that share a common bathroom.

Images provided by designer/architect.

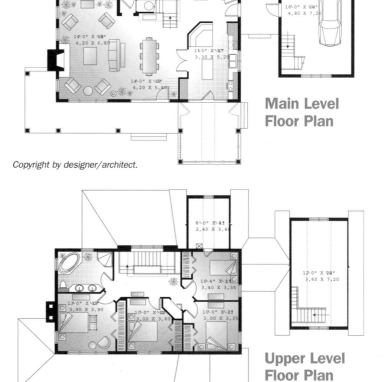

Main Level Floor Plan

Copyright by designer/architect.

Upper Level Floor Plan

Images provided by designer/architect.

Plan #271099

Dimensions: 71' W x 74'2" D
Levels: 2
Square Footage: 2,949
Main Level Sq. Ft.: 2,000
Upper Level Sq. Ft.: 949
Bedrooms: 3
Bathrooms: 2½
Foundation: Crawl space
Materials List Available: No
Price Category: F

Gracious symmetry highlights the lovely facade of this traditional two-story home.

Features:

- Foyer: With a high ceiling and a curved staircase, this foyer gives a warm welcome to arriving guests.

- Family Room: At the center of the home, this room will host gatherings of all kinds. A fireplace adds just the right touch.

- Kitchen: An expansive island with a cooktop anchors this space, which easily serves the adjoining nook and the nearby dining room.

- Master Suite: A cozy sitting room with a fireplace is certainly the highlight here. The private bath is also amazing, with its whirlpool tub, separate shower, dual vanities, and walk-in closet.

- Bonus Room: This generous space above the garage could serve as an art studio or as a place for your teenagers to play their electric guitars.

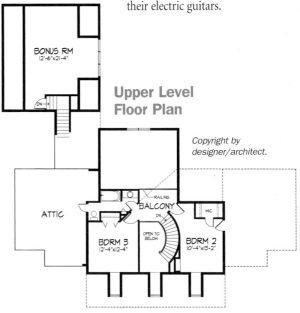

Copyright by designer/architect.

Plan #181151

Dimensions: 50' W x 46' D

Levels: 2

Square Footage: 2,283

Main Level Sq. Ft.: 1,274

Second Level Sq. Ft.: 1,009

Bedrooms: 3

Bathrooms: 2½

Foundation: Basement

Materials List Available: Yes

Price Category: E

Multiple porches, stately columns, and arched multi-paned windows adorn this country home.

CAD FILE AVAILABLE

Features:

- Ceiling Height: 8 ft. unless otherwise noted.

- Great Room: The second-floor mezzanine overlooks this great room. With its soaring ceiling, this dramatic room is the centerpiece of a spacious and flowing design that is just as suited to entertaining as it is to family life.

- Dining Area: Guests will naturally flow into this dining area when it is time to eat. After dinner they can step directly out onto the porch to enjoy coffee and dessert when the weather is fair.

- Kitchen: This efficient and well-designed kitchen has double sinks and offers a separate eating area for those impromptu family meals.

- Master Bedroom: This master retreat has a walk-in closet and its own sumptuous bath.

- Home Office: Whether you work at home or just need a place for the family computer and keeping track of family finances, this home office fills the bill.

Main Level Floor Plan

Upper Level Floor Plan

Plan #121091

Dimensions: 56' W x 50' D
Levels: 2
Square Footage: 2,689
Main Level Sq. Ft.: 1,415
Upper Level Sq. Ft.: 1,274
Bedrooms: 4
Bathrooms: 2½
Foundation: Basement
Materials List Available: Yes
Price Category: F

This home, as shown in the photograph, may differ from the actual blueprints. For more detailed information, please check the floor plans carefully.

Images provided by designer/architect.

You'll love the unusual details that make this home as elegant as it is comfortable.

Features:

- **Entry:** This two-story entry is filled with natural light that streams in through the sidelights and transom window.

- **Den:** To the right of the entry, French doors open to this room, with its 11-ft. high, spider-beamed ceiling. A triple-wide,

transom-topped window brightens this room during the daytime.

- **Family Room:** A fireplace and built-in entertainment center add comfort to this room, and the cased opening to the kitchen area makes it convenient.

- **Kitchen:** With an adjoining breakfast area, this kitchen is another natural gathering spot

Main Level Floor Plan

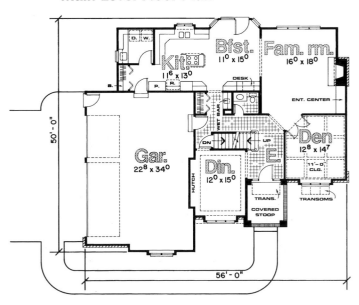

Upper Level Floor Plan

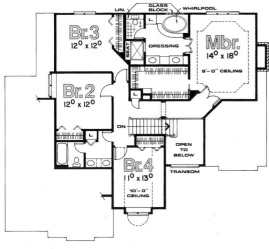

Copyright by designer/architect.

Plan #121083

Dimensions: 72' W x 45'4" D
Levels: 2
Square Footage: 2,695
Main Level Sq. Ft.: 1,881
Upper Level Sq. Ft.: 814
Bedrooms: 4
Bathrooms: 3½
Foundation: Basement
Materials List Available: Yes
Price Category: F

Images provided by designer/architect.

You'll love this home for its soaring entryway ceiling and well-designed layout.

Features:

- **Entry:** A balcony from the upper level looks down into this two-story entry, which features a decorative plant shelf.

- **Great Room:** Comfort is guaranteed in this large room, with its built-in bookcases framing a lovely fireplace and trio of transom-topped windows along one wall.

- **Living Room:** Save both this formal room and the formal dining room, both of which flank the entry, for guests and special occasions.

- **Kitchen:** This convenient work space includes a gazebo-shaped breakfast area where friends and family will gather at any time of day.

Main Level Floor Plan

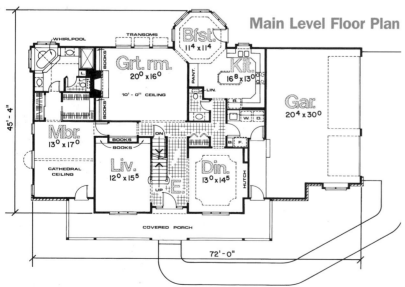

Upper Level Floor Plan

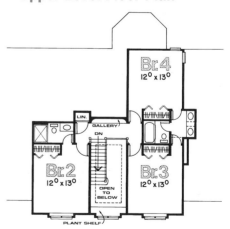

Copyright by designer/architect.

Plan #181094

Dimensions: 50' W x 39' D
Levels: 2
Square Footage: 2,099
Main Level Sq. Ft.: 1,060
Upper Level Sq. Ft.: 1,039
Bedrooms: 4
Bathrooms: 2½
Foundation: Basement
Materials List Available: Yes
Price Category: D

Images provided by designer/architect.

The curved covered porch makes this is a great place to come home to.

CAD FILE AVAILABLE

Features:

- Entry: This air-lock entry area with closet will help keep energy costs down.

- Family Room: This gathering area features a fireplace and is open to the kitchen and the dining area.

- Kitchen: U-shaped and boasting an island and a walk-in pantry, this kitchen is open to the dining area.

- Master Suite: This large retreat features a fireplace and a walk-in closet. The master bath has dual vanities, a separate shower, and a large tub.

- Bedrooms: Located upstairs with the master suite are three additional bedrooms. They share a common bathroom, and each has a large closet.

Rear View

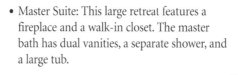

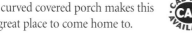

Main Level Floor Plan

Upper Level Floor Plan

Copyright by designer/architect.

Main Level Floor Plan

Plan #141035

Dimensions: 62' W x 36' D

Levels: 2

Square Footage: 2,514

Main Level Sq. Ft.: 1,287

Upper Level Sq. Ft.: 1,227

Bedrooms: 3

Bathrooms: 3½

Foundation: Crawl space, basement

Materials List Available: No

Price Category: E

Images provided by designer/architect.

Upper Level Floor Plan

Copyright by designer/architect.

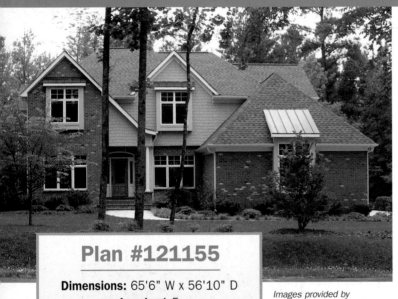

Plan #121155

Dimensions: 65'6" W x 56'10" D

Levels: 1.5

Square Footage: 2,638

Main Level Sq. Ft.: 1,844

Upper Level Sq. Ft.: 794

Bedrooms: 4

Bathrooms: 3½

Foundation: Slab; basement for fee

Material List Available: Yes

Price Category: F

Images provided by designer/architect.

CAD FILE AVAILABLE

Upper Level Floor Plan

Main Level Floor Plan

Copyright by designer/architect.

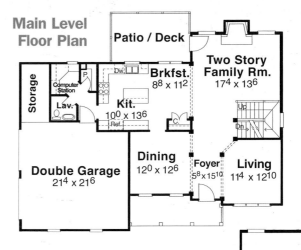

Main Level Floor Plan

Patio / Deck

Storage

Computer Station

P

Lav.

Dw.

Brkfst. 8⁸ x 11²

Kit. 10⁰ x 13⁶

Ref.

C.

Two Story Family Rm. 17⁴ x 13⁶

Up

Dn

Double Garage 21⁴ x 21⁶

Dining 12⁰ x 12⁶

Foyer 5⁸ x 15¹⁰

Living 11⁴ x 12¹⁰

Images provided by designer/architect.

Upper Level Floor Plan

Copyright by designer/architect.

M.Bath Tray Ceil.

Bdrm.2 11⁰ x 11⁶ Opt. Vault W/ Plant Shelf

Bth.2

Two Story Family Rm.

Balcony

Dn

Master Bdrm. 15⁴ x 14⁶ Tray Ceil.

Opt. Vault W/ Plant Shelf

Bdrm.3 11⁸ x 10⁶

W.I.C.

Laund

Opt. Vault W/ Plant Shelf

Open To Foyer

Bdrm.4 11⁴ x 11⁰

Opt. Closet

Sitting 10⁰ x 7⁰

Plan #141032

Dimensions: 52' W x 44' D
Levels: 2
Square Footage: 2,476
Main Level Sq. Ft.: 1,160
Upper Level Sq. Ft.: 1,316
Bedrooms: 4
Bathrooms: 2½
Foundation: Basement
Materials List Available: Yes
Price Category: E

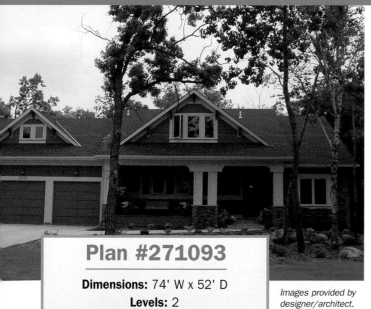

Plan #271093

Dimensions: 74' W x 52' D
Levels: 2
Square Footage: 2,813
Main Level Sq. Ft.: 1,828
Upper Level Sq. Ft.: 985
Bedrooms: 3
Bathrooms: 3
Foundation: Basement
Materials List Available: No
Price Category: F

CAD FILE AVAILABLE

Images provided by designer/architect.

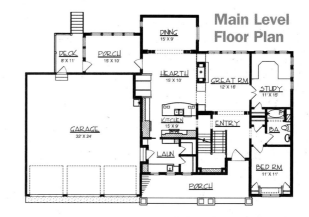

Main Level Floor Plan

DECK 8' X 11'

PORCH 15' X 10'

DINING 15' X 9'

HEARTH 15' X 10'

GREAT RM. 12' X 16'

STUDY 11' X 15'

GARAGE 32' X 24'

KITCHEN 15' X 9'

ENTRY

BA

LAUN

BED RM 11' X 11'

PORCH

Upper Level Floor Plan

W.I.C.

BATH

OWNER'S SUITE 14' X 18'

LOFT

BED RM 11' X 15'

SITTING 13' X 9'

Copyright by designer/architect.

Great Room

Plan #141036

Dimensions: 57' W x 41' D

Levels: 2

Square Footage: 2,527

Main Level Sq. Ft.: 1,236

Upper Level Sq. Ft.: 1,291

Bedrooms: 4

Bathrooms: 3

Foundation: Basement

Materials List Available: No

Price Category: E

Wood shakes and stone make the exterior of this home distinctive, and a fabulous layout and gorgeous features make the interior spectacular.

Features:

• Living Room: This spacious two-story room has a fireplace to make it cozy on chilly nights.

• Guest Wing: Guests will love having their own wing just beyond the computer command center.

• Dining Room: This room is ideal for entertaining or family dinner times.

• Kitchen: This step-saving design features an angled work area and a large pantry.

• Breakfast Room: The door to the patio makes this a perfect gathering place at any time of day.

• Master Suite: You'll love the stepped ceiling and hinged window seat in the bedroom, the walk-in closet, and the vaulted ceiling, tub, shower, and two vanities in the bath.

Images provided by designer/architect.

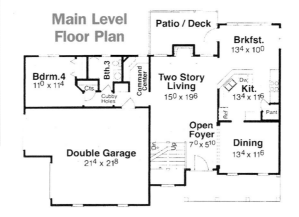

Main Level Floor Plan

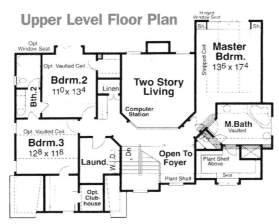

Upper Level Floor Plan

Copyright by designer/architect.

Living Room

Kitchen

Master Bedroom

Plan #131074

Dimensions: 56' W x 41' D
Levels: 2
Square Footage: 2,085
Main Level Sq. Ft.: 1,240
Upper Level Sq. Ft.: 845
Bedrooms: 4
Bathrooms: 2½
Foundation: Slab or basement
Material List Available: Yes
Price Category: E

This farmhouse-style home has much to offer you and your family.

Images provided by designer/architect.

This home, as shown in the photograph, may differ from the actual blueprints. For more detailed information, please check the floor plans carefully.

Features:

- **Family Room:** This vaulted gathering area features a skylight and access to the backyard. The grand fireplace adds a focal point to the room.

- **Kitchen:** This open, island kitchen is ideally located between the formal dining room and the sunny breakfast nook. The bay window in the breakfast nook will keep the space bright.

- **Master Suite:** A vaulted ceiling adds elegance to this private retreat. The master bath features dual vanities and a garden tub.

- **Garage:** A large two-car garage provides the option of parking cars or using the area for additional storage.

Optional Bonus Area Floor Plan

Main Level Floor Plan

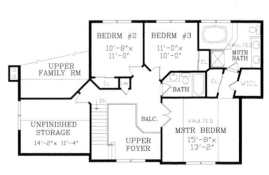

Upper Level Floor Plan

Copyright by designer/architect.

Plan #131055

Dimensions: 62'4" W x 53'6" D
Levels: 1.5
Square Footage: 2,575
Main Level Sq. Ft.: 2,007
Upper Level Sq. Ft.: 568
Bedrooms: 4
Bathrooms: 3
Foundation: Crawl space, slab, or basement
Materials List Available: Yes
Price Category: E

This is a classic-looking farmhouse on the outside, but inside you will find everything today's family wants in a home.

Features:

- Great Room: This room has a large corner fireplace and high ceilings, and it leads directly into a grand master-bedroom suite.

- Dining Room: This open room looks into the great room and across the foyer into an optional fourth bedroom or study.

- Kitchen: With a center island workspace and a snack bar, this large, spacious kitchen opens into the bay window breakfast room.

- Master Suite: This private space is located on the main level away from the secondary bedrooms. It features a large bedroom and sitting area, plus a private bath.

Images provided by designer/architect.

Main Level Floor Plan

Copyright by designer/architect.

Stairs

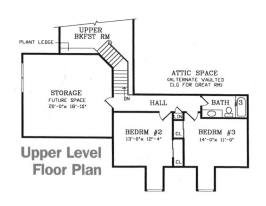

Upper Level Floor Plan

Rear View

Great Room

Kitchen

Dining Room

Master Bedroom

Master Bath

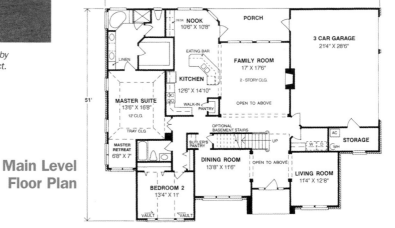

Upper Level Floor Plan

Copyright by designer/architect.

BEDROOM 3
11'4" X 12'6"

OPEN TO BELOW

STUDY
12'6" X 10'10"

WALKWAY

RAIL

DN

RAIL

PLAY ROOM
13'8" X 11'6"

OPEN TO BELOW

BEDROOM 4
11'4" X 12'8"

Plan #121171

Dimensions: 66' W x 51' D

Levels: 1.5

Square Footage: 2,978

Main Level Sq. Ft.: 2,101

Upper Level Sq. Ft.: 877

Bedrooms: 4

Bathrooms: 3

Foundation: Slab; basement for fee

Material List Available: Yes

Price Category: F

Images provided by designer/architect.

66'

DESK

NOOK
10'6" X 10'8"

PORCH

3 CAR GARAGE
21'4" X 28'6"

LINEN

EATING BAR

FAMILY ROOM
17' X 17'6"

2 - STORY CLG.

KITCHEN
12'6" X 14'10"

MASTER SUITE
13'6" X 16'8"
12' CLG.

WALK-IN PANTRY

OPEN TO ABOVE

51'

TRAY CLG.

OPTIONAL BASEMENT STAIRS

BUTLER'S PANTRY

UP

AC

STORAGE

MASTER RETREAT
6'8" X 7'

DINING ROOM
13'8" X 11'6"

OPEN TO ABOVE

W D

WH

LIVING ROOM
11'4" X 12'8"

Main Level Floor Plan

BEDROOM 2
13'4" X 11

VAULT

VAULT

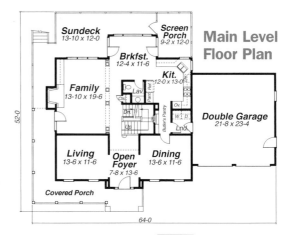

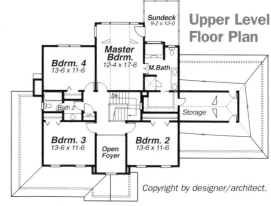

Plan #141016

Dimensions: 64' W x 52' D

Levels: 2

Square Footage: 2,416

Main Level Sq. Ft.: 1,250

Upper Level Sq. Ft.: 1,166

Bedrooms: 4

Bathrooms: 2½

Foundation: Basement

Materials List Available: Yes

Price Category: E

Images provided by designer/architect.

Main Level Floor Plan

Sundeck
13-10 x 12-0

Screen Porch
9-2 x 12-0

Brkfst.
12-4 x 11-6

Kit.
12-0 x 13-0

Family
13-10 x 19-6

Lav.

Pantry

Double Garage
21-8 x 23-4

52-0

W D

Lnd.

Living
13-6 x 11-6

Open Foyer
7-8 x 13-6

Dining
13-6 x 11-6

Covered Porch

64-0

Upper Level Floor Plan

Sundeck
9-2 x 12-0

Master Bdrm.
12-4 x 17-6

M.Bath

Bdrm. 4
13-6 x 11-6

Bath 2

Lin

Storage

Bdrm. 3
13-6 x 11-6

Open Foyer

Bdrm. 2
13-6 x 11-6

Copyright by designer/architect.

Plan #121123

Dimensions: 54' W x 52' D
Levels: 1.5
Square Footage: 2,277
Main Level Sq. Ft.: 1,570
Upper Level Sq. Ft.: 707
Bedrooms: 4
Bathrooms: 2½
Foundation: Basement;
crawl space for fee
Material List Available: Yes
Price Category: E

Images provided by designer/architect.

This country-style home, with its classic wraparound porch, is just the plan you have been searching for.

Features:

- Entry: This two-story entry gives an open and airy feeling when you enter the home. A view into the dining room and great room adds to the open feeling.

- Great Room: This grand gathering area with cathedral ceiling is ready for your friends and family to come and visit. The fireplace, flanked by large windows, adds a cozy feeling to the space.

- Kitchen: The chef in the family will love how efficiently this island kitchen was designed. An abundance of cabinets and counter space is always a plus.

- Master Suite: This main level oasis will help you relieve all the stresses from the day. The master bath boasts dual vanities and a large walk-in closet.

- Secondary Bedrooms: Three generously sized bedrooms occupy the upper level. The full bathroom is located for easy access to all three bedrooms.

Main Level Floor Plan

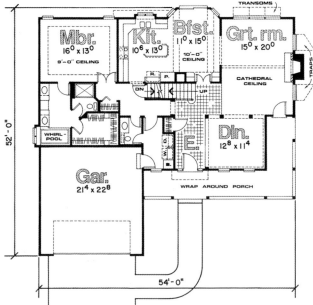

Upper Level Floor Plan

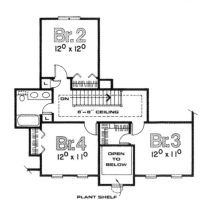

Copyright by designer/architect.

Main Level Floor Plan

Images provided by designer/architect.

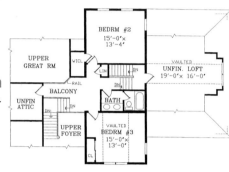

Upper Level Floor Plan

Copyright by designer/architect.

Plan #131050

Dimensions: 72'8" W x 47' D

Levels: 2

Square Footage: 2,874

Main Level Sq. Ft.: 2,146

Upper Level Sq. Ft.: 728

Bedrooms: 4

Bathrooms: 3

Foundation: Crawl space, slab, or basement

Materials List Available: Yes

Price Category: G

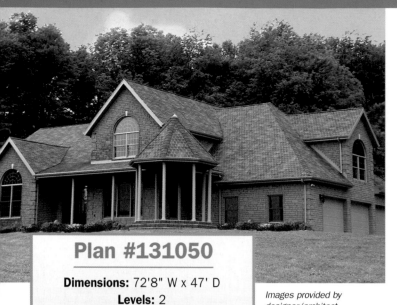

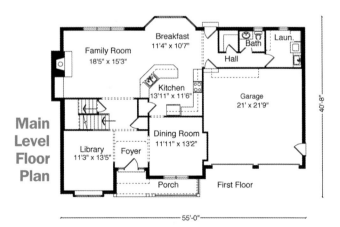

Main Level Floor Plan

Copyright by designer/architect.

Plan #161125

Dimensions: 55' W x 40'8" D

Levels: 2

Square Footage: 2,733

Main Level Sq. Ft.: 1,402

Upper Level Sq. Ft.: 1,331

Bedrooms: 4

Bathrooms: 2½

Foundation: Basement

Material List Available: Yes

Price Category: F

Images provided by designer/architect.

Rear Elevation

Upper Level Floor Plan

Main Level Floor Plan

Plan #151029

Dimensions: 59'4" W x 74'2" D

Levels: 1½

Square Footage: 2,777

Main Level Sq. Ft.: 2,082

Upper Level Sq. Ft.: 695

Bedrooms: 4

Bathrooms: 2½

Foundation: Crawl space, slab; basement for fee

CompleteCost List Available: Yes

Price Category: F

Images provided by designer/architect.

CAD FILE AVAILABLE

Upper Level Floor Plan

Copyright by designer/architect.

Main Level Floor Plan

Plan #131028

Dimensions: 69'2" W x 50'2" D

Levels: 2

Square Footage: 2,696

Main Level Sq. Ft.: 1,960

Upper Level Sq. Ft.: 736

Bedrooms: 4

Bathrooms: 3

Foundation: Crawl space, slab, or basement

Materials List Available: Yes

Price Category: F

Images provided by designer/architect.

Upper Level Floor Plan

Copyright by designer/architect.

Main Level Floor Plan

Kit. 9' x 16'

Eating Area 14'² x 16'

Great Room 16'³ x 22'⁰ Cathedral Ceiling

Mbr. 14'⁰ x 16'⁰ 11'-0" Ceiling

Dining Room 13'⁰ x 13'⁰

Garage 31'⁸ x 24'⁸

Covered Porch

67'-0"

56'-0"

Images provided by designer/architect.

Plan #121203

Dimensions: 67' W x 56' D
Levels: 1.5
Square Footage: 2,690
Main Level Sq. Ft.: 1,792
Upper Level Sq. Ft.: 898
Bedrooms: 4
Bathrooms: 2½
Foundation: Basement; crawl space or slab for fee
Materials List Available: Yes
Price Category: F

Upper Level Floor Plan

Copyright by designer/architect.

Br.3 12'⁴ x 12'⁶

Br.2 16'⁵ x 11'²

Br.4 17'⁶ x 12'⁴ 10'-0" Ceiling

Bonus Area Floor Plan

Unfinished Storage 470 Sq. Ft.

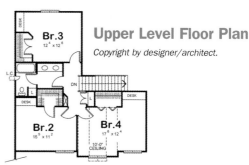

Main Level Floor Plan

fam 13'x16'

brk 11'x10'

k 12'9"x11'6

din 10'5x12'

20'x23' two-car garage

den 11'x11' tray ceiling

liv 12'11x14'8 tray ceiling

FOYER

VERANDAH

Plan #401014

Dimensions: 67'6" W x 47'6" D
Levels: 2
Square Footage: 2,516
Main Level Sq. Ft.: 1,324
Upper Level Sq. Ft.: 1,192
Bedrooms: 4
Bathrooms: 2½
Foundation: Basement
Materials List Available: Yes
Price Category: E

Images provided by designer/architect.

Upper Level Floor Plan

Copyright by designer/architect.

mbr 13'2x18'

br2 13'3x11'5

br3 11'x10' VAULTED

br4 12'11x12'

W.I. Closet

OPEN TO FOYER BELOW

Optional Main Level Floor Plan

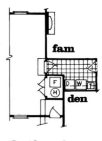

fam

den

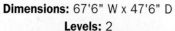

Plan #151030

Dimensions: 59' W x 73' D
Levels: 2
Square Footage: 2,802
Main Level Sq. Ft.: 2,058
Upper Level Sq. Ft.: 744
Bonus Room Sq. Ft.: 493
Bedrooms: 3
Bathrooms: 3½
Foundation: Crawl space, slab; basement for fee
CompleteCost List Available: Yes
Price Category: F

Images provided by designer/architect.

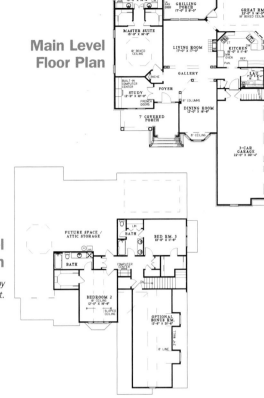

Main Level Floor Plan

Upper Level Floor Plan

Copyright by designer/architect.

Plan #121147

Dimensions: 40' W x 51' D
Levels: 1.5
Square Footage: 2,051
Main Level Sq. Ft.: 1,497
Upper Level Sq. Ft.: 554
Bedrooms: 3
Bathrooms: 2½
Foundation: Basement; crawl space for fee
Material List Available: Yes
Price Category: D

Images provided by designer/architect.

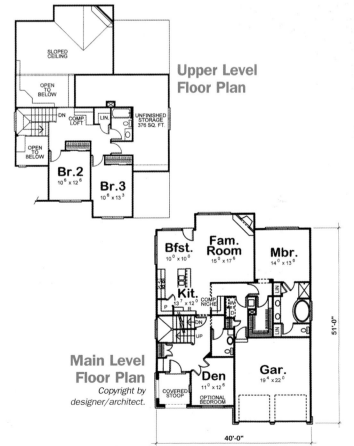

Upper Level Floor Plan

Main Level Floor Plan

Copyright by designer/architect.

Plan #131033

Dimensions: 84'10" W x 48' D
Levels: 2
Square Footage: 2,813
Main Level Sq. Ft.: 1,890
Upper Level Sq. Ft.: 923
Bedrooms: 5
Bathrooms: 3½
Foundation: Crawl space, slab, or basement
Materials List Available: Yes
Price Category: G

Contemporary styling, luxurious amenities, and the classics that make a house a home are all available here.

Features:

- **Family Room:** A sloped ceiling with skylight and a railed overlook to make this large space totally up to date.

- **Living Room:** Sunken for comfort and with a cathedral ceiling for style, this room features a fireplace flanked by windows and sliding glass doors.

- **Master Suite:** Unwind in this room, with its cathedral ceiling, with a skylight, walk-in closet, and private access to the den.

- **Upper Level:** A bridge overlooks the living room and foyer and leads through the family room to three bedrooms and a bath.

- **Optional Guest Suite:** 500 sq. ft. above the master suite and den provides total comfort.

Images provided by designer/architect.

Main Level Floor Plan

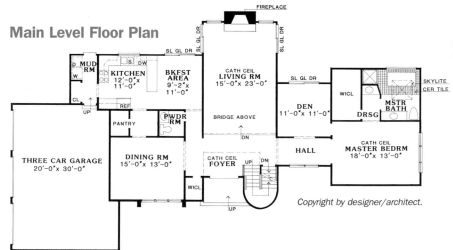

Copyright by designer/architect.

Upper Level Floor Plan

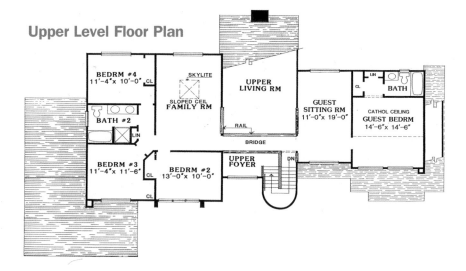

Plan #121212

Dimensions: 54' W x 44' D
Levels: 2
Square Footage: 2,219
Main Level Sq. Ft.: 1,132
Upper Level Sq. Ft.: 1,087
Bedrooms: 4
Bathrooms: 2½
Foundation: Basement;
crawl space for fee
Material List Available: Yes
Price Category: E

Images provided by designer/architect.

Country charm abounds in this lovely home.
Features:

• Entry: The central location of this large entry
allows access to the dining room or great
room. The area features a handy closet.

• Great Room: This gathering area features a
10-ft.-high ceiling and large windows, which
allow plenty of natural light into the space.

• Upper Level: Three bedrooms and the master
suite occupy this level. The master suite features a tray ceiling and a well-appointed bath.

• Garage: A front-loading two-car garage with
additional storage completes the floor plan.

Front View

Main Level Floor Plan

Copyright by designer/architect.

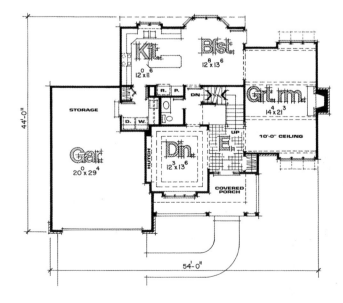

Upper Level
Floor Plan

Plan #321054

Dimensions: 70'6" W x 55'6" D
Levels: 2
Square Footage: 2,828
Main Level Sq. Ft.: 2,006
Upper Level Sq. Ft.: 822
Bedrooms: 5
Bathrooms: 3½
Foundation: Basement
Materials List Available: Yes
Price Category: F

Images provided by designer/architect.

The wraparound porch welcomes visitors to this spacious home built for a large family.

Features:

- **Foyer:** Flanked by the study on one side and the dining room on the other, the foyer leads to the staircase, breakfast room, and family room.

- **Family Room:** You'll feel comfortable in this room, with its vaulted ceiling, wet bar, ample window area, and door to the patio.

- **Kitchen:** A center island adds work space to this well-planned room with large corner windows and a convenient door to the outside patio.

- **Master Suite:** Doors to the covered porch flank the fireplace here, and the luxurious bath includes a corner tub, two vanities, and separate shower. A huge walk-in closet is in the hall.

- **Upper Floor:** You'll find four bedrooms, each with a large closet, and two full baths here. Bay windows grace the two front bedrooms.

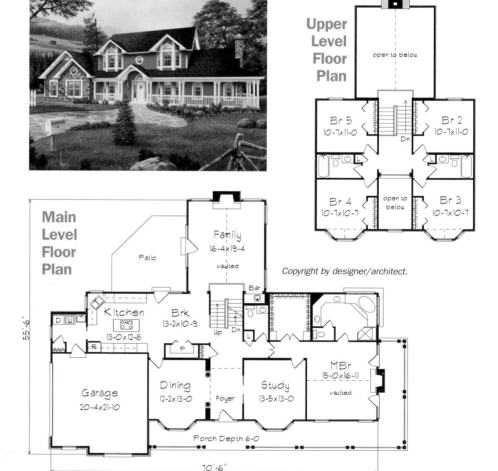

Copyright by designer/architect.

Plan #121190

Dimensions: 80' W x 59' D
Levels: 1.5
Square Footage: 2,252
Main Level Sq. Ft.: 1,736
Upper Level Sq. Ft.: 516
Bedrooms: 4
Bathrooms: 3
Foundation: Slab; crawl space for fee
Materials List Available: Yes
Price Category: E

Images provided by designer/architect.

This classic farmhouse is just what you have been searching for.

Features:

- **Front Porch:** Invite the neighbors over to sit on this fabulous porch and enjoy a glass of lemonade as the kids play in the front yard.

- **Kitchen:** This large kitchen is open into the breakfast nook and features an eating bar. The laundry room and access to the garage are just off the kitchen.

- **Master Suite:** This private retreat, designed just for the two of you, features access to the rear porch. The large walk-in closet has plenty of space for your clothes.

- **Garage:** This large three-car garage is ready to hold whatever you need to store.

Upper Level Floor Plan

Front View

Main Level Floor Plan

Copyright by designer/architect.

Plan #131066

Dimensions: 43'6" W x 48'6" D
Levels: 2
Square Footage: 2,760
Main Level Sq. Ft.: 1,483
Upper Level Sq. Ft.: 1,277
Bedrooms: 4
Bathrooms: 2½
Foundation: Crawl space or basement
Material List Available: Yes
Price Category: G

This two-story home is great for a narrow building lot.

Images provided by designer/architect.

Features:

- **Foyer:** This grand entry rises 23 feet high, giving an open and airy feeling to the home. A nearby coat closet will help keep the area neat and tidy.

- **Family Room:** This casual gathering space is located just a few steps from the kitchen and includes sliding-glass-door access to the rear deck. The corner fireplace adds warmth to the area.

- **Kitchen:** This island kitchen, with its abundance of counter space and cabinets, helps keep the active family in motion. The adjacent breakfast area is a great place to start your day.

- **Master Suite:** Located on the upper level in close proximity to the secondary bedrooms, this master suite features a private balcony for late-night stargazing. The two walk-in closets and well-appointed bath make this area the perfect getaway.

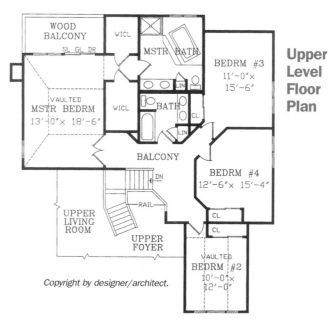

Copyright by designer/architect.

Plan #111049

Dimensions: 60' W x 50' D

Levels: 2

Square Footage: 2,205

Main Level Sq. Ft.: 1,552

Upper Level Sq. Ft.: 653

Bedrooms: 3

Bathrooms: 2

Foundation: Pier

Materials list available: No

Price Code: E

Images provided by designer/architect.

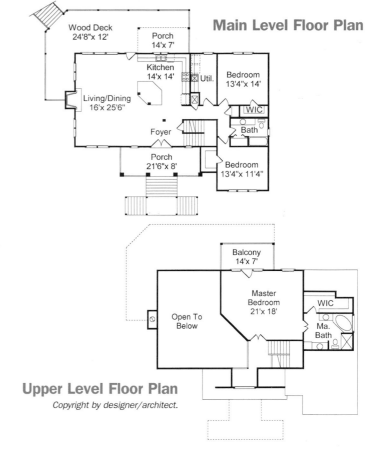

Main Level Floor Plan

Wood Deck 24'8"x 12'
Porch 14'x 7'
Kitchen 14'x 14'
Util.
Bedroom 13'4"x 14'
Living/Dining 16'x 25'6"
WIC
Bath
Foyer
Porch 21'6"x 8'
Bedroom 13'4"x 11'4"

Balcony 14'x 7'
Master Bedroom 21'x 18'
WIC
Ma. Bath
Open To Below

Upper Level Floor Plan

Copyright by designer/architect.

Plan #401016

Dimensions: 40' W x 59' D

Levels: 2

Square Footage: 2,539

Main Level Sq. Ft.: 1,383

Upper Level Sq. Ft.: 1,156

Bedrooms: 4

Bathrooms: 3

Foundation: Basement

Materials List Available: Yes

Price Category: E

Images provided by designer/architect.

This home, as shown in the photograph, may differ from the actual blueprints. For more detailed information, please check the floor plans carefully.

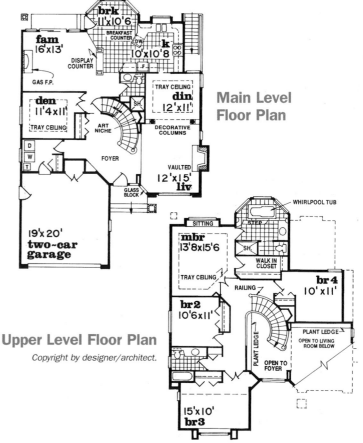

brk 11'x10'6
BREAKFAST COUNTER
fam 16'x13'
DISPLAY COUNTER
k 10'x10'8
GAS F.P.
den 11'4"x11'
TRAY CEILING
din 12'x11'
TRAY CEILING
ART NICHE
DECORATIVE COLUMNS
FOYER
liv 12'x15' VAULTED
GLASS BLOCK
19'x 20' two~car garage

Main Level Floor Plan

WHIRLPOOL TUB
SITTING
STEP
mbr 13'8x15'6
WALK IN CLOSET
br 4 10'x11'
TRAY CEILING
RAILING
PLANT LEDGE
br2 10'6x11'
PLANT LEDGE
OPEN TO LIVING ROOM BELOW
OPEN TO FOYER
15'x10' br3

Upper Level Floor Plan

Copyright by designer/architect.

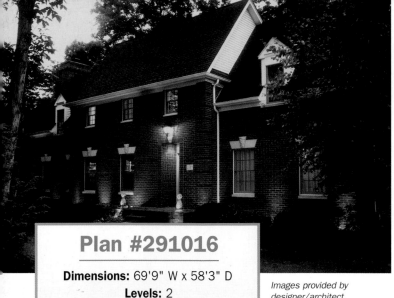

Main Level Floor Plan

Images provided by designer/architect.

Plan #291016

Dimensions: 69'9" W x 58'3" D
Levels: 2
Square Footage: 2,721
Main Level Sq. Ft.: 1,447
Upper Level Sq. Ft.: 1,274
Bedrooms: 3
Bathrooms: 2½
Foundation: Basement
Materials List Available: No
Price Category: F

Upper Level Floor Plan

Copyright by designer/architect.

Plan #391131

Dimensions: 63'4" W x 47'10" D
Levels: 2
Square Footage: 2,183
Main Level Sq. Ft.: 1,584
Upper Level Sq. Ft.: 599
Bedrooms: 3
Bathrooms: 2
Foundation: Basement
Material List Available: Yes
Price Category: D

Images provided by designer/architect.

Main Level Floor Plan

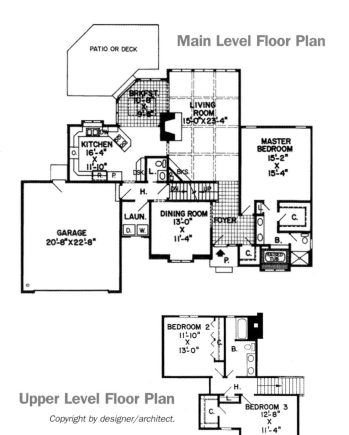

Upper Level Floor Plan

Copyright by designer/architect.

Plan #121149

Dimensions: 75'1 1/2" W x 38' D
Levels: 2
Square Footage: 2,715
Main Level Sq. Ft.: 1,400
Upper Level Sq. Ft.: 1,315
Bedrooms: 4
Bathrooms: 3½
Foundation: Slab; basement for fee
Material List Available: Yes
Price Category: F

This would be the perfect house for raising your family.

Features:

- **Living Room:** This formal gathering area is open to the entry and features a view of the front yard. The open stair railing adds a distinctive design element to the room.

- **Family Room:** This family room provides a place for relatives and friends to gather in a casual environment. The large fireplace adds a cozy feel to the area.

- **Master Suite:** A tray ceiling and a bay window accent this private retreat. The master bath is filled with elegance and includes a whirlpool tub.

- **Secondary Bedrooms:** Three bedrooms accompany the master suite on the upper level. Bedroom 2 boasts a private bathroom, while the remaining bedrooms share a Jack-and-Jill bathroom.

Images provided by designer/architect.

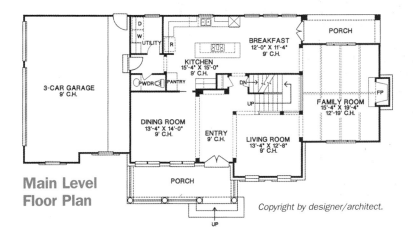

Main Level Floor Plan

Copyright by designer/architect.

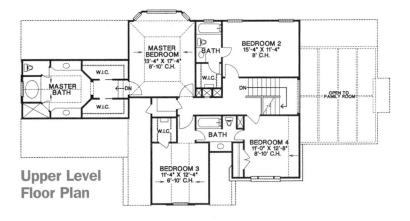

Upper Level Floor Plan

Plan #121127

Dimensions: 58' W x 59'4" D
Levels: 1.5
Square Footage: 2,496
Main Level Sq. Ft.: 1,777
Upper Level Sq. Ft.: 719
Bedrooms: 4
Bathrooms: 2½
Foundation: Basement;
crawl space for fee
Material List Available: Yes
Price Category: E

Images provided by designer/architect.

Beautiful, unique architecture and classic brick combine to make a breathtaking welcome for friends and family alike.

Features:

- **Great Room:** Through the covered stoop and foyer is this welcoming space for coming home after a hard day of work or for entertaining guests. Whether in the brightness of the sun or the warm glow of the fireplace, this will be everyone's favorite place to gather.

- **Kitchen:** With utility space on one side and a window-surrounded breakfast room on the other, this kitchen is the height of convenience. With plenty of work and storage space, as well as a large snack bar, the room makes mealtimes simple.

- **Den:** If you're bringing your work home with you or just need a quiet place to use the computer, what you need is just on the other side of French doors in the foyer.

- **Master Bedroom:** Featuring an entry to the backyard to continue relaxing outside, this master bedroom also includes a full master bath with standing shower, his and her sinks, a whirlpool tub, and a walk-in closet. Take some time for yourself.

- **Second Floor:** Bedrooms for three share the second full bathroom between them. If three is one too many, use the larger space for a study or entertainment area.

- **Garage:** A three-bay garage gives you room for every driver or for extra storage or a workshop.

Main Level Floor Plan

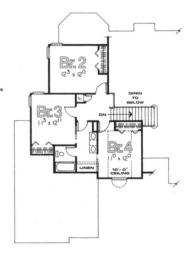

Upper Level Floor Plan

Copyright by designer/architect.

Plan #121148

Dimensions: 36' W x 50' D
Levels: 2
Square Footage: 2,076
Main Level Sq. Ft.: 1,117
Upper Level Sq. Ft.: 959
Bedrooms: 3 or 4
Bathrooms: 2½
Foundation: Basement;
crawl space for fee
Material List Available: Yes
Price Category: D

A compact home with large-home features makes this design perfect for your family.

Features:

• Dining Room: Located just off the entry, this formal eating area has space for a table and a hutch. Easy access to the kitchen will make entertaining a snap.

• Kitchen: This peninsula kitchen features a raised bar open to the breakfast area. The built-in desk will help keep your busy family organized.

• Master Suite: Located on the upper level in close proximity to the secondary bedrooms, this retreat features a walk-in closet. The master bath boasts dual vanities and a separate toilet area.

• Upper Level: There are two options for this upper level, a three-bedroom and a four-bedroom layout. The three-bedroom layout is open to the family room below.

Images provided by designer/architect.

Main Level Floor Plan

Copyright by designer/architect.

Upper Level Floor Plan

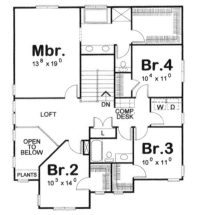

Optional Upper Level Floor Plan

Plan #101017

Dimensions: 57' W x 51' D
Levels: 2
Square Footage: 2,253
Main Level Sq. Ft.: 1,719
Upper Level Sq. Ft.: 534
Opt. Upper Level Bonus Sq. Ft.: 247
Bedrooms: 4
Bathrooms: 3
Foundation: Basement
Materials List Available: No
Price Category: E

Images provided by designer/architect.

This alluring two-story "master-down" design blends a spectacular floor plan with a lovely facade to create a home that's simply irresistible.

Features:

• Entry: You're welcomed by an inviting front porch and greeted by a beautiful leaded glass door leading to this two-story entry.

• Family Room: A corner fireplace and a window wall with arched transoms accent this dramatic room.

• Master Suite: This sumptuous suite includes a double tray ceiling, sitting area, and his and her walk-in closets. The master bathroom features dual vanities, a corner tub, and a shower.

• Bedrooms: Located upstairs, these two additional bedrooms share a Jack-and-Jill bathroom.

Main Level Floor Plan

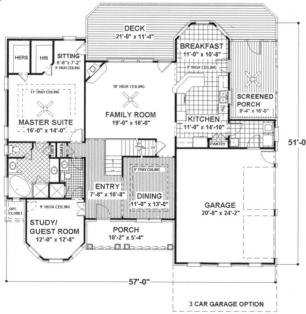

Upper Level Floor Plan

Copyright by designer/architect.

Kitchen

Dining Room

Study

Master Bath

Master Bedroom

Bedroom

Plan #441033

Dimensions: 67' W x 68' D

Levels: 2

Square Footage: 2,986

Main Level Sq. Ft.: 2,162

Upper Level Sq. Ft.: 824

Bedrooms: 3

Bathrooms: 2½

Foundation: Crawl space; slab or basement for fee

Materials List Available: No

Price Category: F

This home, as shown in the photograph, may differ from the actual blueprints. For more detailed information, please check the floor plans carefully.

CAD FILE AVAILABLE

Dramatic design coupled with elegant architectural detailing brings this comfortable home a lovely facade.

Features:

• **Great Room:** This room is two stories tall; the fireplace is flanked by built-ins.

• **Dining Room:** The interior was specifically created for family lifestyles. This formal room, accented with columns, is also graced by the butler's pantry, which connects it to the kitchen for convenience.

• **Master Suite:** The left wing is dedicated to this suite. The extensive master bath, with spa tub, separate shower, and walk-in closet, complements the master salon, which features a tray ceiling and large window over looking the rear yard.

• **Upper Level:** The two family bedrooms are on the second floor; they share the full bathroom with double sinks. The games room opens through double doors just off the loft library.

Main Level Floor Plan

Upper Level Floor Plan

Copyright by designer/architect.

Rear Elevation

Front View

Plan #121114

Dimensions: 64' W x 52' D
Levels: 1.5
Square Footage: 2,115
Main Level Sq. Ft.: 1,505
Upper Level Sq. Ft.: 610
Bedrooms: 4
Bathrooms: 2½
Foundation: Basement;
crawl space for fee
Materials List Available: Yes
Price Category: D

This contemporary home is not only beautifully designed on the outside; it has everything you need on the inside. It will be the envy of the neighborhood.

Features:

- **Great Room:** The cathedral ceiling and cozy fireplace strike a balance that creates the perfect gathering place for family and friends. An abundance of space allows you to tailor this room to your needs.

- **Kitchen/Breakfast Room:** This combined area features a flood of natural light, workspace to spare, an island with a snack bar, and a door that opens to the backyard, creating an ideal space for outdoor meals and gatherings.

- **Dining Room:** A triplet of windows projecting onto the covered front porch creates a warm atmosphere for formal dining.

- **Master Bedroom:** Away from the busy areas of the home, this master suite is ideal for shedding your daily cares and relaxing in a romantic atmosphere. It includes a full master bath with skylight, his and her sinks, a stall shower, a whirlpool tub, and a walk-in closet.

- **Second Floor:** Three more bedrooms and the second full bathroom upstairs give you plenty of room for a large family. Or if you only need two extra rooms, use the fourth bedroom as a study or entertainment area for the kids.

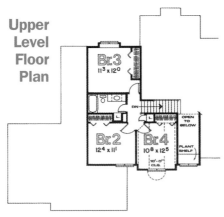

Copyright by designer/architect.

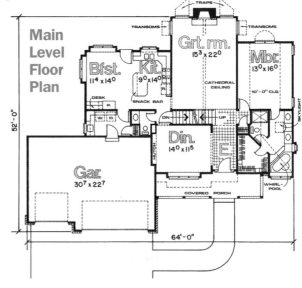

Plan #401029

Dimensions: 37'6" W x 48'4" D
Levels: 2
Square Footage: 2,163
Main Level Sq. Ft.: 832
Upper Level Sq. Ft.: 1,331
Bedrooms: 3
Bathrooms: 2½
Foundation: Basement
Materials List Available: Yes
Price Category: D

This two-level plan has a bonus—a roof deck with hot tub! A variety of additional outdoor spaces makes this one wonderful plan.

Features:

- First Level: Family bedrooms, a full bathroom, and a cozy den are on the first level, along with a two-car garage.

- Living Area: The living spaces are on the second floor and include a living/dining room combination with a deck and fireplace. The dining room has buffet space.

- Family Room: Featuring a fireplace and a built-in entertainment center, the gathering area is open to the breakfast room and sky lighted kitchen.

- Master Bedroom: This room features a private bath with a whirlpool tub and two-person shower, a walk-in closet, and access to still another deck.

Upper Level Floor Plan

CAD FILE AVAILABLE

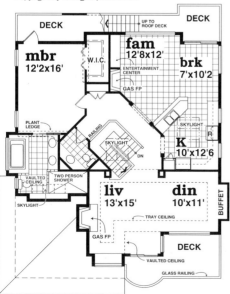

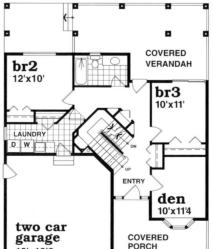

Main Level Floor Plan

Rear Elevation

Dining Room/Kitchen

Plan #121082

Dimensions: 68'8" W x 60' D
Levels: 2
Square Footage: 2,932
Main Level Sq. Ft.: 2,084
Upper Level Sq. Ft.: 848
Bedrooms: 4
Bathrooms: 3½
Foundation: Basement
Materials List Available: Yes
Price Category: F

Images provided by designer/architect.

Enjoy the spacious covered veranda that gives this house so much added charm.

Features:

- Great Room: A volume ceiling enhances the spacious feeling in this room, making it a natural gathering spot for friends and family. Transom-topped windows look onto the veranda, and French doors open to it.

- Den: French doors from the entry lead to this room, with its unusual ceiling detail, gracious fireplace, and transom-topped windows.

- Hearth Room: Three skylights punctuate the cathedral ceiling in this room, giving it an extra measure of light and warmth.

- Kitchen: This kitchen is a delight, thanks to its generous working and storage space.

Main Level Floor Plan

Upper Level Floor Plan

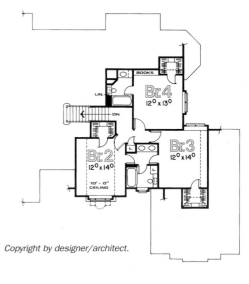

Copyright by designer/architect.

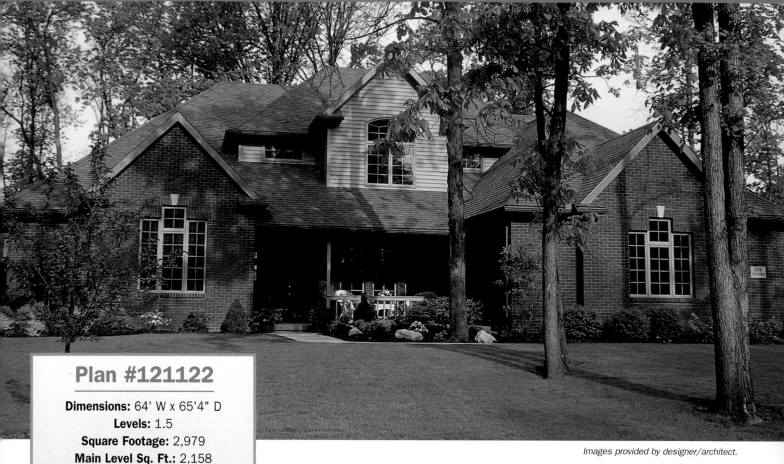

Plan #121122

Dimensions: 64' W x 65'4" D
Levels: 1.5
Square Footage: 2,979
Main Level Sq. Ft.: 2,158
Upper Level Sq. Ft.: 821
Bedrooms: 4
Bathrooms: 3½
Foundation: Basement;
crawl space for fee
Material List Available: Yes
Price Category: F

Images provided by designer/architect.

This classically designed home is the perfect place to raise your family.

Features:

- Great Room: This area was designed for formal entertaining and features an open two-story space. The large group of windows on the back wall will allow an abundance of natural light to fill the room.

- Master Suite: A 10-ft.-high stepped ceiling adds a touch of elegance to the sleeping area of this elegant master suite. The master bath boasts dual vanities and a whirlpool tub.

- Secondary Bedrooms: Three bedrooms are located on the upper level, away from the master suite. Bedroom 2 boasts a private bathroom, while bedrooms 3 and 4 share a Jack-and-Jill bathroom.

- Garage: This side-load three-car garage has room for both cars and storage. Located off of the laundry area close to the kitchen, unloading groceries is a easy and efficient.

Main Level Floor Plan

Upper Level Floor Plan

Copyright by designer/architect.

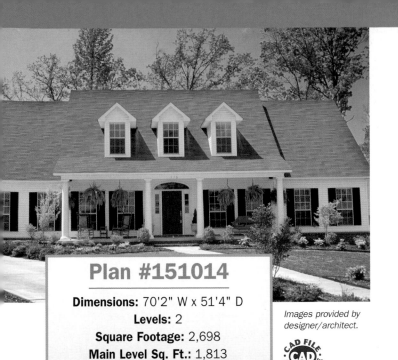

Plan #151014

Dimensions: 70'2" W x 51'4" D

Levels: 2

Square Footage: 2,698

Main Level Sq. Ft.: 1,813

Upper Level Sq. Ft.: 885

Bedrooms: 5

Bathrooms: 3

Foundation: Crawl space, slab, optional basement for fee

CompleteCost List Available: Yes

Price Category: F

Images provided by designer/architect.

CAD FILE AVAILABLE

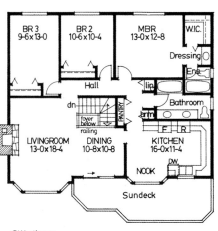

Main Level Floor Plan

Upper Level Floor Plan

Copyright by designer/architect.

Plan #281033

Dimensions: 50'4" W x 47'4" D

Levels: 2

Square Footage: 2,391

Main Level Sq. Ft.: 1,358

Garage Level Sq. Ft.: 1,033

Bedrooms: 4

Bathrooms: 3

Foundation: Basement

Material List Available: Yes

Price Category: E

Images provided by designer/architect.

Main Level Floor Plan

Garage Level Floor Plan

Copyright by designer/architect.

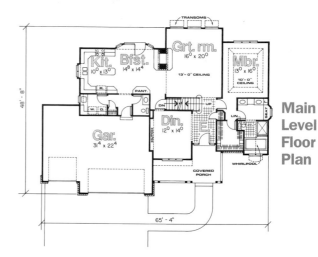

Main Level Floor Plan

Plan #121095

Dimensions: 65'4" W x 48'8" D

Levels: 2

Square Footage: 2,282

Main Level Sq. Ft.: 1,597

Upper Level Sq. Ft.: 685

Bedrooms: 4

Bathrooms: 2½

Foundation: Basement

Materials List Available: Yes

Price Category: E

Images provided by designer/architect.

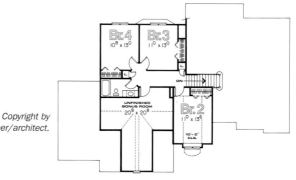

Upper Level Floor Plan

Copyright by designer/architect.

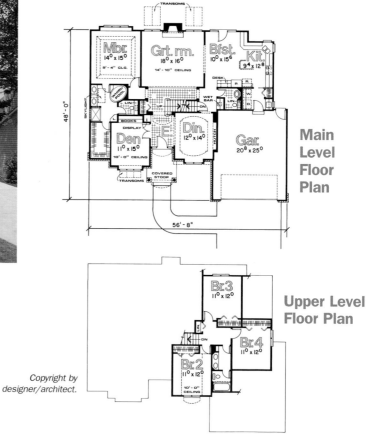

Main Level Floor Plan

Plan #121088

Dimensions: 56'8" W x 48' D

Levels: 2

Square Footage: 2,340

Main Level Sq. Ft.: 1,701

Upper Level Sq. Ft.: 639

Bedrooms: 4

Bathrooms: 2½

Foundation: Basement

Materials List Available: Yes

Price Category: E

Images provided by designer/architect.

Upper Level Floor Plan

Copyright by designer/architect.

Plan #401004

Dimensions: 54' W x 64'4" D
Levels: 2
Square Footage: 2,684
Main Level Sq. Ft.: 1,620
Upper Level Sq. Ft.: 1,064
Bedrooms: 3
Bathrooms: 2 full, 2 half
Foundation: Basement
Materials List Available: Yes
Price Category: F

This home, as shown in the photograph, may differ from the actual blueprints. For more detailed information, please check the floor plans carefully.

Images provided by designer/architect.

Finished in horizontal siding with solid-brick accents, this traditional home stands the test of time.

Features:

- **Foyer:** The sweeping horseshoe-shaped stair case dominates this two-story foyer. The octagonal living room, which is just a few steps away, boasts a masonry fireplace.

- **Kitchen:** The nearby dining room is reached through double doors and connects to this modified U-shaped kitchen with attached breakfast nook. A large walk-in pantry will hold all the supplies needed for your family.

- **Master Suite:** This retreat features an octagonal sleeping area with a vaulted ceiling and a romantic fireplace. The private bath will pamper you with a whirlpool tub and dual vanities.

- **Secondary Bedrooms:** Two additional bedrooms, which share a common bathroom, are located on the upper level with the master suite. The bonus room can act as an additional bedroom if needed.

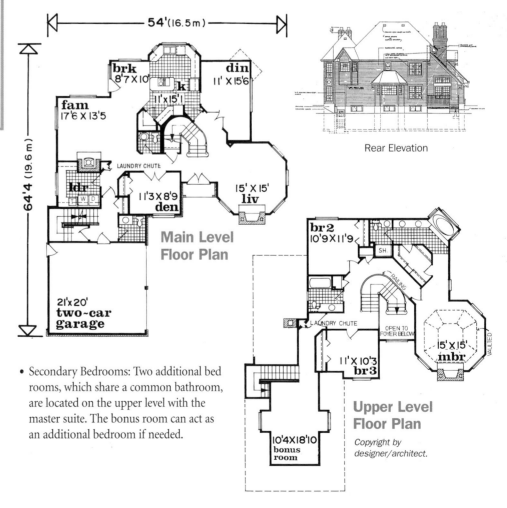

Rear Elevation

Main Level Floor Plan

Upper Level Floor Plan

Copyright by designer/architect.

Plans for Your Landscape

Landscapes change over the years. As plants grow, the overall look evolves from sparse to lush. Trees cast cool shade where the sun used to shine. Shrubs and hedges grow tall and dense enough to provide privacy. Perennials and ground covers spread to form colorful patches of foliage and flowers. Meanwhile, paths, arbors, fences, and other structures gain the comfortable patina of age.

Constant change over the years—sometimes rapid and dramatic, sometimes slow and subtle—is one of the joys of landscaping. It is also one of the challenges. Anticipating how fast plants will grow and how big they will eventually get is difficult, even for professional designers, and was a major concern in formulating the designs for this book.

To illustrate the kinds of changes to expect in a planting, these pages show one of the designs at three different "ages." Even though a new planting may look sparse at first, it will soon fill in. And because of careful spacing, the planting will look as good in 10 to 15 years as it does after 3 to 5. It will, of course, look different, but that's part of the fun.

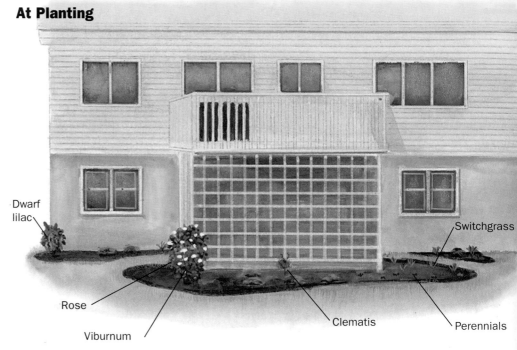

At Planting

Dwarf lilac

Switchgrass

Rose

Clematis

Perennials

Viburnum

Three to Five Years

Rose

Dwarf lilac

Switchgrass

Juniper

Viburnum

Juniper

Clematis

Perennials

At Planting—Here's how the deck planting might appear in late spring immediately after planting. The rose and clematis haven't begun to climb the new lattice trellis. The viburnum and lilac, usually sold in 2- to 5-gal. cans, start blooming as young plants and may have flowers when you buy them, but there will be enough space that you may want to plant some short annuals around them for the first few growing seasons. You can put short annuals between the new little junipers, too. The switchgrass and perennials, transplanted from quart- or gallon-size containers, are just low tufts of foliage now, but they grow fast enough to produce a few flowers the first summer.

Three to Five Years—As shown here in midsummer, the rose and clematis now reach most of the way up the supports. Although they aren't mature yet, the lilac, viburnum, and junipers look nice and bushy, and they're big enough that you don't need to fill around them with annuals. So far, the vines and shrubs have needed only minimal pruning. Most grasses and perennials reach full size about three to five years after planting; after that, they need to be divided and replanted in freshly amended soil to keep them healthy and vigorous.

Ten to Fifteen Years—Shown again in summer, the rose and clematis now cover their supports, and the lilac and viburnum are as tall as they'll get. To maintain all of these plants, you'll need to start pruning out some of the older stems every year in early spring. The junipers have spread sideways to form a solid mass; prunc them as needed along the edge of the lawn and pathways. When the junipers crowd them out, move the daylilies to another part of your property, or move them to the front of the bed to replace the other perennials, as shown here.

Ten to Fifteen Years

Up Front and Formal

Garden Geometry Transforms a Small Front Yard

Formal gardens have a special appeal. Their simple geometry is soothing in a hectic world, and their look is timeless, never going out of style. Traditional two-story homes with symmetrical facades are especially suited to the clean lines and balanced features shown here.

The design creates a small courtyard at the center of four rectangular beds defined by evergreen hedges and flagstone walkways. Inside the hedges, carefree perennial catmint makes a colorful floral carpet during the summer. The flagstone paving reinforces the design's geometry, while providing access to the front door from the sidewalk. (If a driveway runs along one side of the property, the crosswalk could extend to it through an opening in the hedge.) At

the center of the composition, the paving widens to accommodate a planter filled with annuals, a pleasant setting for greetings or good-byes. A bench at one end of the crosswalk provides a spot for longer chats or restful moments enjoying the plantings or, perhaps, contemplating a garden ornament at the other end.

Loose, informal hedges soften the rigid geometry. Deciduous shrubs change with the seasons, offering flowers in the spring and brilliant fall foliage, while the evergreens are a dependably colorful presence year round.

Note: All plants are appropriate for USDA Hardiness *Zones 3, 4, 5, and 6.*

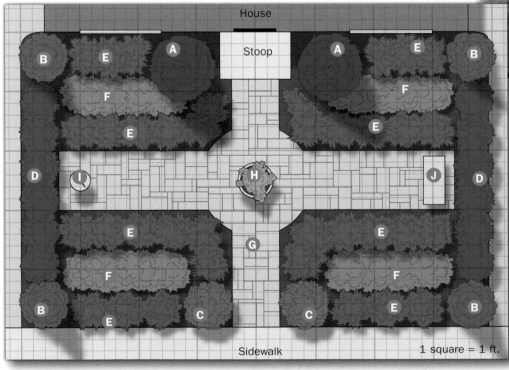

'Nigra' arborvitae Ⓐ

'Techny' Ⓑ arborvitae

Garden Ⓘ ornament

'Blue Wonder' Ⓕ catmint

Plants and Projects

Precise layout is important in a simple design such as this. Start with the flagstone walks; they aren't difficult to build but require some time and muscle. The hedge shrubs are chosen for their compact forms. You'll need to clip the lilacs annually to maintain their shape, but the junipers will require little pruning over the years.

Ⓐ **'Nigra'** *Thuja occidentalis* (use 2 plants)
These upright, pyramidal evergreen trees stand like sentinels at the front door, where their scented foliage greets visitors. Prune to

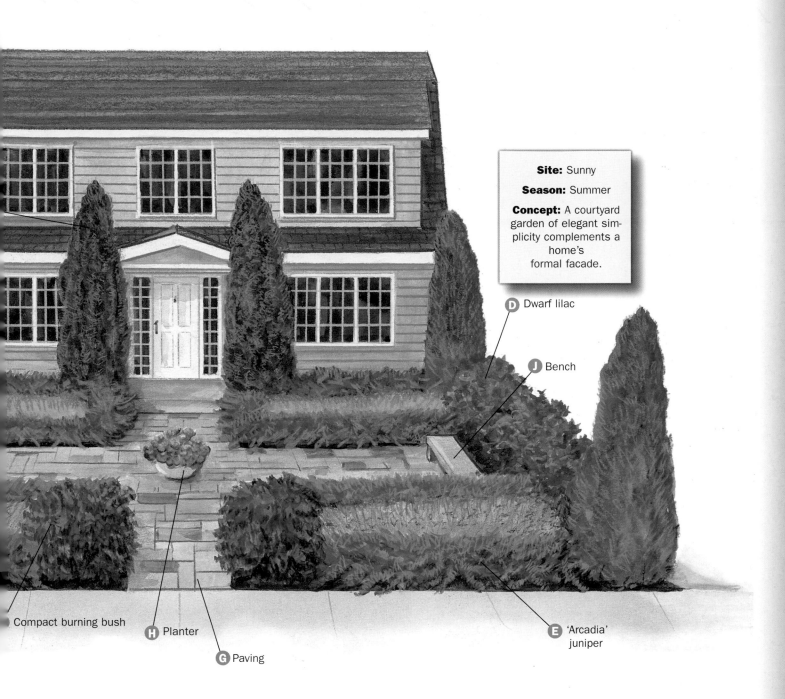

Site: Sunny

Season: Summer

Concept: A courtyard garden of elegant simplicity complements a home's formal facade.

D Dwarf lilac

J Bench

Compact burning bush

H Planter

G Paving

E 'Arcadia' juniper

---

keep their height in scale with the house.

'Techny' arborvitae *Thuja occidentalis* (use 4)
Marking the corners of the design, this evergreen tree forms a shorter, broader cone than its cousin by the door.

Compact burning bush
Euonymus alatus 'Compactus' (use 2)
A deciduous shrub forming a neat globe of green foliage, it turns an attention-grabbing crimson in fall. An excellent choice to mark the property's entrance.

D Dwarf lilac *Syringa meyeri 'Palibin'* (use 12)
This compact deciduous shrub makes an attractive loose hedge offering fragrant springtime flowers and glossy green foliage that has a purplish cast in fall.

E 'Arcadia' juniper *Juniperus sabina* (use 36)
The arching branches of this spreading evergreen shrub line the walks with bright green color through four seasons.

F 'Blue Wonder' catmint *Nepeta × faassenii* (use 40)
Loose spikes of misty blue flowers

rise above the silvery, aromatic foliage of this perennial in June, filling the beds with color. Blooms continue or repeat through the summer.

G Paving
Rectangular flagstones in random sizes suit the style of this house; brick or precast pavers work with other house styles.

H Planter
Nurseries and garden centers offer a range of planters that are suitable for formal settings. Choose one that complements the style of your house and fill it with colorful

annuals such as the geraniums in the round stone planter shown here. If you're ambitious, change the plantings with the seasons.

I Garden ornament
Place a sundial (shown here), reflecting ball, statue, or other ornament as a focal point at the end of the crosswalk.

J Bench
A stone bench is a nice companion for the planter and sundial here, but wood or metal benches can also work well in formal garden settings.

A Neighborly Corner

Beautify a Boundary With Easy-care Plants

The corner where your property meets your neighbor's and the sidewalk can be a kind of grassy no-man's-land. This design defines the boundary with a planting that can be enjoyed by both property owners. Good gardens make good neighbors, so we've used well-behaved low-maintenance plants that won't make extra work for the person next door—or for you.

Because of its exposed location, remote from the house and close to the street, this is a less personal planting than those in other more private and frequently used parts of your property. This design is meant, therefore, to be appreciated from a distance. It showcases five handsome shrubs, arranged in blocks, rather like a patchwork quilt, beneath a fine multi-

trunked tree. (An existing fence on the property line, like the one shown here, can help frame the composition.)

Although several of these plants offer attractive flowers, it is their foliage that makes this planting special. As the seasons progress you'll see blues, greens, reds, and yellows, culminating in an eye-popping display of fiery autumn leaves.

Note: All plants are appropriate for USDA Hardiness *Zones 3, 4, 5, and 6.*

Plants and Projects

For the first few years, mulch the planting well to retain moisture and to keep down weeds until the shrubs fill in. This is a very easy planting to maintain if you choose to prune only to maintain the natural shapes of the shrubs, which soften the geometry imposed by the planting plan.

A **Amur maple** *Acer ginnala* (use 1 plant)
A small but fast-growing deciduous tree; pick one that has multiple trunks. Bears pale flowers in spring, green leaves and red fruits in summer, and crimson foliage in autumn.

B **'Gro-Low'** *Rhus aromatica* (use 4)

These tough deciduous shrubs spread to form low mounds beneath the maple. Shiny green leaves turn scarlet in fall.

C **'Anthony Waterer'** *Spiraea × bumalda* (use 3)
Small, fine blue-green leaves set off the rosy pink flowers of this compact deciduous shrub. Blooms in summer.

D **'Blue Star'** *Juniperus squamata* (use 7)
The prickly, rich blue foliage of this low evergreen shrub makes a striking contrast with its neighbors.

E **'Crimson Pygmy'** *Japanese barberry Berberis thunbergii* (use 3)

The small, deep purple leaves of this deciduous shrub are as eye-catching in summer as in fall, when they turn a rich crimson. The low, rounded mounds are set off by the colors of the nearby juniper and sumac.

F **'Goldflame'** *Spiraea × bumalda* (use 4)
The leaves of this small deciduous shrub have a different look in each season: gold in spring, chartreuse in summer, and orange-red in fall. Bears pale pink flowers in summer.

C 'Anthony Waterer' spirea

D 'Blue Star' juniper

Fence

C

D

A

E

B

Sidewalk

F

Lawn

1 square = 1 ft.

Site: Sunny

Season: Summer

Concept: Enhance the property line with a low-care, neighbor-friendly planting of trees and shrubs.

A Amur maple

B 'Gro-Low' sumac

F 'Goldflame' spirea

E 'Crimson Pygmy' Japanese barberry

Streetwise and Stylish

Give Your Curbside Strip a New Look

Homeowners seldom think much about the strip that runs between the sidewalk and street. At best it is a tidy patch of lawn; at worst, a weed-choked eyesore. Yet this is one of the most public parts of your property. Planting this strip attractively can give pleasure to passersby and to visitors who park next to the curb, as well as enhance the streetscape you view from the house. (This property is usually city-owned, so check local ordinances for restrictions before you start a remake.)

In older neighborhoods, mature trees lining the street create more shade than most grass can tolerate. The design shown here replaces thinning turf in a shady site with a lush planting of hostas, ferns, and ground covers. Leaves in a pleasing variety of sizes, shapes, and colors make an inviting display from spring through fall.

It might help to think of this curbside strip as an island bed between two defined boundaries: the street and the sidewalk. The beds are divided by a pedestrian walkway, providing room for visitors to get in and out of their cars. You can expand the beds to fill a longer strip, or plant lawn next to them. This design, or a variation, would also work nicely in a shady location along a patio, property line, or foundation.

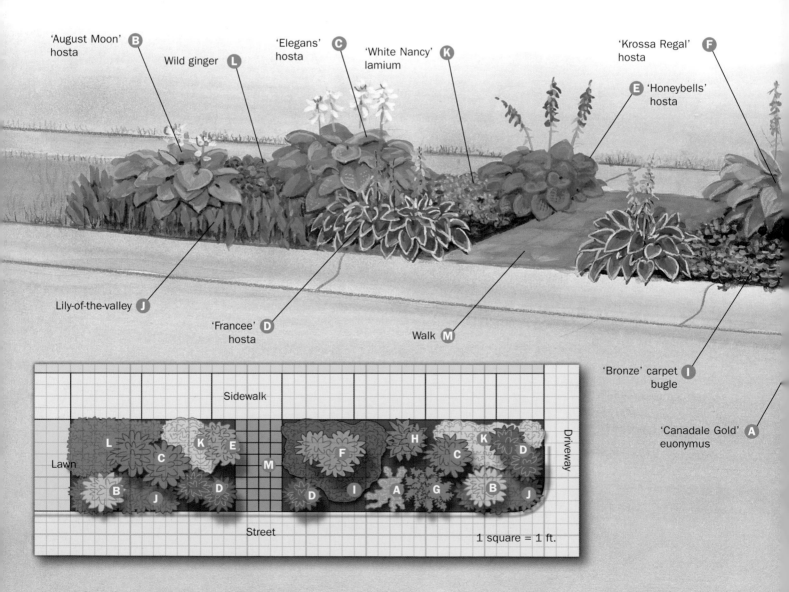

'August Moon' hosta **B**

Wild ginger **L**

'Elegans' hosta **C**

'White Nancy' lamium **K**

'Krossa Regal' hosta **F**

'Honeybells' hosta **E**

Lily-of-the-valley **J**

'Francee' hosta **D**

Walk **M**

'Bronze' carpet bugle **I**

'Canadale Gold' euonymus **A**

1 square = 1 ft.

Plants and Projects

This can be a difficult site. Summer drought and shade, winter road salt, pedestrian and car traffic, and errant dogs are usual conditions along the street. Plants have to be tough to perform well here, but they need not look tough. The ones used here make a dramatic impact during the growing season. Then all but the sturdy low-growing euonymus die back in winter, so piles of snow won't hurt them. To help provide adequate moisture, add plenty of organic matter to the soil when you prepare the beds.

A **'Canadale Gold'** *Euonymus fortunei* (use 1 plant)
A broad-leaved evergreen, this shrub forms a low, spreading mound. The small rounded leaves have yellow margins and contrast attractively with the large-leaved hostas.

B **'August Moon'** *Hosta* (use 2)
A perennial (like all hostas), this cultivar forms a broad clump of textured golden yellow leaves. Thin stalks bear white flowers in mid- to late summer.

C **'Elegans'** *Hosta sieboldiana* (use 3)
This hosta's huge blue, textured leaves form imposing mounds at the center of each bed. White flowers in summer.

D **'Francee'** *Hosta* (use 5)
This hosta's dark green heart-shaped leaves are edged with white, and its flowers are lavender.

E **'Honeybells'** *Hosta* (use 2)
Forms a large, broad clump of pale green oblong leaves. The lilac flowers are scented.

F **'Krossa Regal'** *Hosta* (use 3)
Long, powder blue leaves form a large mound, more erect than the other hostas in the planting. Lilac flowers dangle well above the foliage on tall, thin stalks.

G **Japanese painted fern**
Athyrium goeringianum 'Pictum' (use 6)
This elegant perennial is a subtle accent for the planting, with its fronds delicately painted in glowing tones of green, silver, and maroon.

H **Maidenhair fern**
Adiantum pedatum (use 5)
This perennial forms a dainty mass of lacy green fronds on wiry black stems; looks great with the blue hostas.

I **'Bronze' carpet bugle**
Ajuga reptans (use 22)
The dark bronze-green leaves of this fast-spreading perennial ground cover set off the hostas and ferns handsomely. Small bluish purple flowers add color in late spring and early summer.

J **Lily-of-the-valley**
Convallaria majalis (use 32)
A perennial ground cover, it quickly forms a patch of large erect leaves. In spring, tiny white bell-shaped flowers dangle from slender stalks and produce a wonderful sweet scent.

K **'White Nancy'**
Lamium maculatum (use 26)
This perennial ground cover's small silvery leaves edged with green practically shine in the shade. Bears white flowers in early summer.

L **Wild ginger**
Asarum canadense (use 12)
Another perennial ground cover, this produces fuzzy heart-shaped leaves that create a beautiful dull green carpet beneath the blue hosta leaves.

M **Walk**
Use brick, flagstone, or the simple cement pavers shown here. Choose a color to match your house.

> **Site:** Shady
>
> **Season:** Summer
>
> **Concept:** Striking foliage gives a lush look to a shady curbside planting.

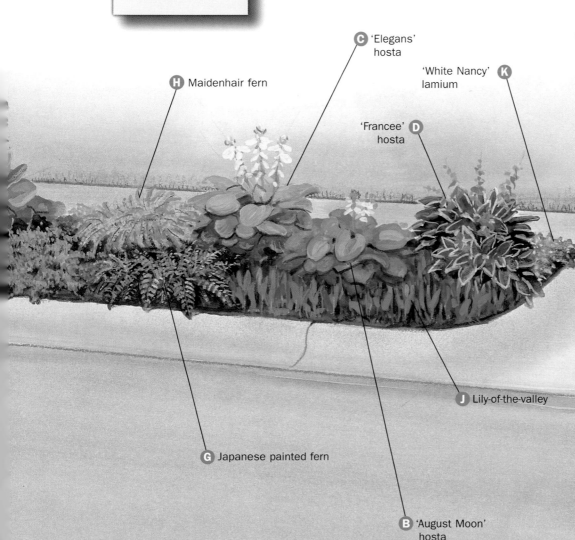

C 'Elegans' hosta

H Maidenhair fern

K 'White Nancy' lamium

D 'Francee' hosta

J Lily-of-the-valley

G Japanese painted fern

B 'August Moon' hosta

Note: All plants are appropriate for USDA Hardiness *Zones 3, 4, 5, and 6.*

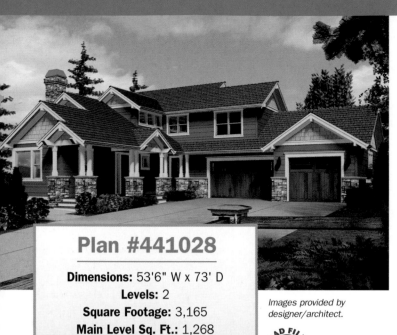

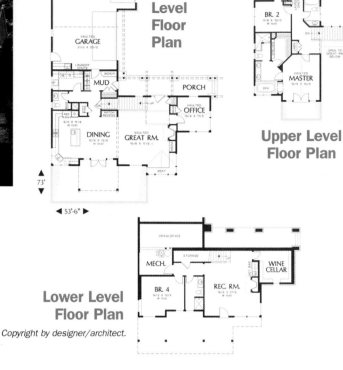

Main Level Floor Plan

Upper Level Floor Plan

Lower Level Floor Plan

Images provided by designer/architect.

Copyright by designer/architect.

Plan #441028

Dimensions: 53'6" W x 73' D

Levels: 2

Square Footage: 3,165

Main Level Sq. Ft.: 1,268

Upper Level Sq. Ft.: 931

Lower Level Sq. Ft.: 966

Bedrooms: 4

Bathrooms: 3½

Foundation: Slab

Materials List Available: No

Price Category: G

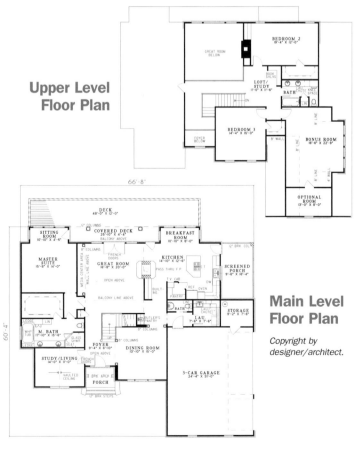

Upper Level Floor Plan

Main Level Floor Plan

Images provided by designer/architect.

Copyright by designer/architect.

Plan #151121

Dimensions: 66'8" W x 60'4" D

Levels: 2

Square Footage: 3,108

Main Level Sq. Ft.: 2,107

Upper Level Sq. Ft.: 1,001

Bedrooms: 3

Bathrooms: 2½

Foundation: Crawl space, slab; basement option for fee

CompleteCost List Available: Yes

Price Category: G

Plan #211111

Dimensions: 66' W x 74' D

Levels: 2

Square Footage: 3,035

Main Level Sq. Ft.: 2,008

Upper Level Sq. Ft.: 1,027

Bedrooms: 4

Bathrooms: 3½

Foundation: Crawl space

Materials List Available: Yes

Price Category: G

Images provided by designer/architect.

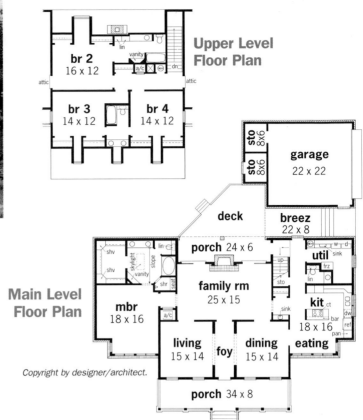

Upper Level Floor Plan

br 2
16 x 12

br 3
14 x 12

br 4
14 x 12

attic   attic

Main Level Floor Plan

sto 8x6
sto 8x6

garage
22 x 22

deck

breez
22 x 8

porch 24 x 6

util

mbr
18 x 16

family rm
25 x 15

sto

kit
18 x 16

living
15 x 14

foy

dining
15 x 14

eating

porch 34 x 8

Copyright by designer/architect.

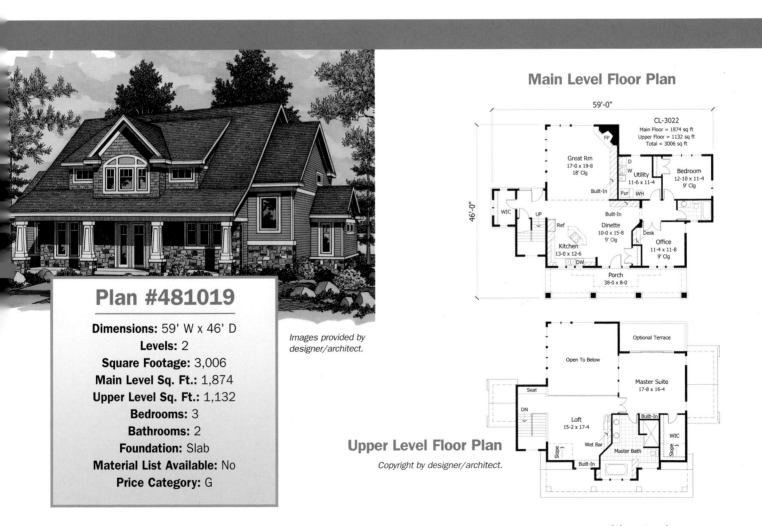

Plan #481019

Dimensions: 59' W x 46' D

Levels: 2

Square Footage: 3,006

Main Level Sq. Ft.: 1,874

Upper Level Sq. Ft.: 1,132

Bedrooms: 3

Bathrooms: 2

Foundation: Slab

Material List Available: No

Price Category: G

Images provided by designer/architect.

Main Level Floor Plan

59'-0"

46'-0"

CL-3022
Main Floor = 1874 sq ft
Upper Floor = 1132 sq ft
Total = 3006 sq ft

Great Rm
17-0 x 19-8
18' Clg

Utility
11-6 x 11-4

Bedroom
12-10 x 11-4
9' Clg

WIC

UP

Ref

Built-In

Dinette
10-0 x 15-8
9' Clg

Desk

Kitchen
13-0 x 12-6

Office
11-4 x 11-8
9' Clg

Porch
38-0 x 8-0

Upper Level Floor Plan

Optional Terrace

Open To Below

Seat

DN

Master Suite
17-8 x 16-4

Loft
15-2 x 17-4

Built-In

WIC

Wet Bar

Master Bath

Built-In

Copyright by designer/architect.

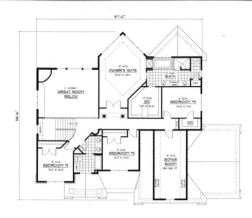

Plan #481131

Dimensions: 69' W x 58' D

Levels: 2

Square Footage: 3,641

Main Level Sq. Ft.: 2,087

Upper Level Sq. Ft.: 1,554

Bedrooms: 4

Bathrooms: 2½

Foundation: Walkout basement

Materials List Available: No

Price Category: H

Images provided by designer/architect.

Upper Level Floor Plan

Main Level Floor Plan

Copyright by designer/architect.

Main Level Floor Plan

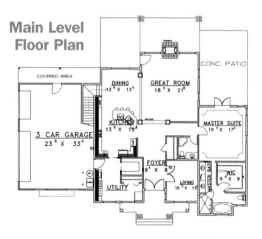

Plan #451269

Dimensions: 73' W x 65'2" D

Levels: 2

Square Footage: 3,952

Main Level Sq. Ft.: 2,080

Upper Level Sq. Ft.: 1,872

Bedrooms: 3

Bathrooms: 3

Foundation: Crawl space

Material List Available: No

Price Category: H

Images provided by designer/architect.

CAD FILE AVAILABLE

Rear Elevation

Upper Level Floor Plan

Copyright by designer/architect.

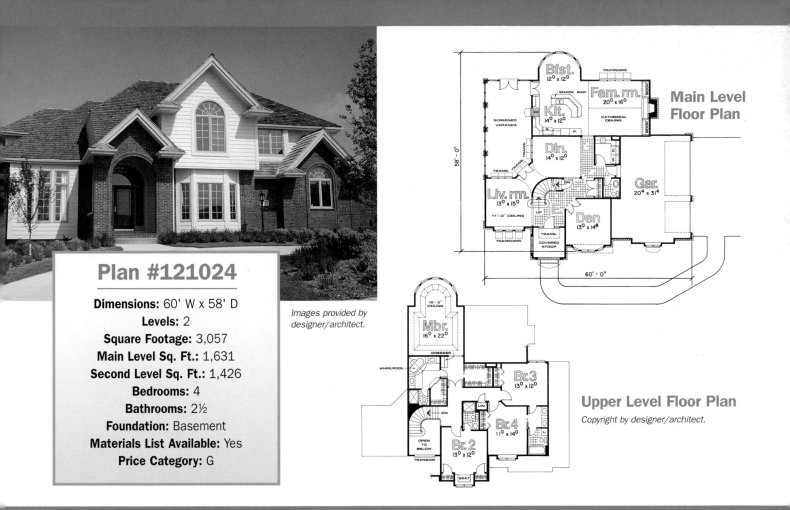

Plan #121024

Dimensions: 60' W x 58' D
Levels: 2
Square Footage: 3,057
Main Level Sq. Ft.: 1,631
Second Level Sq. Ft.: 1,426
Bedrooms: 4
Bathrooms: 2½
Foundation: Basement
Materials List Available: Yes
Price Category: G

Images provided by designer/architect.

Main Level Floor Plan

Upper Level Floor Plan
Copyright by designer/architect.

Plan #441026

Dimensions: 60' W x 52' D
Levels: 2
Square Footage: 3,623
Main Level Sq. Ft.: 1,835
Upper Level Sq. Ft.: 1,788
Bedrooms: 4
Bathrooms: 2½
Foundation: Crawl space
Materials List Available: No
Price Category: H

Images provided by designer/architect.

Main Level Floor Plan

Upper Level Floor Plan
Copyright by designer/architect.

**Upper Level
Floor Plan**

Plan #221025

Dimensions: 69'8" W x 72' D

Levels: 2

Square Footage: 3,009

Main Level Sq. Ft.: 2,039

Upper Level Sq. Ft.: 970

Bedrooms: 4

Bathrooms: 2½

Foundation: Basement

Materials List Available: No

Price Category: G

*Images provided by
designer/architect.*

**Main Level
Floor Plan**

*Copyright by
designer/architect.*

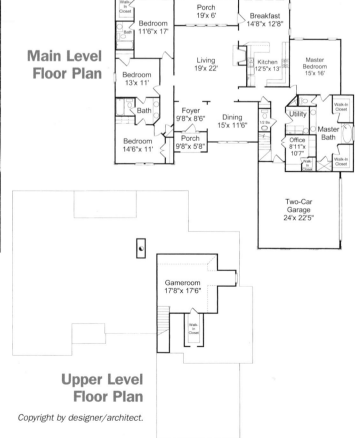

**Main Level
Floor Plan**

Plan #111011

Dimensions: 71'4" W x 74' D

Levels: 2

Square Footage: 3,292

Main Level Sq. Ft.: 2,862

Upper Level Sq. Ft.: 430

Bedrooms: 4

Bathrooms: 3½

Foundation: Crawl space, slab

Materials List Available: No

Price Category: G

*Images provided by
designer/architect.*

**Upper Level
Floor Plan**

Copyright by designer/architect.

Plan #361231

Dimensions: 77' W x 83' D

Levels: 1

Square Footage: 3,026

Bedrooms: 3

Bathrooms: 3

Foundation: Crawl space

Material List Available: No

Price Category: G

Images provided by designer/architect.

Copyright by designer/architect.

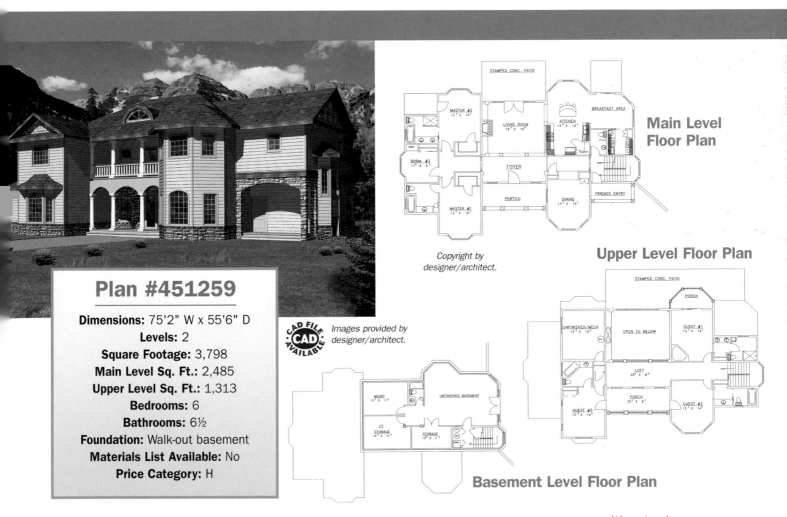

Plan #451259

Dimensions: 75'2" W x 55'6" D

Levels: 2

Square Footage: 3,798

Main Level Sq. Ft.: 2,485

Upper Level Sq. Ft.: 1,313

Bedrooms: 6

Bathrooms: 6½

Foundation: Walk-out basement

Materials List Available: No

Price Category: H

Images provided by designer/architect.

Copyright by designer/architect.

Main Level Floor Plan

Upper Level Floor Plan

Basement Level Floor Plan

Plan #211075

Dimensions: 80' W x 84' D
Levels: 2
Square Footage: 3,568
Main Level Sq. Ft.: 2,330
Upper Level Sq. Ft.: 1,238
Bedrooms: 4
Bathrooms: 3½
Foundation: Crawl space
Materials List Available: Yes
Price Category: H

The porte-cochere—or covered passage over a driveway—announces the quality and beauty of this spacious country home.

Features:

- **Front Porch:** Spot groups of potted plants on this 779-sq.-ft. porch, and add a glider and some rocking chairs to take advantage of its comfort.

- **Family Room:** Let this family room become the heart of the home. With a fireplace to make it cozy and a wet bar for easy serving, it's a natural for entertaining.

- **Game Room:** Expect a crowd in this room, no matter what the weather.

- **Kitchen:** A cooktop island and a pantry are just two features of this fully appointed kitchen.

- **Master Suite:** The bedroom is as luxurious as you'd expect, but the quarter-circle raised tub in the master bath might surprise you. Two walk-in closets and two vanities add a practical touch.

Main Level Floor Plan

Upper Level Floor Plan

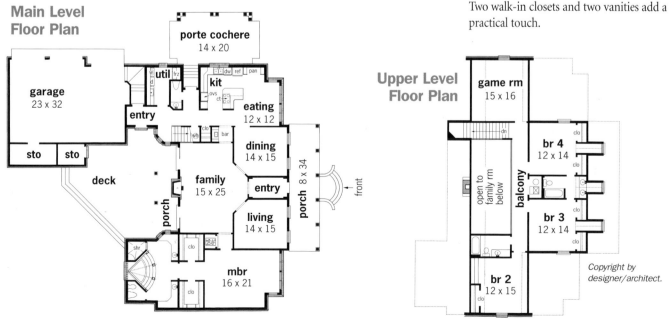

Plan #121026

Dimensions: 66'8" W x 76' D
Levels: 2
Square Footage: 3,926
Main Level Sq. Ft.: 2,351
Upper Level Sq. Ft.: 1,575
Bedrooms: 4
Bathrooms: 3 full, 2 half
Foundation: Basement
Materials List Available: Yes
Price Category: H

Images provided by designer/architect.

Plenty of space and architectural detail make this a comfortable and gracious home.

Features:

- Ceiling Height: 8 ft. unless otherwise noted.

- Great Room: A soaring cathedral ceiling makes this great room seem even more spacious than it is, while the fireplace framed by windows lends warmth and comfort.

- Eating Area: There's a dining room for more formal entertaining, but this informal eating area to the left of the great room will get plenty

of daily use. It features a built-in desk for compiling shopping lists and recipes and access to the backyard.

- Kitchen: Next door to the eating area, this kitchen is designed to make food preparation a pleasure. It features a center cooktop, a recycling area, and a corner pantry.

- Lockers: You'll find a bench and lockers at the service entry and additional lockers in the laundry room next door.

CAD FILE AVAILABLE

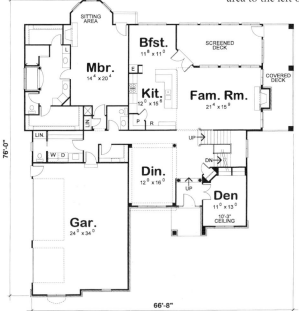

Main Level Floor Plan

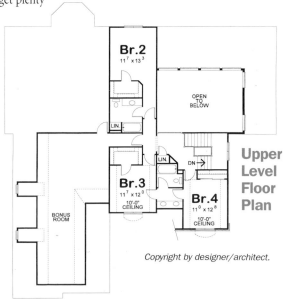

Upper Level Floor Plan

Copyright by designer/architect.

Plan #561002

Dimensions: 61' W x 55' D
Levels: 1.5
Square Footage: 3,416
Main Level Sq. Ft.: 2,479
Upper Level Sq. Ft.: 937
Bedrooms: 4
Bathrooms: 3½
Foundation: Basement
Material List Available: Yes
Price Category: G

Traditional Cape Cod styling provides this home with incredible street appeal.

Features:

- Great Room: There is plenty of room for your family and friends to gather in this large room. The fireplace will add a feeling of coziness to the expansive space

- Kitchen: Open to the great room and a dining area, this island kitchen adds to the open feeling of the home. Additional seating, located at the island, enables guests to mingle with the chef of the family without getting in the way.

- Lower Level: This level (finishing is optional) adds a fourth bedroom suite, enough space for a family room or media room, and a wet bar for entertaining.

- Garage: Split garages allow the daily drivers their spaces plus a separate garage for that special vehicle or even a golf cart.

Main Level Floor Plan

Upper Level Floor Plan

Copyright by designer/architect.

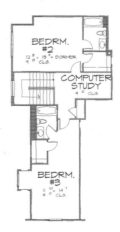

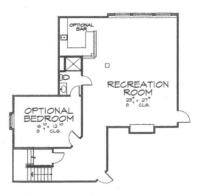

Basement Level Floor Plan

Great Room

Great Room

Kitchen

Office

Master Bedroom

Master Bath

Main Level Floor Plan

DECK (8'0"x25'0")

MASTER BEDROOM (20'2"x14'0")

LIVING ROOM (16'0"x19'8")

SUNROOM (13'2"x14'0")

BREAKFAST AREA (11'0"x14'0")

STUDY/ SITTING AREA (7'10"x15'8")

FOYER

DINING ROOM (15'0"x13'4")

KITCHEN (13'2"x14'0")

FRONT PORCH

CART AREA

2-CAR GARAGE (31'4"x20'0")

BEDROOM #2 (12'0"x12'4")

BEDROOM #3 (12'4"x11'10")

LOFT AREA

STORAGE

Upper Level Floor Plan

BONUS ROOM (27'10"x20'0")

Copyright by designer/architect.

Plan #521003

Dimensions: 72' W x 100' D
Levels: 2
Square Footage: 3,373
Main Level Sq. Ft.: 2,515
Upper Level Sq. Ft.: 858
Bedrooms: 3
Bathrooms: 2 full, 2 half
Foundation: Crawl space
Material List Available: No
Price Category: G

Images provided by designer/architect.

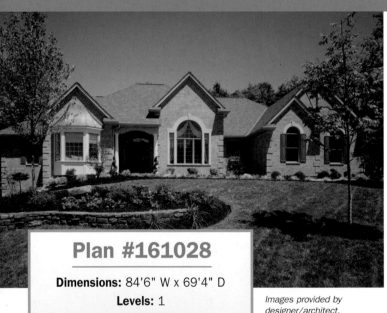

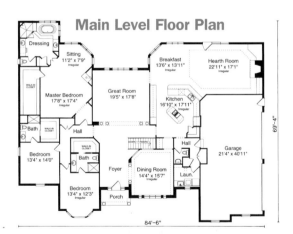

Main Level Floor Plan

Dressing

Sitting 11'2" x 7'9" Irregular

Breakfast 13'6" x 13'11" Irregular

Hearth Room 22'11" x 17'1" Irregular

Master Bedroom 17'8" x 17'4" Irregular

Great Room 19'5" x 17'8"

Kitchen 16'10" x 17'11" Irregular

Bath

Bedroom 13'4" x 14'0"

Hall

Bath

Foyer

Hall

Garage 21'4" x 40'11"

Dining Room 14'4" x 15'7" Irregular

Laun.

Bedroom 13'4" x 12'3" Irregular

Porch

69'-4"

84'-6"

Copyright by designer/architect.

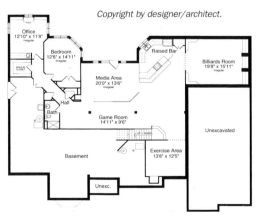

Optional Basement Level Floor Plan

Office 12'10" x 11'8" Irregular

Bedroom 12'6" x 14'11" Irregular

Raised Bar

Billiards Room 19'8" x 15'11" Irregular

Media Area 20'0" x 13'6" Irregular

Hall

Bath

Game Room 14'11" x 9'6"

Unexcavated

Basement

Exercise Area 13'8" x 12'5"

Unexc.

Plan #161028

Dimensions: 84'6" W x 69'4" D
Levels: 1
Square Footage: 3,570
Optional Finished Basement Sq. Ft.: 2,367
Bedrooms: 3
Bathrooms: 3½
Foundation: Basement
Materials List Available: Yes
Price Category: H

Images provided by designer/architect.

Plan #151129

Dimensions: 70' W x 75'10" D
Levels: 2
Square Footage: 3,947
Main Level Sq. Ft.: 2,777
Upper Level Sq. Ft.: 1,170
Bedrooms: 4
Bathrooms: 3 full, 2 half
Foundation: Crawl space or slab; basement or walkout for fee
CompletCost List Available: Yes
Price Category: H

Images provided by designer/architect.

CAD FILE AVAILABLE

Main Level Floor Plan

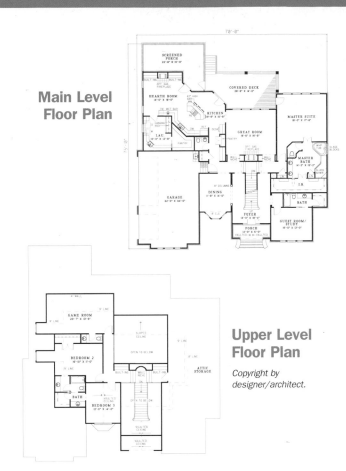

Upper Level Floor Plan

Copyright by designer/architect.

Plan #241014

Dimensions: 66'6" W x 55'6" D
Levels: 2
Square Footage 3,046
Main Level Sq. Ft.: 2,292
Upper Level Sq. Ft.: 754
Bedrooms: 4
Bathrooms: 3
Foundation: Slab
Materials List Available: No
Price Category: G

Images provided by designer/architect.

Main Level Floor Plan

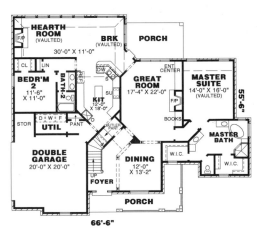

Upper Level Floor Plan

Copyright by designer/architect.

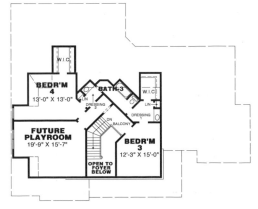

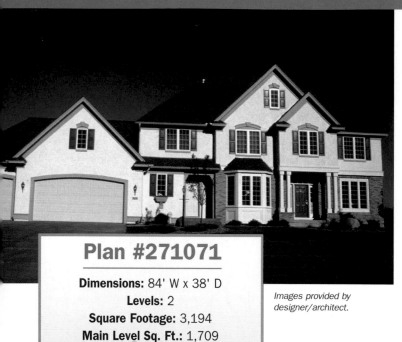

Main Level Floor Plan

DECK

DINETTE 14⁶ x 11⁶ 9⁰ clg

FAMILY RM 22⁸ x 15⁴ 18⁰ clg

STUDY 11⁴ x 11⁰ 9⁰ clg

GARAGE 33⁶ x 25⁴

KITCHEN 14⁴ x 14² 9⁰ clg

DINING RM 11⁸ x 13⁴ 9⁰ clg

FOYER 18⁰ clg

LIVING RM 11⁴ x 13⁴ 9⁰ clg

Plan #271071

Dimensions: 84' W x 38' D

Levels: 2

Square Footage: 3,194

Main Level Sq. Ft.: 1,709

Upper Level Sq. Ft.: 1,485

Bedrooms: 4

Bathrooms: 2½

Foundation: Crawl space or basement

Materials List Available: No

Price Category: G

Images provided by designer/architect.

Upper Level Floor Plan

MSTR SUITE 14⁴ x 17⁴ 10⁰ tray clg

BEDRM 4 10¹⁰ x 10⁴

MSTR BATH 11⁸ x 15⁴

BEDRM 2 11⁸ x 13⁴

BEDRM 3 11⁴ x 13⁰

Copyright by designer/architect.

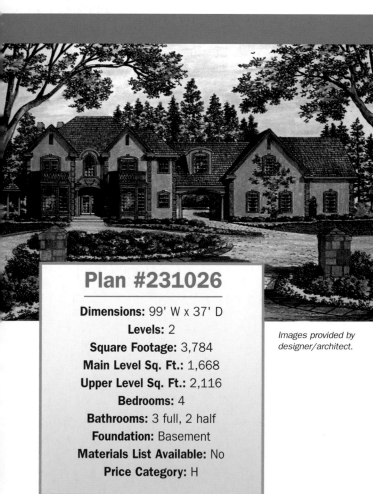

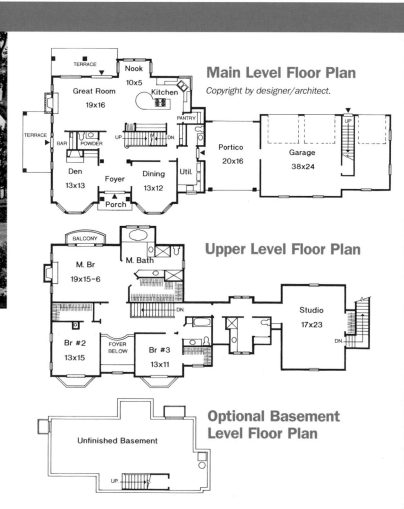

TERRACE

Nook 10x5

Main Level Floor Plan

Copyright by designer/architect.

Great Room 19x16

Kitchen

PANTRY

TERRACE

BAR POWDER

UP.

DN.

Portico 20x16

UP

Garage 38x24

Den 13x13

Foyer

Dining 13x12

Util.

Porch

Plan #231026

Dimensions: 99' W x 37' D

Levels: 2

Square Footage: 3,784

Main Level Sq. Ft.: 1,668

Upper Level Sq. Ft.: 2,116

Bedrooms: 4

Bathrooms: 3 full, 2 half

Foundation: Basement

Materials List Available: No

Price Category: H

Images provided by designer/architect.

BALCONY

M. Br 19x15-6

M. Bath

Upper Level Floor Plan

DN.

Studio 17x23

DN.

Br #2 13x15

FOYER BELOW

Br #3 13x11

Optional Basement Level Floor Plan

Unfinished Basement

UP

Plan #211117

Dimensions: 74' W x 78' D

Levels: 2

Square Footage: 3,284

Main Level Sq. Ft.: 2,655

Upper Level Sq. Ft.: 629

Bedrooms: 4

Bathrooms: 4

Foundation: Slab

Materials List Available: Yes

Price Category: G

Images provided by designer/architect.

Main Level Floor Plan

veranda
br 3 14 x 15 • books • balc • br 4 14 x 13
open to foyer

Upper Level Floor Plan

Copyright by designer/architect.

sto 6x14 • sto 6x8
garage 22 x 22
sto
eating
kit
books
pan
dw
bar
shv
dining 14 x 12
sink
ice
terrace
sun rm
guest br 12 x 14
vanity
shr seat
util
mbr 16 x 18
living 19 x 19
books
foy
niche
study 13 x 12
books
porch

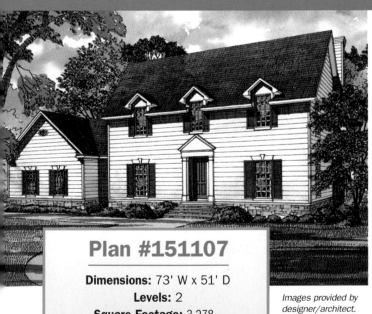

Plan #151107

Dimensions: 73' W x 51' D

Levels: 2

Square Footage: 3,278

Main Level Sq. Ft.: 1,921

Upper Level Sq. Ft.: 1,357

Bedrooms: 4

Bathrooms: 3½

Foundation: Crawl space or slab; basement or walkout for fee

CompletCost List Available: Yes

Price Category: E

Images provided by designer/architect.

CAD FILE AVAILABLE

Main Level Floor Plan

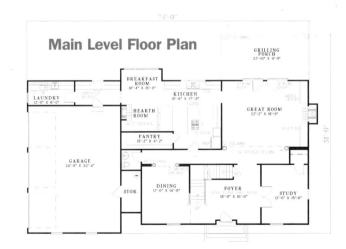

GRILLING PORCH 22'-10" X 11'-8"
BREAKFAST ROOM 10'-4" X 15'-9"
KITCHEN 15'-6" X 17'-3"
LAUNDRY 12'-0" X 6'-0"
HEARTH ROOM
GREAT ROOM 22'-2" X 16'-9"
PANTRY 13'-2" X 4'-2"
GARAGE 24'-0" X 32'-4"
STOR
DINING 12'-0" X 14'-8"
FOYER 18'-0" X 9'-0"
STUDY 12'-0" X 15'-0"

Upper Level Floor Plan

Copyright by designer/architect.

BALCONY DECK 22'-10" X 11'-8"
M. BATH 17'-4" X 15'-9"
MASTER SUITE 12'-8" X 16'-9"
BEDROOM 3 12'-0" X 12'-3"
BATH
BALCONY
BATH
BEDROOM 4 12'-0" X 12'-4"
OPEN TO BELOW
BEDROOM 2 12'-0" X 12'-6"

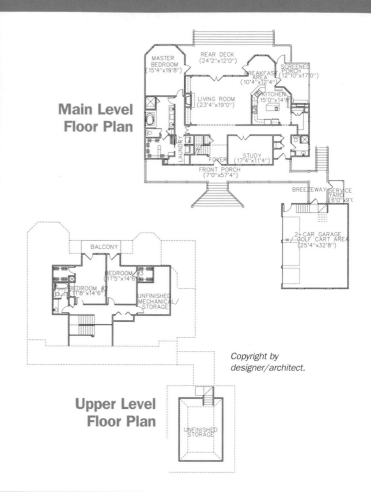

Main Level Floor Plan

Images provided by designer/architect.

CAD FILE AVAILABLE

Plan #521004

Dimensions: 79'6" W x 95'8" D

Levels: 2

Square Footage: 3,131

Main Level Sq. Ft.: 2,357

Upper Level Sq. Ft.: 774

Bedrooms: 3

Bathrooms: 3

Foundation: Crawl space

Material List Available: No

Price Category: G

Copyright by designer/architect.

Upper Level Floor Plan

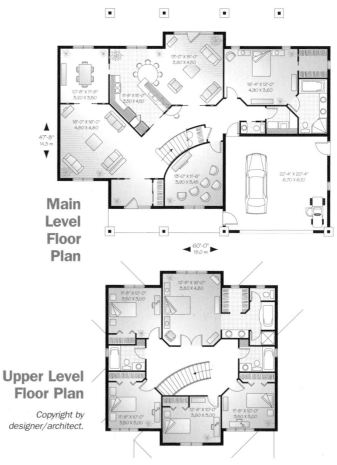

Plan #181079

Dimensions: 60' W x 47'8" D

Levels: 2

Square Footage: 3,016

Main Level Sq. Ft.: 1,716

Upper Level Sq. Ft.: 1,300

Bedrooms: 6

Bathrooms: 4½

Foundation: Crawl space

Materials List Available: Yes

Price Category: G

Images provided by designer/architect.

CAD FILE AVAILABLE

Main Level Floor Plan

Upper Level Floor Plan

Copyright by designer/architect.

Main Level Floor Plan

Plan #161049

Dimensions: 69'2" W x 53' D

Levels: 2

Square Footage: 3,213

Main Level Sq. Ft.: 1,967

Basement Level Sq. Ft.: 1,246

Bedrooms: 3

Bathrooms: 2 full, 2 half

Foundation: Slab

Materials List Available: Yes

Price Category: G

Images provided by designer/architect.

Basement Level Floor Plan

Copyright by designer/architect.

Rear Elevation

Main Level Floor Plan

Plan #271067

Dimensions: 72'2" W x 46'5" D

Levels: 2

Square Footage: 3,015

Main Level Sq. Ft.: 1,367

Upper Level Sq. Ft.: 1,648

Bedrooms: 3

Bathrooms: 2½

Foundation: Crawl space or basement

Materials List Available: No

Price Category: G

Images provided by designer/architect.

Upper Level Floor Plan

Copyright by designer/architect.

Plan #451054

Dimensions: 50'4" W x 54' D
Levels: 2
Square Footage: 3,489
Main Level Sq. Ft.: 1,269
Upper Level Sq. Ft.: 851
Lower Level Sq. Ft.: 1,369
Bedrooms: 2
Bathrooms: 3
Foundation: Walkout
Material List Available: No
Price Category: G

Experience the rustic charm and modern amenities of the log home.

Features:

• **Great Room:** This gathering area, complete with a cathedral ceiling, welcomes you into the home. The room is open to the dining room and kitchen, which gives an airy feeling to the home.

• **Kitchen:** This island kitchen stands ready when it's time to prepare your meals. The additional seating at the island can handle the overflow from the adjacent dining room.

• **Master Suite:** Filling the entire upper level, this retreat boasts its own private balcony and a walk-in closet. The loft acts as a private sitting area and has a view down to the great room.

• **Lower Level:** A large recreation room resides on this level; double doors lead to the outside. The full bathroom is an added convenience.

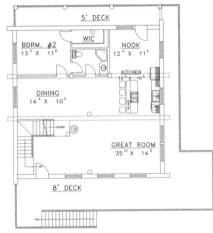

Main Level Floor Plan

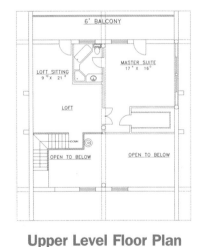

Upper Level Floor Plan
Copyright by designer/architect.

Basement Level Floor Plan

Rear Elevation

Plan #121081

Dimensions: 76'8" W x 68' D
Levels: 2
Square Footage: 3,623
Main Level Sq. Ft.: 2,603
Upper Level Sq. Ft.: 1,020
Bedrooms: 4
Bathrooms: 4½
Foundation: Basement
Materials List Available: Yes
Price Category: G

This home, as shown in the photograph, may differ from the actual blueprints. For more detailed information, please check the floor plans carefully.

Images provided by designer/architect.

You'll love this impressive home if you're looking for perfect spot for entertaining as well as a home for comfortable family living.

Features:

- **Entry:** Walk into this grand two-story entryway through double doors, and be greeted by the sight of a graceful curved staircase.

- **Great Room:** This two-story room features stacked windows, a fireplace flanked by an entertainment center, a bookcase, and a wet bar.

- **Dining Room:** A corner column adds formality to this room, which is just off the entryway for the convenience of your guests.

- **Hearth Room:** Connected to the great room by a lovely set of French doors, this room features another fireplace as well as a convenient pantry.

Main Level Floor Plan

Upper Level Floor Plan

Copyright by designer/architect.

Main Level Floor Plan

Two-Car Garage 22'6"x 24'9"

Patio 19'x 10'

Porch 19'x 9'5"

Storage 12'4"x 7'7"

Utility

Master Bath

Walk-In Closet

Bath

Master Bedroom 14'x 20'

Family Room 20'x 20'

Kitchen 13'2"x 18'8"

Walk-In Closet

Bedroom 13'2" 12'

Living 12'1"x 14'

Foyer

Dining 12'1"x 14'

Breakfast 13'2"x 11'

Porch 32'10"x 6'

Images provided by designer/architect.

Unfinished Gameroom

Upper Level Floor Plan

Copyright by designer/architect.

Storage

Open to Below

Balcony

Bedroom 12'x 13'

Bedroom 13'x 13'

Bath

Plan #111034

Dimensions: 67' W x 79' D

Levels: 2

Square Footage: 3,085

Main Level Sq. Ft.: 2,439

Upper Level Sq. Ft.: 646

Bedrooms: 4

Bathrooms: 3

Foundation: Basement

Materials List Available: No

Price Category: G

Plan #391053

Dimensions: 76' W x 63' D

Levels: 2

Square Footage: 3,128

Main Level Sq. Ft.: 2,277

Upper Level Sq. Ft.: 851

Bedrooms: 4

Bathrooms: 3½

Foundation: Crawl space, slab, or basement

Material List Available: Yes

Price Category: G

Images provided by designer/architect.

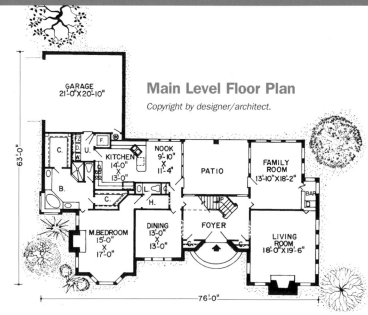

Main Level Floor Plan

Copyright by designer/architect.

GARAGE 21'-0"X 20'-10"

KITCHEN 14'-0" X 13'-0"

NOOK 9'-10" X 11'-4"

PATIO

FAMILY ROOM 13'-10"X18'-2"

M.BEDROOM 15'-0" X 17'-0"

DINING 13'-0" X 13'-0"

FOYER

LIVING ROOM 18'-0"X 19'-6"

63'-0"

76'-0"

Upper Level Floor Plan

BEDROOM 12'-10"X11'-0"

BEDROOM 12'-10"X11'-0"

BEDROOM 13'-0"X11'-0"

LIBRARY

Main Level Floor Plan

Images provided by designer/architect.

CAD FILE AVAILABLE

Plan #101024

Dimensions: 53' W x 57' D

Levels: 2

Square Footage: 3,135

Main Level Sq. Ft.: 1,600

Upper Level Sq. Ft.: 1,535

Bedrooms: 5

Bathrooms: 4

Foundation: Basement

Materials List Available: No

Price Category: G

Upper Level Floor Plan

Copyright by designer/architect.

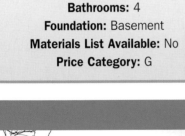

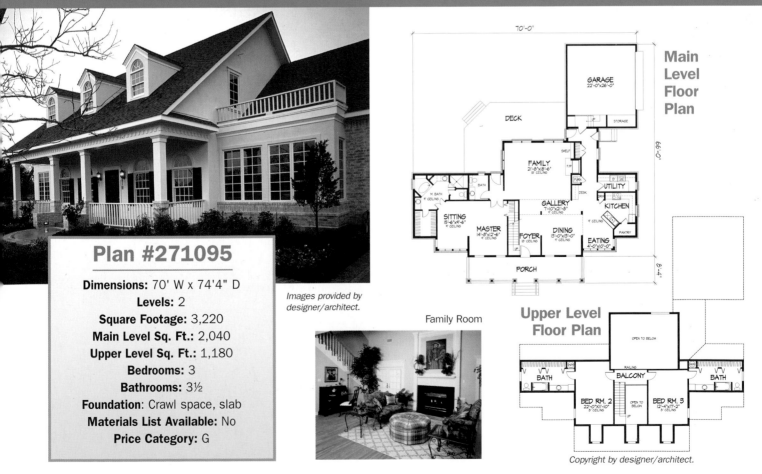

Plan #271095

Dimensions: 70' W x 74'4" D

Levels: 2

Square Footage: 3,220

Main Level Sq. Ft.: 2,040

Upper Level Sq. Ft.: 1,180

Bedrooms: 3

Bathrooms: 3½

Foundation: Crawl space, slab

Materials List Available: No

Price Category: G

Images provided by designer/architect.

Main Level Floor Plan

Family Room

Upper Level Floor Plan

Copyright by designer/architect.

Plan #561003

Dimensions: 58'8" W x 50' D

Levels: 1.5

Square Footage: 3,164

Main Level Sq. Ft.: 2,085

Upper Level Sq. Ft.: 1,079

Bedrooms: 4

Bathrooms: 3½

Foundation: Basement

Material List Available: Yes

Price Category: G

Images provided by designer/architect.

This European-styled two-story home has something for everyone.

Features:

- Great Room: A large two-story gathering area will be the location of many great family memories. The fireplace is the centerpiece of the room.

- Formal Dining: Set off by two columns at the entry, this area features a 9-ft.-high ceiling. The walk-in storage room is an added bonus.

- Den: Located off the entry foyer, this space can also be used as a home office.

- Upper Level: Three large secondary bedrooms occupy this level. Bedroom 2 features its own bathroom, while the two remaining bedrooms share a Jack-and-Jill bathroom.

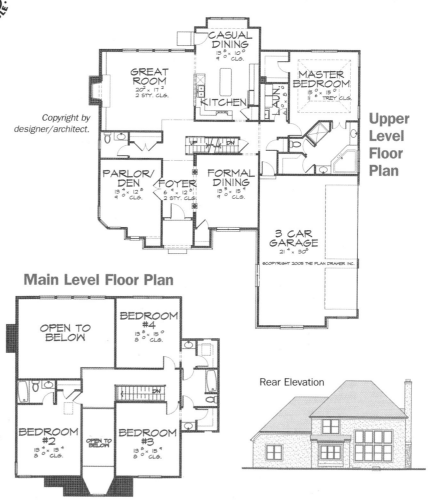

Copyright by designer/architect.

Main Level Floor Plan

Upper Level Floor Plan

Rear Elevation

Plan #121113

Dimensions: 73'4" W x 57'4" D
Levels: 1.5
Square Footage: 3,172
Main Level Sq. Ft.: 2,252
Upper Level Sq. Ft.: 920
Bedrooms: 4
Bathrooms: 3½
Foundation: Basement;
crawl space for fee
Material List Available: Yes
Price Category: G

A brick and stucco home provides a
solid foundation to raise a family.

Images provided by designer/architect.

Features:

- Den: Located just off the entry, this unique den features a 10-ft.-high ceiling. The built-in bookcases are a welcome addition to the room.

- Dining Room: This large formal dining area boasts a stepped ceiling, which adds elegance to this space. A nook for the hutch allows more usable space for the dining table.

- Kitchen: An island kitchen aids in the preparation of meals and acts as the communication center for the home. Open to the breakfast area and hearth room, the kitchen area function as one large space.

- Master Suite: Located on the main level for convenience and privacy, this retreat offers a large sleeping area with an 11-ft.-high ceiling. The master bath boasts a whirlpool tub and a separate toilet room.

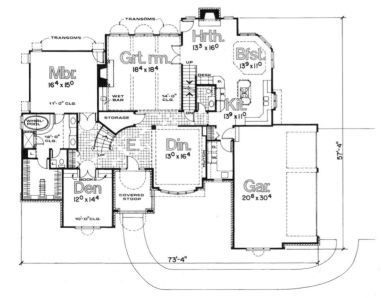

Main Level Floor Plan

Upper Level Floor Plan
Copyright by designer/architect.

Plan #111037

Dimensions: 66' W x 84' D
Levels: 2
Square Footage: 3,176
Main Level Sq. Ft.: 2,183
Upper Level Sq. Ft.: 993
Bedrooms: 4
Bathrooms: 3½
Foundation: Slab
Materials List Available: No
Price Category: G

Images provided by designer/architect.

Main Level Floor Plan

Upper Level Floor Plan

Copyright by designer/architect.

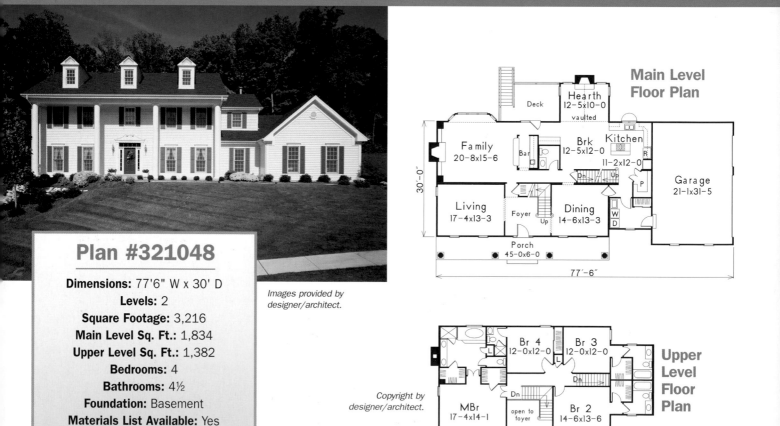

Plan #321048

Dimensions: 77'6" W x 30' D
Levels: 2
Square Footage: 3,216
Main Level Sq. Ft.: 1,834
Upper Level Sq. Ft.: 1,382
Bedrooms: 4
Bathrooms: 4½
Foundation: Basement
Materials List Available: Yes
Price Category: G

Images provided by designer/architect.

Main Level Floor Plan

Copyright by designer/architect.

Upper Level Floor Plan

Plan #121076

Dimensions: 64' W x 60'8" D
Levels: 2
Square Footage: 3,067
Main Level Sq. Ft.: 2,169
Upper Level Sq. Ft.: 898
Bedrooms: 4
Bathrooms: 3½
Foundation: Basement
Materials List Available: Yes
Price Category: G

Images provided by designer/architect.

Main Level Floor Plan

Upper Level Floor Plan

Copyright by designer/architect.

Plan #111029

Dimensions: 65' W x 77' D
Levels: 1.5
Square Footage: 2,781
Main Level Sq. Ft.: 2,781
Bonus Area Sq. Ft.: 319
Bedrooms: 4
Bathrooms: 3
Foundation: Crawl space
Materials List Available: No
Price Category: F

Images provided by designer/architect.

Bonus Area Floor Plan

Copyright by designer/architect.

Main Level Floor Plan

Main Level Floor Plan

Upper Level Floor Plan

Copyright by designer/architect.

Images provided by designer/architect.

CAD FILE AVAILABLE CAD

Basement Level Floor Plan

Plan #181221

Dimensions: 60' W x 44' D

Levels: 2

Square Footage: 3,411

Main Level Sq. Ft.: 1,488

Upper Level Sq. Ft.: 603

Basement Level Sq. Ft.: 1,321

Bedrooms: 3

Bathrooms: 2½

Foundation: Basement

Materials List Available: Yes

Price Category: G

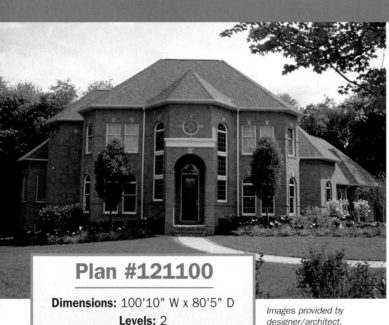

Upper Level Floor Plan

Copyright by designer/architect.

Images provided by designer/architect.

Main Level Floor Plan

Plan #121100

Dimensions: 100'10" W x 80'5" D

Levels: 2

Square Footage: 3,750

Main Level Sq. Ft.: 2,274

Upper Level Sq. Ft.: 1,476

Bedrooms: 4

Bathrooms: 3½

Foundation: Slab

Materials List Available: No

Price Category: G

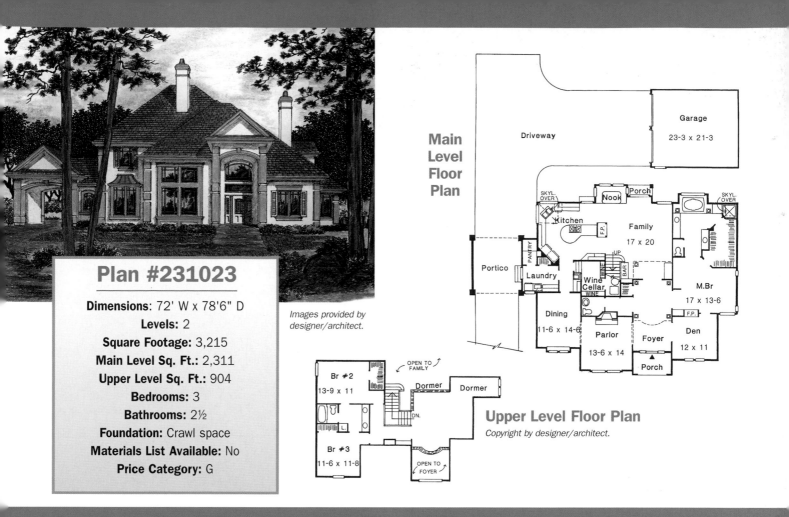

Plan #231023

Dimensions: 72' W x 78'6" D

Levels: 2

Square Footage: 3,215

Main Level Sq. Ft.: 2,311

Upper Level Sq. Ft.: 904

Bedrooms: 3

Bathrooms: 2½

Foundation: Crawl space

Materials List Available: No

Price Category: G

Images provided by designer/architect.

Main Level Floor Plan

Garage
23-3 x 21-3

Driveway

Portico

SKYL.
OVER

Nook   Porch

Kitchen

Pantry

F.P.

Family
17 x 20

SKYL.
OVER

M.Br
17 x 13-6

Laundry

Wine
Cellar
WINE

UP
BAR

Dining
11-6 x 14-6

Parlor
13-6 x 14

Foyer

Porch

Den
12 x 11

F.P.

Upper Level Floor Plan

Copyright by designer/architect.

Br #2
13-9 x 11

OPEN TO
FAMILY

Dormer   Dormer

DN.

Br #3
11-6 x 11-8

OPEN TO
FOYER

Plan #261001

Dimensions: 77'8" W x 49' D

Levels: 2

Square Footage: 3,746

Main Level Sq. Ft.: 1,965

Upper Level Sq. Ft.: 1,781

Bedrooms: 4

Bathrooms: 3½

Foundation: Basement

Materials List Available: No

Price Category: H

Images provided by designer/architect.

DECK

KITCHEN
12 x 16

DINETTE
12 x 16

FAMILY
16 x 20
TRAY CLG

DINING
14 x 14
STEPPED CLG

DESK

PANTRY

ENTRY
BENCH

GARAGE
24 x 35-6

LIVING
14 x 18

OPEN
ABOVE

UP   DN

HALL

B C

LDY

FOYER

STUDY
14 x 14-6

BOOKS   BOOKS

Main Level Floor Plan

Upper Level Floor Plan

ROOF

ROOF

FAMILY
(BELOW)

ROOF

M/BATH

BATH 2

BR 3
14-4 x 13

STORAGE

HALL

MBR
14 x 18
TRAY CLG

LIN

BATH 3

DESK

BR 4
12-8 x 15

BALCONY
BOOKS
BENCH

FOYER
(BELOW)
RAILING

BR 2
14 x 14

TWL

Copyright by designer/architect.

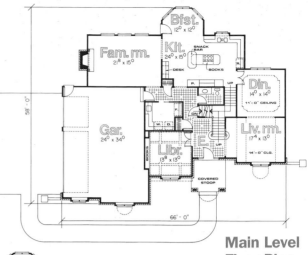

Main Level Floor Plan

Plan #121096

Dimensions: 66' W x 58' D
Levels: 2
Square Footage: 3,611
Main Level Sq. Ft.: 1,857
Upper Level Sq. Ft.: 1,754
Bedrooms: 4
Bathrooms: 2½
Foundation: Basement
Materials List Available: Yes
Price Category: G

Images provided by designer/architect.

CAD FILE AVAILABLE CAD

Upper Level Floor Plan

Copyright by designer/architect.

Upper Level Floor Plan

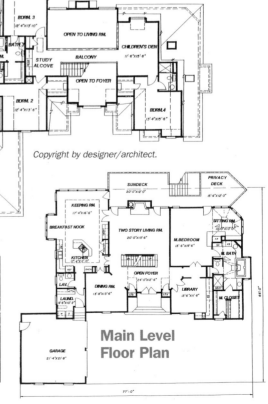

Copyright by designer/architect.

Plan #141034

Dimensions: 77' W x 66' D
Levels: 2
Square Footage: 3,588
Main Level Sq. Ft.: 2,329
Upper Level Sq. Ft.: 1,259
Bedrooms: 4
Bathrooms: 3½
Foundation: Basement
Materials List Available: Yes
Price Category: H

Images provided by designer/architect.

Main Level Floor Plan

Plan #391040

Dimensions: 69' W x 55'6" D
Levels: 2
Square Footage: 3,276
Main Level Sq. Ft.: 1,786
Upper Level Sq. Ft.: 1,490
Bedrooms: 4
Bathrooms: 2½
Foundation: Basement
Materials List Available: Yes
Price Category: G

Main Level Floor Plan

Copyright by designer/architect.

Images provided by designer/architect.

Upper Level Floor Plan

Plan #321065

Dimensions: 80' W x 52' D
Levels: 2
Square Footage: 3,420
Main Level Sq. Ft.: 1,894
Upper Level Sq. Ft.: 1,526
Bedrooms: 4
Bathrooms: 3½
Foundation: Daylight basement
Materials List Available: Yes
Price Category: G

Main Level Floor Plan

Images provided by designer/architect.

Upper Level Floor Plan

Copyright by designer/architect.

Plan #121170

Dimensions: 68'4" W x 68' D
Levels: 1.5
Square Footage: 3,459
Main Level Sq. Ft.: 2,348
Upper Level Sq. Ft.: 1,111
Bedrooms: 4
Bathrooms: 3½
Foundation: Basement;
crawl space for fee
Material List Available: Yes
Price Category: G

This home, as shown in the photograph, may differ from the actual blueprints. For more detailed information, please check the floor plans carefully.

CAD FILE AVAILABLE

Images provided by designer/architect.

Large rooms make this home very attractive.
Features:

• Dining Room: When you enter this home, your eyes are drawn to this elegant formal eating area. The stepped ceiling adds to the feeling of grandeur.

• Den: Featuring French door access to the front porch, this den could function as a home office. The fireplace adds a focal point to the room.

• Master Suite: This main-level master suite boasts a 10-ft.-high ceiling. The master bath features a stall shower and dual vanities.

• Upper Level: Three secondary bedrooms are located on this level. Bedroom 2 boasts a private bathroom.

Front View

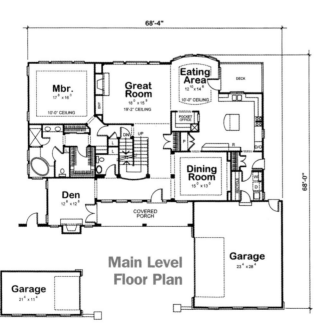

Main Level Floor Plan

Upper Level Floor Plan

Copyright by designer/architect.

Plan #121182

Dimensions: 56' W x 74' D
Levels: 1.5
Square Footage: 3,397
Main Level Sq. Ft.: 2,496
Upper Level Sq. Ft.: 901
Bedrooms: 4
Bathrooms: 4½
Foundation: Slab; basement for fee
Material List Available: Yes
Price Category: G

This home, as shown in the photograph, may differ from the actual blueprints. For more detailed information, please check the floor plans carefully.

Images provided by designer/architect.

Front View

This stone home will look great in any location.

Features:

- **Living Room:** This formal gathering area features a 14-ft.-high ceiling. The back wall of windows will allow an abundance of natural light into the space.

- **Family Room:** A fireplace, flanked by windows, sets a calm and casual mood in this gathering area. The vaulted ceiling adds an elegant look to the space.

- **Kitchen:** This island kitchen features a raised bar, which is perfect for a quick snack. The walk-in pantry adds needed storage space.

- **Garage:** This three-car garage can be used for parking the cars or for additional storage space.

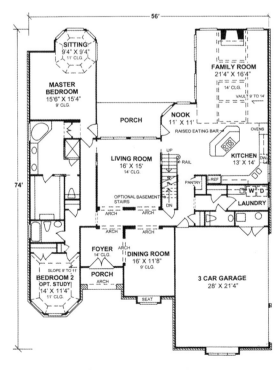

Main Level Floor Plan

Upper Level Floor Plan

Copyright by designer/architect.

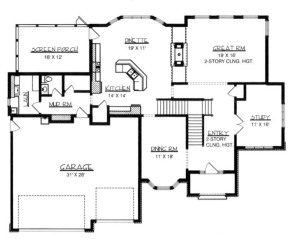

Main Level Floor Plan

Upper Level Floor Plan

Copyright by designer/architect.

Images provided by designer/architect.

CAD FILE AVAILABLE

Plan #271055

Dimensions: 68' W x 53' D
Levels: 2
Square Footage: 3,159
Main Level Sq. Ft.: 1,819
Upper Level Sq. Ft.: 1,340
Bedrooms: 4
Bathrooms: 2½
Foundation: Daylight basement
Materials List Available: No
Price Category: G

Upper Level Floor Plan

Images provided by designer/architect.

Main Level Floor Plan

Copyright by designer/architect.

Plan #101126

Dimensions: 67' W x 56' D
Levels: 2
Square Footage: 3,431
Main Level Sq. Ft.: 2,005
Upper Level Sq. Ft.: 1,426
Bedrooms: 3
Bathrooms: 3½
Foundation: Basement
Material List Available: No
Price Category: G

Main Level Floor Plan

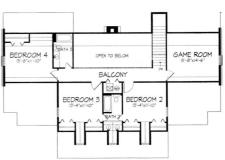

Plan #271098

Dimensions: 68'10" W x 81'5" D

Levels: 2

Square Footage: 3,382

Main Level Sq. Ft.: 2,136

Upper Level Sq. Ft.: 1,246

Bedrooms: 4

Bathrooms: 3½

Foundation: Slab

Materials List Available: No

Price Category: G

Images provided by designer/architect.

CAD FILE AVAILABLE

Upper Level Floor Plan

Copyright by designer/architect.

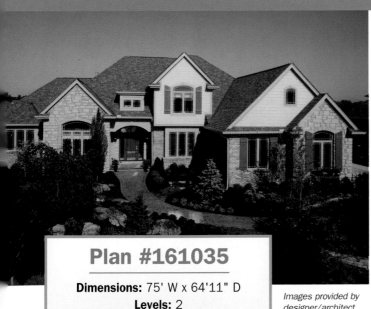

Upper Level Floor Plan

Copyright by designer/architect.

Plan #161035

Dimensions: 75' W x 64'11" D

Levels: 2

Square Footage: 3,688

Main Level Sq. Ft.: 2,702

Upper Level Sq. Ft.: 986

Bedrooms: 4

Bathrooms: 3½

Foundation: Basement

Materials List Available: No

Price Category: H

Images provided by designer/architect.

CAD FILE AVAILABLE

Main Level Floor Plan

Plan #141051

Dimensions: 44' W x 50' D
Levels: 2
Square Footage: 3,011
Main Level Sq. Ft.: 1,285
Upper Level Sq. Ft.: 1,726
Bedrooms: 4
Bathrooms: 3½
Foundation: Basement
Material List Available: No
Price Category: G

This country home has a hint of craftsman styling to make it a neighborhood standout.

Features:

- Family Room: Exposed beams and a fireplace flanked by built-in shelves add to the charm of this gathering area. French doors lead to the backyard patio.

- Kitchen: This large, open kitchen features additional seating at the island. The layout allows guests in the family room to overflow into the kitchen during parties. The generously sized pantry is available to hold all of the supplies needed for your family.

- Master Suite: This retreat features a tray ceiling in the sleeping area plus an additional sitting area. The master bath boasts a stall shower and a large walk-in closet.

- Secondary Bedrooms: Bedrooms 2 and 3 share a Jack-and-Jill bathroom. Bedroom 4 has a private bathroom.

Images provided by designer/architect.

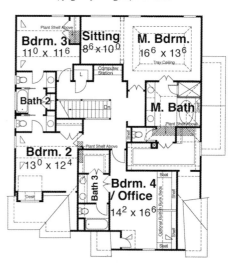

Main Level Floor Plan

Upper Level Floor Plan

Copyright by designer/architect.

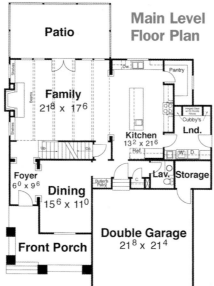

Kitchen

Kitchen/Family Room

Plan #221022

Dimensions: 79' W x 55' D
Levels: 2
Square Footage: 3,382
Main Level Sq. Ft.: 2,376
Upper Level Sq. Ft.: 1,006
Bedrooms: 4
Bathrooms: 3½
Foundation: Basement
Materials List Available: No
Price Category: G

The traditional-looking facade of stone, brick, and siding opens into a home you'll love for its spaciousness, comfort, and great natural lighting.

Features:

- Ceiling Height: 9 ft.

- Great Room: The two-story ceiling here emphasizes the dimensions of this large room, and the huge windows make it bright and cheery.

- Sunroom: Use this area as a den or an indoor conservatory where you can relax in the midst of health-promoting and beautiful plants.

- Kitchen: This well-planned kitchen features a snacking island and opens into a generous dining nook where everyone will gather.

- Master Suite: Located on the main floor for privacy, this area includes a walk-in closet and a deluxe full bathroom.

- Upper Level: Look into the great room and entryway as you climb the stairs to the three large bedrooms and full bath on this floor.

Rear View

Main Level Floor Plan

Upper Level Floor Plan

Copyright by designer/architect.

Main Level Floor Plan

Images provided by designer/architect.

Garage 22'6"x 24'6"

Covered Porch

Master Bedroom 17'2"x 16'4"

Living 22'2"x 18'

Bedroom 11'2"x 10'6"

Dining 11'6"x 14'

Breakfast 12'6"x 10'

Gameroom 13'6"x 15'6"

Upper Level Floor Plan

Copyright by designer/architect.

Bedroom 12'x 11'

Bedroom 11'x 16'

Bedroom 11'x 16'

Open to Below

Plan #111035

Dimensions: 68'6" W x 74'7" D
Levels: 2
Square Footage: 3,064
Main Level Sq. Ft.: 2,143
Upper Level Sq. Ft.: 921
Bedrooms: 4
Bathroom: 3½
Foundation: Slab
Materials List Available: No
Price Category: G

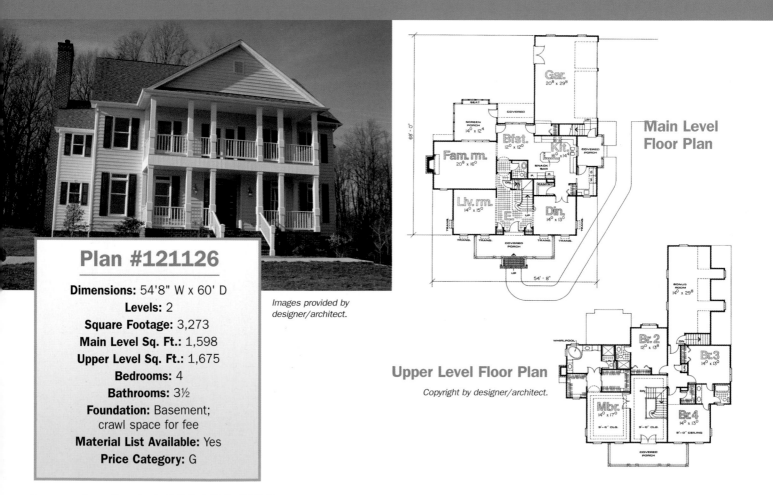

Gar. 20⁸ x 29⁸

Screen Porch 14⁰ x 12⁴

Bfst. 12⁰ x 12⁰

Kit.

Fam. rm. 20⁸ x 16⁰

Snack Bar

Covered Porch

Pantry

Liv. rm. 14⁰ x 15⁰

Din. 14⁰ x 13⁰

Covered Porch

66' - 0"

54' - 8"

Main Level Floor Plan

Images provided by designer/architect.

Bonus Room 14⁰ x 29⁸

Whirlpool

Br. 2 12⁰ x 13⁸

Br. 3 14⁰ x 13⁰

Mbr. 14⁰ x 17⁰

Br. 4 14⁰ x 13⁰

Covered Porch

Upper Level Floor Plan

Copyright by designer/architect.

Plan #121126

Dimensions: 54'8" W x 60' D
Levels: 2
Square Footage: 3,273
Main Level Sq. Ft.: 1,598
Upper Level Sq. Ft.: 1,675
Bedrooms: 4
Bathrooms: 3½
Foundation: Basement; crawl space for fee
Material List Available: Yes
Price Category: G

Main Level Floor Plan

Upper Level Floor Plan

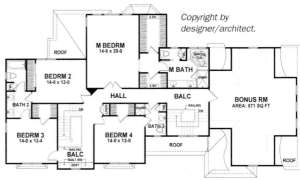

Copyright by designer/architect.

Rear Elevation

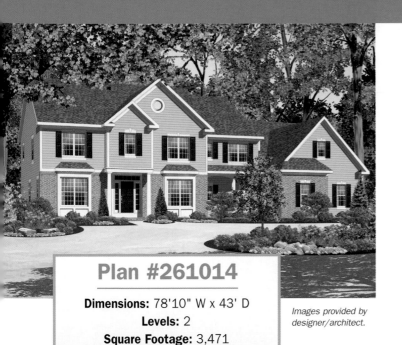

Images provided by designer/architect.

Plan #261014

Dimensions: 78'10" W x 43' D
Levels: 2
Square Footage: 3,471
Main Level Sq. Ft.: 1,873
Upper Level Sq. Ft.: 1,598
Bedrooms: 4
Bathrooms: 3½
Foundation: Basement
Materials List Available: No
Price Category: G

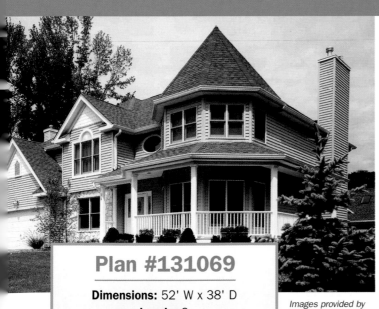

Images provided by designer/architect.

Plan #131069

Dimensions: 52' W x 38' D
Levels: 2
Square Footage: 3,169
Main Level Sq. Ft.: 1,535
Upper Level Sq. Ft.: 1,634
Bedrooms: 5
Bathrooms: 3½
Foundation: Crawl space or basement
Material List Available: Yes
Price Category: H

Main Level Floor Plan

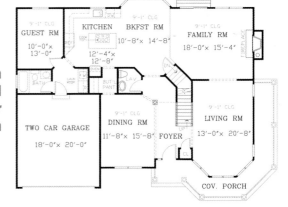

Upper Level Floor Plan

Copyright by designer/architect.

Plan #261015

Dimensions: 79'4" W x 48' D
Levels: 2
Square Footage: 3,200
Main Level Sq. Ft.: 1,766
Upper Level Sq. Ft.: 1,434
Bedrooms: 4
Bathrooms: 3½
Foundation: Basement
Materials List Available: No
Price Category: G

Images provided by designer/architect.

This traditional design has all the comforts of family-friendly home.

Features:

- Living Room: Located off of the entry, this formal gathering area features a bay window for added styling. Guests can seamlessly flow from here into the formal dining room.

- Family Room: This casual gathering area boasts windows on three walls, which flood the area with natural light. The fireplace adds cozy warmth to the area.

- Den: This is the perfect room in which to relax. Or you can use the space as a home office. The built-in cabinets are a nice feature.

- Rear Deck: Accessible from the dinette area, this outdoor entertainment space lets the fun spill out into the backyard.

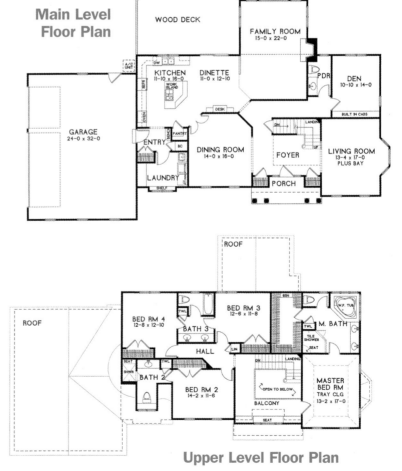

Main Level Floor Plan

Upper Level Floor Plan

Copyright by designer/architect.

Plan #371092

Dimensions: 71'6" W x 70'8" D
Levels: 2
Square Footage: 3,836
Main Level Sq. Ft.: 2,981
Upper Level Sq. Ft.: 855
Bedrooms: 5
Bathrooms: 4
Foundation: Slab
Materials List Available: No
Price Category: H

CAD FILE AVAILABLE

This grand home has an arched covered entry and great styling that would make this home a focal point of the neighborhood.

Features:

- **Family Room:** This large gathering area boasts a fireplace flanked by a built-in media center. Large windows flood the room with natural light, and there is access to the rear porch.

- **Kitchen:** This large island kitchen has a raised bar and is open to the family room. Its walk-in pantry has plenty of room for supplies.

- **Master Suite:** This retreat features a stepped ceiling and a see-through fireplace to the master bath, which has a large walk-in closet, dual vanities, a glass shower, and a marble tub.

- **Secondary Bedrooms:** Bedrooms 2 and 3 are located on the main level and share a common bathroom. Bedrooms 4 and 5 are located on the upper level and share a Jack-and-Jill bathroom.

Front View

Copyright by designer/architect.

Main Level Floor Plan

Upper Level Floor Plan

Plan #121152

Dimensions: 67'1" W x 65'10⅛" D
Levels: 1.5
Square Footage: 3,094
Main Level Sq. Ft.: 2,112
Upper Level Sq. Ft.: 982
Bedrooms: 4
Bathrooms: 3½
Foundation: Slab; basement for fee
Material List Available: Yes
Price Category: G

Images provided by designer/architect.

This home, as shown in the photograph, may differ from the actual blueprints. For more detailed information, please check the floor plans carefully.

Main Level Floor Plan

Upper Level Floor Plan

Copyright by designer/architect.

Plan #131025

Dimensions: 62'4" W x 65'10" D
Levels: 1½
Square Footage: 3,204
Main Level Sq. Ft.: 2,196
Upper Level Sq. Ft.: 1,008
Bedrooms: 4
Bathrooms: 4
Foundation: Crawl space, slab, or basement
Materials List Available: Yes
Price Category: H

Images provided by designer/architect.

Rear Elevation

Main Level Floor Plan
Copyright by designer/architect.

Upper Level Floor Plan

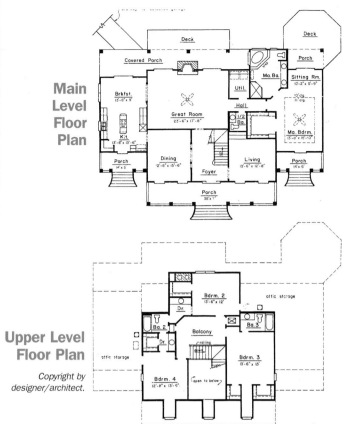

Plan #111036

Dimensions: 66' W x 47' D

Levels: 2

Square Footage: 3,149

Main Level Sq. Ft.: 2,033

Upper Level Sq. Ft.: 1,116

Bedrooms: 4

Bathrooms: 3½

Foundation: Pier

Materials List Available: No

Price Category: G

Images provided by designer/architect.

Main Level Floor Plan

Upper Level Floor Plan

Copyright by designer/architect.

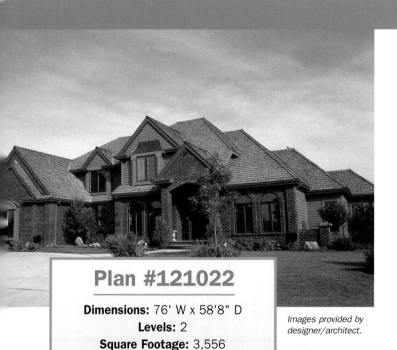

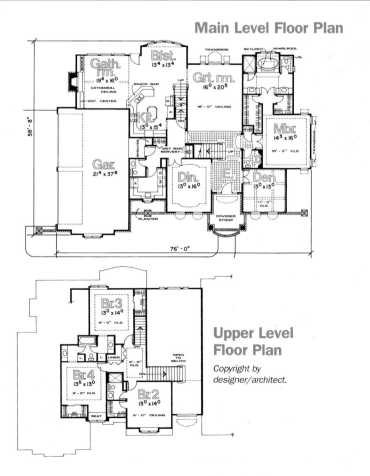

Plan #121022

Dimensions: 76' W x 58'8" D

Levels: 2

Square Footage: 3,556

Main Level Sq. Ft.: 2,555

Upper Level Sq. Ft.: 1,001

Bedrooms: 4

Bathrooms: 3 full, 2 half

Foundation: Basement

Materials List Available: Yes

Price Category: H

Images provided by designer/architect.

Main Level Floor Plan

Upper Level Floor Plan

Copyright by designer/architect.

Plan #271031

Dimensions: 87'4" W x 66' D
Levels: 2
Square Footage: 3,062
Main Level Sq. Ft.: 2,389
Upper Level Sq. Ft.: 673
Bedrooms: 4
Bathrooms: 3½
Foundation: Basement
Materials List Available: Yes
Price Category: G

The distinctive look of this elegant, trendsetting estate reflects a refined sense of style and taste.

Features:

- **Parlor/Dining:** Off the vaulted foyer, this cozy sunken parlor boasts a vaulted ceiling and a warm fireplace. Opposite the parlor, this formal dining room is serviced by a stylish wet bar.

- **Kitchen:** This open room features an angled snack bar and serves a skylighted breakfast room.

- **Family Room:** Defined by columns, this skylighted, vaulted family room offers a handsome fireplace with a built-in log bin. Sliding glass doors open to a backyard deck.

- **Master Suite:** This deluxe getaway boasts a vaulted ceiling and unfolds to a skylighted sitting area and a private deck. The garden tub in the master bath basks under its own skylight.

- **Library/Guest Room:** This versatile room enjoys a high ceiling and a walk-in closet.

- **Secondary Bedrooms:** Two reside on the upper floor.

Main Level Floor Plan

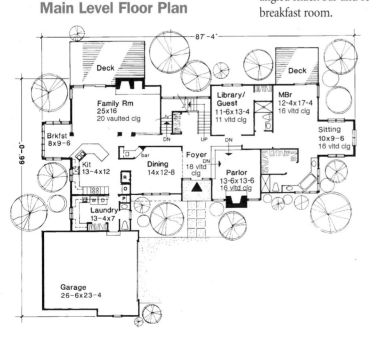

Upper Level Floor Plan

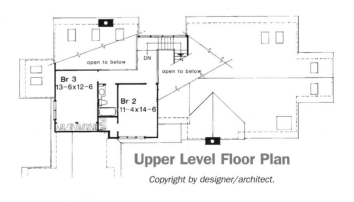

Copyright by designer/architect.

Plan #161096

Dimensions: 67'6" W x 75'6" D
Levels: 2
Square Footage: 3,435
Main Level Sq. Ft.: 2,479
Upper Level Sq. Ft.: 956
Bedrooms: 4
Bathrooms: 3½
Foundation: Walkout basement; basement for fee
Material List Available: No
Price Category: G

Images provided by designer/architect.

A stone-and-brick exterior is excellently coordinated to create a warm and charming showplace.

CAD FILE AVAILABLE

Features:

- **Great Room:** The spacious foyer leads directly into this room, which visually opens to the rear yard, providing natural light and outdoor charm.

- **Kitchen:** This fully equipped kitchen is located to provide the utmost convenience in serving the formal dining room and the breakfast area, which is surrounded by windows and has a double-soffit ceiling treatment. The combination of breakfast room, hearth room, and kitchen creatively forms a comfortable family gathering place.

- **Master Suite:** A tray ceiling tops this suite and its luxurious dressing area, which will pamper you after a hard day.

- **Balcony:** Wood rails decorate the stairs leading to this balcony, which offers a dramatic view of the great room and foyer below.

- **Bedrooms:** A secondary private bedroom suite with personal bath, plus two bedrooms that share a Jack-and-Jill bathroom, complete the exciting home.

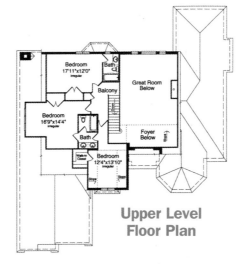

Upper Level Floor Plan

Rear Elevation

Main Level Floor Plan

Copyright by designer/architect.

Hearth Room

Family Kitchens

From every standpoint, the importance of the kitchen and its design cannot be underestimated. The heart of the home beats in the kitchen. There's the hum of the refrigerator, the whir of the food processor, the crunch of the waste-disposal unit, and the bubbling of dinner simmering on the stove. These are the reassuring sounds of a home in action. The kitchen is also a warehouse, a communications center, a place to socialize, and the hub of family life. According to industry studies, 90 percent of American families eat some or all of their meals in the kitchen. It is also the command center where household bills are paid and vacations are planned. The kitchen is even a playroom at times. Emotions, as well as tasks, reside here. When you were little, this is where you could find mom whenever you needed her. It's where the cookies were kept. When other rooms were cold and empty, the kitchen was a place of warmth and companionship. It is from the kitchen that the family sets off into the day. And it is to the kitchen that they return at nightfall.

The Great Room Concept

Today, the family life that was once contained by the kitchen is spilling into an adjoining great room. Usually a large, open room, great rooms and kitchens are often considered part of the same space. It is here where the family gathers to watch TV, share meals, and do homework. In short, great rooms/kitchens are the new heart of the home and the places where families do most of their living. In most designs, a kitchen and great room are separated by a snack counter, an island, or a large pass-through.

Kitchen Layouts That Work

The basic layout of your kitchen will depend on the home design you choose. Look for aisles that have at least 39 inches between the front of the cabinets and appliances or an opposite-facing island. If it's possible, a clearance of 42 inches is better. And given more available space, a clear-

Large kitchen/great rooms, below, are now considered the true heart of the family home.

In large kitchens, opposite, look for plenty of counter and storage space, but insist on compact, efficient work areas.

ance of 48 to 49 inches is ideal. It means that you can open the dishwasher to load or unload it, and someone will still be able to walk behind you without doing a side-to-side shuffle or a crab walk. It also means that two people can work together in the same area. Any more than 49 inches, and the space is too much and involves a lot of walking back and forth. Fifty-four inches, for example, is too big a stretch. In large kitchens, look for balance; the work areas should have generous proportions, but to be truly efficient they should be compact and well designed.

Food Prep Areas and Surfaces. In many families, much of the food preparation takes place between the sink and the refrigerator. When you think of the work triangle, think of how much and how often you use an appliance. For example, sinks are generally used the most, followed by the refrigerator. The use of the cooktop is a matter of personal habit. Some families use it everyday, others use it sporadically. How close does it really need to be in relation to

the sink and refrigerator? Make your primary work zone the link between the sink and the refrigerator; then make the cooktop a secondary zone that's linked to them.

Cabinets Set the Style

Cabinets are the real furniture of a kitchen, making their selection both an aesthetic and functional choice. They are also likely to account for the largest portion of the budget.

Laminate. There are different brands and grades of plastic laminate, but cabinets made from this material generally are the least expensive you can buy. For the most part, they are devoid of detail and frameless, so don't look for raised panels, moldings, or inlaid beads on plastic laminate cabinets.

Although the surface is somewhat vulnerable (depending on the quality) to scratches and chips, plastic laminate cabinets can be refaced relatively inexpensively. Laminates come in a formidable range of

colors and patterns. Some of the newer speckled and patterned designs, which now even include denim and canvas, not only look great but won't show minor scratches and scars.

Wood. Wood cabinets offer the greatest variety of type, style, and finish. Framed cabinets (the full frame across the face of the cabinets may show between the doors) are popular for achieving a traditional look, but they are slightly less roomy inside. That's because you lose the width of the frame, which can be as much as an inch on each side. Frameless cabinets have full overlay doors and drawer fronts. With frameless cabinets, you gain about 2 inches of interior space per cabinet unit. Multiply that by the number of cabinet doors or drawer units you have, and add it up. It's easy to see that if space is at a premium, choose the frameless or full-overlay type. Besides, most cabinet companies now offer enough frameless styles to give you a traditional look in cabinetry, if that's your style.

The Decorative Aspect of Cabinets

While the trend in overall kitchen style is toward more decorative moldings and carvings, the trend in cabinet doors is toward simpler designs. Plain panels, for instance, are now more popular than raised panels. They allow you to have more decoration elsewhere. Ornamentation is effective when it is used to provide a focal point over a hood, fridge, or sink. Instead of installing a single crown profile, you might create a three- or four-piece crown treatment, or add a carving of grapevines, acanthus leaves, or another decorative motif. In the traditional kitchen, add them, but sparingly.

Finishes. Of all of the choices you will need to make regarding wood cabinets, the selection of the finish may be the hardest. Wood can be stained, pickled, painted, or oiled. Your selection will be determined in part by whether you order stock or custom cabinets. Finishing options on stock cabinets are usually limited, and variations are offered as an upgrade. Translation: more money. Try working with the manufacturer's stock cabinets. It not only costs less but also speeds up the process. There is usually a reason why manufacturers offer certain woods in certain choices: it's because those choices work best with other elements in the room.

Wood Stains. Today, stains that are close to natural wood tones are popular, particularly natural wood finishes. Cherry is quickly becoming the number-one wood in the country. Pickled finishes, very popular in the early 1990s, are now looking dated. Some woods, particularly oak, have more grain than others. Some, such as maple, are smoother. And others, such as birch, dent more easily. The quality and inherent characteristics of the wood you choose will help determine whether it is better to stain, pickle, or paint. For staining, you need a good-quality clear wood. Pickling, because it has pigment in the stain, masks more of the grain but is still translucent. Because paint completely covers the grain, painted wood cabinets are usually made of lesser-quality paint-grade wood.

Painted Wood. Paint gives wood a smooth, clean finish. You can paint when you want a change or if the finish starts to show wear. This comes at no small expense, though, because the painter will have to sand the surfaces well before applying several coats of paint. If you choose painted cabinets, be sure to obtain a small can of the exact same paint from your kitchen vendor. There is usually a charge for this, but it allows you to do small touch-ups yourself, ridding your cabinets of particularly hideous scars without a complete repainting. While in theory the color choice for painted cabinets is infinite, manufacturers generally offer four shades of white and a few other standard color options from which to choose.

Pickled Wood. Pickled cabinets fall midway between full-grain natural cabinets and painted ones. Pickling is a combination of stain and paint, allowing some of the grain to show. It subdues the strongest patterns, while it covers over the lesser ones. The degree depends on your choice and on the options available from the manufacturer.

Be creative with storage, above. Here a tall cabinet tops a drawer unit that holds dish towels and tablecloths.

A great room, below, works best when a well-defined kitchen area flows effortlessly into the living area.

Hardware. Handles are easier to maneuver than knobs. Advocates of universal design, which takes into consideration the capabilities of all people—young and old, with and without physical limitations—recommend them. Knobs do not work easily for children or elderly people with arthritis. A handle with a backplate will keep fingerprints off the cabinet door.

Fitting Cabinets into Your Layout

This calls for attention to the kitchen layout. In specifying cabinets, first let common sense and budget be your guide. Kitchen geography can help you determine how much storage you need and where it should be. Mentally divide your kitchen into zones: food preparation, food consumption, and so on. And don't forget about the nonfood areas. Do you see yourself repotting plants or working on a hobby in the kitchen? You'll need work space and cabinet space for those extra activities.

A kitchen workhorse, the island, is not new to kitchen design. It's as old as the solid, slightly elevated, central table of medieval kitchens in England. But where that table was a work surface, today's island can hold cabinets, a sink, a cooktop, a beverage refrigerator, and it can serve to divide areas of the kitchen.

How Tall Is Too Tall?

Upper cabinets are typically 12 inches deep; base, or lower, cabinets are 24 inches deep. With the exception of a desk unit, standard base cabinets are always the same height, 36 inches. Although most people prefer clean lines and planes as much as possible, some circumstances call for variations in the height of lower cabinets. There may be an often-used area where you want a countertop at which you can work while seated, for example.

Upper cabinets come in two or three standard heights: 30, 36, and 42 inches. The 30-inch ones look short; 36-inch cabinets look standard, and 42-inch ones can look too tall if your ceiling is not unusually high. In general, there is a slight up-charge for 30-inch cabinets and a big jump in price for 42-inch units. Order another size and you will pay double-custom prices. But you don't need to. For greater variation, install upper cabinets at varying heights. The old standard was to install 30-inch upper cabinets under a soffit—the often,

but not always, boxed-in area just under the ceiling and above the wall cabinets. Now, unless you have very tall ceilings, soffits are practically obsolete. Provided you have standard-height, 8-foot ceilings, the way to go now seems to be 36-inch cabinets with the remaining space of 6 inches or so filled with decorative trim up to the ceiling. It is a nicer, more refined look than cabinets that extend all the way to the ceiling, unless you prefer something contemporary and totally sleek and without ornament.

Size and Space. You don't want a massive bank of cabinets, either. Add up the dimensions wherever you're considering wall units. The counter is 36 inches high; backsplashes typically range from 15 to 17 inches. So with 36-inch-high upper cabinets, we're talking 7½ feet in all, 8 feet if you chose 42-inch-high wall units. Your own size can help determine which ones to choose. Determine what's comfortable by measuring your reach. A petite person will lose access to the top third of a cabinet. An inch or two can make a very big difference.

Also, be sure that the small appliances you keep on the countertop fit under the wall cabinets. Having them sit at the front edge of a countertop is an accident waiting to happen. A lot of people who have "appliance garages" discovered this. Whenever they pulled out the appliance, which places it nearer the counter's edge, they watched their mixer or coffeemaker tumble to the floor.

Often people need extra storage, so they extend the cabinets up to the ceiling. This provides the added extra storage space, but it can only be reached by a step stool. An open soffit above the upper cabinets provides just as much space for oversize, infrequently used objects, and it is equally accessible by stepladder. Plus it can be both a display area and perfect home for hard-to-store items: pitchers, trays, salad bowls, vases, collectibles, platters, covered servers, and so forth.

Light, natural wood finishes, left, are a popular cabinet choice.

Kitchen offices, left, are becoming increasingly popular. This desk and office storage matches the kitchen cabinets.

Just remember to allow plenty of room for air to circulate around the TV.

Kitchen Storage Solutions

There are many storage options that are extremely useful. At the top of the list is a spice drawer or rack attached to an upper cabinet or door. Both drawer and door spice racks are offered as factory options when you order cabinets, or you can retro-fit them into existing cabinets. They provide visible access to all spices, so you don't end up with three tins of cinnamon, nine jars of garlic salt, four tiny bottles of vanilla, and no red pepper.

Lazy Susans. These rotating trays make items in the back of corner cabinets accessible. Consider adding inexpensive, plastic lazy Susans in a small upper cabinet. They will make the seasonings and cooking items you use everyday easily accessible.

Pie-cut door attachments can provide the same accessibility as a lazy Susan. Your choice depends on how much and what kind of storage you need. If a corner cabinet is home to sodas, chips, and cooking materials, install a pie-cut. A lazy Susan is more stable, best for pots, bowls, and larger, heavier objects.

The Kitchen Desk

Consider whether you will actually sit at a kitchen desk. Many people don't. Instead, they use it as the family message center and generally stand or perch on a stool. An additional, taller counter simply introduces more clutter to a room that is already overburdened with paraphernalia. And forget a desk-high cabinet, too. Instead use a standard counter-height cabinet to streamline whenever and wherever you can in the room.

Think about outfitting the desk area with a phone and answering machine and a corkboard for notes, your family's social schedule, invitations, and reminders. If you have room, a file drawer makes sense for storing school and business papers that

need to be easy to retrieve. Also, if you don't have a separate study, and there's room, the kitchen may be a place to keep the family computer. Not only will you likely be using it more in the future for household record-keeping, but you can also help the kids with their homework and monitor their Internet use. In those cases, it makes sense to add a desk for comfort.

A Niche for the TV. Many people also want a TV in the kitchen. Plan for it. Who wants to see the back of the set or look at cords stretching across work areas, atop the refrigerator or the stove? Space and an outlet can be built into the lower portion of a well-placed wall cabinet or an open unit.

Pullouts, Rollouts, and Dividers.
Pullout fittings maximize the use of very narrow spaces. There are just two options for these areas: vertical tray-storage units or pullout pantries. You can find a 12-inch-wide base cabinet that is a pullout pantry with storage for canned goods and boxed items.

Pullout racks for cabinets and lid-rack dividers for drawers are also available from some cabinet suppliers. They are handy, but if you have enough cabinet storage space, the best thing is to store pots and pans with the lids on them in a couple of large cabinets.

Rollout cabinets are great and offer a lot of flexibility. They are adjustable to accommodate bulky countertop appliances and

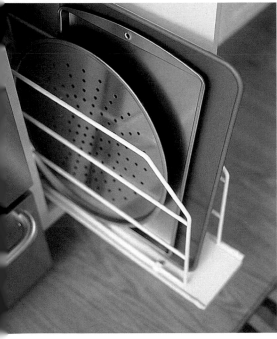

Pullout cutting boards, above left, increase usable counter space.

Accessories for tall, narrow cabinets, left, home in handy for storing cookie sheets and trays.

Decorative molding, above, can enhance any cabinet. Most manufacturers offer a variety of molding options.

stock pots, and they can save a lot of steps and banging around.

You can also divide a base cabinet vertically into separate parts. Some of the vertical spaces are further subdivided horizontally—good places for storing cutting boards, cookie trays, baking tins, and big glass baking dishes.

Other Organizers

Buy cutlery drawers carefully. They are often too big and too clumsy, and they fail to take advantage of the full interior of the drawer. They are as bad as bookshelves spread too far apart. Consider cutlery dividers that are almost no wider than a spoon, with separate sections for teaspoons, cereal spoons, breakfast and dinner knives, lunch forks, dinner forks, and serving pieces. Add to this a section for miscellaneous utensils such as spoons for iced tea, chopsticks, and so on. Drawer dividers should be adjustable in case your needs, or your cutlery, change.

Knife, Towel, and Bread Storage. If you want a place to store knives, use slotted storage on a countertop. Frequently islands have false backs because they are deeper than base cabinets. Slots for knives can be cut into the area of the countertop that covers the void behind the base cabinet.

You can obtain all these storage options at the time you buy your cabinets. But you don't have to and may not even want to until you see how you really end up using your kitchen. A carpenter or handyman can often make them or install off-the-shelf units. Think outside of the box. We get in a rut; it is hard to be objective. Ask friends where they keep their kitchen stuff, and analyze every aspect of how you use your kitchen. Store things at point of use, such as leftover containers and sandwich bags near the refrigerator; mixing bowls and carving knives near the sink.

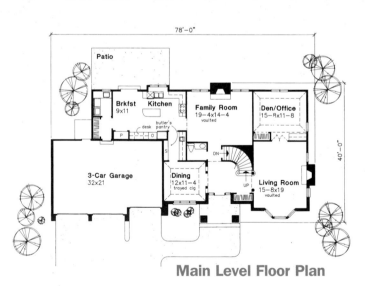

Upper Level Floor Plan

Images provided by designer/architect.

Main Level Floor Plan

Copyright by designer/architect.

Plan #271042

Dimensions: 69'8" W x 71'4" D

Levels: 2

Square Footage: 3,469

Main Level Sq. Ft.: 2,132

Upper Level Sq. Ft.: 1,337

Bedrooms: 5

Bathrooms: 3½

Foundation: Basement

Materials List Available: No

Price Category: G

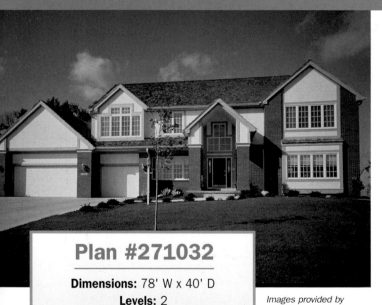

Main Level Floor Plan

Images provided by designer/architect.

Upper Level Floor Plan

Copyright by designer/architect.

Plan #271032

Dimensions: 78' W x 40' D

Levels: 2

Square Footage: 3,195

Main Level Sq. Ft.: 1,758

Upper Level Sq. Ft.: 1,437

Bedrooms: 4

Bathrooms: 2½

Foundation: Basement

Materials List Available: No

Price Category: E

Plan #211074

Dimensions: 64' W x 89' D
Levels: 2
Square Footage: 3,486
Main Level Sq. Ft.: 2,575
Upper Level Sq. Ft.: 911
Bedrooms: 4
Bathrooms: 3
Foundation: Crawl space
Materials List Available: Yes
Price Category: G

Images provided by designer/architect.

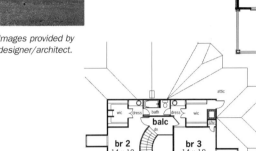

Main Level Floor Plan

Upper Level Floor Plan

Copyright by designer/architect.

Plan #161023

Dimensions: 71'8" W x 39'10" D
Levels: 2
Square Footage: 3,445
Main Level Sq. Ft.: 1,666
Mid Level Sq. Ft.: 743
Upper Level Sq. Ft.: 1,036
Bedrooms: 4
Bathrooms: 3½
Foundation: Basement
Materials List Available: No
Price Category: G

Images provided by designer/architect.

CAD FILE AVAILABLE

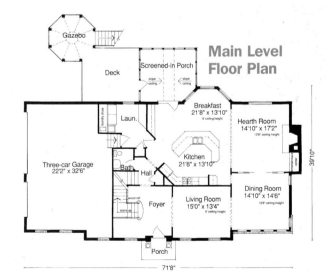

Main Level Floor Plan

Copyright by designer/architect.

Upper Level Floor Plan

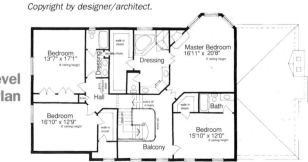

Plan #271072

Dimensions: 76' W x 38' D

Levels: 2

Square Footage: 3,081

Main Level Sq. Ft.: 1,358

Upper Level Sq. Ft.: 1,723

Bedrooms: 3

Bathrooms: 2½

Foundation: Crawl space or basement

Materials List Available: No

Price Category: G

This updated farmhouse design features a wraparound porch for savoring warm afternoons.

Features:

- **Living Room:** Striking columns invite visitors into this relaxing space. Double doors provide direct access to the casual family room beyond.

- **Family Room:** A focal-point fireplace warms this friendly space, while windows overlook impressive backyard vistas.

- **Kitchen:** An island cooktop and a menu desk simplify meal preparation here. A versatile dinette offers outdoor access through sliding glass doors.

- **Dining Room:** Neatly situated near the kitchen, this room will host important meals with style.

- **Master Suite:** Double doors and a tray ceiling make a good first impression. Two walk-in closets organize lots of clothes. A spa tub anchors the private bath.

- **Bonus Room:** A unique phone booth is found in this versatile room, which could serve as a playroom or an art studio.

Images provided by designer/architect.

Main Level Floor Plan

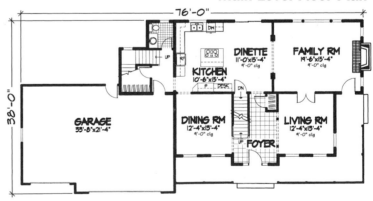

Upper Level Floor Plan

Copyright by designer/architect.

Plan #151022

Dimensions: 79' W x 77'8" D
Levels: 2
Square Footage: 3,059
Main Level Sq. Ft.: 2,650
Upper Level Sq. Ft.: 409
Bedrooms: 4
Bathrooms: 4
Foundation: Crawl space, slab, or basement
CompleteCost List Available: Yes
Price Category: G

Images provided by designer/architect.

The two front porches, a rear covered porch, and a huge rear deck are your first clues to the comfort you'll enjoy in this home.

Features:

- Great Room: This versatile room with a 10-ft. ceiling has a gas fireplace, built-in shelves and entertainment center, a place for an optional staircase, and access to the rear covered porch.

- Dining Room: The 10-ft. ceiling lets you decorate for formal dining but still allows a casual feeling.

- Breakfast Room: This bright space is open to the kitchen, so you can enjoy it at any time of day.

- Hobby Room: Use this space just off the garage for almost any activity.

- Master Suite: Enjoy the 10-ft. boxed ceiling, built-in cabinets, and access to the rear covered porch. The split design gives privacy. The bath has a corner whirlpool tub, separate glass shower, and split vanities.

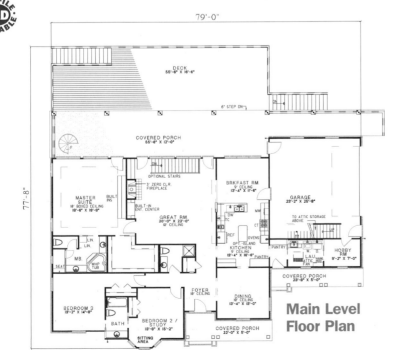

Main Level Floor Plan

Upper Level Floor Plan

Copyright by designer/architect.

Plan #121049

Dimensions: 82' W x 60'8" D
Levels: 2
Square Footage: 3,335
Main Level Sq. Ft.: 2,054
Upper Level Sq. Ft.: 1,281
Bedrooms: 4
Bathrooms: 3½
Foundation: Slab; basement for fee
Materials List Available: Yes
Price Category: G

This charming Craftsman-style home creates a welcoming environment with its covered porch, two-story foyer, and attractive accommodations.

CAD FILE AVAILABLE

Features:

• Great Room: Bask in the quiet glow of abundant natural light; cozy up to the smoldering fireplace; or gather with the family in this large, relaxing area.

• Kitchen: This design creates a great balance between workspace and play space. The kitchen surrounds the household chef with workspace without feeling closed-in.

A breakfast bar opens into the large breakfast area, making life a little simpler in the mornings.

• Master Bedroom: This spacious room is yours for the styling, a private space that features a walk-in closet and full bath, which includes his and her sinks, a standing shower, and a large tub.

• Second Floor: "Go to your room" sounds much better when that room is separated by a story. Identically sized bedrooms with ample closet space save you from family squabbles. The second floor has everything you need, with a compartmentalized full bathroom and computer loft.

Upper Level Floor Plan

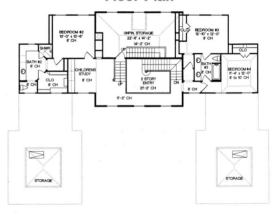

Third Floor Bedroom Floor Plan

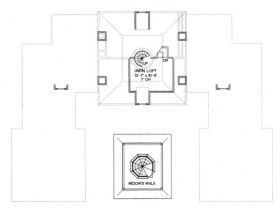

Main Level Floor Plan

Copyright by designer/ architect.

Plan #221023

Dimensions: 90'3" W x 65'8" D
Levels: 2
Square Footage: 3,511
Main Level Sq. Ft.: 1,931
Upper Level Sq. Ft.: 1,580
Bedrooms: 4
Bathrooms: 3½
Foundation: Basement
Materials List Available: No
Price Category: H

The curb appeal of this traditional two-story home, with its brick-and-stucco facade, is well matched by the luxuriousness you'll find inside.

CAD FILE AVAILABLE · CAD

Images provided by designer/architect.

Features:

- Ceiling Height: 9 ft.

- Family Room: This large room is open to the kitchen and the dining nook, making it an ideal spot in which to entertain.

- Living Room: The high ceiling in this room contributes to its somewhat formal feeling, and the fireplace and built-in bookcase allow you to decorate for a classic atmosphere.

- Master Suite: The bedroom in this suite has a luxurious feeling, partially because of the double French doors that are flanked by niches for displaying small art pieces or

collectables. The bathroom here is unusually large and features a walk-in closet.

- Upper Level: You'll find four bedrooms, three bathrooms, and a large bonus room to use as a study or play room on this floor.

Rear View

Main Level Floor Plan

Upper Level Floor Plan

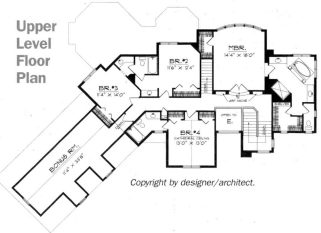

Copyright by designer/architect.

Plan #391066

Dimensions: 78' W x 60' D
Levels: 2
Square Footage: 3,526
Main Level Sq. Ft.: 2,054
Upper Level Sq. Ft.: 1,472
Bedrooms: 4
Bathrooms: 3½
Foundation: Crawl space, slab, or basement
Material List Available: No
Price Category: H

This is the manor house you have always wanted.

Features:

- **Foyer:** This dramatic two-story foyer welcomes you to the home. The coat closet and powder room are in close proximity.

- **Kitchen:** This efficient kitchen features a breakfast room and opens on a deck. A large walk-in pantry has plenty of storage space.

- **Master Suite:** Upstairs, this master suite with vaulted ceilings features two large walk-in closets. The master bath will pamper you with dual vanities and a whirlpool tub.

- **Secondary Bedrooms:** Three secondary bedrooms share two full bathrooms and are close by to the master suite. Bedrooms 2 and 4 feature walk-in closets.

Alternate Foundation Option

Main Level Floor Plan

Living Room

Upper Level Floor Plan

Plan #481021

Dimensions: 98'4" W x 55'8" D
Levels: 2
Square Footage: 3,289
Main Level Sq. Ft.: 1,680
Upper Level Sq. Ft.: 1,609
Bedrooms: 3
Bathrooms: 2½
Foundation: Walkout
Material List Available: No
Price Category: G

A large front porch welcomes visitors to this luxury home.

Features:

- **Family Room:** This two-story entertaining area features a beautiful fireplace and is open to the kitchen. The wall of windows will make the space feel light and airy.

- **Dining Room:** A stepped ceiling adds to the elegance of this formal dining area. The butler's pantry is a welcome amenity when it comes to entertaining.

- **Master Suite:** This retreat features a vaulted ceiling and built-in cabinets in the sleeping area. The master bath boasts dual vanities and a private toilet enclosure.

- **Bedrooms:** Two secondary bedrooms share the upper level with the master suite. Both of these bedrooms feature built-in desks.

Images provided by designer/architect.

Family Room

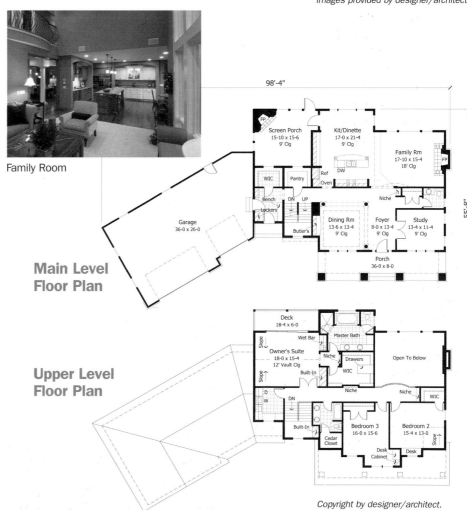

Main Level Floor Plan

Upper Level Floor Plan

Copyright by designer/architect.

Plan #161036

Dimensions: 74'10" W x 65' D
Levels: 2
Square Footage: 3,664
Main Level Sq. Ft.: 2,497
Upper Level Sq. Ft.: 1,167
Bedrooms: 4
Bathrooms: 2½
Foundation: Basement
Materials List Available: No
Price Category: H

Images provided by designer/architect.

The traditional European brick-and-stone facade on the exterior of this comfortable home will thrill you and make your guests feel welcome.

Features:

• Pub: The beamed ceiling lends a casual feeling to this pub and informal dining area between the kitchen and the great room.

• Dining Room: Columns set off this formal dining room, from which you can see the fireplace in the expansive great room.

• Library: Close to the master suite, this room lends itself to quiet reading or work.

• Master Suite: The ceiling treatment makes the bedroom luxurious, while the whirlpool tub, double-bowl vanity, and large walk-in closet make the bath a pleasure.

• Upper Level: Each of the three bedrooms features a large closet and easy access to a convenient bathroom.

CAD FILE AVAILABLE

Main Level Floor Plan

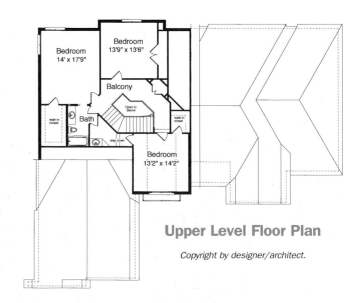

Upper Level Floor Plan

Copyright by designer/architect.

Rear Elevation

Left Elevation

Right Elevation

Kitchen

Dining Room

Living Room

Living Room

Plan #121019

Dimensions: 70' W x 60' D
Levels: 2
Square Footage: 3,775
Main Level Sq. Ft.: 1,923
Upper Level Sq. Ft.: 1,852
Bedrooms: 4
Bathrooms: 3
Foundation: Basement
Materials List Available: Yes
Price Category: H

Images provided by designer/architect.

The grand exterior presence is carried inside, beginning with the dramatic curved staircase.

Features:

• Ceiling Height: 8 ft.

• Den: French doors lead to this sophisticated den, with its bayed windows and wall of bookcases.

• Living Room: A curved wall and a series of arched windows highlight this large space.

• Formal Dining Room: This room shares the curved wall and arched windows found in the living room.

• Screened Porch: This huge space features skylights and is accessible by another French door from the dining room.

• Family Room: Family and guests alike will be drawn to this room, with its trio of arched windows and fireplace flanked by bookcases.

• Kitchen: An island adds convenience and distinction to this large, functional kitchen.

• Garage: This spacious three-bay garage provides plenty of space for cars and storage.

Main Level Floor Plan

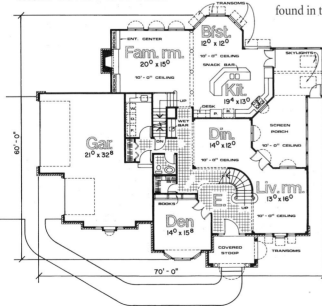

Upper Level Floor Plan

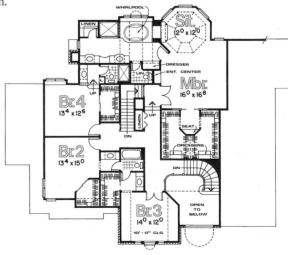

Copyright by designer/architect.

Plan #321049

Dimensions: 77'6" W x 30' D
Levels: 2
Square Footage: 3,144
Main Level Sq. Ft.: 1,724
Upper Level Sq. Ft.: 1,420
Bedrooms: 4
Bathrooms: 3½
Foundation: Basement
Materials List Available: Yes
Price Category: G

This stunning brick home would look great on your property.

Features:

- Family Room: This expansive family room includes a wet bar, fireplace, and attractive bay window. A powder room is centrally located between it and the kitchen.

- Kitchen: This kitchen offers a large pantry and an island cooktop. A conveniently located laundry room is nearby. The French doors provide light and access to the patio.

- Bedrooms: Located on the upper level are the master suite and three secondary bedrooms. The master suite and bedroom 4 each have a private bathroom. Bedrooms 2 and 3 share a "Jack-and-Jill" bathroom.

- Garage: A large side-load three-car garage has ample space for cars and storage.

Images provided by designer/architect.

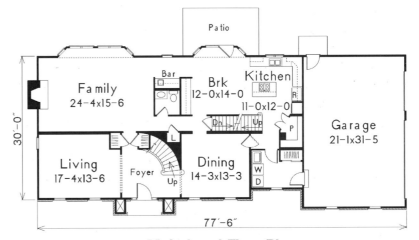

Main Level Floor Plan

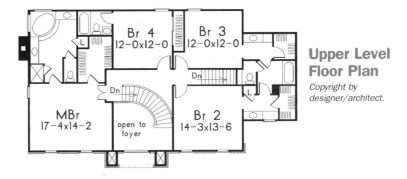

Upper Level Floor Plan

Copyright by designer/architect.

Plan #151232

Dimensions: 79'6" W x 71'4" D
Levels: 1.5
Square Footage: 3,901
Main Level Sq. Ft.: 3,185
Upper Level Sq. Ft.: 716
Bedrooms: 3
Bathrooms: 4
Foundation: Crawl space or slab
CompleteCost List Available: Yes
Price Category: H

Images provided by designer/architect.

This elegant brick home has something for everyone

Features:

- Great Room: This large gathering area has a fireplace and access to the rear grilling porch.

- Hearth Room: Relaxing and casual, this cozy area has a fireplace and is open to the kitchen.

- Kitchen: This large island kitchen has a built-in pantry and is open to the breakfast nook.

- Master Suite: A private bathroom with a corner whirlpool tub and a large walk-in closet turn this area into a spacious retreat.

- Bonus Room: This large space located upstairs near the two secondary bedrooms can be turned into a media room.

Main Level Floor Plan

Copyright by designer/architect.

Upper Level Floor Plan

Kitchen

Great Room

Plan #121061

Dimensions: 56' W x 52' D
Levels: 2
Square Footage: 3,025
Main Level Sq. Ft.: 1,583
Upper Level Sq. Ft.: 1,442
Bedrooms: 4
Bathrooms: 3½
Foundation: Basement
Materials List Available: Yes
Price Category: G

Images provided by designer/architect.

This large home with a contemporary feeling is ideal for the family looking for comfort and amenities.

Features:

• Entry: Stacked windows bring sunlight into this two-story entry, with its stylish curved staircase.

• Library: French doors off the entry lead to this room, with its built-in bookcases flanking a large, picturesque window.

• Family Room: Located in the rear of the home, this family room is sunken to set it apart. A spider-beamed ceiling gives it a contemporary feeling, and a bay window, wet bar, and pass-through fireplace add to this impression.

• Kitchen: The island in this kitchen makes working here a pleasure. The corner pantry joins a breakfast area and hearth room to this space.

Main Level Floor Plan

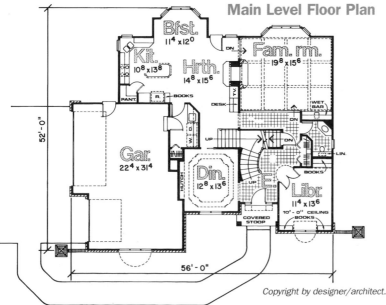

Copyright by designer/architect.

Upper Level Floor Plan

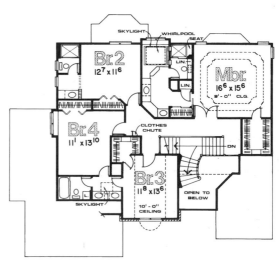

Plan #481035

Dimensions: 99' W x 64' D
Levels: 2
Square Footage: 3,204
Main Level Sq. Ft.: 1,701
Upper Level Sq. Ft.: 1,503
Bedrooms: 3
Bathrooms: 2½
Foundation: Walkout
Material List Available: No
Price Category: G

Images provided by designer/architect.

Rear Elevation

Distinctive design details set this home apart from others in the neighborhood.

Features:

- **Foyer:** This large foyer welcomes you home and provides a view through the home and into the family room. The adjoining study can double as a home office.

- **Family Room:** This two-story gathering space features a fireplace flanked by built-in cabinets. The full-height windows on the rear wall allow natural light to flood the space.

- **Kitchen:** This island kitchen flows into the nearby family room, allowing mingling between both spaces when friends or family are visiting. The adjacent dinette is available for daily meals.

- **Master Suite:** This private retreat waits for you to arrive home. The tray ceiling in the sleeping area adds elegant style to the area.

Porch

Kitchen

Main Level Floor Plan

Copyright by designer/architect.

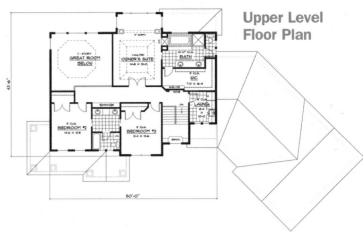

Upper Level Floor Plan

Breakfast Room/Kitchen

Great Room

Master Bedroom

Balcony

Plan #151021

Dimensions: 75'2" W x 89'6" D
Levels: 2
Square Footage: 3,385
Main Level Sq. Ft.: 2,633
Upper Level Sq. Ft.: 752
Bedrooms: 4
Bathrooms: 4
Foundation: Crawl space, or slab
CompleteCost List Available: Yes
Price Category: G

Images provided by designer/architect.

CAD FILE AVAILABLE

Main Level Floor Plan

Upper Level Floor Plan

Copyright by designer/architect.

Plan #111039

Dimensions: 59' W x 64' D
Levels: 2
Square Footage: 3,335
Main Level Sq. Ft.: 2,129
Upper Level Sq. Ft.: 1,206
Bedrooms: 4
Bathrooms: 4
Foundation: Basement
Materials List Available: No
Price Category: G

Images provided by designer/architect.

Main Level Floor Plan

Copyright by designer/architect.

Optional Lower Level Floor Plan

Upper Level Floor Plan

Main Level Floor Plan

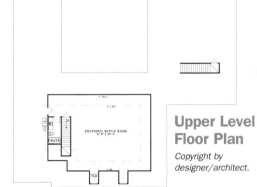

Images provided by designer/architect.

CAD FILE AVAILABLE

Plan #151126

Dimensions: 89' W x 86'4" D

Levels: 1.5

Square Footage: 3,474

Bedrooms: 4

Bathrooms: 5

Foundation: Crawl space or slab; walkout or basement for fee

CompleteCost List Available: Yes

Price Category: E

Upper Level Floor Plan

Copyright by designer/architect.

Main Level Floor Plan

Plan #121062

Dimensions: 70' W x 62' D

Levels: 2

Square Footage: 3,448

Main Level Sq. Ft.: 2,375

Upper Level Sq. Ft.: 1,073

Bedrooms: 4

Bathrooms: 3½

Foundation: Basement

Materials List Available: Yes

Price Category: G

Images provided by designer/architect.

Upper Level Floor Plan

Copyright by designer/architect.

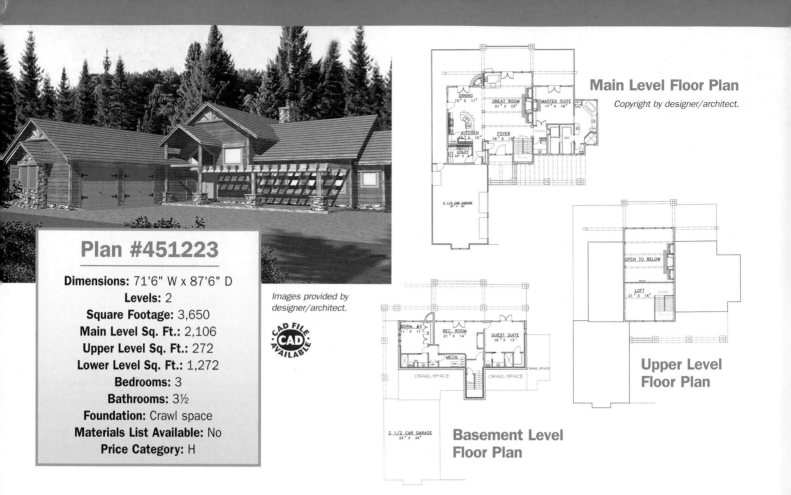

Main Level Floor Plan

Copyright by designer/architect.

Images provided by designer/architect.

CAD FILE AVAILABLE

Basement Level Floor Plan

Upper Level Floor Plan

Plan #451223

Dimensions: 71'6" W x 87'6" D
Levels: 2
Square Footage: 3,650
Main Level Sq. Ft.: 2,106
Upper Level Sq. Ft.: 272
Lower Level Sq. Ft.: 1,272
Bedrooms: 3
Bathrooms: 3½
Foundation: Crawl space
Materials List Available: No
Price Category: H

Upper Level Floor Plan

Copyright by designer/architect.

Images provided by designer/architect.

CAD FILE AVAILABLE

Main Level Floor Plan

Plan #121130

Dimensions: 66' W x 66' D
Levels: 1.5
Square Footage: 3,040
Main Level Sq. Ft.: 2,215
Upper Level Sq. Ft.: 825
Bedrooms: 4
Bathrooms: 3½
Foundation: Basement; crawl space for fee
Material List Available: Yes
Price Category: G

Main Level Floor Plan

Plan #271100

Dimensions: 69'10" W x 66'5" D

Levels: 2

Square Footage: 3,263

Main Level Sq. Ft.: 2,017

Upper Level Sq. Ft.: 1,246

Bedrooms: 4

Bathrooms: 2½

Foundation: Basement

Material List Available: No

Price Category: G

Images provided by designer/architect.

CAD FILE AVAILABLE

Upper Level Floor Plan

Copyright by designer/architect.

Main Level Floor Plan

Plan #151024

Dimensions: 60' W x 73'8" D

Levels: 2

Square Footage: 3,623

Main Level Sq. Ft.: 2,391

Upper Level Sq. Ft.: 1,232

Bedrooms: 3

Bathrooms: 3½

Foundation: Crawl space, slab; full basement for fee

CompleteCost List Available: Yes

Price Category: H

Images provided by designer/architect.

CAD FILE AVAILABLE

Upper Level Floor Plan

Copyright by designer/architect.

Plan #151011

Dimensions: 59'6" W x 74'4" D
Levels: 2
Square Footage: 3,437
Main Level Sq. Ft.: 2,184
Upper Level Sq. Ft.: 1,253
Bedrooms: 5
Bathrooms: 4
Foundation: Crawl space or slab; basement or daylight basement for fee
CompleteCost List Available: Yes
Price Category: G

Beauty, comfort, and convenience are yours in this luxurious, split-level home.

Features:

- Ceiling Height: 10 ft. unless otherwise noted.

- Master Suite: The 11-ft. pan ceiling sets the tone for this secluded area, with a lovely bay window that opens onto a rear porch, a pass-through fireplace to the great room, and a sitting room.

- Great Room: The pass-through fireplace makes this spacious room a cozy spot,

while the French doors leading to a rear porch make it a perfect spot for entertaining.

- Dining Room: Gracious 8-in. columns set off the entrance to this room.

- Kitchen: An island bar provides an efficient work area that's fitted with a sink.

- Breakfast Room: Open to the kitchen, this room is defined by a bay window and a spiral staircase to the second floor.

- Laundry Room: Large enough to accommodate a folding table, this room can also be fitted with a swinging pet door.

- Play Room: French doors in the children's playroom open onto a balcony where they can continue their games.

- Bedrooms: The 9-ft. ceilings on the second story make the rooms feel bright and airy.

CAD FILE AVAILABLE

**Main Level
Floor Plan**

**Upper Level
Floor Plan**

Plan #271029

Dimensions: 53' W x 55'8" D
Levels: 2
Square Footage: 3,039
Main Level Sq. Ft.: 1,612
Upper Level Sq. Ft.: 1,427
Bedrooms: 4
Bathrooms: 2½
Foundation: Basement
Materials List Available: Yes
Price Category: G

Image provided by designer/architect.

This English cottage-style home is packed with fabulous amenities.

Features:

• Living Room: The vaulted entry reveals an elegant stairway and this vaulted formal living room, which boasts oversized windows and a dramatic corner fireplace.

• Dining Room: Decorative columns introduce this adjoining formal dining room, which opens to a screened porch.

• Kitchen: An island cooktop punctuates this large kitchen, which flows into a spacious breakfast room.

• Family Room: The certain hot spot of the home, this generously proportioned room boasts a warming fireplace and access to a jaw-dropping wraparound deck that promises truly awesome views.

• Master Suite: Secluded to a corner of the upper floor, the master bedroom features its own fireplace and private bath. Two more bedrooms and a bonus room finish the floor.

Main Level Floor Plan

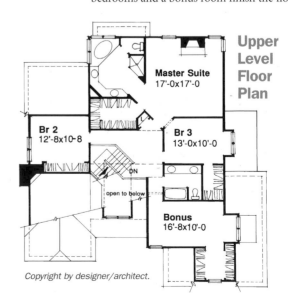

Upper Level Floor Plan

Copyright by designer/architect.

Main Level Floor Plan

sto | sto | sto

garage
22 x 22

Main Level Floor Plan

porch 18 x 6

w d
14x9
util

family rm
25 x 16
built-in entertainment ctr and library

bath 17 x 9

kit 14x13

built-in entertainment ctr and library

sitting
14 x 12

mbr
16 x 13

foy

dining
16 x 12

eating
14 x 10

porch 34 x 8

future space 28 x 12

*Images provided by
designer/architect.*

Upper Level Floor Plan

outline of lower level

br 4
11 x 12

balcony

br 2
13 x 13

br 3
13 x 12

hand rail

open to lower level

Copyright by designer/architect.

Plan #211072

Dimensions: 62' W x 86' D

Levels: 2

Square Footage: 3,012

Main Level Sq. Ft.: 2,202

Upper Level Sq. Ft.: 810

Bedrooms: 4

Bathrooms: 3½

Foundation: Crawl space, optional basement

Materials List Available: Yes

Price Category: G

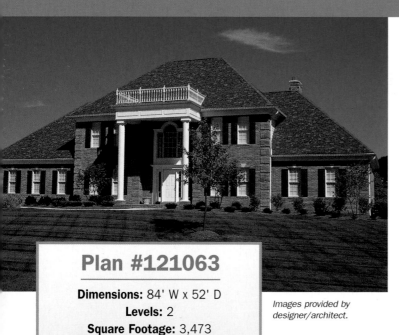

Main Level Floor Plan

Bkfst
13 x 13

Kit.

Grt. rm.
21 x 19

Mbr.
15 x 19

Gar.
23 x 35

Dn.
15 x 13

Liv. rm.
14 x 12

*Images provided by
designer/architect.*

Upper Level Floor Plan

Br.

Br.
14 x 13

OPEN TO BELOW

Br.
14 x 13

Copyright by designer/architect.

Plan #121063

Dimensions: 84' W x 52' D

Levels: 2

Square Footage: 3,473

Main Level Sq. Ft.: 2,500

Upper Level Sq. Ft.: 973

Bedrooms: 4

Bathrooms: 3½

Foundation: Basement

Materials List Available: Yes

Price Category: G

Main Level Floor Plan

Images provided by designer/architect.

CAD FILE AVAILABLE

Plan #161094

Dimensions: 68'8" W x 56'8" D

Levels: 2

Square Footage: 3,366

Main Level Sq. Ft.: 1,759

Upper Level Sq. Ft.: 1,607

Bedrooms: 5

Bathrooms: 4

Foundation: Walkout basement

Material List Available: No

Price Category: G

Upper Level Floor Plan

Copyright by designer/architect.

Main Level Floor Plan

Images provided by designer/architect.

CAD FILE AVAILABLE

Plan #151025

Dimensions: 71' W x 55' D

Levels: 2

Square Footage: 3,914

Main Level Sq. Ft.: 2,291

Upper Level Sq. Ft.: 1,623

Bedrooms: 3

Bathrooms: 3

Foundation: Crawl space, slab; full basement for fee

CompleteCost List Available: Yes

Price Category: H

Upper Level Floor Plan

Copyright by designer/architect

Plan #151031

Dimensions: 60'2" W x 60'2" D
Levels: 2
Square Footage: 3,130
Main Level Sq. Ft.: 1,600
Upper Level Sq. Ft.: 1,530
Bedrooms: 3
Bathrooms: 3½
Foundation: Crawl space, slab
CompleteCost List Available: Yes
Price Category: G

Images provided by designer/architect.

If you love traditional Southern plantation homes, you'll want this house with its wraparound porches that are graced with boxed columns.

Features:

- **Great Room:** Use the gas fireplace for warmth in this comfortable room, which is open to the kitchen.

- **Living Room:** 8-in. columns add formality as you enter this living and dining room.

- **Kitchen:** You'll love the island bar with a sink. An elevator here can take you to the other floors.

- **Master Suite:** A gas fireplace warms this area, and the bath is luxurious.

- **Bedrooms:** Each has a private bath and built-in bookshelves for easy organizing.

- **Optional Features:** Choose a 2,559-sq.-ft. basement and add a kitchen to it, or finish the 1,744-sq.-ft. bonus room and add a spiral staircase and a bath.

Main Level Floor Plan

Upper Level Floor Plan

Copyright by designer/architect.

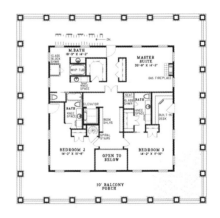

Basement Level Floor Plan

Optional Upper Level Floor Plan

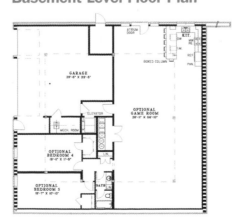

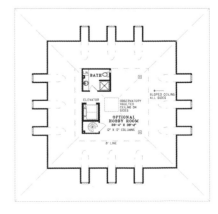

Plan #441024

Dimensions: 90'6" W x 84' D
Levels: 2
Square Footage: 3,517
Main Level Sq. Ft.: 2,698
Upper Level Sq. Ft.: 819
Bedrooms: 3
Bathrooms: 3½
Foundation: Crawl space; slab or basement available for fee
Materials List Available: No
Price Category: H

You'll feel like royalty every time you pull into the driveway of this European-styled manor house.

Images provided by designer/architect.

Features:

- **Kitchen:** This gourmet chef's center hosts an island with a vegetable sink. The arched opening above the primary sink provides a view of the fireplace and entertainment center in the great room. A walk-in food pantry and a butler's pantry are situated between this space and the dining room.

- **Master Suite:** Located on the main level, this private retreat boasts a large sleeping area and a sitting area. The grand master bath features a large walk-in closet, dual vanities, a large tub, and a shower.

- **Bedrooms:** Two secondary bedrooms are located on the upper level, and each has its own bathroom.

- **Laundry Room:** This utility room houses cabinets, a folding counter, and an ironing board.

- **Garage:** This large three-car garage has room for storage. Family members entering the home from this area will find a coat closet and a place to stash briefcases and backpacks.

Main Level Floor Plan

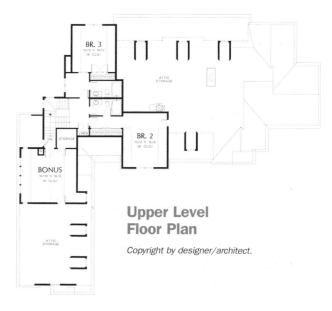

Upper Level Floor Plan

Copyright by designer/architect.

Plan #321061

Dimensions: 55' W x 49'4" D
Levels: 2
Square Footage: 3,169
Main Level Sq. Ft.: 1,679
Upper Level Sq. Ft.: 1,490
Bedrooms: 4
Bathrooms: 2½
Foundation: Basement
Materials List Available: Yes
Price Category: G

Images provided by designer/architect.

You'll love the spacious interior of this gorgeous home, which is built for comfortable family living but includes amenities for gracious entertaining.

Features:

• **Entry:** This large entry gives a view of the handcrafted staircase to the upper floor.

• **Living Room:** Angled French doors open into this generously sized room with a vaulted ceiling.

• **Family Room:** You'll love to entertain in this huge room with a masonry fireplace, built-in entertainment area, gorgeous bay window, and well-fitted wet bar.

• **Breakfast Room:** A door in the bayed area opens to the outdoor patio for dining convenience.

• **Kitchen:** The center island provides work space and a snack bar, and the walk-in pantry is a delight.

• **Master Suite:** Enjoy the vaulted ceiling, two walk-in closets, and luxurious bath in this suite.

Main Level Floor Plan

Upper Level Floor Plan

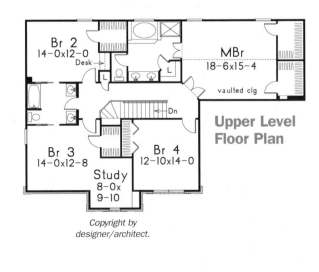

Copyright by designer/architect.

Plan #141033

Dimensions: 38' W x 79' D
Levels: 2
Square Footage: 3,223
Main Level Sq. Ft.: 1,388
Upper Level Sq. Ft.: 1,835
Bedrooms: 4
Bathrooms: 3½
Foundation: Basement
Materials List Available: No
Price Category: G

Images provided by designer/architect.

This brick home with a hint of Craftsman styling adds charm to any neighborhood.

Features:

- Front Porch: This covered front porch welcomes guests to your home. It's the perfect spot to sit and sip lemonade while visiting with friends or family.

- Living Room: The fireplace, flanked by optional built-in cabinets, is the focal point of this gathering area. On nice days you can expand the area onto the adjacent screened-in porch.

- Kitchen: This large island kitchen features a built-in pantry and direct access to the dining room. The bay window in the adjacent breakfast nook will bring in an abundance of natural light.

- Master Suite: This upper-level oasis boasts a private sitting area off of the sleeping area. The large master bath pampers you with amenities such as a Jacuzzi tub, dual vanities, and a compartmentalized lavatory.

Main Level Floor Plan

Copyright by designer/architect.

Upper Level Floor Plan

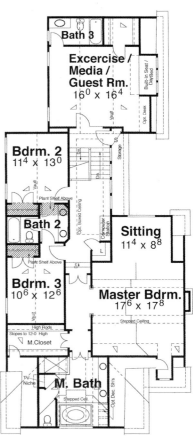

Plan #131021

Dimensions: 60' W x 52'4" D
Levels: 2
Square Footage: 3,110
Main Level Sq. Ft.: 1,818
Upper Level Sq. Ft.: 1,292
Bedrooms: 5
Bathrooms: 2½
Foundation: Crawl space, slab, or basement
Materials List Available: Yes
Price Category: H

This home, as shown in the photograph, may differ from the actual blueprints. For more detailed information, please check the floor plans carefully.

Images provided by designer/architect.

Amenities abound in this luxurious two-story beauty with a cozy gazebo on one corner of the spectacular wraparound front porch. Comfort, functionality, and spaciousness characterize this home.

Features:

- Ceiling Height: 8 ft.

- Foyer: This two-story high foyer is breathtaking.

- Family Room: Roomy with open views of the kitchen, the family room has a vaulted ceiling and boasts a functional fireplace and a built-in entertainment center.

- Dining Room: Formal yet comfortable, this spacious dining room is perfect for entertaining family and friends.

- Kitchen: Perfectly located with access to a breakfast room and the family room, this U-shaped kitchen with large center island is charming as well as efficient.

- Master Suite: Enjoy this sizable room with a vaulted ceiling, two large walk-in closets, and a lovely compartmented bath.

Main Level Floor Plan

Upper Level Floor Plan

Plan #481022

Dimensions: 85'8" W x 48' D
Levels: 2
Square Footage: 3,217
Main Level Sq. Ft.: 1,667
Upper Level Sq. Ft.: 1,550
Bedrooms: 3
Bathrooms: 2½
Foundation: Walkout
Material List Available: No
Price Category: G

This elegant house has an open interior design that is made for family living.

Images provided by designer/architect.

Features:

- **Family Room:** An 18-ft.-high ceiling and an angled fireplace flanked with built-ins add to the great atmosphere in this gathering area. The large windows allow for a view of the backyard.

- **Dining Room:** This formal dining area features columns, which define its boundaries. The stepped ceiling adds an elegant feature to the area.

- **Kitchen:** This island kitchen features a built-in pantry and large center island. The dinette area has access to the rear screened porch.

- **Bedrooms:** The master suite and two secondary bedrooms are located on the upper level. Bedrooms 2 and 3 share a "Jack-and-Jill" bathroom.

Rear Elevation

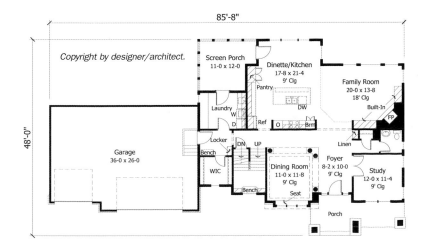

Main Level Floor Plan

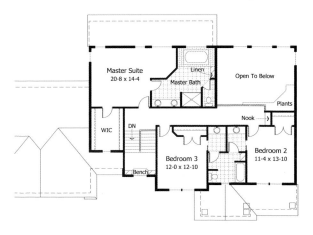

Upper Level Floor Plan

Plan #271028

Dimensions: 48' W x 39'6" D
Levels: 2
Square Footage: 2,335
Main Level Sq. Ft.: 1,168
Upper Level Sq. Ft.: 1,167
Bedrooms: 4
Bathrooms: 2½
Foundation: Daylight basement
Materials List Available: Yes
Price Category: E

Images provided by designer/architect.

Main Level Floor Plan

Upper Level Floor Plan

Copyright by designer/architect.

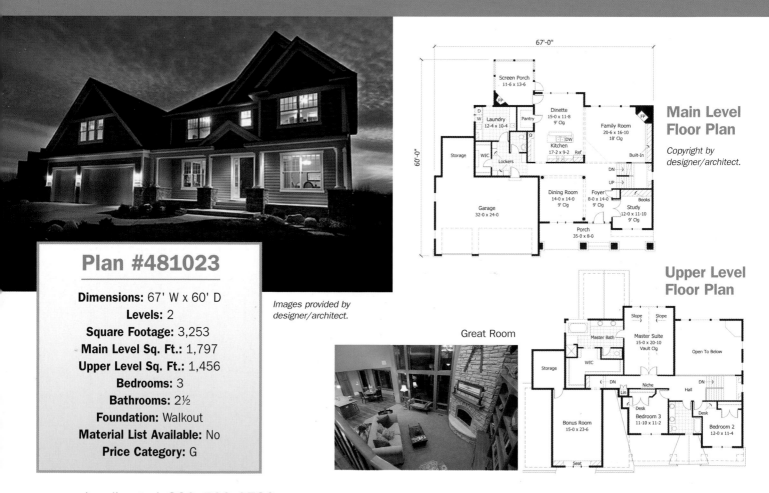

Plan #481023

Dimensions: 67' W x 60' D
Levels: 2
Square Footage: 3,253
Main Level Sq. Ft.: 1,797
Upper Level Sq. Ft.: 1,456
Bedrooms: 3
Bathrooms: 2½
Foundation: Walkout
Material List Available: No
Price Category: G

Images provided by designer/architect.

Main Level Floor Plan

Copyright by designer/architect.

Upper Level Floor Plan

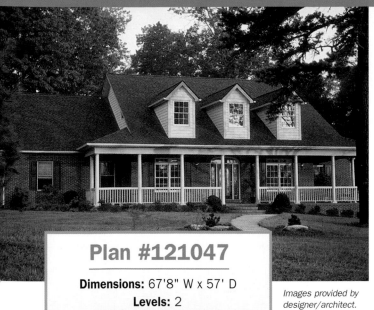

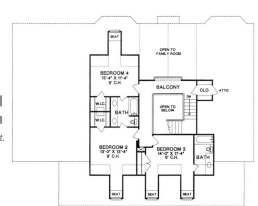

**Main Level
Floor Plan**

*Images provided by
designer/architect.*

**Upper Level
Floor Plan**

Copyright by designer/architect.

Plan #121047

Dimensions: 67'8" W x 57' D

Levels: 2

Square Footage: 3,072

Main Level Sq. Ft.: 2,116

Upper Level Sq. Ft.: 956

Bedrooms: 4

Bathrooms: 3½

Foundation: Slab

Materials List Available: Yes

Price Category: G

Plan #151023

Dimensions: 60' W x 96'6" D

Levels: 2

Square Footage: 3,203

Main Level Sq. Ft.: 2,328

Upper Level Sq. Ft.: 875

Bedrooms: 4

Bathrooms: 3½

Foundation: Crawl space, slab;
full basement available for fee

CompleteCost List Available: Yes

Price Category: G

*Images provided by
designer/architect.*

**Main Level
Floor Plan**

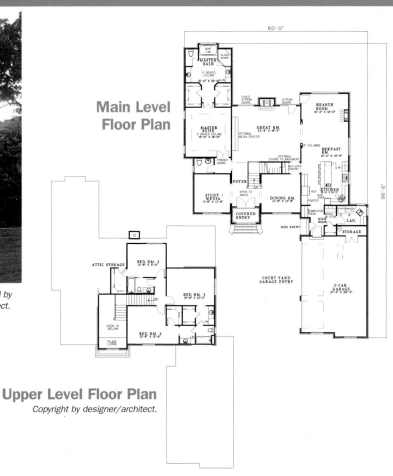

Upper Level Floor Plan
Copyright by designer/architect.

Plan #131078

Dimensions: 72'8" W x 47' D
Levels: 2
Square Footage: 3,278
Main Level Sq. Ft.: 2,146
Upper Level Sq. Ft.: 1,132
Bedrooms: 3
Bathrooms: 3
Foundation: Crawl space, slab, or basement
Material List Available: Yes
Price Category: H

This attractive home is a delight when viewed from the outside and features a great floor plan inside.

Images provided by designer/architect.

Features:

- Great Room: This spacious room, with a vaulted ceiling and skylights, is the place to curl up by the fireplace on a cold winter night. Sliding glass doors lead out to the backyard.

- Kitchen: A center island adds convenience to this well-planned kitchen. The bayed breakfast area adds extra room for a table.

- Master Suite: The 10-ft.-high stepped ceiling sets the tone for this secluded area, which features a large walk-in closet. The master bath boasts a whirlpool tub and dual vanities.

- Bonus Room: Located above the garage, this space can be finished as a fourth bedroom or home office.

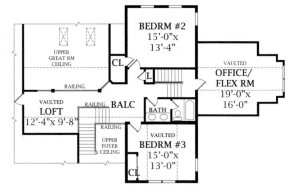

Rear View

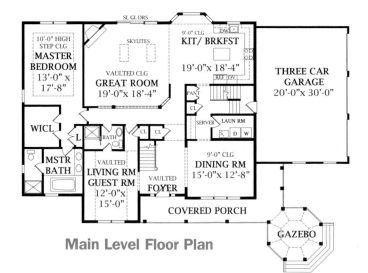

Main Level Floor Plan

Upper Level Floor Plan

Copyright by designer/architect.

Plan #321062

Dimensions: 54' W x 57'4" D
Levels: 2
Square Footage: 3,138
Main Level Sq. Ft.: 1,958
Upper Level Sq. Ft.: 1,180
Bedrooms: 4
Bathrooms: 3½
Foundation: Basement
Materials List Available: Yes
Price Category: G

Images provided by designer/architect.

This home, as shown in the photograph, may differ from the actual blueprints. For more detailed information, please check the floor plans carefully.

This elegant home is spacious enough for an active family and lovely enough for entertaining.

Features:

- Family Room: Host a crowd in this enormous room, or enjoy a cozy chat beside the fireplace.

- Breakfast Room: Open to the family room, this breakfast room leads to the outdoor patio.

- Study: Situated for privacy and quiet, this study has large windows and handsome double doors.

- Dining Room: This large, private room is equally suitable for formal parties and family dinners.

- Master Suite: The vaulted ceiling and bay window make the bedroom elegant, while the two walk-in closets, linen closet, double vanity, tub, and separate shower make the suite luxurious.

- Loft: Use this spacious area as a playroom when the children are small and a media area later on.

Main Level Floor Plan

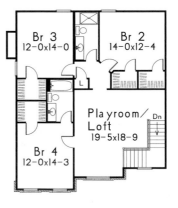

Upper Level Floor Plan

Copyright by designer/architect.

Main Level Floor Plan

Copyright by designer/architect.

Upper Level Floor Plan

Images provided by designer/architect.

Rear Elevation

Plan #261013

Dimensions: 81'8" W x 34' D

Levels: 2

Square Footage: 3,193

Main Level Sq. Ft.: 1,735

Upper Level Sq. Ft.: 1,458

Bedrooms: 4

Bathrooms: 3½

Foundation: Basement

Materials List Available: No

Price Category: G

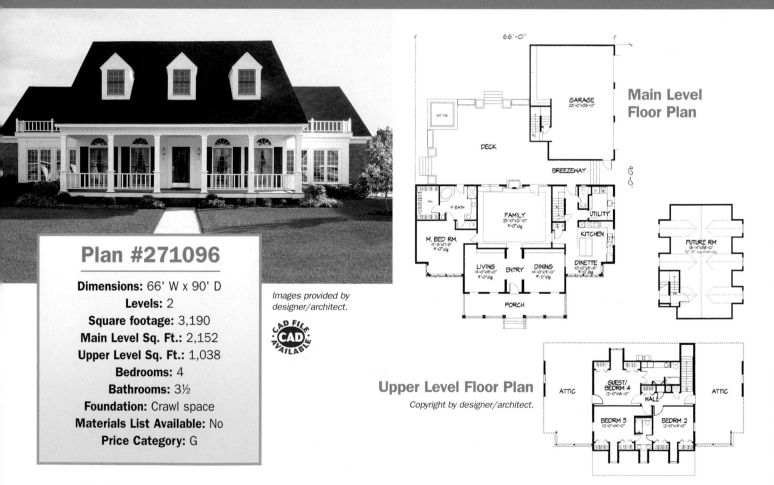

Main Level Floor Plan

Upper Level Floor Plan

Copyright by designer/architect.

Images provided by designer/architect.

Plan #271096

Dimensions: 66' W x 90' D

Levels: 2

Square footage: 3,190

Main Level Sq. Ft.: 2,152

Upper Level Sq. Ft.: 1,038

Bedrooms: 4

Bathrooms: 3½

Foundation: Crawl space

Materials List Available: No

Price Category: G

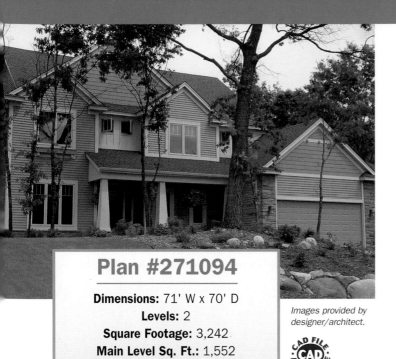

Main Level Floor Plan

GREAT RM.
21' X 18'

DINING
21' X 10'

KITCHEN
15' X 14'

STUDY
11' X 13'

MUD RM.

PORCH

GARAGE
40' X 24'

Images provided by designer/architect.

CAD FILE AVAILABLE

BED RM.
10' X 14'

BED RM.
10' X 14'

OWNER'S SUITE
14' X 18'

BATH

LAUN.

BATH

WLC

BED RM.
11' X 13'

BED RM.
11' X 13'

Upper Level Floor Plan

Copyright by designer/architect.

Plan #271094

Dimensions: 71' W x 70' D

Levels: 2

Square Footage: 3,242

Main Level Sq. Ft.: 1,552

Upper Level Sq. Ft.: 1,690

Bedrooms: 5

Bathrooms: 2½

Foundation: Full basement

Materials List Available: No

Price Category: G

Plan #141020

Dimensions: 58' W x 40'4" D

Levels: 2

Square Footage: 3,140

Main Level Sq. Ft.: 1,553

Upper Level Sq. Ft.: 1,587

Bedrooms: 5

Bathrooms: 4

Foundation: Basement

Materials List Available: No

Price Category: G

Images provided by designer/architect.

Main Level Floor Plan

Sundeck
18-0 x 12-0

Guest Bdrm.
12-2 x 10-0

Guest Bath

Two Story Family Rm.
18-8 x 15-4

Brkfst.
10-10 x 11-10

Kit.
12-6 x 14-0

Dbl. Garage
21-8 x 21-8

Living
11-4 x 13-4

Two Story Foyer
11-8 x 11-6

Dining
11-4 x 13-6

58-0

40-4

9-8

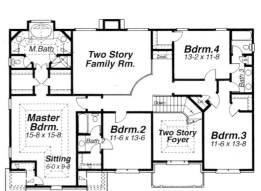

Upper Level Floor Plan

Copyright by designer/architect.

M. Bath

Two Story Family Rm.

Bdrm.4
13-2 x 11-8

Bath 3

Master Bdrm.
15-8 x 15-8

Bath 2

Bdrm.2
11-6 x 13-6

Two Story Foyer

Bdrm.3
11-6 x 13-8

Sitting
6-0 x 9-8

Plan #331004

Dimensions: 81' W x 49'10" D
Levels: 2
Square Footage: 3,125
Main Level Sq. Ft.: 2,147
Upper Level Sq. Ft.: 978
Bedrooms: 4
Bathrooms: 3½
Foundation: Crawl space, slab, or basement
Materials List Available: No
Price Category: G

This inviting home has great curb appeal.

Features:

- Foyer: This foyer contains a curved stairway that adds an elegant focal point and welcomes you to the home. The two-story space feels open and airy as it flows seamlessly into the dining room.

- Living Room: Open to the floor above, this living room boasts a cozy fireplace flanked by built-in cabinets. Large windows and access to the rear patio allow an abundance of natural light to flood this space.

- Master Suite: This main-level retreat boasts a tray ceiling and bay window in the sleeping area. The large master bath features dual vanities, his and her closets, and a whirlpool tub.

- Secondary Bedrooms: Located on the upper level, the three bedrooms share two full bathrooms. Bedrooms 2 and 3 have tray ceilings and direct access to a full bathroom.

Images provided by designer/architect.

This home, as shown in the photograph, may differ from the actual blueprints. For more detailed information, please check the floor plans carefully.

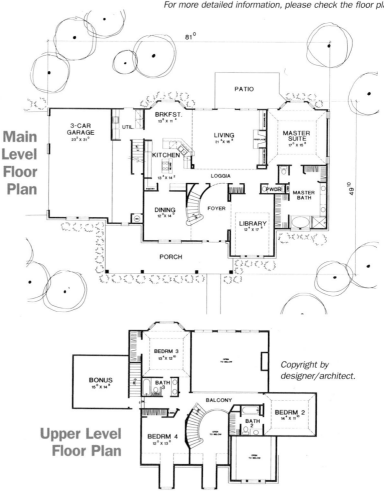

Main Level Floor Plan

Upper Level Floor Plan

Copyright by designer/architect.

Plan #391018

Dimensions: 93' W x 54' D
Levels: 2
Square Footage: 3,746
Main Level Sq. Ft.: 1,978
Upper Level Sq. Ft.: 1,768
Bedrooms: 4
Bathrooms: 3½
Foundation: Basement
Materials List Available: Yes
Price Category: H

This home, as shown in the photograph, may differ from the actual blueprints. For more detailed information, please check the floor plans carefully.

Images provided by designer/architect.

While the facade of this house suggests the level of detail within, it gives no hint of the home's uniquely designed rooms.

Features:

- Kitchen: This L-shape kitchen, with its large, angled island, provides plenty of workspace and storage.

- Built-ins: Shelving, bookcases, and a built-in desk add extra usefulness throughout the home.

- Porch: This three-season porch is an ideal place to relax and enjoy the outdoors when the weather doesn't permit use of either of the two decks.

- Garage: This garage holds up to three vehicles, though the third bay can be used as storage or shop space.

- Fireplaces: The master suite, great room, and kitchen/breakfast area are all warmed by fireplaces.

Main Level Floor Plan

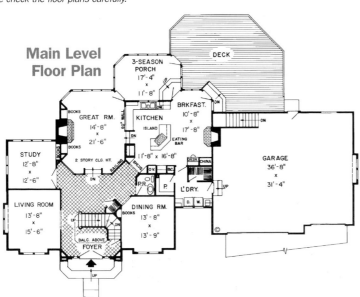

Upper Level Floor Plan

Copyright by designer/architect.

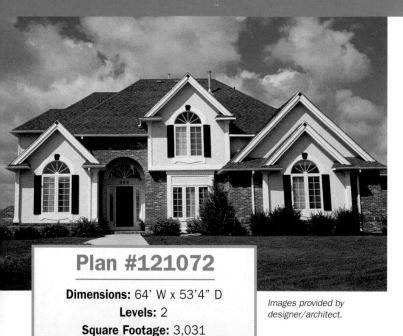

Main Level Floor Plan

Images provided by designer/architect.

Upper Level Floor Plan

Copyright by designer/architect.

Plan #121072

Dimensions: 64' W x 53'4" D

Levels: 2

Square Footage: 3,031

Main Level Sq. Ft.: 1,640

Upper Level Sq. Ft.: 1,391

Bedrooms: 4

Bathrooms: 3½

Foundation: Basement

Materials List Available: Yes

Price Category: G

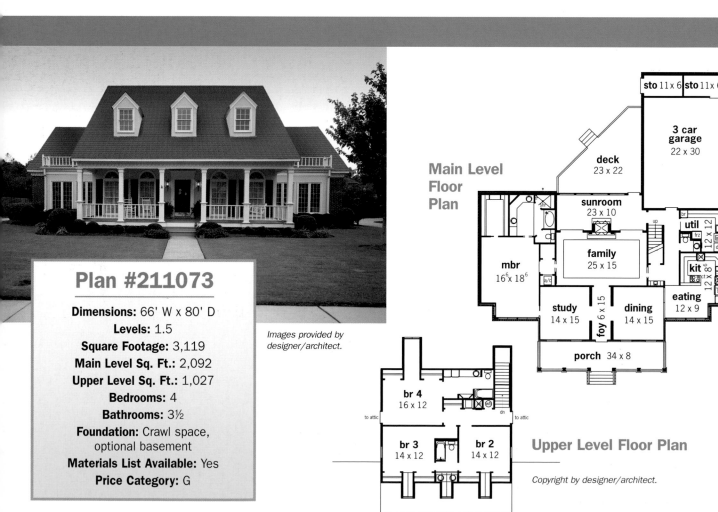

Main Level Floor Plan

Images provided by designer/architect.

Upper Level Floor Plan

Copyright by designer/architect.

Plan #211073

Dimensions: 66' W x 80' D

Levels: 1.5

Square Footage: 3,119

Main Level Sq. Ft.: 2,092

Upper Level Sq. Ft.: 1,027

Bedrooms: 4

Bathrooms: 3½

Foundation: Crawl space, optional basement

Materials List Available: Yes

Price Category: G

Main Level Floor Plan

Upper Level Floor Plan

Copyright by designer/architect.

Plan #481018

Dimensions: 90'8" W x 61'10" D
Levels: 2
Square Footage: 3,071
Main Level Sq. Ft.: 1,705
Upper Level Sq. Ft.: 1,366
Bedrooms: 3
Bathrooms: 2½
Foundation: Walkout
Material List Available: No
Price Category: G

Images provided by designer/architect.

This home, as shown in the photograph, may differ from the actual blueprints. For more detailed information, please check the floor plans carefully.

Plan #151012

Dimensions: 47' W x 94'1" D
Levels: 2
Square Footage: 3,730
Main Level Sq. Ft.: 2,648
Upper Level Sq. Ft.: 1,082
Bedrooms: 3
Bathrooms: 2½
Foundation: Crawl space or slab; basement for fee
CompleteCost List Available: Yes
Price Category: H

Images provided by designer/architect.

CAD FILE AVAILABLE
CAD

Upper Level Floor Plan

Copyright by designer/architect.

Main Level Floor Plan

Plan #121023

Dimensions: 85'5" W x 74'8" D

Levels: 2

Square Footage: 3,904

Main Level Sq. Ft.: 2,813

Upper Level Sq. Ft.: 1,091

Bedrooms: 4

Bathrooms: 3½

Foundation: Basement

Materials List Available: Yes

Price Category: H

Spacious and gracious, here are all the amenities you expect in a fine home.

Features:

- Ceiling Height: 8 ft. except as noted.

- Foyer: This magnificent entry features a graceful curved staircase with balcony above.

- Sunken Living Room: This sunken room is filled with light from a row of bowed windows. It's the perfect place for social gatherings both large and small.

- Den: French doors open into this truly distinctive den with its 11-ft. ceiling and built-in bookcases.

- Formal Dining Room: Entertain guests with style and grace in this dining room with corner column.

- Master Suite: Another set of French doors leads to this suite that features two walk-in closets, a whirlpool flanked by vanities, and a private sitting room with built-in bookcases.

Main Level Floor Plan

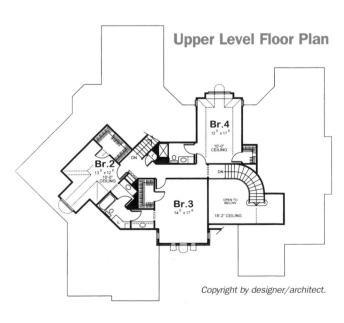

Upper Level Floor Plan

Copyright by designer/architect.

Plan #121065

Dimensions: 62' W x 55'4" D
Levels: 2
Square Footage: 3,407
Main Level Sq. Ft.: 1,719
Upper Level Sq. Ft.: 1,688
Bedrooms: 4
Bathrooms: 2½
Foundation: Basement
Materials List Available: Yes
Price Category: G

If you love contemporary design, the unusual shapes of the rooms in this home will delight you.

Features:

- Entry: You'll see a balcony from the upper level that overlooks this entryway, as well as the lovely curved staircase to this floor.

- Great Room: This room is sunken to set it apart. A fireplace, wet bar, spider-beamed ceiling, and row of arched windows give it character.

- Dining Room: Columns define this lovely octagon room, where you'll love to entertain guests or create lavish family dinners.

- Master Suite: A multi-tiered ceiling adds a note of grace, while the fireplace and private library create a real retreat. The gracious bath features a gazebo ceiling and a skylight.

Main Level Floor Plan

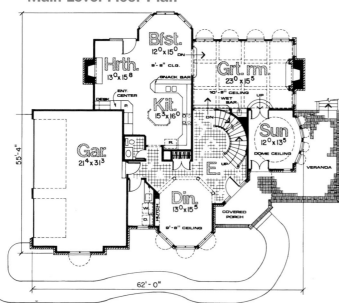

Upper Level Floor Plan

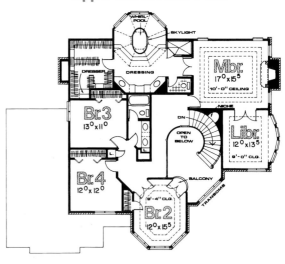

Main Level Floor Plan

porch 40 x 10

family 23 x 20

kit & den 35 x 17

util

mbr 20 x 16

wet bar

built in entertainment center and library

built in entertainment center and library

clo

gallery

sto

bar

phone niche

dining 18 x 12

study 18 x 12

br 2 13 x 12

clo

clo

lin

foy

golf cart & sto 18 x 17

garage 22 x 22

work bench

future space 36 x 12

Upper Level Floor Plan

open to lower level

Bonus Area Floor Plan

library

to attic

clo

clo

to attic

br 3 18 x 12

br 4 18 x 12

open to lower level

books desk

desk books

Images provided by designer/architect.

Copyright by designer/architect.

Plan #211125

Dimensions: 94' W x 92' D

Levels: 2

Square Footage: 4,440

Main Level Sq. Ft.: 3,465

Upper Level Sq. Ft.: 975

Bedrooms: 4

Bathrooms: 5½

Foundation: Crawl space

Materials List Available: Yes

Price Category: I

87' 0"

12"X12" BRK COL

SCREENED PORCH 28'-0" X 12'-0"

PATIO 50'-0" X 19'-4"

ATRIUM DOORS

HEARTH ROOM 14'-8" X 14'-10"

GAS FIREPLACE

MASTER SUITE 18'-4" X 20'-0" 9" BOXED CEILING

GREAT ROOM 20'-10" X 20'-6"

KITCHEN 20'-4" X 15'-8"

70' 0"

KNEE SPACE

MBATH

STUDY 14'-0" X 15'-6"

GLASS SHOWER

SEAT

WET BAR

FOYER

DINING ROOM 14'-0" X 15'-6"

3-CAR GARAGE 23'-4" X 34'-0"

FRENCH DOORS

TERRACE 43'-2" X 18'-6"

Main Level Floor Plan

Images provided by designer/architect.

CAD FILE AVAILABLE

BEDROOM 2 13'-0" X 15'-6"

BATH

BEDROOM 3 13'-0" X 15'-6"

BONUS AREA

GUEST ROOM 14'-0" X 12'-0"

PLAY ROOM 14'-0" X 15'-6"

OPEN TO BELOW

Upper Level Floor Plan

Copyright by designer/architect.

Plan #151095

Dimensions: 87' W x 70' D

Levels: 2

Square Footage: 4,446

Main Level Sq. Ft.: 3,086

Upper Level Sq. Ft.: 1,360

Bedrooms: 4

Bathrooms: 3 full, 2 half

Foundation: Crawl space or slab; basement or walkout for fee

CompleteCost List Available: Yes

Price Category: I

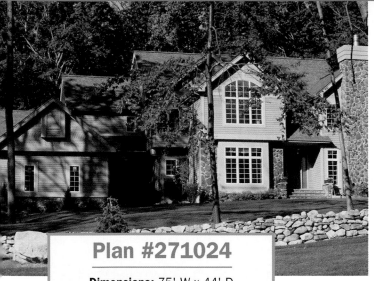

Plan #271024

Dimensions: 75' W x 44' D
Levels: 2
Square Footage: 3,107
Main Level Sq. Ft.: 1,639
Upper Level Sq. Ft.: 1,468
Bedrooms: 4
Bathrooms: 2½
Foundation: Basement
Materials List Available: Yes
Price Category: G

Images provided by designer/architect.

Main Level Floor Plan

Upper Level Floor Plan

Copyright by designer/architect.

Plan #161044

Dimensions: 90'6" W x 78'9" D
Levels: 2
Square Footage: 4,652
Main Level Sq. Ft.: 3,414
Upper Level Sq. Ft.: 1,238
Bedrooms: 4
Bathrooms: 3½
Foundation: Basement
Materials List Available: No
Price Category: I

Images provided by designer/architect.

Rear Elevation

Main Level Floor Plan

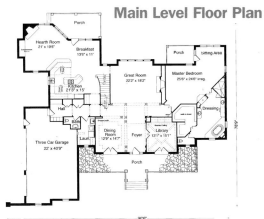

Upper Level Floor Plan

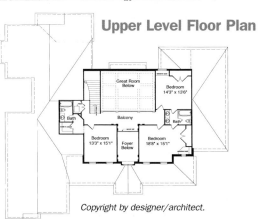

Copyright by designer/architect.

Plan #291013

Dimensions: 72' W x 75' D
Levels: 2
Square Footage: 3,553
Main Level Sq. Ft.: 1,830
Upper Level Sq. Ft.: 1,723
Bedrooms: 4
Bathrooms: 2½
Foundation: Basement
Materials List Available: No
Price Category: H

Images provided by designer/architect.

Copyright by designer/architect.

Main Level Floor Plan

Upper Level Floor Plan

Plan #151112

Dimensions: 67'8" W x 49' D
Levels: 2
Square Footage: 3,661
Main Level Sq. Ft.: 2,018
Upper Level Sq. Ft.: 1,643
Bedrooms: 4
Bathrooms: 2½
Foundation: Crawl space or slab; basement or walkout available for fee
CompleteCost List Available: Yes
Price Category: F

Images provided by designer/architect.

Main Level Floor Plan

Upper Level Floor Plan

Copyright by designer/architect.

Front View

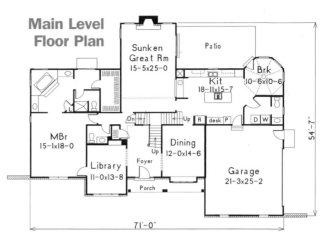

Main Level Floor Plan

Sunken Great Rm 15-5x25-0

Patio

Brk 10-6x10-6

Kit 18-11x15-7

MBr 15-1x18-0

Dining 12-0x14-6

Library 11-0x13-8

Foyer

Porch

Garage 21-3x25-2

54'-7"

71'-0"

Images provided by designer/architect.

Upper Level Floor Plan

Copyright by designer/architect.

open to below

Br 2 13-6x14-9

Br 4 14-9x11-8

Furn Room

storage

Br 3 13-2x14-6

open to below

Plan #321042

Dimensions: 71' W x 54'7" D

Levels: 2

Square Footage: 3,368

Main Level Sq. Ft.: 2,150

Upper Level Sq. Ft.: 1,218

Bedrooms: 4

Full Bathrooms: 3

Half Bathrooms: 2

Foundation: Basement

Materials List Available: Yes

Price Category: G

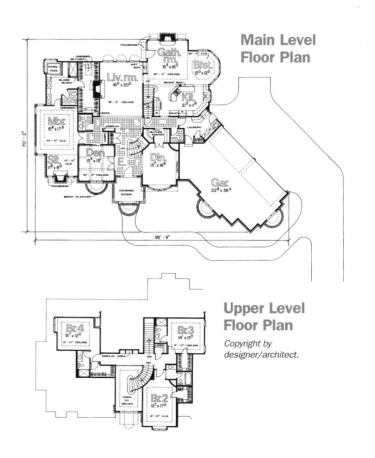

Main Level Floor Plan

Gath. rm. 15'x16'

Bfst. 12'0x12'0

Liv. rm. 16'x20'

Kit. 21'0x11'8

Mbr. 15'8x17'3

Den 13'3x13'

Din. 13'x16'8

Gar. 22'8x36'4

Sit. 11'8x8'0

70'-2"

95'-9"

Images provided by designer/architect.

CAD FILE AVAILABLE

Upper Level Floor Plan

Copyright by designer/architect.

Br4 15'8x12'0

Br3 14'4x13'0

display area

open to below

Br2 12'x17'0

Plan #121018

Dimensions: 95'9" W x 70'2" D

Levels: 2

Square Footage: 3,950

Main Level Sq. Ft.: 2,839

Upper Level Sq. Ft.: 1,111

Bedrooms: 4

Bathrooms: 4 full, 2 half

Foundation: Basement

Materials List Available: Yes

Price Category: H

Plan #161061

Dimensions: 90' W x 69'10" D
Levels: 2
Square Footage: 3,816
Main Level Sq. Ft.: 2,725
Upper Level Sq. Ft.: 1,091
Bedrooms: 4
Bathrooms: 3½
Foundation: Basement, walkout basement
Materials List Available: No
Price Category: H

Images provided by designer/architect.

Luxurious amenities make living in this spacious home a true pleasure for the whole family.

Features:

• Great Room: A fireplace, flanking built-in shelves, a balcony above, and three lovely windows create a luxurious room that's always comfortable.

• Hearth Room: Another fireplace with surrounding built-ins and double doors to the outside deck (with its own fireplace) highlight this room.

• Kitchen: A butler's pantry, laundry room, and mudroom with a window seat and two walk-in closets complement this large kitchen.

• Library: Situated for privacy and quiet, this spacious room with a large window area may be reached from the master bedroom as well as the foyer.

• Master Suite: A sloped ceiling and windows on three walls create a lovely bedroom, and the huge walk-in closet, dressing room, and luxurious bath add up to total comfort.

Main Level Floor Plan

Upper Level Floor Plan

Copyright by designer/architect.

Plan #531040

Dimensions: 42' W x 81' D
Levels: 2
Square Footage: 3,325
Main Level Sq. Ft.: 1,272
Upper Level Sq. Ft.: 2,053
Bedrooms: 3
Bathrooms: 3½
Foundation: Slab
Material List Available: No
Price Category: G

This home is tailor-made for a site with dramatic views.

Features:

- **Dining Room:** This dining room is located just off the foyer and features a built-in butler's pantry. Large windows will flood this area with natural light.

- **Kitchen:** This island kitchen is open to the family room and has access to the tower above. The breakfast nook offers great views and additional seating at the bar.

- **Master Suite:** Also located on the upper level, this oasis has access to the rear lanai. The master bath features a large walk-in closet and a whirlpool tub.

- **Lower Level:** The third bedroom, with a large walk-in closet, is located on this level. The game room and office make their home here as well.

Main Level Floor Plan

Upper Level Floor Plan

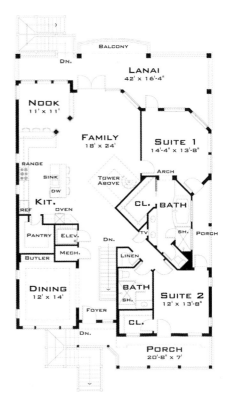

Plan #211076

Dimensions: 95' W x 90' D
Levels: 2
Square Footage: 4,242
Main Level Sq. Ft.: 3,439
Upper Level Sq. Ft.: 803
Bedrooms: 4
Bathrooms: 4 full, 3 half
Foundation: Raised slab
Materials List Available: Yes
Price Category: I

Build this country manor home on a large lot with a breathtaking view to complement its beauty.

Images provided by designer/architect.

Features:

- Foyer: You'll love the two-story ceiling here.

- Living Room: A sunken floor, two-story ceiling, large fireplace, and generous balcony above combine to create an unusually beautiful room.

- Kitchen: Use the breakfast bar at any time of the day. The layout guarantees ample working space, and the pantry gives room for extra storage.

- Master Suite: A sunken floor, wood-burning fireplace, and 200-sq.-ft. sitting area work in concert to create a restful space.

- Bedrooms: The guest room is on the main floor, and bedrooms 2 and 3, both with built-in desks in special study areas, are on the upper level.

- Outdoor Grilling Area: Fitted with a bar, this area makes it a pleasure to host a large group.

Kitchen

Kitchen

Main Level Floor Plan

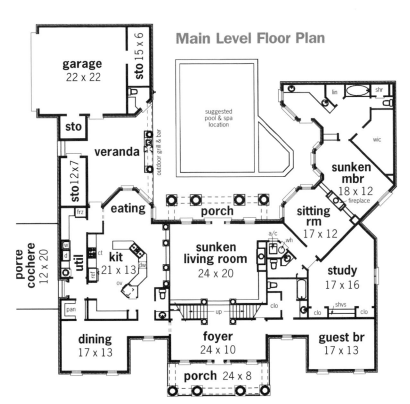

- **garage** 22 x 22
- **sto** 15 x 6
- **sto**
- **veranda**
- **sto** 12 x 7
- **eating**
- suggested pool & spa location
- outdoor grill & bar
- **porch**
- **sunken mbr** 18 x 12 — fireplace
- **sitting rm** 17 x 12
- **porte cochere** 12 x 20
- **util**
- **kit** 21 x 13
- **sunken living room** 24 x 20
- a/c
- wh
- **study** 17 x 16
- lin
- shr
- wic
- **dining** 17 x 13
- **foyer** 24 x 10
- up
- clo
- shvs
- clo
- **guest br** 17 x 13
- **porch** 24 x 8

frz, w, d, ct, ref, dw, ov, pan

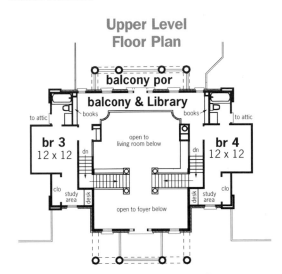

Master Bathroom

Upper Level Floor Plan

- **balcony por**
- **balcony & Library**
- to attic
- books
- books
- to attic
- **br 3** 12 x 12
- open to living room below
- **br 4** 12 x 12
- dn
- dn
- clo
- study area
- desk
- desk
- study area
- clo
- open to foyer below

Dining Room

Living Room

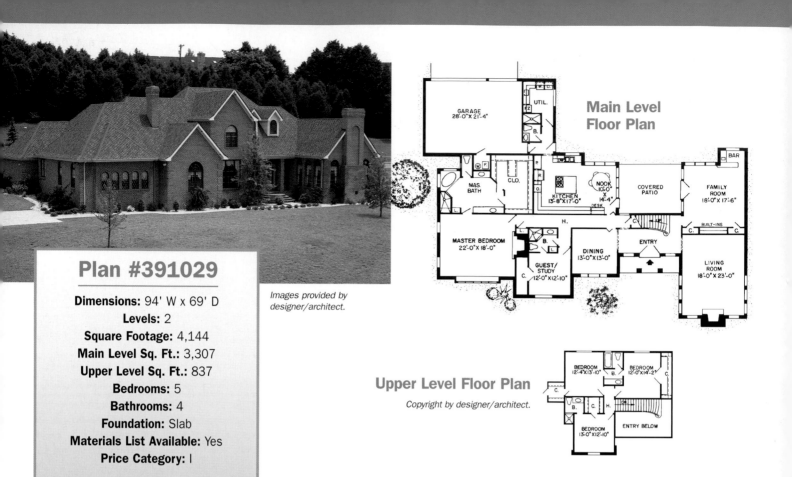

Plan #391029

Dimensions: 94' W x 69' D
Levels: 2
Square Footage: 4,144
Main Level Sq. Ft.: 3,307
Upper Level Sq. Ft.: 837
Bedrooms: 5
Bathrooms: 4
Foundation: Slab
Materials List Available: Yes
Price Category: I

Images provided by designer/architect.

Main Level Floor Plan

Upper Level Floor Plan

Copyright by designer/architect.

Plan #451075

Dimensions: 110'4" W x 65' D
Levels: 2
Square Footage: 4,910
Main Level Sq. Ft.: 2,913
Basement Level Sq. Ft.: 1,997
Bedrooms: 4
Bathrooms: 4½
Foundation: Walkout insulated concrete form
Material List Available: No
Price Category: I

Images provided by designer/architect.

CAD FILE AVAILABLE

Copyright by designer/architect.

Main Level Floor Plan

Upper Level Floor Plan

Basement Level Floor Plan

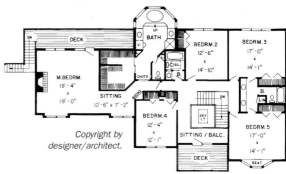

Upper Level Floor Plan

Copyright by designer/architect.

Main Level Floor Plan

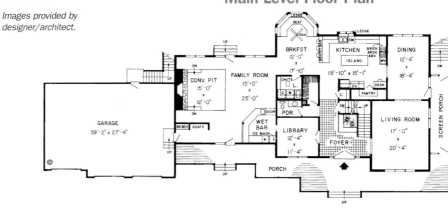

Images provided by designer/architect.

Plan #391010

Dimensions: 122' W x 52'6" D
Levels: 2
Square Footage: 4,963
Main Level Sq. Ft.: 2,573
Upper Level Sq. Ft.: 2,390
Bedrooms: 5
Bathrooms: 3½
Foundation: Crawl space
Materials List Available: Yes
Price Category: E

Upper Level Floor Plan

Copyright by designer/architect.

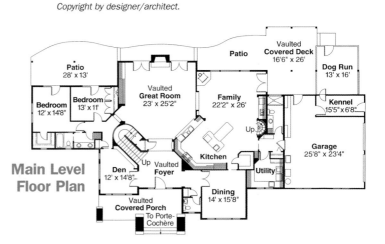

Plan #361450

Images provided by designer/architect.

Dimensions: 108' W x 66'6" D
Levels: 2
Square Footage: 4,021
Main Level Sq. Ft.: 3,028
Upper Level Sq. Ft.: 993
Bedrooms: 3
Bathrooms: 3½
Foundation: Crawl space
Material List Available: No
Price Category: I

Main Level Floor Plan

Plan #151020

Dimensions: 96'10" W x 75'10" D
Levels: 2
Square Footage: 4,532
Main Level Sq. Ft.: 3,732
Upper Level Sq. Ft.: 800
Bedrooms: 3
Bathrooms: 3½
Foundation: Crawl space or slab; basement available for fee
CompleteCost List Available: Yes
Price Category: I

From the arched entry to the lanai and exercise and game rooms, this elegant home is a delight.

Images provided by designer/architect.

Features:

• Foyer: This spacious foyer with 12-ft. ceilings sets an open-air feeling for this home.

• Hearth Room: This cozy hearth room shares a 3-sided fireplace with the breakfast room. French doors open to the rear lanai.

• Dining Room: Entertain in this majestic dining room, with its arched entry and 12-ft. ceilings.

• Master Suite: This stunning suite includes a sitting room and access to the lanai. The bath

features two walk-in closets, a step-up whirlpool tub with 8-in. columns, and glass-block shower.

• Upper Level: You'll find an exercise room, a game room, and attic storage space upstairs.

Rear View

Main Level Floor Plan

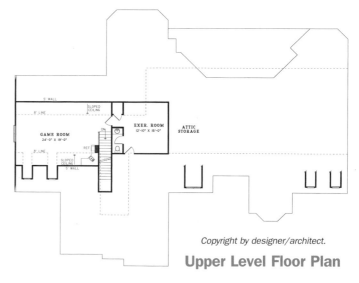

Copyright by designer/architect.

Upper Level Floor Plan

Plan #161029

Dimensions: 87' W x 82' D
Levels: 2
Square Footage: 4,470
Main Level Sq. Ft.: 3,300
Upper Level Sq. Ft.: 1,170
Bedrooms: 4
Bathrooms: 3 full, 2 half
Foundation: Basement
Materials List Available: Yes
Price Category: I

This gracious home is so impressive — inside and out — that it suits the most discriminating tastes.

Features:

- Foyer: A balcony overlooks this gracious area decorated by tall columns.

- Hearth Room: Visually open to the kitchen and the breakfast area, this room is ideal for any sort of gathering.

- Great Room: Colonial columns also form the entry here, and a magnificent window treatment that includes French doors leads to the terrace.

- Library: Built-in shelving adds practicality to this quiet retreat.

- Kitchen: Spread out on the oversized island with a cooktop and seating.

- Additional Bedrooms: Walk-in closets and private access to a bath define each bedroom.

Main Level Floor Plan

Upper Level Floor Plan

Copyright by designer/architect.

Plan #151855

Dimensions: 65'2" W x 108'10" D
Levels: 2
Square Footage: 4,134
Main Level Sq. Ft.: 3,258
Upper Level Sq. Ft.: 876
Bedrooms: 10
Bathrooms: 3½
Foundation: Crawl space or slab
CompleteCost List Available: Yes
Price Category: I

Images provided by designer/architect.

Main Level Floor Plan

Copyright by designer/architect.

Upper Level Floor Plan

Plan #361485

Dimensions: 70' W x 74'6" D
Levels: 2
Square Footage: 4,633
Main Level Sq. Ft.: 2,823
Upper Level Sq. Ft.: 1,810
Bedrooms: 5
Bathrooms: 4 full, 2 half
Foundation: Crawl space
Material List Available: No
Price Category: I

Images provided by designer/architect.

Main Level Floor Plan

Upper Level Floor Plan

Copyright by designer/architect.

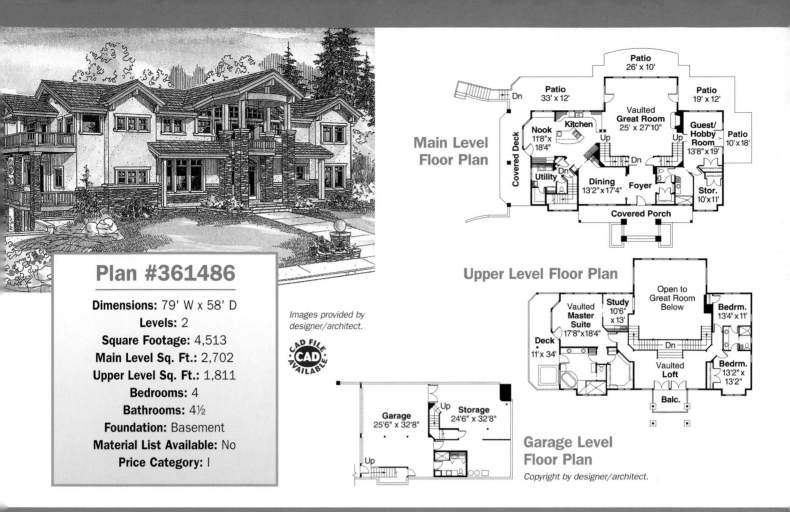

Plan #361486

Dimensions: 79' W x 58' D

Levels: 2

Square Footage: 4,513

Main Level Sq. Ft.: 2,702

Upper Level Sq. Ft.: 1,811

Bedrooms: 4

Bathrooms: 4½

Foundation: Basement

Material List Available: No

Price Category: I

Images provided by designer/architect.

Main Level Floor Plan

Patio 26' x 10'

Patio 33' x 12'

Patio 19' x 12'

Nook 11'8" x 18'4"

Kitchen

Vaulted Great Room 25' x 27'10"

Guest/Hobby Room 13'8" x 19'

Patio 10' x 18'

Covered Deck

Utility

Dining 13'2" x 17'4"

Foyer

Stor. 10' x 18'

Covered Porch

Upper Level Floor Plan

Vaulted Master Suite 17'8" x 18'4"

Study 10'6" x 13'

Open to Great Room Below

Bedrm. 13'4" x 11'

Deck 11' x 34'

Vaulted Loft

Bedrm. 13'2" x 13'2"

Balc.

Garage Level Floor Plan

Garage 25'6" x 32'8"

Storage 24'6" x 32'8"

Up

Up

Up

Copyright by designer/architect.

Plan #451318

Dimensions: 64' W x 36'8" D

Levels: 2

Square Footage: 4,256

Main Level Sq. Ft.: 3,582

Upper Level Sq. Ft.: 674

Bedrooms: 4

Bathrooms: 3½

Foundation: Crawl space

Material List Available: No

Price Category: I

Images provided by designer/architect.

Main Level Floor Plan

LAUNDRY 12' x 18'

GARAGE 23' x 23'

GATHERING ROOM 30' x 18' FIREPLACE

BDRM. #3 15' x 14'

BDRM. #2 12' x 12'

NOOK

DINING 20' x 18'

BDRM. #4 14' x 14'

KITCHEN 15' x 20'

FOYER 12' x 12'

OFFICE 15' x 14'

COVERED DECK

Upper Level Floor Plan

BALCONY

MASTER BATH

MASTER BDRM.

OPEN TO BELOW

Basement Level Floor Plan

UNFINISHED BASEMENT

UNFINISHED BASEMENT

Copyright by designer/architect

Plan #331005

Dimensions: 85'11" W x 55'7" D

Levels: 2

Square Footage: 3,585

Main Level Sq. Ft.: 2,691

Upper Level Sq. Ft.: 894

Bedrooms: 4

Bathrooms: 3½

Foundation: Crawl space, slab, or basement

Materials List Available: No

Price Category: H

Images provided by designer/architect.

You'll love the stately, traditional exterior design and the contemporary, casual interior layout as they are combined in this elegant home.

Features:

- Foyer: The highlight of this spacious area is the curved stairway to the balcony over head.

- Family Room: The two-story ceiling and second-floor balcony overlooking this room add to its spacious feeling, but you can decorate around the fireplace to create a cozy, intimate area.

- Study: Use this versatile room as a guest room, home office or media room.

- Kitchen: Designed for the modern cook, this kitchen features a step-saving design, an island for added work space, and ample storage space.

- Master Suite: Step out to the rear deck from the bedroom to admire the moonlit scenery or bask in the morning sun. The luxurious bath makes an ideal place to relax in privacy.

Rear View

Copyright by designer/architect.

Main Level Floor Plan

Upper Level Floor Plan

Plan #391055

Dimensions: 76'4" W x 55' D
Levels: 2
Square Footage: 4,217
Main Level Sq. Ft.: 2,108
Upper Level Sq. Ft.: 2,109
Bedrooms: 4
Bathrooms: 2½
Foundation: Basement
Material List Available: Yes
Price Category: I

Images provided by designer/architect.

This home, as shown in the photograph, may differ from the actual blueprints. For more detailed information, please check the floor plans carefully.

The exterior veranda and the formal tiled foyer define the entry to this home.

Features:

- **Gathering Room:** Located just off the kitchen, this family space boasts a vaulted ceiling. The fireplace adds warmth and a focal point to the area.

- **Kitchen:** This island kitchen features an abundance of cabinets and counter space. Additional storage can be found in the walk-in pantry.

- **Master Suite:** This large retreat is located on the upper level and features a sitting area. The master bath boasts a large walk-in closet and a whirlpool tub.

- **Secondary Bedrooms:** Located on the upper level in close proximity to the master suite are three bedrooms, which share a common bathroom. Two bedrooms have walk-in closets.

Main Level Floor Plan

Upper Level Floor Plan

Copyright by designer/architect.

Plan #181483

Dimensions: 70' W x 50' D

Levels: 2

Square Footage: 4,183

Main Level Sq. Ft.: 2,423

Upper Level Sq. Ft.: 1,760

Bedrooms: 4

Bathrooms: 3½

Foundation: Basement

Material List Available: Yes

Price Category: I

This house has single-family styling with extended-family amenities.

CAD FILE AVAILABLE

Images provided by designer/architect.

Features:

- **Grandparents' Suite:** Just off the foyer and complete with a kitchenette, living room, full bathroom, and laundry area, this suite gives grandparents the independence and privacy they need while still being close by.

- **Kitchen:** This main kitchen features a snack counter, compact U-shaped work area, and nearby breakfast nook. It connects to the garage to make carrying and putting away groceries easy. A conveniently located laundry room is just a few steps away.

- **Home Offices:** Located off both levels, these spaces are perfect for telecommuting, running a home-based business, or relaxing and getting away for some peace and quiet.

- **Upper Level:** The two secondary bedrooms share a common bathroom and have a generous amount of closet space. The master suite boasts a bedroom, large walk-in closet, and private bath.

Rear Elevation

Main Level Floor Plan

Copyright by designer/architect.

Upper Level Floor Plan

Images provided by designer/architect.

Plan #271037

Dimensions: 66' W x 65' D

Levels: 2

Square Footage: 4,220

Main Level Sq. Ft.: 2,768

Upper Level Sq. Ft.: 1,452

Bedrooms: 3

Bathrooms: 4½

Foundation: Basement

Materials List Available: No

Price Category: I

This design allows family members to carry out their work and leisure activities inside the home. The options for leisure and study are almost countless!

Features:

- "Us" Room: The home's sunken "Us" room is the center of attention, with its vaulted ceiling and two-story fireplace. The room is surrounded by the family living areas.

- Master Suite: Relax in this oasis, which offers twin walk-in closets and a lovely bath.

- Upper Floor: Study areas, an office, and an exercise space are just the beginning!

CAD FILE AVAILABLE

Main Level Floor Plan

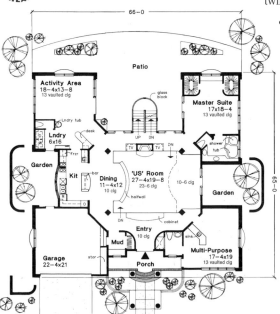

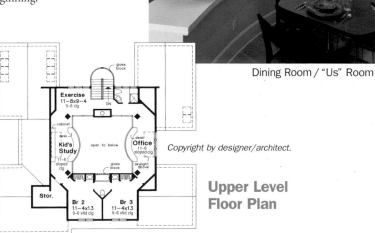

Dining Room / "Us" Room

Copyright by designer/architect.

Upper Level Floor Plan

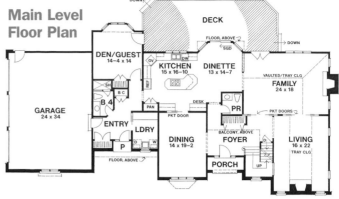

Main Level Floor Plan

Images provided by designer/architect.

Copyright by designer/architect.

Upper Level Floor Plan

Plan #261009

Dimensions: 90' W x 46' D

Levels: 2

Square Footage: 4,048

Main Level Sq. Ft.: 2,388

Upper Level Sq. Ft.: 1,660

Bedrooms: 5

Bathrooms: 4½

Foundation: Basement

Materials List Available: No

Price Category: I

Upper Level Floor Plan

Copyright by designer/architect.

Main Level Floor Plan

Plan #241058

Dimensions: 93' W x 57'2" D

Levels: 2

Square Footage: 4,216

Main Level Sq. Ft.: 2,384

Upper Level Sq. Ft.: 1,832

Bedrooms: 4

Bathrooms: 3½

Foundation: Slab

Material List Available: No

Price Category: I

Images provided by designer/architect.

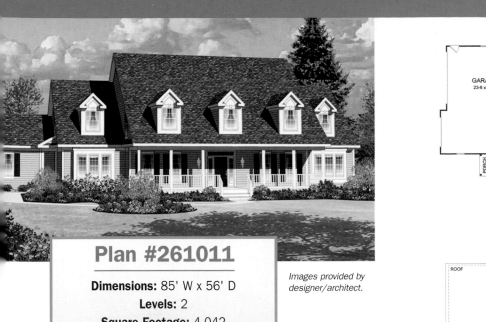

Main Level Floor Plan

Images provided by designer/architect.

GARAGE 23-6 X 33-0

SCREENED PORCH 13-8 X 11-8

WOOD DECK 21-10 X 11-8

DINETTE 13-8 X 12-10

KITCHEN 11-8 X 14-6

GATHERING RM 20-0 X 16-6

WHIRLPOOL TUB SHWR

M BATH

WIC

M BEDRM 13-8 X 17-6

ENTRY

PDR LAUND

DINING RM 13-6 X 13-6

FOYER

DEN 13-6 X 13-6

WOOD PORCH 41-0 X 8-0

Plan #261011

Dimensions: 85' W x 56' D

Levels: 2

Square Footage: 4,042

Main Level Sq. Ft.: 2,492

Upper Level Sq. Ft.: 1,550

Bedrooms: 4

Bathrooms: 3½

Foundation: Walkout basement

Materials List Available: No

Price Category: I

Rear Elevation

Upper Level Floor Plan

Copyright by designer/architect.

HOME OFFICE 23-4 x 26-4

GATHERING RM BELOW

BATH 3

BEDRM 4 13-4 x 19-10

BALCONY

BEDRM 2 13-6 x 19-2

BATH 2

BEDRM 3 13-6 x 19-2

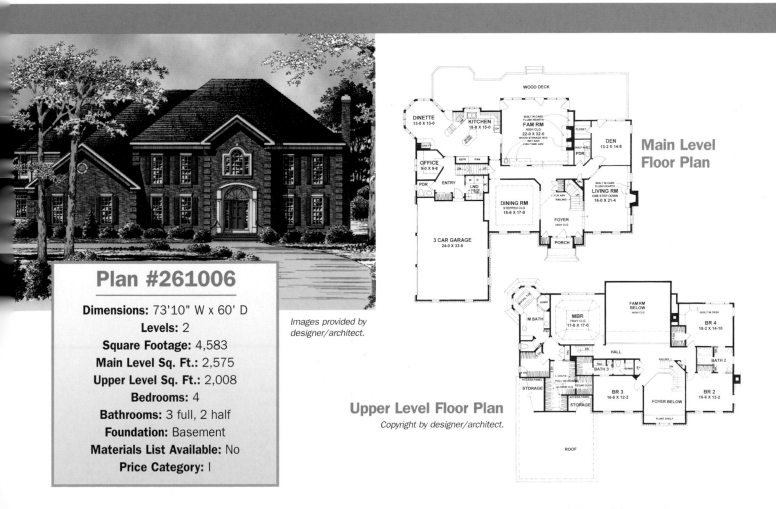

Main Level Floor Plan

DINETTE 13-0 X 13-0

KITCHEN 18-8 X 15-0

FAM RM 22-0 X 32-0

DEN 13-2 X 14-8

OFFICE 9-0 X 9-8

PDR ENTRY

DINING RM 15-6 X 17-0

LIVING RM 16-0 X 21-4

3 CAR GARAGE 24-0 X 33-6

FOYER

PORCH

WOOD DECK

Images provided by designer/architect.

Plan #261006

Dimensions: 73'10" W x 60' D

Levels: 2

Square Footage: 4,583

Main Level Sq. Ft.: 2,575

Upper Level Sq. Ft.: 2,008

Bedrooms: 4

Bathrooms: 3 full, 2 half

Foundation: Basement

Materials List Available: No

Price Category: I

Upper Level Floor Plan

Copyright by designer/architect.

M BATH

MBR TRAY CLG 17-8 X 17-0

FAM RM BELOW

BR 4 18-2 X 14-10

BATH 3

STORAGE

BR 3 16-6 X 12-2

FOYER BELOW

BR 2 16-6 X 13-2

Plan #401049

Dimensions: 77'10" W x 55'8" D
Levels: 2
Square Footage: 4,087
Main Level Sq. Ft.: 2,403
Upper Level Sq. Ft.: 1,684
Bedrooms: 4
Bathrooms: 4½
Foundation: Basement
Materials List Available: Yes
Price Category: I

Images provided by designer/architect.

Finished in stucco, with an elegant entry, this dramatic two-story home is the essence of luxury.

Features:

• Foyer: Double doors open to this foyer, with a sunken living room on the right and a den on the left.

• Dining Room: An archway leads to this formal room, mirroring its own bow window and the curved window in the living room.

• Den: This den and the nearby computer room have use of a full bathroom – making them handy as extra guest rooms when needed.

• Family Room: This room, like the living room, is sunken and warmed by a hearth, but it also has built-in bookcases.

• Kitchen: A snack-bar counter separates this U-shaped kitchen from the light-filled breakfast room.

• Master Suite: This gigantic space has his and her vanities, an oversized shower, a walk-in closet, and a sitting area.

Main Level Floor Plan

Optional Upper Level Floor Plan

Copyright by designer/architect.

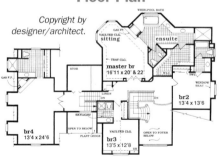

Upper Level Floor Plan

Basement Level Floor Plan

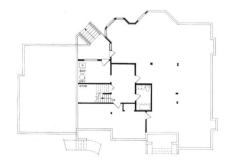

Plan #161097

Dimensions: 70' W x 56'10" D
Levels: 2
Square Footage: 4,594
Main Level Sq. Ft.: 2,237
Upper Level Sq. Ft.: 900
Optional Basement Level Sq. Ft.:
1,450
Bedrooms: 3
Bathrooms: 2½
Foundation: Walkout; basement for fee
Material List Available: No
Price Category: I

The design of this contemporary home complements many rating styles.

Features:

• Foyer: A graceful staircase anchors this traditional foyer. A closet and powder room complete the design. The foyer leads directly to the two-story great room.

• Master Suite: This first-floor retreat includes a circular sitting area with 11-ft.-high ceiling. A super bath adds to the luxurious atmosphere, boasting dual vanities and a private toilet enclosure.

• Loft: Overlooking the first floor, this delightful loft area is perfect for the family computer or as a hobby area. A built-in desk provides a good environment for the kids to do their homework.

Images provided by designer/architect.

• Secondary Bedrooms: These two bedrooms on the second level, each with large walk-in closet and private access to a shared bathroom, complete the exciting family-size home.

Upper Level Floor Plan

CAD FILE AVAILABLE

Main Level Floor Plan

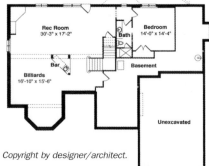

Optional Basement Level Floor Plan

Copyright by designer/architect.

Main Level Floor Plan

Upper Level Floor Plan

Plan #291014

Dimensions: 104' W x 60' D
Levels: 2
Square Footage: 4,372
Main Level Sq. Ft.: 3,182
Upper Level Sq. Ft.: 1,190
Bedrooms: 3
Bathrooms: 3 full, 2 half
Foundation: Basement
Materials List Available: No
Price Category: I

Images provided by designer/architect.

Rear View

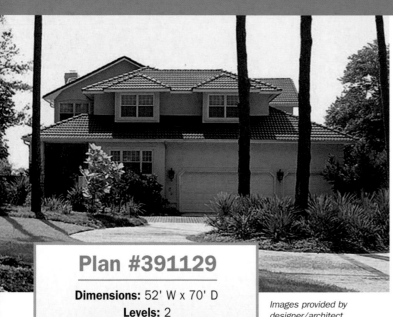

Main Level Floor Plan

Copyright by designer/architect.

Plan #391129

Dimensions: 52' W x 70' D
Levels: 2
Square Footage: 4,441
Main Level Sq. Ft.: 2,409
Upper Level Sq. Ft.: 2,032
Bedrooms: 4
Bathrooms: 3
Foundation: Slab
Material List Available: Yes
Price Category: I

Images provided by designer/architect.

Upper Level Floor Plan

Rear View

Plan #391177

Dimensions: 90' W x 73'8" D

Levels: 2

Square Footage: 4,562

Main Level Sq. Ft.: 3,625

Upper Level Sq. Ft.: 937

Bedrooms: 5

Bathrooms: 3½

Foundation: Crawl space, slab, or basement

Material List Available: Yes

Price Category: I

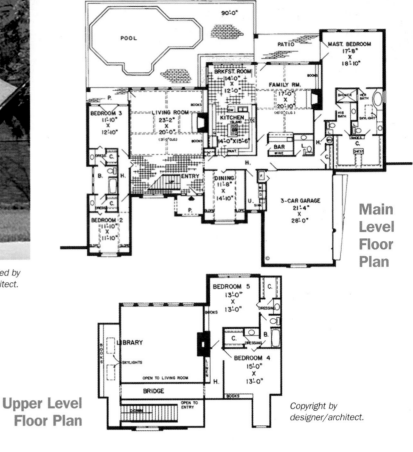

Images provided by designer/architect.

Main Level Floor Plan

Upper Level Floor Plan

Copyright by designer/architect.

Plan #481032

Dimensions: 139' W x 73'4" D

Levels: 2

Square Footage: 4,113

Main Level Sq. Ft.: 3,033

Upper Level Sq. Ft.: 1,080

Bedrooms: 3

Bathrooms: 2 full, 2 half

Foundation: Walkout

Material List Available: No

Price Category: I

Images provided by designer/architect.

Main Level Floor Plan

Upper Level Floor Plan

Copyright by designer/architect.

Plan #161030

Dimensions: 98'6" W x 61'5" D
Levels: 2
Square Footage 4,562
Main Level Sq. Ft.: 3,364
Upper Level Sq. Ft.: 1,198
Bedrooms: 4
Bathrooms: 3½
Foundation: Basement
Materials List Available: Yes
Price Category: I

You'll be charmed by this impressive home, with its stone-and-brick exterior.

Features:

- Great Room: The two-story ceiling here adds even more dimension to this expansive space.

- Hearth Room: A tray ceiling and molding help to create a cozy feeling in this room, which is located so your guests will naturally gravitate to it.

- Dining Room: This formal room features columns at the entry and a butler's pantry for entertaining.

- Master Suite: A walk-in closet, platform whirlpool tub, and 2-person shower are only a few of the luxuries in the private bath, and tray ceilings and moldings give extra presence to the bedroom.

- Upper Level: A balcony offers a spectacular view of the great room and leads to three large bedrooms, each with a private bath.

Main Level Floor Plan

Upper Level Floor Plan

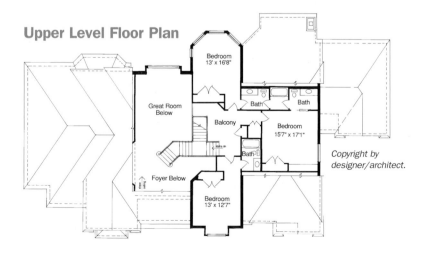

Plan #441031

Dimensions: 78'2" W x 68' D
Levels: 2
Square Footage: 4,150
Main Level Sq. Ft.: 2,572
Upper Level Sq. Ft.: 1,578
Bedrooms: 4
Bathrooms: 4½
Foundation: Crawl space; slab or basement available for fee
Materials List Available: No
Price Category: I

Images provided by designer/architect.

Features:

- Great Room: The main level offers this commodious room, with its beamed ceiling, alcove, fireplace, and built-ins.

- Kitchen: Go up a few steps to the dining nook and this kitchen, and you'll find a baking center, walk-in pantry, and access to a covered side porch.

- Formal Dining Room: This formal room lies a few steps up from the foyer and sports a bay window and hutch space.

- Guest Suite: This suite, which is located at the end of the hall, features a private bathroom and walk-in closet.

- Master Suite: A fireplace flanked by built-ins warms this suite. Its bath contains a spa tub, compartmented toilet, and huge shower.

Graceful and gracious, this superb shingle design delights with handsome exterior elements. A whimsical turret, covered entry, upper-level balcony, and bay window all bring their charm to the facade.

CAD FILE AVAILABLE — CAD

Main Level Floor Plan

Upper Level Floor Plan

Copyright by designer/architect.

Plan #441015

Dimensions: 130'3" W x 79'3" D
Levels: 1
Square Footage: 4,732
Main Level Sq. Ft.: 2,902
Lower Level Sq. Ft.: 1,830
Bedrooms: 4
Bathrooms: 3 full, 2 half
Foundation: Walkout basement
Materials List Available: No
Price Category: I

CAD FILE AVAILABLE

An artful use of stone was employed on the exterior of this rustic hillside home to complement other architectural elements, such as the angled, oversize four-car garage and the substantial roofline.

Features:

- **Great Room:** This massive vaulted room features a large stone fireplace at one end and a formal dining area at the other. A built-in media center and double doors separate the great room from a home office with its own hearth and built-ins.

- **Kitchen:** This kitchen features a walk-in pantry and snack counter and opens to a skylighted outdoor kitchen. Its appointments include a cooktop and a corner fireplace.

- **Home Theatre:** This space has a built-in viewing screen, a fireplace, and double terrace access.

- **Master Suite:** This private space is found at the other side of the home. Look closely for expansive his and her walk-in closets, a spa tub, a skylighted double vanity area, and a corner fireplace in the salon.

- **Bedrooms:** Three family bedrooms are on the lower level; bedroom 4 has a private bathroom and walk-in closet.

- **Garage:** This large garage has room for four cars; don't miss the dog shower and grooming station just off the garage.

Entry

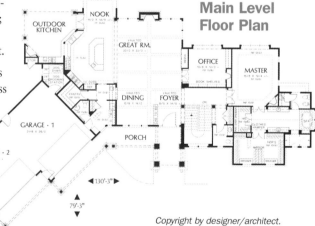

Main Level Floor Plan

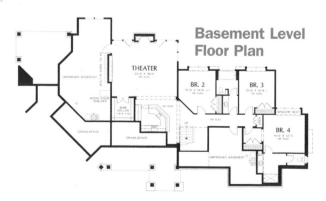

Basement Level Floor Plan

Plan #181100

Dimensions: 74'6" W x 44' D
Levels: 2
Square Footage: 4,200
Main Level Sq. Ft.: 2,207
Upper Level Sq. Ft.: 1,993
Bedrooms: 4
Bathrooms: 3½
Foundation: Basement
Material List Available: Yes
Price Category: I

This stone-and-stucco home has a contemporary flair that is just what you have been searching for.

Images provided by designer/architect.

Features:

- **Family Room:** This gathering area boasts a beautiful fireplace and access to the rear yard. The many windows will flood this space with natural light.

- **Den:** Located just off the entry, this comfortable room is the perfect spot for relaxing after a busy day. The fireplace adds a cozy feel to the room.

- **Master Suite:** A complete getaway from the day is yours once you enter this master suite. The master bath features dual vanities and a large tub.

- **Secondary Bedrooms:** Three additional bedrooms are located on the second floor, close by the master suite. Two bedrooms feature walk-in closets.

Main Level Floor Plan

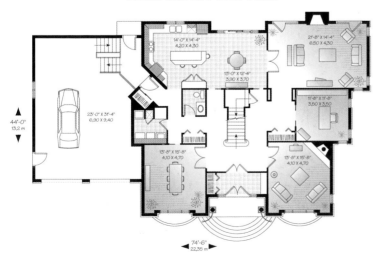

Upper Level Floor Plan

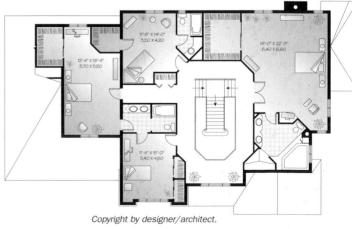

Copyright by designer/architect.

Plan #161032

Dimensions: 75'8" W x 70'6" D
Levels: 2
Square Footage: 4,517
Main Level Sq. Ft.: 2,562
Lower Level Sq. Ft.: 1,955
Bedrooms: 3
Bathrooms: 2 full, 2 half
Foundation: Basement
Materials List Available: Yes
Price Category: I

SMARTtip

Art Underfoot

Make a simple geometric pattern with your flooring materials. Create a focal point in a courtyard or a small area of a patio by fashioning an intricate mosaic with tile, stone, or colored concrete. By combining elements and colors, a simple garden room floor becomes a wonderful work of art. Whether you commission a craftsman or do it yourself, you'll have a permanent art installation right in your own backyard.

Images provided by designer/architect.

The brick-and-stone exterior, a recessed entry, and a tower containing a large library combine to convey the strength and character of this enchanting house.

Features:

• **Hearth Room:** Your family or guests will enjoy this large, comfortable hearth room, which has a gas fireplace and access to the rear deck, perfect for friendly gatherings.

• **Kitchen:** This spacious kitchen features a walk-in pantry and a center island.

• **Master Suite:** Designed for privacy, this master suite includes a sloped ceiling and opens to the rear deck. It also features a deluxe whirlpool bath, walk-in shower, separate his and her vanities, and a walk-in closet.

• **Lower Level:** This lower level includes a separate wine room, exercise room, sauna, two bedrooms, and enough space for a huge recreation room.

Rear Elevation

Main Level Floor Plan

Copyright by designer/architect.

Basement Level Floor Plan

Plan #151524

Dimensions: 79'10" W x 60'6" D
Levels: 2
Square Footage: 4,461
Main Level Sq. Ft.: 2,861
Upper Level Sq. Ft.: 1,600
Bedrooms: 5
Bathrooms: 4½
Foundation: Crawl space or slab; basement or walkout available for fee
CompleteCost List Available: Yes
Price Category: I

Images provided by designer/architect.

Features:

- **Great Room:** This gathering area features a vaulted ceiling and a built-in media center. Step through the French doors to the rear porch.

- **Kitchen:** An island kitchen is the most desirable layout in today's home. The raised bar in this kitchen is open to the breakfast room.

- **Master Suite:** The tray ceiling in this room adds a unique look to the sleeping area. The master bath features a large walk-in closet, vaulted ceiling, and whirlpool tub.

- **Secondary Bedrooms:** Four bedrooms and three bathrooms are located on the upper level.

This home is the culmination of classic French design and ambiance.

Upper Level Floor Plan

Copyright by designer/architect.

Main Level Floor Plan

Main Level Floor Plan

Images provided by designer/architect.

CAD FILE AVAILABLE CAD

Upper Level Floor Plan

Copyright by designer/architect.

Rear View

Plan #221119

Dimensions: 82'8" W x 65' D

Levels: 2

Square Footage: 4,422

Main Level Sq. Ft.: 2,555

Upper Level Sq. Ft.: 1,867

Bedrooms: 4

Bathrooms: 3 full, 2 half

Foundation: Basement

Material List Available: No

Price Category: I

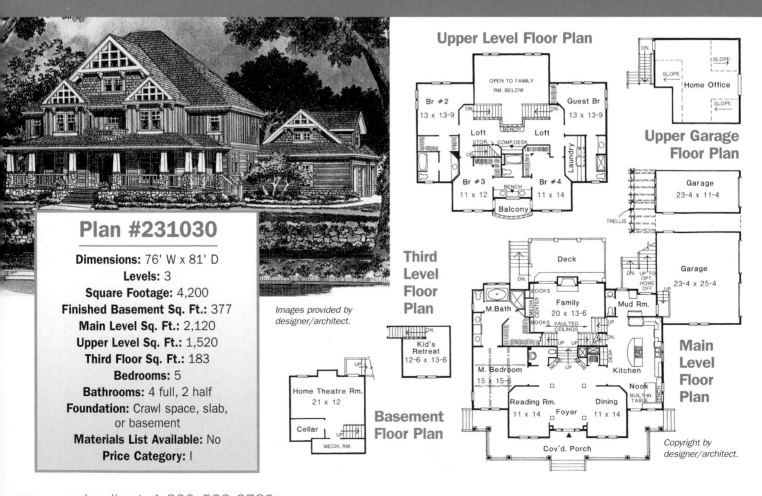

Upper Level Floor Plan

Upper Garage Floor Plan

Third Level Floor Plan

Images provided by designer/architect.

Basement Floor Plan

Main Level Floor Plan

Copyright by designer/architect.

Plan #231030

Dimensions: 76' W x 81' D

Levels: 3

Square Footage: 4,200

Finished Basement Sq. Ft.: 377

Main Level Sq. Ft.: 2,120

Upper Level Sq. Ft.: 1,520

Third Floor Sq. Ft.: 183

Bedrooms: 5

Bathrooms: 4 full, 2 half

Foundation: Crawl space, slab, or basement

Materials List Available: No

Price Category: I

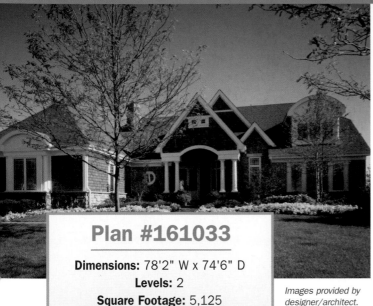

Plan #161033

Dimensions: 78'2" W x 74'6" D

Levels: 2

Square Footage: 5,125

Main Level Sq. Ft.: 2,782

Upper Level Sq. Ft.: 1,027

Optional Basement Level Sq. Ft.: 1,316

Bedrooms: 4

Bathrooms: 3½

Foundation: Basement

Materials List Available: Yes

Price Category: I

Images provided by designer/architect.

Main Level Floor Plan

Copyright by designer/architect.

Upper Level Floor Plan

Optional Basement Level Floor Plan

Plan #221087

Dimensions: 112'6¼" W x 72'6" D

Levels: 2

Square Footage: 5,009

Main Level Sq. Ft.: 3,378

Upper Level Sq. Ft.: 1,631

Bedrooms: 5

Bathrooms: 3 full, 2 half

Foundation: Basement

Material List Available: No

Price Category: J

Images provided by designer/architect.

CAD FILE AVAILABLE

Main Level Floor Plan

Upper Level Floor Plan

Copyright by designer/architect.

Rear Elevation

Main Level Floor Plan

Images provided by designer/architect.

Upper Level Floor Plan

Copyright by designer/architect.

Plan #561001

Dimensions: 55'4" W x 59'8" D

Levels: 2

Square Footage: 5,079

Main Level Sq. Ft.: 3,301

Upper Level Sq. Ft.: 1,778

Bedrooms: 3

Bathrooms: 2½

Foundation: Basement

Material List Available: Yes

Price Category: J

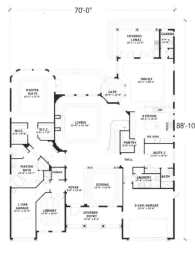

Main Level Floor Plan

Images provided by designer/architect.

Upper Level Floor Plan

Copyright by designer/architect.

Plan #151252

Dimensions: 70' W x 88'10" D

Levels: 2

Square Footage: 5,412

Main Level Sq. Ft.: 3,874

Upper Level Sq. Ft.: 1,538

Bedrooms: 5

Bathrooms: 5 full, 2 half

Foundation: Slab

CompleteCost List Available: Yes

Price Category: I

Plan #291038

Dimensions: 72'10" W x 104'4" D

Levels: 2

Square Footage: 5,884

Main Level Sq. Ft.: 3,584

Upper Level Sq. Ft.: 2,300

Bedrooms: 5

Bathrooms: 5½

Foundation: Basement

Material List Available: No

Price Category: J

Images provided by designer/architect.

Main Level Floor Plan

Upper Level Floor Plan

Copyright by designer/architect.

Rear View

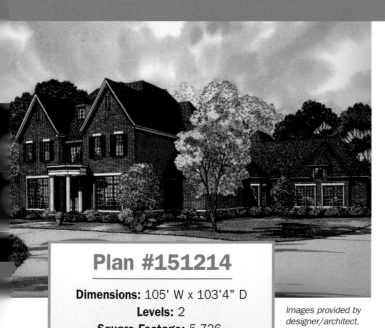

Plan #151214

Dimensions: 105' W x 103'4" D

Levels: 2

Square Footage: 5,726

Main Level Sq. Ft.: 3,908

Upper Level Sq. Ft.: 1,818

Bedrooms: 4

Bathrooms: 4 full, 2 half

Foundation: Crawl space or slab; basement or walkout for fee

CompletCost List Available: Yes

Price Category: J

Images provided by designer/architect.

CAD FILE AVAILABLE

Main Level Floor Plan

Upper Level Floor Plan

Copyright by designer/architect.

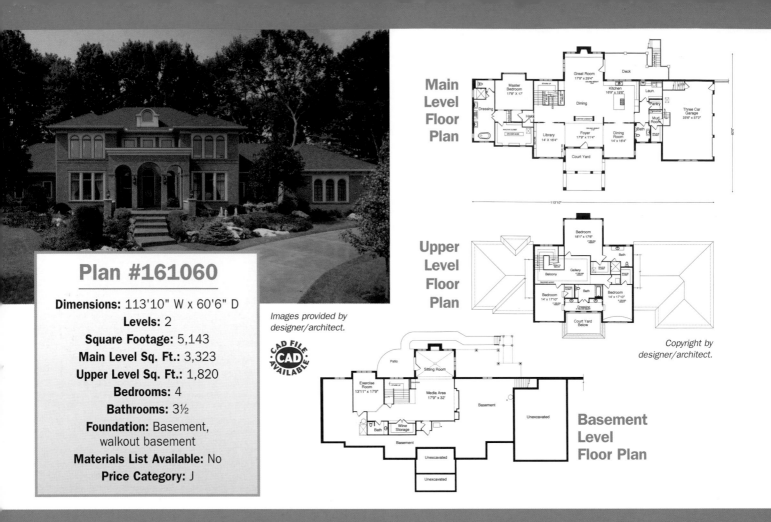

Plan #161060

Dimensions: 113'10" W x 60'6" D
Levels: 2
Square Footage: 5,143
Main Level Sq. Ft.: 3,323
Upper Level Sq. Ft.: 1,820
Bedrooms: 4
Bathrooms: 3½
Foundation: Basement, walkout basement
Materials List Available: No
Price Category: J

Images provided by designer/architect.

Copyright by designer/architect.

Main Level Floor Plan

Upper Level Floor Plan

Basement Level Floor Plan

Plan #441030

Dimensions: 117'6" W x 63'6" D
Levels: 2
Square Footage: 5,180
Main Level Sq. Ft.: 3,030
Upper Level Sq. Ft.: 2,150
Bedrooms: 6
Bathrooms: 5
Foundation: Crawl space; slab or basement available for fee
Materials List Available: No
Price Category: J

Images provided by designer/architect.

Main Level Floor Plan

Upper Level Floor Plan

Copyright by designer/architect.

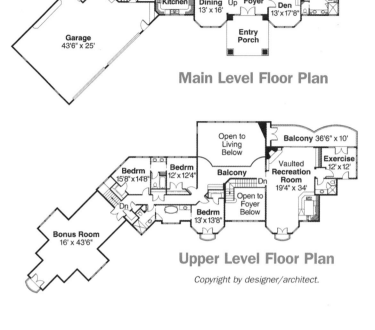

Main Level Floor Plan

Upper Level Floor Plan

Copyright by designer/architect.

Plan #361535

Dimensions: 141'10" W x 76'9" D

Levels: 2

Square Footage: 5,389

Main Level Sq. Ft.: 3,112

Upper Level Sq. Ft.: 2,277

Bedrooms: 4

Bathrooms: 4 full, 2 half

Foundation: Crawl space

Material List Available: No

Price Category: J

Images provided by designer/architect.

CAD FILE AVAILABLE

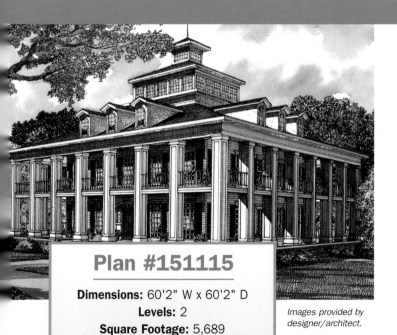

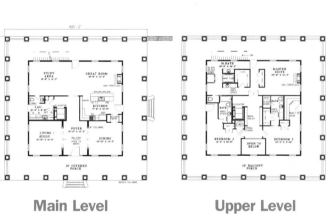

Main Level Floor Plan

Upper Level Floor Plan

Basement Level Floor Plan

Bonus Area Floor Plan

Plan #151115

Dimensions: 60'2" W x 60'2" D

Levels: 2

Square Footage: 5,689

Main Level Sq. Ft.: 1,600

Upper Level Sq. Ft.: 1,530

Lower Level Sq. Ft.: 2,559

Bedrooms: 5

Bathrooms: 5½

Foundation: Walkout

CompleteCost List Available: Yes

Price Category: J

Images provided by designer/architect.

CAD FILE AVAILABLE

Copyright by designer/architect.

Plan #131031

Dimensions: 69'8" W x 48'4" D
Levels: 2
Square Footage: 4,027
Main Level Sq. Ft.: 2,198
Upper Level Sq. Ft.: 1,829
Bedrooms: 5
Bathrooms: 4½
Foundation: Crawl space, slab, or basement
Materials List Available: Yes
Price Category: I

If you love dramatic lines and contemporary design, you'll be thrilled by this lovely home.

Features:

- Foyer: A gorgeous vaulted ceiling sets the stage for a curved staircase flanked by a formal living room and dining room.

- Living Room: The foyer ceiling continues in this room, giving it an unusual presence.

- Family Room: This sunken family room features a fireplace and a wall of windows that look out to the backyard. It's open to the living room, making it an ideal spot for entertaining.

- Kitchen: With a large island, this kitchen flows into the breakfast room.

- Master Suite: The luxurious bedroom has a dramatic tray ceiling and includes two-walk-in closets. The dressing room is fitted with a sink, and the spa bath is sumptuous.

Images provided by designer/architect.

Main Level Floor Plan

Copyright by designer/architect.

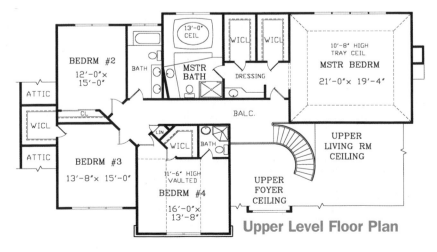

Upper Level Floor Plan

Plan #151033

Dimensions: 81'6" W x 93'2" D
Levels: 2
Square Footage: 5,548
Main Level Sq. Ft.: 3,276
Upper Level Sq. Ft.: 2,272
Bedrooms: 5
Bathrooms: 4½
Foundation: Crawl space or slab; basement option for fee
CompleteCost List Available: Yes
Price Category: J

Images provided by designer/architect.

From the exercise room to the home theatre, you'll love the spaciousness and comfort in this beautifully-designed home.

Features:

- **Family Room:** Everyone can gather around the stone fireplace and built-in media center.
- **Hearth Room:** Open to the breakfast/kitchen area, this room also has a lovely gas fireplace.
- **Computer Areas:** Set up work areas in the computer room, as well as the kid's nook.
- **Dining Room:** Sit by the bay window or go through the swinging door to the adjoining hearth room.
- **Master Suite:** Somewhat secluded, the bedroom has a vaulted 10-ft. boxed ceiling while the bath features a TV, whirlpool tub, a separate shower, and corner vanities.
- **Porch:** The rear screened-in porch lets in extra light through skylights on its roof.

Main Level Floor Plan

Upper Level Floor Plan

Copyright by designer/architect.

Plan #211127

Dimensions: 94' W x 71' D

Levels: 2

Square Footage: 5,474

Main Level Sq. Ft.: 4,193

Upper Level Sq. Ft.: 1,281

Bedrooms: 4

Bathrooms: 4 full, 2 half

Foundation: Slab, crawl space

Materials List Available: No

Price Category: I

This is a truly grand southern-style home, with stately columns and eye-pleasing symmetry.

Features:

• Ceiling Height: 12 ft.

• Foyer: A grand home warrants a grand entry, and here it is. The graceful curved staircase will impress your guests as they move from this foyer to the fireplace.

• Family Room: Great for entertaining, this family room features a vaulted ceiling. A handsome fireplace adds warmth and ambiance.

• Den: Another fireplace enhances this smaller and cozier den. Here the kids can play, supervised by the family chef working in the adjacent kitchen.

• Verandas: As is fitting for a gracious southern home, you'll find verandas at front and rear.

• Master Suite: A romantic third fireplace is found in this sprawling master bedroom. The master bath provides the utmost in privacy and organization.

Main Level Floor Plan

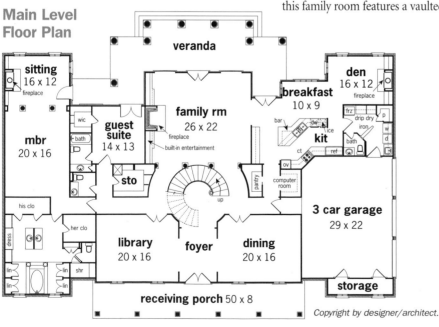

Upper Level Floor Plan

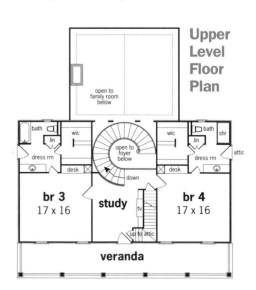

Plan #581016

Dimensions: 80' W x 74'5" D
Levels: 2
Square Footage: 4,043
Main Level Sq. Ft.: 2,746
Upper Level Sq. Ft.: 1,297
Bedrooms: 4
Bathrooms: 4
Foundation: Slab or basement
Material List Available: No
Price Category: I

Images provided by designer/architect.

This home is designed for gracious living and is distinguished by many architectural details.

Features:

- Family Room: Create a sitting area around the fireplace in this room so that the whole family can enjoy the warmth on chilly days and winter evenings. A door from the family room leads to the rear deck, making this space the heart of the home.

- Kitchen: This island kitchen is large enough for friends or family to join you while you are cooking without getting in the way of your culinary creativity. The walk-in pantry features an abundance of shelves.

- Breakfast Room: A stepped ceiling and an abundance of windows make this breakfast room the ideal spot for family brunches.

- Master Suite: A sitting area and a tray ceiling make the bedroom in this suite luxurious, while the private bath featuring a whirlpool tub creates a spa atmosphere.

Main Level Floor Plan

Copyright by designer/architect.

Upper Level Floor Plan

Plan #151103

Dimensions: 80'8" W x 94'2" D

Levels: 1.5

Square Footage: 5,129

Main Level Sq. Ft.: 1,755

Upper Level Sq. Ft.: 3,374

Bedrooms: 4

Bathrooms: 4½

Foundation: Crawl space, slab, basement or walkout

CompletCost List Available: Yes

Price Category: J

Images provided by designer/architect.

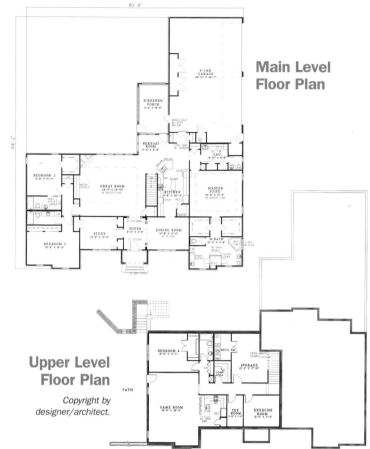

Main Level Floor Plan

Upper Level Floor Plan

Copyright by designer/architect.

Plan #401048

Dimensions: 57'8" W x 103'6" D

Levels: 2

Square Footage: 5,159

Main Level Sq. Ft.: 2,473

Upper Level Sq. Ft.: 2,686

Bedrooms: 4

Bathrooms: 4½

Foundation: Basement

Materials List Available: Yes

Price Category: I

Images provided by designer/architect.

Rear Elevation

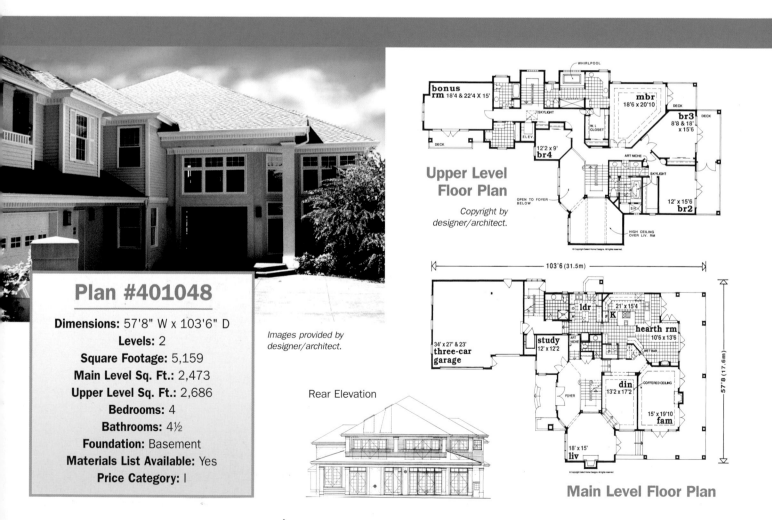

Upper Level Floor Plan

Copyright by designer/architect.

Main Level Floor Plan

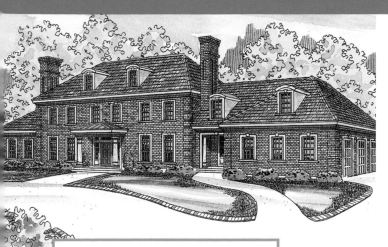

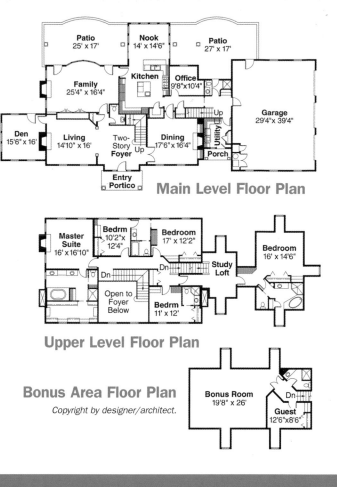

Patio 25' x 17'
Nook 14' x 14'6"
Patio 27' x 17'
Family 25'4" x 16'4"
Kitchen
Office 9'8"x10'4"
Garage 29'4"x 39'4"
Den 15'6" x 16'
Living 14'10" x 16'
Two-Story Foyer
Dining 17'6" x 16'4"
Utility
Porch
Entry Portico

Main Level Floor Plan

Master Suite 16' x 16'10"
Bedrm 10'2"x 12'4"
Bedroom 17' x 12'2"
Bedroom 16' x 14'6"
Open to Foyer Below
Study Loft
Bedrm 11' x 12'

Upper Level Floor Plan

Bonus Area Floor Plan

Copyright by designer/architect.

Bonus Room 19'8" x 26'
Guest 12'6"x8'6"

Plan #361432

Dimensions: 111'6" W x 59' D
Levels: 2
Square Footage: 5,269
Main Level Sq. Ft.: 2,801
Upper Level Sq. Ft.: 2,468
Bedrooms: 6
Bathrooms: 6½
Foundation: Crawl space
Material List Available: No
Price Category: J

Images provided by designer/architect.

 CAD FILE AVAILABLE

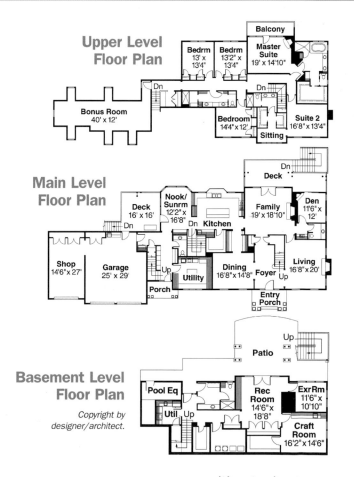

Plan #361038

Dimensions: 116' W x 61' D
Levels: 2
Square Footage: 5,384
Main Level Sq. Ft.: 2,928
Upper Level Sq. Ft.: 2,456
Bedrooms: 5
Bathrooms: 4 full, 2 half
Foundation: Basement
Material List Available: No
Price Category: J

Images provided by designer/architect.

CAD FILE AVAILABLE

Upper Level Floor Plan
Bedrm 13' x 13'4"
Bedrm 13'2" x 13'4"
Master Suite 19' x 14'10"
Balcony
Bonus Room 40' x 12'
Bedroom 14'4" x 12'
Sitting
Suite 2 16'8" x 13'4"

Main Level Floor Plan
Deck 16' x 16'
Nook/Sunrm 12'2" x 16'8"
Kitchen
Deck
Family 19' x 18'10"
Den 11'6" x 12'
Shop 14'6" x 27'
Garage 25' x 29'
Utility
Porch
Dining 16'8" x 14'8"
Foyer
Living 16'8" x 20'
Entry Porch

Basement Level Floor Plan
Patio
Pool Eq
Rec Room 14'6" x 18'8"
ExrRm 11'6" x 10'10"
Util
Craft Room 16'2" x 14'6"

Copyright by designer/architect.

Main Level Floor Plan

Plan #391054

Dimensions: 111' W x 72'6" D

Levels: 2

Square Footage: 5,254

Main Level Sq. Ft.: 4,075

Upper Level Sq. Ft.: 1,179

Bedrooms: 5

Bathrooms: 5

Foundation: Slab

Material List Available: Yes

Price Category: J

Images provided by designer/architect.

Rear View

Upper Level Floor Plan

Copyright by designer/architect.

Main Level Floor Plan

Copyright by designer/architect.

Plan #451169

Dimensions: 97'7" W x 70'10" D

Levels: 2

Square Footage: 5,241

Main Level Sq. Ft.: 2,226

Upper Level Sq. Ft.: 1,028

Basement Level Sq. Ft.: 1,987

Bedrooms: 5

Bathrooms: 4½

Foundation: Walkout

Material List Available: No

Price Category: J

Images provided by designer/architect.

Upper Level Floor Plan

Basement Level Floor Plan

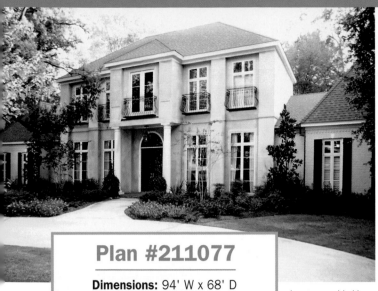

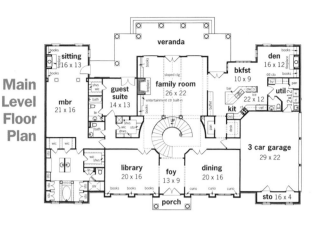

Main Level Floor Plan

Plan #211077

Dimensions: 94' W x 68' D

Levels: 2

Square Footage: 5,560

Main Level Sq. Ft.: 4,208

Upper Level Sq. Ft.: 1,352

Bedrooms: 4

Bathrooms: 4 full, 2 half

Foundation: Slab; crawl space for fee

Materials List Available: Yes

Price Category: J

Images provided by designer/architect.

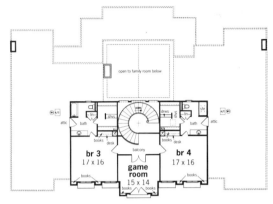

Upper Level Floor Plan

Copyright by designer/architect.

Main Level Floor Plan

Plan #221121

Dimensions: 102'4" W x 89' D

Levels: 1.5

Square Footage: 5,140

Main Level Sq. Ft.: 3,989

Upper Level Sq. Ft.: 1,151

Bedrooms: 4

Bathrooms: 4½

Foundation: Walkout

Material List Available: No

Price Category: J

Images provided by designer/architect.

Upper Level Floor Plan

Rear View

Copyright by designer/architect.

Plan #121168

Dimensions: 75'4" W x 73'9" D

Levels: 1.5

Square Footage: 5,203

Main Level Sq. Ft.: 3,148

Upper Level Sq. Ft.: 2,055

Bedrooms: 4

Bathrooms: 4½

Foundation: Slab; basement for fee

Material List Available: No

Price Category: J

This luxurious Spanish villa is the perfect place to enjoy the good life.

Images provided by designer/architect.

Features:

- **Dining Room:** The 11-ft.-high ceiling of this room provides the perfect setting for serving elegant meals. An adjoining butler's pantry makes serving meals a breeze.

- **Kitchen:** This two-story island kitchen features a walk-in pantry and an eating area. Access to the rear loggia provides the opportunity to eat outside on nice days.

- **Master Suite:** Located on the main level for convenience and privacy, this retreat boasts a tray ceiling in the sleeping area. The master bath features a dual vanity and a stall shower.

- **Upper Level:** Three secondary bedrooms, each with a private bathroom, are located on this level. A game room with a built-in TV cabinet is the perfect place for the kids to play.

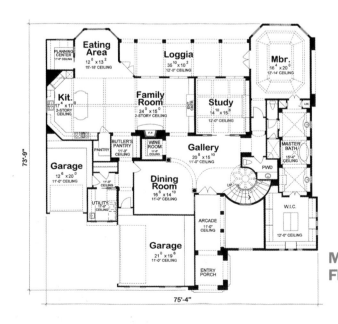

Main Level Floor Plan

Upper Level Floor Plan

Copyright by designer/architect.

Plan #161103

Dimensions: 89'10" W x 89'4" D
Levels: 2
Square Footage: 5,633
Main Level Sq. Ft.: 3,850
Upper Level Sq. Ft.: 1,783
Bedrooms: 4
Bathrooms: 3½
Foundation: Walkout; basement for fee
Material List Available: No
Price Category: J

The brick and stone exterior, with its arches and balcony overlooking the entry, creates a home that showcases artistic and historic architectural elements.

CAD FILE AVAILABLE

Images provided by designer/architect.

Features:

- **Kitchen:** The heart of the home centers around this gourmet kitchen, which features a large island and a breakfast area that opens to a delightful terrace. The adjacent hearth room boasts a cozy fireplace.

- **Master Suite:** This main-level retreat has private access to the rear porch and a stepped ceiling in the sleeping area. The master bath will pamper you with amenities such as a platform whirlpool tub and a two-person shower.

- **Secondary Bedrooms:** Three bedrooms are located on the upper level and each have a walk-in closets. Two bedrooms share a Jack-and-Jill bathroom, while the third has a private bathroom.

- **Lower Level:** For fun times, this lower level is finished to provide a wet bar, a billiard room, and a recreation room. Future expansion can include an additional bedroom and an exercise room.

Main Level Floor Plan

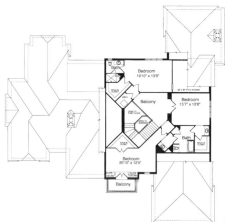

Upper Level Floor Plan

Optional Basement Level Floor Plan

Copyright by designer/architect.

Brick Materials

In one form or another, brick has been used as a building material for thousands of years. It is durable, attractive, and noncombustible, among other things, and installing it is a straightforward job. The work is well suited to do-it-yourselfers because you can do it a little at a time.

Bricks are bonded together with mortar. But most projects will also require accessories such as anchors, ties, or joint reinforcements. These materials can strengthen the overall structure, will anchor masonry to existing construction, and will control expansion and contraction.

Types of Brick

Brick is made from molded clay that is fired at very high temperatures in a kiln. The clay color and firing temperature determine the brick color, although some manufacturers combine clays to produce tones from off-white to almost black. Brick textures vary too, depending on the molding process.

Brick made in the United States and Canada today is extremely dense, hard, and durable. If the bricks are shaped by extruding clay through a die, they usually have large holes through the middle. The holes make the bricks lighter and improve the mortar bond. This type of brick is most commonly used for wall construction, where the holes are not visible.

To choose brick for your project, visit a local supplier and look at sample panels. Bear in mind that bricks with a wide range of light and dark shades can be more difficult to work with than bricks of a single color.

Face Brick. A batch of face brick will be quite uniform in color, size, and texture. It comes in three types. Type FBA (architectural) brick has no limits on size variations or on the amount of chips and cracks that are permitted. This type is popular for residential work because the units resemble old brick. Type FBS (standard) and FBX (extra) have tighter limits on variations and are generally used on commercial jobs.

Bricks similar to those used in historic buildings are still produced by some manufacturers.

order direct: 1-800-523-6789

Common Brick Types

Face Bricks are uniform in color and texture.

Modular Building Bricks are often rough-faced.

Locking Pavers nestle together without mortar.

Firebrick is baked at high temperature to resist heat.

Brick Pavers are strong and weatherproof.

Veneer Bricks are thin slices of real brick.

But they will absorb more water than extruded bricks. You could also work with genuine used brick, but unpredictable durability makes them risky for exterior use.

Modular Building Brick. Building bricks, or common bricks, are rougher in appearance and less expensive than face bricks, but are structurally sound. Most building bricks today are sold with interior holes that reduce weight.

Paving Brick. Paving brick is manufactured to be denser than the other bricks because in paving, the widest faces are visible. The clay is machine-pressed densely into molds and baked longer than either extruded or molded face bricks. This process reduces the amount of water that will be absorbed by the brick.

With pavers, low absorption is critical because the materials must be able to withstand repeated cycles of winter freezing and thawing as well as heavy traffic. Paving brick is classified by its appearance in the same way as face brick: PA (architectural), PS (standard), and PX (extra).

Firebrick. Firebrick is made of a special clay that is baked at an extremely high temperature. It is used to line fireplaces and is generally a yellowish off-white color. You must install it with a special fireclay mortar.

Water Testing and Grading

Very dry brick absorbs much of the water in fresh mortar, weakening the bond. To test for excessive absorption, place 12 drops of water on any spot on the brick. If the water is absorbed in less than one minute, the brick is too dry, and you should wet the bricks as you install them. Overall grading is based on resistance to freeze-thaw damage. Grade MW (moderate weathering) can be exposed to moisture but not freezing. Grade SW (severe weathering) is used when the bricks are likely to be frozen when saturated. Grade NW (no weathering), is for indoor use only.

Using a Brick Splitter

1 **Measure your brick** and mark the length required to fill the void, allowing for mortar joints.

2 **Line up your squared mark** with the angled cutting blades in the jaws of the brick splitter.

Layouts and Estimates

Laying out bricks is simple when you set them to a multiple of 4 inches. This multiple also applies against 8 x 8 x 16-inch concrete block. With 8-inch brick, the 4-inch module is the length of half bricks that create a staggered layout. For example, make a brick wall a multiple of 4 inches long (80 inches long rather than 78 inches). For estimating purposes, figure about seven bricks (nominally 4 x 8 inches) for every square foot of area in a wall. Estimate about 4½ bricks for every square foot when laying paving bricks broad faced, horizontally on the ground.

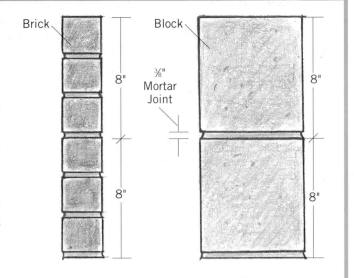

Common Brick Sizes

The basic modular unit is 3⅝ inches wide, 2¼ inches thick, and 7⅝ inches long. When laid with standard ⅜-inch mortar joints, the nominal length becomes about 8 inches. Three bricks laid on top of one another with ⅜-inch mortar joints measure 8 inches high. Paving bricks designed to butt together without mortar have a full 4 x 8-inch face. The most common are 1 inch thick for light traffic areas and 2¼ inches for heavy traffic areas, such as driveways and streets. Some suppliers offer special shapes such as copings and angled corner bricks that fit a modular system.

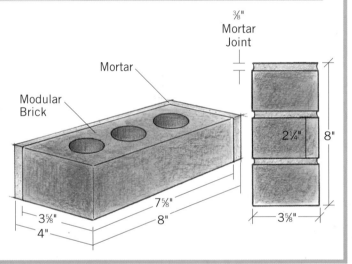

3 **Push down** slowly on the lever, compressing the upper and lower jaws until the brick snaps.

4 **The blades** of a brick splitter produce a cleaner cut than you can make with hammer and chisel.

Brick Patterns

Bricks and pavers come in so many sizes and shapes that you can create an almost endless number of patterns.

The most common bond pattern is called a running bond. In a wall with this pattern bricks are laid flat on their wide surface and run lengthwise. Each brick in a course of stretchers is offset by one-half brick from the bricks in the courses above and below.

This bond is also generally used on walks, which don't present the same structural considerations as walls do. And staggered joints tend to hold together better than joints that are aligned in a row. There are variations, such as using an offset of one-third or one-quarter brick in each course. But a running bond works well in any landscape and is easy to keep consistent, whether you are using

bricks set with mortar joints or pavers butted without mortar.

Bear in mind that any layout becomes more complicated when you introduce curves, more common in walks than in walls. You can make some adjustments in the joints to run the brick in line with the walk or set the running bond so that the bricks are all parallel with each other.

This mortared running bond curves with the walk.

This curved walk has a rigid, parallel running bond.

Paver Patterns

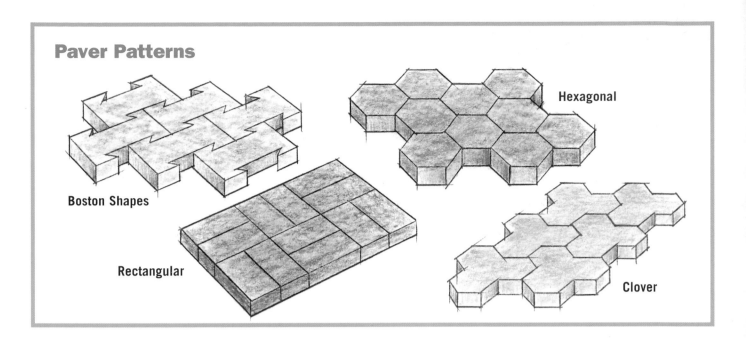

Boston Shapes

Rectangular

Hexagonal

Clover

This informal garden walk has an organic pattern.

A herringbone pattern is more complex to lay out.

When you need to turn a corner in a wall, bricks called headers are turned perpendicular to the stretcher courses. Also by alternating header and stretcher bricks in different ways, you can create a variety of patterns. And because header units help hold the two wythes, or brick widths, of a wall together, they are functional as well as decorative. A number of decorative bond patterns mimic the look of historic masonry buildings.

Other popular bond patterns include the common, or American, bond. It is similar to the running bond, except that it has courses of headers spaced every sixth course. The English bond consists of alternating courses of stretchers and headers; the headers are centered over the stretchers, and the vertical joints of all the stretcher courses align.

A stack bond lays all the bricks as either headers or stretchers with all joints aligning vertically. But the stack bond is weak structurally, and generally not permitted for load-bearing walls without reinforcement in the joints.

The Flemish bond is a complex pattern in which every course has alternating stretchers and headers. The pattern is offset by courses so that the headers center over stretchers and vice versa. Remember that more complex patterns often require more cutting.

Brick lends itself well to traditional home exteriors like this one.

order direct: 1-800-523-6789

Brick Patterns

RUNNING

ENGLISH

COMMON

DUTCH

GARDEN WALL

FLEMISH

Plan #161113

Dimensions: 120'2" W x 60'4" D
Levels: 2
Square Footage: 6,126
Main Level Sq. Ft.: 3,298
Upper Level Sq. Ft.: 1,067
Lower Level Sq. Ft.: 1,761
Bedrooms: 5
Bathrooms: 3½
Foundation: Basement
Materials List Available: No
Price Category: K

A covered porch welcomes friends and family to this elegant home.

Features:

- Library: Just off the foyer is this library, which can be used as a home office. Notice the connecting door to the master bathroom.

- Kitchen: Release the chef inside of you into this gourmet kitchen, complete with seating at the island and open to the breakfast area. Step through the triple sliding door, and arrive on the rear porch.

- Master Suite: This luxurious master suite features a stepped ceiling in the sleeping area and private access to the rear patio. The master bath boasts an oversized stall shower, a whirlpool bath, dual vanities, and an enormous walk-in closet.

- Lower Level: For family fun times, this lower level is finished to provide a wet bar, billiard room, and media room. The area also includes two additional bedrooms and an exercise room.

- Garage: You'll have storage galore in this four-car garage, complete with an additional set of stairs to the unfinished part of the basement.

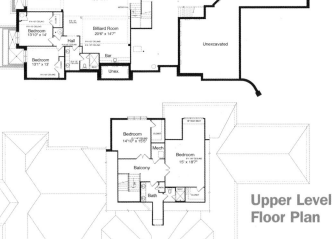

Basement Level Floor Plan

Main Level Floor Plan

Upper Level Floor Plan

Plan #151146

Dimensions: 113" W x 72" D
Levels: 2
Square Footage: 7,870
Finished Basement Sq. Ft.: 3,026
Main Level Sq. Ft.: 2,181
Upper Level Sq. Ft.: 2,663
Bedrooms: 6
Bathrooms: 5
Foundation: Walkout basement
CompleteCost List Available: Yes
Price Category: I

Main Level Floor Plan

Upper Level Floor Plan

Images provided by designer/architect.

Basement Level Floor Plan

Copyright by designer/architect.

Plan #241059

Dimensions: 107'4" W x 87'4" D
Levels: 2
Square Footage: 6,508
Main Level Sq. Ft.: 4,063
Upper Level Sq. Ft.: 2,445
Bedrooms: 6
Bathrooms: 5½
Foundation: Slab
Material List Available: No
Price Category: K

Images provided by designer/architect.

Main Level Floor Plan
Copyright by designer/architect.

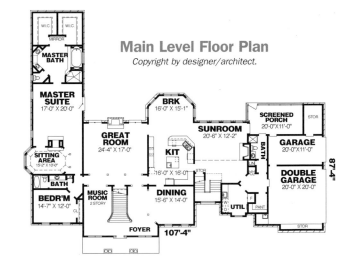

Upper Level Floor Plan

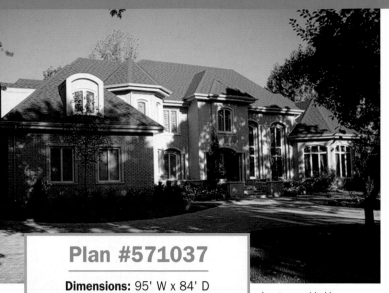

95'-0"

84'-0"

**Main Level
Floor Plan**

*Images provided by
designer/architect.*

76'-0"

64'-0"

**Upper Level
Floor Plan**

*Copyright by
designer/architect.*

Plan #571037

Dimensions: 95' W x 84' D

Levels: 2

Square Footage: 6,440

Main Level Sq. Ft.: 4,409

Upper Level Sq. Ft.: 2,031

Bedrooms: 4

Bathrooms: 3½

Foundation: Basement

Material List Available: Yes

Price Category: K

Main Level Floor Plan

**Guest
Suite**

*Images provided by
designer/architect.*

Upper Level Floor Plan
Copyright by designer/architect.

**Optional Garage
Level Floor Plan**

**Optional
Garage Level
Floor Plan**

Plan #361539

Dimensions: 136' W x 99' D

Levels: 2

Square Footage: 6,455

Main Level Sq. Ft.: 4,319

Upper Level Sq. Ft.: 2,136

Bedrooms: 5

Bathrooms: 6 full, 2 half

Foundation: Crawl space

Material List Available: No

Price Category: K

Plan #571036

Dimensions: 87'6" W x 51'3" D
Levels: 2
Square Footage: 6,175
Main Level Sq. Ft.: 2,628
Upper Level Sq. Ft.: 3,024
Bonus Area Sq. Ft.: 523
Bedrooms: 4
Bathrooms: 2½
Foundation: Basement
Material List Available: Yes
Price Category: K

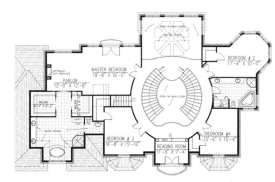

Main Level Floor Plan

Copyright by designer/architect.

Images provided by designer/architect.

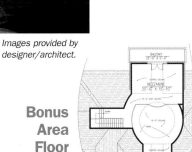

Bonus Area Floor Plan

Upper Level Floor Plan

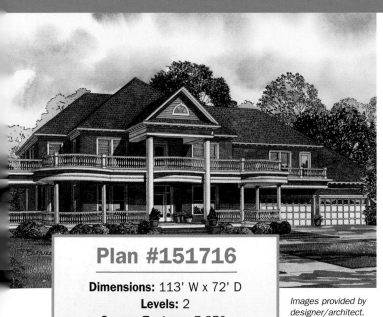

Plan #151716

Dimensions: 113' W x 72' D
Levels: 2
Square Footage: 7,870
Main Level Sq. Ft.: 2,181
Upper Level Sq. Ft.: 2,663
Lower Level Sq. Ft.: 3,026
Bedrooms: 6
Bathrooms: 5
Foundation: Walkout
CompleteCost List Available: Yes
Price Category: L

Images provided by designer/architect.

Main Level Floor Plan

Upper Level Floor Plan

Basement Level Floor Plan

Copyright by designer/architect.

Plan #401050

Dimensions: 81' W x 61' D
Levels: 2
Square Footage: 6,841
Main Level Sq. Ft.: 2,596
Upper Level Sq. Ft.: 2,233
Finished Basement Sq. Ft.: 2,012
Bedrooms: 4
Bathrooms: 3 full, 2 half
Foundation: Basement
Materials List Available: Yes
Price Category: I

Images provided by designer/architect.

This grand two-story European home is adorned with a facade of stucco and brick, meticulously appointed with details for gracious living.

Features:

- Foyer: Guests enter through a portico to find this stately two-story foyer.

- Living Room: This formal area features a tray ceiling and a fireplace and is joined by a charming dining room with a large bay window.

- Kitchen: A butler's pantry joins the dining room to this gourmet kitchen, which holds a separate wok kitchen, an island work center, and a breakfast room with double doors that lead to the rear patio.

- Family Room: Located near the kitchen, this room enjoys a built-in aquarium, media center, and fireplace.

- Den: This room with a tray ceiling, window seat, and built-in computer center is tucked in a corner for privacy.

- Master Suite: The second floor features this spectacular space, which has a separate sitting room, an oversized closet, and a bath with a spa tub.

Right Side Elevation

Kitchen

Rear Elevation

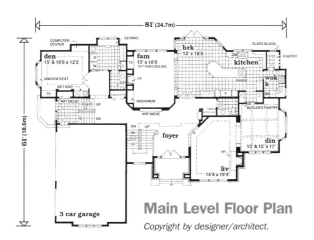

Main Level Floor Plan
Copyright by designer/architect.

Upper Level Floor Plan

Basement Level Floor Plan

Master Bedroom

Great Room

Master Bathroom

Plan #181680

Dimensions: 86'4" W x 98'4"D
Levels: 2
Square Footage: 9,028
Main Level Sq. Ft.: 3,663
Upper Level Sq. Ft.: 882
Lower Level Sq. Ft.: 4,483
Bedrooms: 7
Bathrooms: 6 full, 2 half
Foundation: Walkout
Material List Available: Yes
Price Category: L

There is plenty of room for the extended family in this large home.

Features:

- Kitchen: This island kitchen has an abundance of counter space and cabinets. The extended bar makes additional seating available when the dining room is full.

- Guest Suite: The entire second level of the home is devoted to this guest suite, complete with a kitchenette. The one-bedroom suite boasts a rear deck with a view of the yard.

- Master Suite: There are two master suites in this beautiful home. Each suite features a large walk-in closet and private bath with dual vanities and separate tubs and showers.

- Lower Level: Every item on your wish list is located on this level. There are four bedrooms, a home theater room, exercise room, and an indoor pool.

Upper Level Floor Plan

Basement Level Floor Plan

Main Level Floor Plan

Copyright by designer/architect.

Plan #151557

Dimensions: 117'8" W x 84'8" D

Levels: 2

Square Footage: 6,388

Main Level Sq. Ft.: 5,338

Upper Level Sq. Ft.: 1,050

Bedrooms: 4

Bathrooms: 4 full, 2 half

Foundation: Crawl space or slab

CompleteCost List Available: Yes

Price Category: K

The exquisite design and extensive amenities of this home make it a dream-come-true.

Images provided by designer/architect.

Features:

- **Entry:** This two-story entry gives the home an open feeling. It separates the formal living room from the dining room. The stairs lead to a balcony, which overlooks the enormous great room.

- **Kitchen:** This expansive kitchen adjoins both the breakfast nook and the hearth room. It is located near the guest suite, providing an abundance of options. The walk-in pantry is a bonus.

- **Master Suite:** This main-level master suite has a large sitting bay and private access to the study. Enter through the French doors to a luxurious master bath complete with a double vanity and whirlpool tub.

- **Upper Level:** Located above the four-car garage, this large bonus room contains skylights and stairs that lead to the hearth room. Two secondary bedrooms, each with a full bathroom, are located on this level.

Main Level Floor Plan

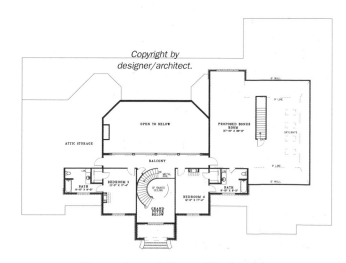

Copyright by designer/architect.

Upper Level Floor Plan

Plan #161105

Dimensions: 90'2" W x 104'5" D
Levels: 2
Square Footage: 6,806
Main Level Sq. Ft.: 4,511
Upper Level Sq. Ft.: 2,295
Bedrooms: 4
Bathrooms: 4 full, 2 half
Foundation: Walkout basement
Material List Available: No
Price Category: K

The opulence and drama of this European-inspired home features a solid brick exterior with limestone detail, arched dormers, and a parapet.

Images provided by designer/architect.

Features:

- **Foyer:** A large octagonal skylight tops a water fountain feature displayed in this exquisite entryway. The formal dining room and library flank the entry and enjoy a 10-ft. ceiling height.

- **Family Living Area:** The gourmet kitchen, breakfast area, and cozy hearth room comprise this family activity center of the home. Wonderful amenities such as a magnificent counter with seating, a celestial ceiling over the dining table, an alcove for an entertainment center, a stone-faced wood-burning fireplace, and access to the rear porch enhance the informal area.

- **Master Suite:** This luxurious suite enjoys a raised ceiling, a seating area with bay window, and access to the terrace. The dressing room pampers the homeowner with a whirlpool tub, a ceramic tile shower enclosure, two vanities, and a spacious walk-in closet.

- **Upper Level:** Elegant stairs lead to the second-floor study loft and two additional bedrooms, each with a private bathroom and large walk-in closet. On the same level, and located for privacy, the third bedroom serves as a guest suite, showcasing a cozy sitting area and private bathroom.

Upper Level Floor Plan

Main Level Floor Plan

Copyright by designer/architect.

Optional Basement Level Floor Plan

Plan #451079

Dimensions: 224'6" W x 112'11" D
Levels: 2
Square Footage: 12,410
Main Level Sq. Ft.: 4,515
Upper Level Sq. Ft.: 7,895
Bedrooms: 7
Bathrooms: 7½
Foundation: Walkout, insulated concrete form
Material List Available: No
Price Category: L

This expansive house is full of cozy, homey details.

CAD FILE AVAILABLE

Images provided by designer/architect.

Features:

- Foyer: This elegant circular foyer greets you as you enter the home. There is easy access to the library, parlor, dining room, and great room. Circular stairs allow access to the upper level.

- Kitchen: This island kitchen features a circular eating area that adjoins the family room. The large walk-in pantry is just off the garage to ease unloading the car.

- Master Suite: This large retreat features two walk-in closets and a spa area. The master bath spoils you with his and her vanities, a large stall shower, and a separate toilet enclosure.

- Lower Level: This level is dedicated to entertainment and features a game room and a home theater. There are even your own private bowling alley and an exercise room. After all of this excitement you can relax by going for a swim in the indoor pool.

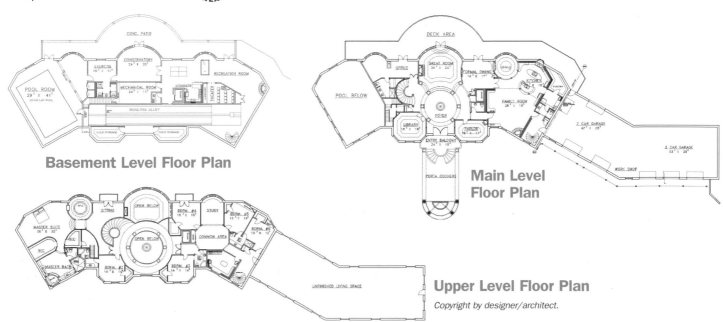

Basement Level Floor Plan

Main Level Floor Plan

Upper Level Floor Plan

Copyright by designer/architect.

Plan #161104

Dimensions: 130' W x 84'6" D
Levels: 2
Square Footage: 8,088
Main Level Sq. Ft.: 5,418
Upper Level Sq. Ft.: 2,670
Bedrooms: 4
Bathrooms: 4 full, 2 half
Foundation: Basement
Material List Available: No
Price Category: L

Images provided by designer/architect.

Spectacular exterior with solid brick, limestone trim, and custom wood door reflects an authentic European manor.

CAD FILE AVAILABLE

Features:

- **Kitchen:** A 17-ft. high ceiling with arched timber beams, wall oven, island with vegetable sink, and second island with seating all create a true gourmet working space that overlooks the breakfast room and the cozy hearth room.

- **Master Suite:** This palatial suite with curved ceilings, fireplace-side whirlpool tub, large shower, sunken solarium, dressing room with two vanities and dressing table will pamper you. Four closets, including a compartmented double-entry master and secondary laundry area provide unmatched convenience.

- **Bedrooms:** Two sets of stairs lead to the second floor bedrooms—two with private sitting areas. Each bedroom enjoys a private bath and walk-in closet.

- **Additional Space:** A sunken covered porch, enhances the rear-yard enjoyment, while a finished lower level creates additional rooms for fun and entertainment.

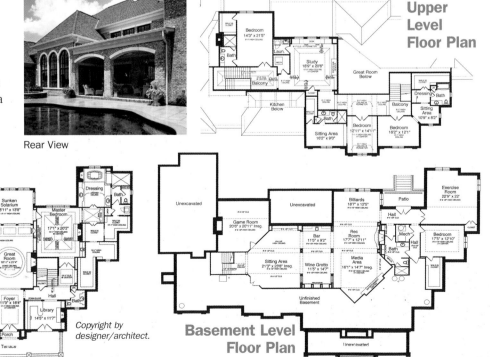

Rear View

Upper Level Floor Plan

Main Level Floor Plan

Copyright by designer/architect.

Basement Level Floor Plan

Foyer

Media Room

Master Bedroom

Bar

Kitchen

Master Bedroom

Balcony

Plan #451103

Dimensions: 180' W x 161'10" D
Levels: 2
Square Footage: 13,865
Main Level Sq. Ft.: 5,477
Upper Level Sq. Ft.: 3,473
Lower Level Sq. Ft.: 4,915
Bedrooms: 13
Bathrooms: 10½
Foundation: Walkout,
insulated concrete form
Material List Available: No
Price Category: L

This home features all the amenities of a private resort.

CAD FILE AVAILABLE

Features:

• **Living Room:** Entertain your guests in this large formal living room, which features a beautiful fireplace. Open the sliding doors to the formal dining room, and allow your guests to flow into the area.

• **Great Room:** This family gathering area is open to the kitchen and has access to the rear screened porch. The corner fireplace adds warmth and charm to the area.

• **Kitchen:** The chef in the family will love the abundance of counter space and cabinets. The large walk-in pantry and attached baking area will make life much easier.

Images provided by designer/architect.

• **Master Suite:** Located on the main level for privacy, this retreat boasts a corner fireplace and a private courtyard. The master bath pampers you with dual vanities and a private toilet enclosure.

**Main Level
Floor Plan**

**Upper Level
Floor Plan**

**Basement Level
Floor Plan**

**Bonus Area
Floor Plan**

*Copyright by
designer/architect.*

Plan #151259

Dimensions: 99'2" W x 127'10" D
Levels: 2
Square Footage: 10,575
Main Level Sq. Ft.: 6,504
Upper Level Sq. Ft.: 4,071
Bedrooms: 7
Bathrooms: 7 full, 2 half
Foundation: Slab
CompleteCost List Available: Yes
Price Category: L

This Mediterranean villa provides an escape from your busy life.

Images provided by designer/architect.

CAD FILE AVAILABLE

Features:

- Library: Grab a great book, and relax in front of the fireplace in this comfortable room. The coffered ceiling gives the area an elegant feeling.

- Kitchen: This enormous island kitchen will please the chef in the family. The raised bar is open to the breakfast area and family room. A large pantry is located close by.

- Maid's Quarters: Located in the wing by the garage, this area is complete with a full bathroom, bedroom, and living area. A kitchenette is an added bonus.

- Master Suite: You'll find this private oasis on the upper level-but separated from the secondary bedrooms. Complete with his-and-her bathrooms and walk-in closets, this is truly and elegant space.

Main Level Floor Plan

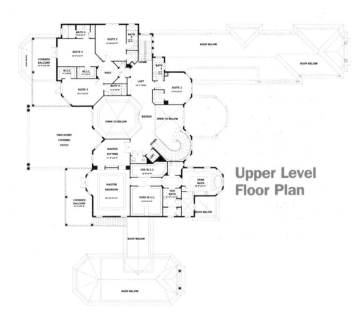

Upper Level Floor Plan

Copyright by designer/architect.

Plan #161101

Dimensions: 136'3" W x 69' D
Levels: 2
Square Footage: 8,414
Main Level Sq. Ft.: 4,011
Upper Level Sq. Ft.: 2,198
Optional Lower Level Sq. Ft.: 2,205
Bedrooms: 4
Bathrooms: 4 full, 2 half
Foundation: Walkout; basement for fee
Material List Available: Yes
Price Category: L

Images provided by designer/architect.

The grandeur of this mansion-style home boasts period stone, two-story columns, an angular turret, a second-floor balcony, and a gated courtyard.

CAD FILE AVAILABLE

Features:

- **Formal Living:** Formal areas consist of the charming living room and adjacent music room, which continues to the library, with its sloped ceilings and glass surround. Various ceiling treatments, with 10-ft. ceiling heights, and 8-ft.-tall doors add luxury and artistry to the first floor.

- **Hearth Room:** This large room, with false wood-beamed ceiling, adds a casual yet rich atmosphere to the family gathering space. Dual French doors on each side of the fireplace create a pleasurable indoor-outdoor relationship.

- **Kitchen:** This space is an enviable work place for the gourmet cook. Multiple cabinets and expansive counter space create a room that may find you spending a surprisingly enjoyable amount of time on food preparation. The built-in grill on the porch makes outdoor entertaining convenient and fun.

- **Master Suite:** This suite offers a vaulted ceiling, dual walk-in closets, and his and her vanities. The whirlpool tub is showcased on a platform and surrounded by windows for a relaxing view of the side yard. Private access to the deck is an enchanting surprise.

Rear View

Copyright by designer/architect.

Main Level Floor Plan

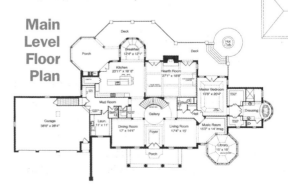

Upper Level Floor Plan

Basement Level Floor Plan

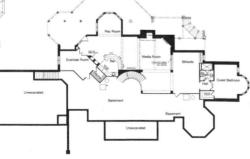

Let Us Help You Plan Your Dream Home

Whether you've always dreamed of building your own home or you can't find the right house from among the dozens you've toured, our collection of affordable plans can help you achieve the home of your dreams. You could have an architect create a one-of-a-kind home for you, but the design services alone could end up costing up to 15 percent of the cost of construction—a hefty premium for any building project. Isn't it a better idea to select from among the hundreds of unique designs shown in our collection for a fraction of the cost?

What does Creative Homeowner Offer?

In this book, Creative Homeowner provides hundreds of home plans from the country's best architects and designers. Our designs are among the most popular available. Whether your taste runs from traditional to contemporary, Victorian to early American, you are sure to find the best house design for you and your family. Our plans packages include detailed drawings to help you or your builder construct your dream house. **(See page 374.)**

Can I Make Changes to the Plans?

Creative Homeowner offers three ways to help you achieve a truly unique home design. Our customizing service allows for extensive changes to our designs. **(See page 375.)** We also provide reverse images of our plans, or we can give you and your builder the tools for making minor changes on your own. **(See page 378.)**

Can You Help Me Stay on Budget?

Building a house is a large financial investment. To help you stay within your budget, Creative Homeowner can provide you with general construction costs based on your zip code. **(See page 378.)** Also, many of our plans come with the option of buying detailed materials lists to help you price out construction costs.

How Can I Get Started with the Building Process?

We've teamed up with the leading estimating company to provide one of the most accurate, complete, and reliable building material take-offs in the industry. **(See page 376.)** If you plan on doing all or part of the work yourself, or want to keep tabs on your builder, we offer best-selling building and design books at attractive prices. See our Web site at www.creativehomeowner.com.

Our Plans Packages Offer:

"Square footage" refers to the total "heated square feet" of this plan. This number does not include the garage, porches, or unfinished areas. All of our home plans are the result of many hours of work by leading architects and professional designers. Most of our home plans include each of the following:

Frontal Sheet

This artist's rendering of the front of the house gives you an idea of how the house will look once it is completed and the property landscaped.

Detailed Floor Plans

These plans show the size and layout of the rooms. They also provide the locations of doors, windows, fireplaces, closets, stairs, and electrical outlets and switches.

Foundation Plan

A foundation plan gives the dimensions of basements, walk-out basements, crawl spaces, pier foundations, and slab construction. Each house design lists the type of foundation included. If the plan you choose does not have the foundation type you require, our customer service department can help you customize the plan to meet your needs.

Roof Plan

In addition to providing the pitch of the roof, these plans also show the locations of dormers, skylights, and other elements.

Exterior Elevations

These drawings show the front, rear, and sides of the house as if you were looking at it head on. Elevations also provide information about architectural features and finish materials.

Interior Elevations and Details

Interior elevations show specific details of such elements as fireplaces, kitchen and bathroom cabinets, built-ins, and other unique features of the design.

Cross Sections

These show the structure as if it were sliced to reveal construction requirements, such as insulation, flooring, and roofing details.

Frontal Sheet

Floor Plan

Foundation Plan

Roof Plan

Cross Sections

Stair Details

Elevation

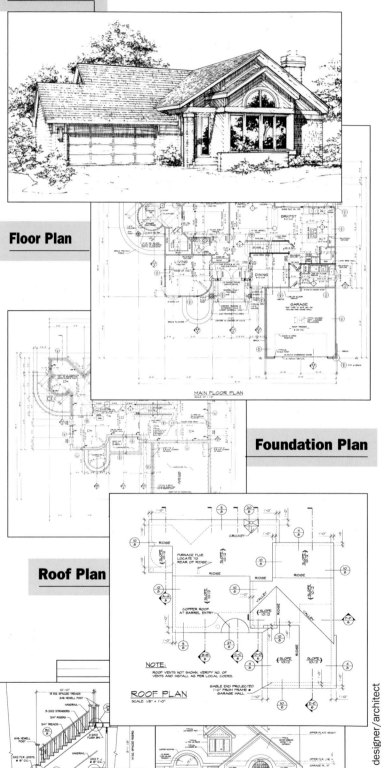

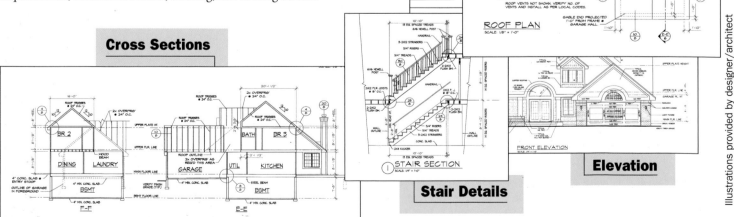

Illustrations provided by designer/architect

Customize Your Plans in 4 Easy Steps

1 **Select the home plan** that most closely meets your needs. Purchase of a reproducible master is necessary in order to make changes to a plan.

2 **Call 1-800-523-6789 to place your order.** Tell our sales representative you are interested in customizing your plan. To receive your customization cost estimate, we will send you a checklist (via fax or email) for you to complete indicating the changes you would like to make to your plan. There is a $50 nonrefundable consultation fee for this service. If you decide to continue with the custom changes, the $50 fee is credited to the total amount charged.

3 **Fax the completed checklist** to 1-201-760-2431 or email it to us at customize@creativehomeowner.com. Within three business days of receipt of your checklist, a detailed cost estimate will be provided to you.

4 **Once you approve the estimate,** a 75% retainer fee is collected and customization work begins. Preliminary drawings typically take 10 to 15 business days. After approval, we will collect the balance of your customization order cost before shipping the completed plans. You will receive five sets of blueprints or a reproducible master, plus a customized materials list if desired.

Terms & Copyright

These home plans are protected under the terms of United States Copyright Law and may not be copied or reproduced in any way, by any means, unless you have purchased reproducible masters, which clearly indicate your right to copy or reproduce. We authorize the use of your chosen home plan as an aid in the construction of one single-family home only. You may not use this home plan to build a second or multiple dwellings without purchasing another blueprint or blueprints, or paying additional home plan fees.

Architectural Seals

Because of differences in building codes, some cities and states now require an architect or engineer licensed in that state to review and "seal" a blueprint, or officially approve it, prior to construction. Delaware, Nevada, New Jersey, and New York require that all plans for houses built in those states be redrawn by an architect licensed in the state in which the home will be built. We strongly advise you to consult with your local building official for information regarding architectural seals.

Modification Pricing Guide

Categories	Average Cost For Modification
Add or remove living space	Quote required
Bathroom layout redesign	Starting at $120
Kitchen layout redesign	Starting at $120
Garage: add or remove	Starting at $400
Garage: front entry to side load or vice versa	Starting at $300
Foundation changes	Starting at $220
Exterior building materials change	Starting at $200
Exterior openings: add, move, or remove	$65 per opening
Roof line changes	Starting at $360
Ceiling height adjustments	Starting at $280
Fireplace: add or remove	Starting at $90
Screened porch: add	Starting at $280
Wall framing change from 2x4 to 2x6	Starting at $200
Bearing and/or exterior walls changes	Quote required
Non-bearing wall or room changes	$65 per room
Metric conversion of home plan	Starting at $400
Adjust plan for handicapped accessibility	Quote required
Adapt plans for local building code requirements	Quote required
Engineering stamping only	Quote required
Any other engineering services	Quote required
Interactive illustrations (choices of exterior materials)	Quote required

Note: Any home plan can be customized to accommodate your desired changes. The average prices above are provided only as examples of the most commonly requested changes, and are subject to change without notice. Prices for changes will vary according to the number of modifications requested, plan size, style, and method of design used by the original designer. To obtain a detailed cost estimate, please contact us.

Before Customization

After

Turn your dream home into reality with

UltimateEstimate

When purchasing a home plan with Creative Homeowner, we recommend you order one of the most complete materials lists in the industry.

What comes with an Ultimate Estimate?

Quote

- Basis of the entire estimate.

- Detailed list of all the framing materials needed to build your project, listed from the bottom up, in the order that each one will actually be used.

Comments

- Details pertinent information beyond the cost of materials.

- Includes any notes from our estimator.

Express List

- A version of the Quote with space for SKU numbers listed for purchasing the items at your local lumberyard.

- Your local lumberyard can then price out the materials list.

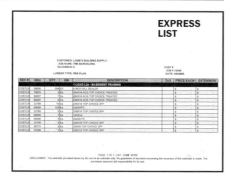

Construction-Ready Framing Diagrams

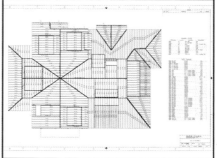

- Your "map" to exact roof and floor framing.

Millwork Report

- A complete count of the windows, doors, molding, and trim.

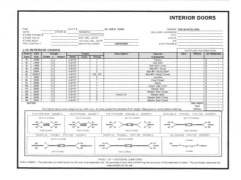

Man-Hour Report

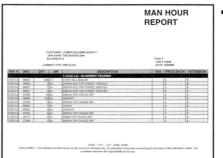

- Calculates labor on a line-by-line basis for all items quoted and presented in man-hours.

2 Why an Ultimate Estimate?

Accurate. Professional estimators break down each individual item from the blueprints using advanced software, techniques, and equipment.

Timely. You will be able to start your home-building project quickly — knowing the exact framing materials you need to order from your local lumberyard.

Detailed. Work with your local lumberyard associate to complete your quote with the remaining products needed for your new home.

3 So how much does it cost?

Pricing is determined by the total square feet of the home plan — including living area, garages, decks, porches, finished basements, and finished attics.

Square Feet Range	UE Tier*	Price
2,001 to 5,000 total square feet	XB	$299.00
5,001 to 10,000 total square feet	XC	$499.00

*Please see the Plan Index to determine your plan's Material Take-off Tier (MT Tier).
 Note: All prices subject to change.

Call our toll-free number (800-523-6789), or visit ultimateplans.com to order your Material Take-off.

4 What else do I need to know?

Call our toll-free number (800-523-6789), or visit
ultimateplans.com to order your Ultimate Estimate.

Turn your dream home into reality.

Decide What Type of Plan Package You Need

How many Plans Should You Order?

Standard 8-Set Package. We've found that our 8-set package is the best value for someone who is ready to start building. Once the process begins, a number of people will require their own set of blueprints. The 8-set package provides plans for you, your builder, the subcontractors, mortgage lender, and the building department.

Minimum 5-Set Package. If you are in the bidding process, you may want to order only five sets for the bidding round and reorder additional sets as needed.

1-Set Study Package. The 1-set package allows you to review your home plan in detail. The plan will be marked as a study print, and it is illegal to build a house from a study print alone. It is a violation of copyright law to reproduce a blueprint without permission.

Buying Additional Sets

If you require additional copies of blueprints for your home construction, you can order additional sets within 60 days of the original order date at a reduced price. The cost is $45.00 for each additional set. For more information, contact customer service.

Reproducible Masters

If you plan to make minor changes to one of our home plans, you can purchase reproducible masters. Printed on vellum paper, an erasable paper that you can reproduce in a copying machine, reproducible masters allow an architect, designer, or builder to alter our plans to give you a customized home design. This package also allows you to print as many copies of the modified plans as you need for construction.

CAD Files

CAD files are the complete set of home plans in an electronic file format. Choose this option if there are multiple changes you wish made to the home plans and you have a local design professional able to make the changes. Not available for all plans. Please contact our order department or visit our website to check the availability of CAD files for your plan.

Mirror-Reverse Sets/Right-Reading Reverse

Plans can be printed in mirror-reverse—we can "flip" plans to create a mirror image of the design. This is useful when the house would fit your site or personal preferences if all the rooms were on the opposite side than shown. As the image is reversed, the lettering and dimensions will also be reversed, meaning they will read backwards. Therefore, when ordering mirror-reverse drawings, you must order at least one set of right-reading plans. A $50.00 fee per plan order will be charged for mirror-reverse (regardless of the number of mirror-reverse sets ordered). Some plans are available in right-reading reverse, this feature will show the plan in reverse, but the writing on the plan will be readable. A $150.00 fee per plan order will be charged for right-reading reverse (regardless of the number of right-reading reverse sets ordered). Please contact our order department or visit our website to check the availibility of this feature for your chosen plan.

EZ Quote: Home Cost Estimator

EZ Quote is our response to one of the most frequently asked questions we hear from customers: "How much will the house cost me to build?" EZ Quote: Home Cost Estimator will enable you to obtain a calculated building cost to construct your home, based on labor rates and building material costs within your zip code area. This summary is useful for those who want to get an idea of the total construction costs before purchasing sets of home plans. It will also provide a level of comfort when you begin soliciting bids. The cost is $29.95 for the first EZ Quote and $14.95 for each additional one. Available only in the U.S. and Canada.

Materials List

Available for most of our plans, the Materials List provides you an invaluable resource in planning and estimating the cost of your home. Each Materials List outlines the quantity, dimensions, and type of materials needed to build your home (with the exception of mechanical systems). You will get faster, more-accurate bids from your contractors and building suppliers. A Materials List may only be ordered with the purchase of at least five sets of home plans.

CompleteCost Estimator

CompleteCost Estimator is a valuable tool for use in planning and constructing your new home. It provides more detail than a materials list and will act as a checklist for all items you will need to select or coordinate during your building process. CompleteCost Estimator is only available for certain plans (please see Plan Index) and may only be ordered with the purchase of at least five sets of home plans. The cost is $125.00 for CompleteCost Estimator.

Order Toll Free by Phone
1-800-523-6789
By Fax: 201-760-2431

Regular office hours are
8:30AM–7:30PM ET, Mon–Fri
Orders received 3PM ET, will be processed and
shipped within two business days.

Order Online
www.ultimateplans.com

Mail Your Order
Creative Homeowner
Attn: Home Plans
24 Park Way
Upper Saddle River, NJ 07458

Canadian Customers
Order Toll Free 1-800-393-1883

Mail Your Order (Canada)
Creative Homeowner Canada
Attn: Home Plans
113-437 Martin St., Ste. 215
Penticton, BC V2A 5L1

Before You Order

Our Exchange Policy

Blueprints are nonrefundable. However, should you find that the plan you have purchased does not fit your needs, you may exchange that plan for another plan in our collection within 60 days from the date of your original order. The entire content of your original order must be returned before an exchange will be processed. You will be charged a processing fee of 20% of the amount of the original order, the cost difference between the new plan set and the original plan set (if applicable), and all related shipping costs for the new plans. Contact our order department for more information. Please note: reproducible masters may only be exchanged if the package is unopened and CAD files cannot be exchanged and are nonrefundable.

Building Codes and Requirements

At the time of creation, our plans meet the building code requirements published by the Building Officials and Code Administrators International, the Southern Building Code Congress International, the International Conference of Building Officials, or the Council of American Building Officials. Because building codes vary from area to area, some drawing modifications and/or the assistance of a professional designer or architect may be necessary to comply with your local codes or to accommodate specific building site conditions. We strongly advise you to consult with your local building official for information regarding codes governing your area.

Blueprint Price Schedule

Price Code	1 Set	5 Sets	8 Sets	Reproducible Masters	CAD	Materials List
A	$315	$360	$415	$560	$950	$85
B	$395	$455	$505	$630	$1,100	$85
C	$450	$525	$580	$680	$1,200	$85
D	$515	$590	$640	$745	$1,300	$95
E	$580	$650	$695	$810	$1,400	$95
F	$640	$715	$760	$870	$1,500	$95
G	$705	$780	$820	$935	$1,600	$95
H	$800	$870	$915	$1,030	$1,700	$95
I	$900	$975	$1020	$1,135	$1,800	$105
J	$1,010	$1,080	$1,125	$1,250	$1,900	$105
K	$1,125	$1,210	$1,250	$1,380	$2,030	$105
L	$1,240	$1,335	$1,375	$1,535	$2,170	$105

Note: All prices subject to change

Ultimate Estimate Tier (UE Tier)

MT Tier*	Price
XB	$299
XC	$499

* Please see the Plan Index to determine your plan's Ultimate Estimate Tier (UE Tier).

Shipping & Handling

Shipping & Handling	1-4 Sets	5-7 Sets	8+ Sets or Reproducibles	CAD
US Regular (7–10 business days)	$18	$20	$25	$25
US Priority (3–5 business days)	$25	$30	$35	$35
US Express (1–2 business days)	$40	$45	$50	$50
Canada Express (1–2 business days)	$80	$80	$80	$80
Worldwide Express (3–5 business days)	$100	$100	$100	$100

Note: All delivery times are from date the blueprint package is shipped (typically within 1-2 days of placing order).

Order Form Please send me the following:

Plan Number: _____ **Price Code:** _____ (See Plan Index.)

Indicate Foundation Type: (Select ONE. See plan page for availability.)

❏ Slab ❏ Crawl space ❏ Basement ❏ Walk-out basement

❏ Optional Foundation for Fee _____ $_____
(Please enter foundation here)

*Please call all our order department or visit our website for optional foundation fee

Basic Blueprint Package	Cost
❏ Reproducible Masters	$_____
❏ 8-Set Plan Package	$_____
❏ 5-Set Plan Package	$_____
❏ 1-Set Study Package	$_____
❏ Additional plan sets: __ sets at $45.00 per set	$_____
❏ Print in mirror-reverse: $50.00 per order	$_____

*Please call all our order department or visit our website for availbility

❏ Print in right-reading reverse: $150.00 per order $_____
*Please call all our order department or visit our website for availbility

Important Extras

❏ Materials List $_____

❏ CompleteCost Materials Report at $125.00 $_____
Zip Code of Home/Building Site _____

❏ EZ Quote for Plan #_____ at $29.95 $_____

❏ Additional EZ Quotes for Plan #s_____ at $14.95 each $_____

❏ Ultimate Estimate (See Price Tier above.) $_____

Shipping (see chart above) $_____

SUBTOTAL $_____

Sales Tax (NJ residents only, add 7%) $_____

TOTAL $_____

Order Toll Free: 1-800-523-6789 By Fax: 201-760-2431
Creative Homeowner
24 Park Way
Upper Saddle River, NJ 07458

Name _____
(Please print or type)

Street _____
(Please do not use a P.O. Box)

City _____ State _____

Country _____ Zip _____

Daytime telephone (___)_____

Fax (___)_____
(Required for reproducible orders)

E-Mail _____

Payment ❏ Bank check/money order. No personal checks.
Make checks payable to Creative Homeowner

❏ VISA ❏ MasterCard ❏ American Express Cards ❏ Discover

Credit card number _____

Expiration date (mm/yy) _____

Signature _____

Please check the appropriate box:

❏ Licensed builder/contractor ❏ Homeowner ❏ Renter

| SOURCE CODE | CA353 |

Copyright Notice

All home plans sold through this publication are protected by copyright. Reproduction of these home plans, either in whole or in part, including any form and/or preparation of derivative works thereof, for any reason without prior written permission is strictly prohibited. The purchase of a set of home plans in no way transfers any copyright or other ownership interest in it to the buyer except for a limited license to use that set of home plans for the construction of one, and only one, dwelling unit. The purchase of additional sets of the home plans at a reduced price from the original set or as a part of a multiple-set package does not convey to the buyer a license to construct more than one dwelling.

Similarly, the purchase of reproducible home plans (sepias, mylars) carries the same copyright protection as mentioned above. It is gener-ally allowed to make up to a maximum of 10 copies for the construction of a single dwelling only. To use any plans more than once, and to avoid any copyright license infringement, it is necessary to contact the plan designer to receive a release and license for any extended use. Whereas a purchaser of reproducible plans is granted a license to make copies, it should be noted that because blueprints are copyrighted, making photocopies from them is illegal.

Copyright and licensing of home plans for construction exist to protect all parties. Copyright respects and supports the intellectual property of the original architect or designer. Copyright law has been reinforced over the past few years. Willful infringement could cause settlements for statutory damages to $150,000.00 plus attorney fees, damages, and loss of profits.

Plan #	Price Code	Page	Total Finished Area Square Feet	Materials List	CompleteCost	Ue Tier
101014	1,598	12	C	N	N	XB
101015	1,647	35	C	N	N	XB
101017	2,253	196	E	N	N	XB
101017	2,253	197	E	N	N	XB
101024	3,135	233	G	N	N	XB
101126	3,431	244	G	N	N	XB
111008	2,011	114	D	N	N	XB
111009	2,514	123	E	N	N	XB
111010	1,804	45	D	N	N	XB
111011	3,292	218	G	N	N	XB
111029	2,781	237	F	N	N	XB
111034	3,088	232	G	N	N	XB
111035	3,064	248	G	N	N	XB
111036	3,149	253	G	N	N	XB
111037	3,176	236	G	N	N	XB
111039	3,335	278	G	N	N	XB
111040	1,650	64	C	N	N	XB
111041	1,743	47	C	N	N	XB
111042	1,779	68	C	N	N	XB
111043	1,737	54	C	N	N	XB
111044	1,819	51	D	N	N	XB
111046	1,768	43	C	N	N	XB
111047	1,863	39	D	N	N	XB
111049	2,205	191	E	N	N	XB
121014	1,869	73	D	Y	N	XB
121015	1,999	26	D	Y	N	XB
121018	3,950	307	H	Y	N	XB
121019	3,775	272	H	Y	N	XB
121021	2,270	139	E	Y	N	XB
121022	3,556	253	H	Y	N	XB
121023	3,904	302	H	Y	N	XB
121024	3,057	217	G	Y	N	XB
121025	2,562	125	E	Y	N	XB
121026	3,926	221	H	Y	N	XB
121027	1,660	48	C	Y	N	XB
121029	2,576	115	E	Y	N	XB
121031	1,772	11	C	Y	N	XB
121033	1,987	49	D	Y	N	XB
121035	1,463	53	B	Y	N	XB
121036	1,297	56	B	Y	N	XB
121040	1,818	59	D	Y	N	XB
121044	1,923	40	D	Y	N	XB
121045	1,575	41	C	Y	N	XB
121047	3,072	293	G	Y	N	XB
121049	3,335	266	G	Y	N	XB
121061	3,025	275	G	Y	N	XB
121062	3,448	279	G	Y	N	XB
121063	3,473	284	G	Y	N	XB
121064	1,846	36	D	Y	N	XB
121065	3,407	303	G	Y	N	XB
121066	2,078	95	D	Y	N	XB
121072	3,031	300	G	Y	N	XB
121076	3,067	237	G	Y	N	XB
121078	2,248	160	E	Y	N	XB
121079	2,688	86	F	Y	N	XB
121081	3,623	231	G	Y	N	XB
121082	2,932	201	F	Y	N	XB
121083	2,695	172	F	Y	N	XB
121084	1,728	29	C	Y	N	XB
121085	1,948	44	D	Y	N	XB
121086	1,998	32	D	Y	N	XB
121088	2,340	204	E	Y	N	XB
121089	1,976	72	D	Y	N	XB
121090	2,645	128	F	Y	N	XB
121091	2,689	171	F	Y	N	XB
121093	2,603	133	F	Y	N	XB
121094	1,768	28	C	Y	N	XB
121095	2,282	204	E	Y	N	XB
121096	3,611	240	G	Y	N	XB
121097	2,417	115	E	Y	N	XB
121098	2,292	111	E	Y	N	XB
121100	3,750	238	G	N	N	XB
121110	1,855	60	D	Y	N	XB
121111	1,685	38	C	Y	N	XB
121112	1,650	22	C	Y	N	XB
121113	3,172	235	G	Y	N	XB
121114	2,115	199	D	Y	N	XB
121115	1,993	68	D	Y	N	XB
121120	2,131	131	D	Y	N	XB
121122	2,979	202	F	Y	N	XB
121123	2,277	181	E	Y	N	XB
121126	3,273	248	G	Y	N	XB
121127	2,496	194	E	Y	N	XB
121129	2,198	136	D	Y	N	XB
121130	3,040	280	G	Y	N	XB
121147	2,051	185	D	Y	N	XB
121148	2,076	195	D	N	N	XB
121149	2,715	193	F	Y	N	XB
121150	2,639	166	F	Y	N	XB
121152	3,094	252	G	Y	N	XB
121153	1,984	69	D	Y	N	XB
121155	2,638	174	F	Y	N	XB
121160	2,188	162	D	Y	N	XB
121168	5,203	348	J	N	N	XC
121170	3,459	242	G	Y	N	XB
121171	2,978	180	F	Y	N	XB
121172	1,897	66	D	Y	N	XB
121182	3,397	243	G	Y	N	XB
121190	2,252	189	E	Y	N	XB
121203	2,690	184	F	Y	N	XB
121212	2,219	187	E	Y	N	XB
131021	3,110	290	H	Y	N	XB
131022	2,092	142	E	Y	N	XB
131023	2,460	138	F	Y	N	XB
131024	1,635	52	D	Y	N	XB
131025	3,204	252	H	Y	N	XB
131026	2,796	132	G	Y	N	XB
131027	2,567	165	F	Y	N	XB
131028	2,696	183	G	Y	N	XB
131029	2,718	129	G	Y	N	XB
131030	2,470	121	F	Y	N	XB
131031	4,027	340	J	Y	N	XC
131032	2,455	117	F	Y	N	XB
131033	2,813	186	G	Y	N	XB
131041	1,679	64	D	Y	N	XB
131050	2,874	182	G	Y	N	XB
131051	2,431	107	F	Y	N	XB
131055	2,575	178	F	Y	N	XB
131055	2,575	179	F	Y	N	XB
131056	1,396	67	C	Y	N	XB
131066	2,760	190	G	Y	N	XB
131067	1,909	63	E	Y	N	XB
131069	3,169	249	H	Y	N	XB
131071	1,992	61	E	Y	N	XB
131074	2,085	177	E	Y	N	XB
131078	3,278	294	G	Y	N	XB
141012	1,870	57	D	Y	N	XB
141014	2,091	87	D	Y	N	XB
141016	2,416	180	E	Y	N	XB
141017	2,480	93	E	N	N	XB
141020	3,140	297	G	N	N	XB
141023	1,715	71	C	Y	N	XB
141024	1,792	66	C	Y	N	XB
141025	1,721	13	C	Y	N	XB
141026	1,993	61	D	Y	N	XB
141028	2,215	140	E	Y	N	XB
141029	2,289	164	E	Y	N	XB
141030	2,323	161	E	Y	N	XB
141032	2,476	175	E	Y	N	XB
141033	3,223	289	G	N	N	XB
141034	3,588	240	H	Y	N	XB
141035	2,514	174	E	Y	N	XB
141036	2,527	176	E	Y	N	XB
141037	1,735	60	C	Y	N	XB
141044	1,855	62	D	N	N	XB
141051	3,011	246	G	N	N	XB
151011	3,437	282	G	N	Y	XB
151012	3,730	301	H	N	Y	XB
151014	2,698	203	F	N	Y	XB
151015	2,798	161	F	N	Y	XB
151016	1,783	21	C	N	Y	XB
151018	2,755	164	F	N	Y	XB
151019	2,653	166	F	N	Y	XB
151020	4,532	314	I	N	Y	XB
151021	3,385	278	G	N	Y	XB
151022	3,059	265	G	N	Y	XB
151023	3,203	293	G	N	Y	XB
151024	3,623	281	H	N	Y	XB

Index *For pricing, see page 379.*

Plan #	Price Code	Page	Total Finished Area Square Feet	Materials List	CompleteCost	Ue Tier
151025	3,914	285	H	N	Y	XB
151026	1,574	42	C	N	Y	XB
151027	2,323	167	E	N	Y	XB
151028	2,252	167	E	N	Y	XB
151029	2,777	183	F	N	Y	XB
151030	2,949	185	F	N	Y	XB
151031	3,130	286	G	N	Y	XB
151033	5,548	341	J	N	Y	XC
151095	4,446	304	I	N	Y	XB
151103	5,129	344	J	N	Y	XC
151107	3,278	227	G	N	Y	XB
151112	3,661	306	H	N	Y	XB
151115	5,689	339	J	N	Y	XC
151121	3,108	214	G	N	Y	XB
151126	3,474	279	G	N	Y	XB
151129	3,947	225	H	N	Y	XB
151146	7,870	359	L	N	Y	XC
151213	1,231	37	B	N	Y	XB
151214	5,726	337	J	N	Y	XC
151232	3,901	274	H	N	Y	XB
151252	5,412	336	J	N	Y	XC
151259	10,575	371	L	N	Y	XC
151384	2,742	165	F	N	Y	XB
151484	2,211	160	E	N	Y	XB
151524	4,461	333	I	N	Y	XB
151530	2,146	146	D	N	Y	XB
151534	2,237	141	E	N	Y	XB
151557	6,388	365	K	N	Y	XC
151716	7,870	361	L	N	Y	XC
151855	4,134	316	I	N	Y	XB
161015	1,768	19	C	Y	N	XB
161017	2,653	100	F	N	N	XB
161018	2,816	141	F	N	N	XB
161019	2,428	146	E	N	N	XB
161020	2,082	137	D	Y	N	XB
161022	1,898	23	D	N	N	XB
161023	3,445	263	G	Y	N	XB
161024	1,698	10	C	N	N	XB
161025	2,738	140	F	N	N	XB
161027	2,388	137	E	N	N	XB
161028	3,570	224	H	N	N	XB
161029	4,470	315	I	Y	N	XB
161030	4,562	328	I	Y	N	XB
161032	4,517	332	I	Y	N	XB
161033	5,125	335	J	Y	N	XC
161034	2,156	147	D	N	N	XB
161035	3,688	245	H	N	N	XB
161036	3,664	270	H	N	N	XB
161036	3,664	271	H	N	N	XB
161037	2,469	104	E	Y	N	XB
161037	2,469	105	E	Y	N	XB
161041	2,738	135	F	Y	N	XB
161044	4,652	305	I	N	N	XB
161045	2,077	96	D	N	N	XB
161049	3,213	229	G	Y	N	XB
161060	5,143	338	J	N	N	XC
161061	3,816	308	H	N	N	XB
161094	3,366	285	G	N	N	XB
161096	3,435	255	G	N	N	XB
161097	4,594	325	I	N	N	XB
161101	8,414	372	L	Y	N	XC
161103	5,633	349	J	N	N	XC
161104	8,088	368	L	N	N	XC
161104	8,088	369	L	N	N	XC
161105	6,806	366	K	N	N	XC
161113	6,126	358	K	N	N	XC
161125	2,733	182	F	Y	N	XB
171007	1,650	51	C	Y	N	XB
171017	2,558	134	E	Y	N	XB
171018	2,599	131	E	Y	N	XB
181034	2,687	88	F	N	N	XB
181063	2,037	144	D	Y	N	XB
181074	1,760	34	C	N	N	XB
181079	2,292	148	E	Y	N	XB
181079	3,016	228	G	N	N	XB
181081	2,350	94	E	Y	N	XB

Plan #	Price Code	Page	Total Finished Area Square Feet	Materials List	CompleteCost	Ue Tier
181085	2,183	101	D	Y	N	XB
181094	2,099	173	D	Y	N	XB
181100	4,200	331	I	Y	N	XB
181120	1,480	20	B	Y	N	XB
181126	1,468	18	B	Y	N	XB
181128	1,634	14	C	Y	N	XB
181133	1,832	24	D	Y	N	XB
181151	2,283	170	E	Y	N	XB
181221	3,411	238	G	Y	N	XB
181224	1,727	8	C	Y	N	XB
181224	1,727	9	C	Y	N	XB
181228	2,393	168	E	Y	N	XB
181483	4,183	320	I	Y	N	XB
181680	9,028	364	L	Y	N	XC
211070	1,700	50	C	Y	N	XB
211071	2,954	130	F	Y	N	XB
211072	3,012	284	G	Y	N	XB
211073	3,119	300	G	Y	N	XB
211074	3,486	263	G	Y	N	XB
211075	3,568	220	H	Y	N	XB
211076	4,242	310	I	Y	N	XB
211076	4,242	311	I	Y	N	XB
211077	5,560	347	J	Y	N	XC
211111	3,035	215	G	Y	N	XB
211117	3,284	227	G	Y	N	XB
211125	4,440	304	I	Y	N	XB
211127	5,474	342	J	Y	N	XC
221022	3,291	247	G	N	N	XB
221023	3,511	267	H	N	N	XB
221025	3,009	218	G	N	N	XB
221087	5,009	335	J	N	N	XC
221119	4,422	334	I	N	N	XB
221121	5,140	347	J	N	N	XC
231023	3,215	239	G	N	N	XB
231026	3,784	226	H	N	N	XB
231030	4,200	334	I	N	N	XB
241046	3,046	225	G	N	N	XB
241058	4,216	322	I	N	N	XB
241059	6,508	359	K	N	N	XC
251009	1,829	50	D	N	N	XB
251014	2,210	90	E	Y	N	XB
261001	3,746	239	H	N	N	XB
261006	4,583	323	I	N	N	XB
261009	4,048	322	I	N	N	XB
261011	4,042	323	I	N	N	XB
261012	2,648	130	F	N	N	XB
261013	3,193	296	G	N	N	XB
261014	3,471	249	G	N	N	XB
261015	3,200	250	G	N	N	XB
271009	1,909	46	D	Y	N	XB
271010	1,724	17	C	Y	N	XB
271011	1,296	33	B	Y	N	XB
271012	1,359	25	B	Y	N	XB
271024	3,107	305	G	Y	N	XB
271028	3,502	292	H	Y	N	XB
271029	3,039	283	G	Y	N	XB
271031	3,062	254	G	Y	N	XB
271032	3,195	262	G	N	N	XB
271037	4,220	321	I	N	N	XB
271042	3,469	262	G	N	N	XB
271055	3,159	244	G	N	N	XB
271067	3,015	229	G	N	N	XB
271071	3,194	226	G	N	N	XB
271072	3,081	264	G	N	N	XB
271090	2,708	124	F	N	N	XB
271091	2,854	123	F	N	N	XB
271092	2,636	122	F	N	N	XB
271093	2,813	175	F	N	N	XB
271094	3,242	297	G	N	N	XB
271095	3,220	233	G	N	N	XB
271096	3,190	296	G	N	N	XB
271097	1,645	43	C	N	N	XB
271098	3,382	245	G	N	N	XB
271099	2,949	169	F	N	N	XB
271100	3,263	281	G	N	N	XB
281001	2,423	163	E	Y	N	XB

Index

For pricing, see page 379.

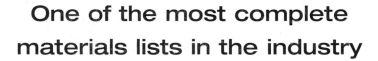